Business Planning in Transport

This book provides a set of practical business planning tools aimed at developing a business in the public transport sector, primarily – railways, ferry, long distance bus/coach and air transport services.

Adam Simmons covers a wide range of subject areas, including economics, statistical & forecasting techniques, marketing and investment appraisal.

No manager can go far without needing to make decisions based on customer prices, company costs and income (microeconomics) or, on the global and national effects of financial decisions (macroeconomics). These decisions affect all our lives and are too important to be left to economists!

'Business Planning in Transport' includes a wide range of numerical techniques from the mundane (probability) to the esoteric (Holt Winters Exponential Smoothing).

It is critical to bear in mind that businesses cannot be assessed or planned without numbers, costs, demand, revenue capacity or an understanding of the impacts of seasonality. This book places a heavy emphasis on tools to enable the user to understand how a business can quantify many of the important issues it faces.

Adam Simmons MBA MSc BSc

All Rights Reserved

The right of Adam Simmons to be identified as the author of this work has been asserted by him in accordance with Sections 77 and 78 of the Copyright, Designs and Patent Act 1988. No part of this publication may be reproduced or transmitted by any means, electronic, mechanical, photocopy or otherwise, without the prior permission of the publisher. Trademark Notice: product or corporate names may be registered / trademarks and are used only for identification and explanation, without the intent to infringe. This is a non-fiction work and includes information of public historical record. The data, names, places, characters, examples and incidents are as researched and recorded by the author and are reproduced here in good faith without the intention to defame. The author and publisher have made every effort possible to ensure that all the information in this book was correct at the point of publication and hereby disclaim any liability to any party for any loss, damage, or disruption caused by any errors or omissions.

Front Picture copyright © nerthuz #116318920
Cover Design copyright © U P Publications 2017
Maps © OpenStreetMap contributors
Fonts Caviar, Caviar Dreams © Lauren Thompson
Dustimo © 2002 Dustin Norlander

Copyright © 2016, 2017 Adam Simmons MBA, MSc, BSc

Adam Simmons has asserted his moral rights
www.facebook.com/BusinessPlanningInTransport/

Published in Great Britain, 2017, by
U P Publications
St George's House,
George Street,
Huntingdon,
Cambridgeshire,
PE29 3GH. UK

A CIP Catalogue record of this book
is available from the British Library

ISBN 978-1908135827

FIRST EDITION

Also published as an e-book
by U P Publications

ISBN 978-1908135834

9 3 7 0 8 1 6 4 2 5

Printed in England by
The Lightning Source Group

www.AdamSimmons.co.uk
www.uppbooks.com

2017

Adam Simmons
MBA MSc BSc

Business Planning in Transport

CONTENTS

1 INTRODUCTION — 23
1.1 For Whom This Book is Written — 23
1.2 Why this Book? — 23
1.3 About the Author — 26
1.4 How this Book is Structured — 27
1.5 Excel — 30

2 PRINCIPLES OF DATA PRESENTATION — 31
2.1 Introduction — 31
2.2 Presentation of Data — 32
2.3 What is the Message? — 32
2.4 Plotting Data with Different Orders of Magnitude — 34
2.5 Chapter 2 Exercises — 36

3 MARKETS, SUPPLY AND DEMAND — 37
3.1 Introduction — 37
3.2 Markets — 37
3.3 Demand — 38
   3.3.1 Definition — 38
   3.3.2 The Law of Demand — 38
3.4 Supply — 39
   3.4.1 Introduction — 39
   3.4.2 Supply Curve and Schedule — 40
3.5 Equilibrium Point — 41
3.6 Changes in Demand — 41
3.7 Changes in Supply — 42
3.8 Luxury Goods — 43
3.9 Chapter 3 Exercises — 43

4 INDUSTRY STRUCTURE — 45
4.1 Overview — 45
4.2 Perfect Competition — 45
4.3 Oligopoly — 47
   4.3.1 Bangkok-Singapore Air Market — 47
   4.3.2 Perfect Competition or Oligopoly — 47
   4.3.3 How Competitive is this Oligopoly — 48
   4.3.4 Price Setting in an Oligopoly — 48
4.4 Duopoly — 50
   4.4.1 Overview — 50
   4.4.2 Jersey – Gatwick Market — 50
   4.4.3 Tests for Collusion — 51

4.5 MONOPOLY	51
4.5.1 OCCURRENCE OF MONOPOLIES	51
4.5.2 REASONS FOR THE OCCURRENCE OF MONOPOLIES	52
4.5.3 MONOPOLY IN THAILAND	53
4.6 ECONOMIC REGULATION	54
4.6.1 TYPES OF REGULATION	54
4.6.1 PRICE REGULATION	54
4.6.3 RATE OF RETURN REGULATION	55
4.6.1 CONDITIONS OF SERVICE REGULATION	55
4.7 CHAPTER 4 EXERCISES	56

5 CONSUMER SURPLUS & ELASTICITIES   57

5.1 PRICE SETTING & CONSUMER SURPLUS	57
5.2 GENERALISED JOURNEY TIME (GJT)	60
5.2.1 TYPES OF REGULATION	60
5.3 ELASTICITIES	61
5.3.1 PRINCIPLE OF ELASTICITY	61
5.3.2 PRICE ELASTICITY	62
CASE STUDY 1 - PART 1	64
5.3.3 JOURNEY TIME ELASTICITY	64
5.3.4 INCOME ELASTICITY	65
5.4 CROSS ELASTICITIES	65
CASE STUDY 1 - PART 2	67
5.5 CHAPTER 5 EXERCISES	68

6 COMPETITION WITH OTHER MODES   69

6.1 OVERVIEW OF HOW MODES COMPARE	69
6.2 PRIVATE AND PUBLIC TRANSPORT	69
6.2.1 INTRODUCTION	69
6.3 CAR'S PERCEIVED COMPETITIVE ADVANTAGES	71
6.3.1 NO GJT PENALTIES	71
6.3.2 GROUP SIZE	71
6.3.3 DISTANCE	72
6.3.4 OTHER CONSIDERATIONS ON COMPARATIVE COST	73
6.4 ASSESSMENT OF EUROPEAN AIR-RAIL COMPETITION	74
6.4.1 PHASE1(TO 1983): INAUGURATION OF HIGH SPEED RAIL	74
6.4.2 PHASE 2 (1983 TO THE MID 1990S): CONSOLIDATION OF HIGH SPEED RAIL	75
6.4.3 PHASE 3 (MID 1990S ONWARDS): AIR SERVICE DEREGULATION	75
6.4.4 PHASE 4 (2013 ON): LONG DISTANCE BUS DEREGULATION	76
6.4.5 LESSONS DERIVED FROM CHANGES IN SUPPLY OF MODES	77
6.5 RAIL, FERRY & AIR: UK-FRANCE CROSS CHANNEL	77
6.5.1 ASSESSMENT OF MODAL SPLIT	77
6.6 RAIL, ROAD & AIR: BARCELONA-ZARAGOZA-MADRID	79
6.6.1 ASSESSMENT OF MODAL SPLIT	79

6.6.2 Converting Average Daily Road Figures	82
6.6.3 Coach Travel on the Madrid-Zaragoza-Barcelona Corridor	83
6.6.4 Conclusions from Modal Split Analysis	84
6.6.5 Lessons Learned	85
6.7 Chapter 6 Exercises	86

7 INFLATION AND GROSS DOMESTIC PRODUCT — 87

7.1 Inflation	87
7.2 Fuel Costs	89
7.3 Real Economic Growth	91
7.3.1 Calculating Real GDP	91
7.3.2 Real GDP and Transport Demand	93
7.3.3 Real GDP and Inter-Island Transport	94
7.4 Chapter 7 Exercises	97

8. SUMMARISING DATA, PROBABILITY & SAMPLING — 99

8.1 Summarising Data	99
8.1.1. Why Summarise?	99
8.1.2 Tools to Summarise Data	100
8.2 Probability Distributions	102
8.2.1. How Probability Distributions Work	102
8.2.2 Basic Probability Theory	102
8.3 Binomial Distribution	103
8.4 Poisson Distribution	104
8.5 Sampling of Data	106
8.5.1 Introduction	106
8.5.2 Introduction to the T Distribution	109
8.5.3 Use of T Distribution for Probability	110
8.5.4 T Distribution for Confidence Intervals	112
8.5.5 Confidence and Degrees of Freedom	114
8.5.6 Sampling of Passenger Counts	116
8.5.7 How Sample Size Affects the Size of Confidence Intervals	116
8.5.8 Probability Method	117
8.5.9 Confidence Interval Method	119
8.5.10 Probability And Confidence Interval Methods Compared	121
8.5.11 Trade-off between Sample Size and Cost	121
8.5.12 Case Study: Measuring Tourism Demand	121
8.5.13 More Complicated Example – Airline Punctuality	124
8.5.14 Confidence Intervals for Proportions	126
8.5.15 Samples Should Be Representative	126
8.6 Chapter 8 Exercises	128
8.7 Annex – Standard Deviation in Airline Punctuality Example	130

9 CORRELATION & REGRESSION — 131

9.1 Introduction — 131
9.2 Relationships between Variables — 132
9.3 Correlation — 133
9.3.1 Description of Correlation — 133
9.3.2 Significance of the Correlation Coefficient — 134
9.3.3 Correlation is not Necessarily Causation — 135
9.4 Regression — 136
9.4.1 Regression Method Outcome — 136
9.4.2 The Problem — 137
9.4.3 Undertaking the Regression — 139
9.4.4 Developing the Model – Unemployment only — 143
9.4.5 How Useful is our Model? — 143
9.4.6 Bringing in the Car Unemployment Variable — 144
9.4.7 Comparing Modelled & Actual Rail Demand — 145
9.4.8 Checking for Bias — 147
9.4.9 Relevant Range — 148
9.5 Chapter 9 Exercise — 149

10. REGRESSION ANALYSIS: FURTHER CONSIDERATIONS — 151

10.1 Chapter Overview — 151
10.2 Time as an Independent Variable — 151
10.3 The Illusion of Time — 153
10.4 How to Deal with Outlying Values — 154
10.4.1 What is an Outlier? — 154
10.4.2 Dealing with Outliers — 155
10.5 Dummy Variables — 156
10.5.1 What is a Dummy Variable? — 156
10.5.2 Dummy Variables in Transportation — 157
10.5.3 Application of a Dummy Variable to Performance Data — 158
10.5.4 Results from Using the Dummy Variable — 159
10.5.5 Closing Notes on Dummy Variables — 161
10.6 Updating Forecasts — 161

11 QUEUING AND SIMULATION — 165

11.1 Introduction — 165
11.2 Queuing Behaviour — 166
11.2.1 Fairness and Equity — 166
11.2.2 Baulking and Reneging — 166
11.3 Single Server Queue — 167
11.3.1 Mathematics of a Single Queue — 167
11.3.2 Varying the Rate of Arrivals — 168

- 11.4 Single Server Queue Simulation — 168
  - 11.4.1 Developing Probability Distributions — 168
  - 11.4.2 Random Numbers — 169
  - 11.4.3 Simulation Results — 170
  - 11.4.4 Full Simulation Results — 170
- 11.5 Business Impact of Simulations — 173
  - 11.5.1 Available Options — 173
  - 11.5.2 Improve the Service Rate — 173
  - 11.5.3 Add a Server — 174
  - 11.5.4 One Queue or Two? — 176
- 11.6 Simulations for Significant Events — 178
  - 11.6.1 Taking Account of Significant Events — 178
- 11.7 Lessons Learned — 179
- 11.8 Rare Incidents – An Advanced Example — 180
  - 11.8.1 Introduction — 180
  - 11.8.2 Modelling the Simulation Variables — 180
  - 11.8.3 Output from the Simulation — 182
- 11.9 Chapter Exercises — 184

12 COSTS — 185

- 12.1 The Importance of Costs — 185
  - 12.1.1 How Costs Influence Price — 185
  - 12.1.2 How Costs Influence Investment Decisions — 186
- 12.2 Sunk, Fixed and Variable Costs — 187
  - 12.2.1. Which Type of Cost? — 187
  - 12.2.2 Sunk Costs — 187
  - 12.2.3 Fixed, Semi-fixed and Variable Costs — 188
  - 12.2.4 More Considerations on Labour Costs — 191
- 12.3 Marginal Costs and Revenues — 191
  - 12.3.1 Overview of the Marginal Concept — 191
  - 12.3.2 Marginal Costs per Journey — 192
  - 12.3.3 Marginal Costs by Company — 192
- 12.4 Costs for Investment Appraisal — 196
- 12.5 Benchmarking — 197
  - 12.5.1 Introduction to Benchmarking — 197
  - 12.5.2 Obstacles to Benchmarking — 198
  - 12.5.3 Intensity of Asset Use — 199
  - 12.5.4 Seasonality — 199
  - 12.5.5 Average Trip Length — 200
  - 12.5.6 Vehicle/Building Size — 201
- 12.6 Breakdown of Costs – GB Rail — 202
  - 12.6.1 Overall Cost Structure — 202
  - 12.6.2 Drivers of TOC Costs — 203
- 12.7 Airline Costs — 205

12.8 Depreciation	207
12.9 Chapter 12 Exercises	208
12.10 Annex: Proof of Profit Maximisation	209

13 COMPANY SIZE AND STRUCTURE — 211

13.1 Introduction	211
13.2 Company Size	211
13.3 Economies of Scale	212
13.4 Long Run Average Cost	213
13.5 Company Structure	214
13.5.1 Outright Takeover	214
13.5.2 Wholly Owned Subsidiary	215
13.5.3 Conglomerate	216

14 LINEAR PROGRAMMING — 217

14.1 Introduction	217
14.2 A Simple Example of Linear Programming	218
14.3 Constraints	219
14.3.1 Aircraft Variables	219
14.3.2 Integers and Non-Negative Responses	219
14.3.3 Demand	219
14.3.4 Aircraft Supply	220
14.3.5 Route-specific Constraints	220
14.3.6 Summary of Constraints	220
14.4 Defining the Objective Function	221
14.5 Excel's Solver	221
14.6 Solution	222
14.7 Sensitivities	223
14.8 Conclusion	224

15 SUBSIDIES — 225

15.1 Introduction	225
15.2 Types of Subsidy	225
15.3 Fixed Subsidy	226
15.4 Variable/Ad Valorem Subsidies	227
15.5 Cross Subsidy	228
15.5.1 Time of Year	228
15.5.2 Subsidies between Short & Long-Haul Routes	229
15.5.3 Pricing Strategies for Different Markets	231
15.6 Arguments against Subsidies	233
15.6.1 Market Distortion	233
15.6.2 Who Benefits from Subsidies?	234
15.6.3 Flat Fares by Distance	235
15.6.4 Fares by Time of Day	236

15.7 Chapter 15 Exercise	237

16 PRINCIPLES OF MARKETING I — 239

16.1 Introduction	239
16.2 Consumer Behaviour	240
16.2.1 Dynamics of Consumer Behaviour	240
16.2.2 Culture, Demographics, Social Status	241
16.2.3 Influencers	241
16.2.4 Internal Influencers	242
16.2.5 Purchase Decision	242
16.2.6 Revealed & Stated Preference Techniques	243
16.2.7 "In the factory we make cosmetics. In the drugstore we sell hope."	244
16.3 Core and Augmented Product	244
16.3.1 Core Product	244
16.3.2 Features are a Competitive Battleground	245
16.3.3 Reservation and Ticket Purchase	245
16.3.4 Features at the Terminal	246
16.4 Product Augmented by Geography	247
16.4.1 Bringing the Core Product Closer to Home	247
16.4.2 Getting to the Port	248
16.4.3 Integration between Modes 1	248
16.4.4 Integration between Modes 2	248
16.4.5 An Example of Poor Integration	249
16.5 Difficulties in Defining the Market	250
16.6 Chapter 16 Exercise	252

17 PRINCIPLES OF MARKETING II — 253

17.1 Overview of this Chapter	253
17.2 Overall Pricing Strategy by Mode	253
17.2.1 Airline Pricing	253
17.2.2 Hotel Pricing	254
17.2.3 Rail Pricing	254
17.3 Pricing and Market Segmentation	257
17.3.1 Introduction	257
17.3.2 Traditional Segmentation Methods	257
17.3.3 Wealth/disposable income	257
17.3.4 Lifestyle Segmentation	258
17.3.5 Trade-off between Segmentation & Efficiency	259
17.4 Segmentation Barriers	260
17.4.1 Overview of Barriers	260
17.4.2 Time of Purchase – Elapsed Time	260
17.4.3 Last-Minute Bookings	261
17.5 Failure to Capture Markets	262

18 PRINCIPLES OF MARKETING III — 265

- 18.1 Chapter Overview — 265
- 18.2 Product or Service? — 265
- 18.3 Physical Evidence, People, Process — 267
  - 18.3.1 Physical Evidence — 267
  - 18.3.2 People — 267
  - 18.3.3 Process — 268
- 18.4 Service Profit Chain – the 3 'Rs' — 268
  - 18.4.1 An Alternative Approach to the 'P's' of Marketing — 268
  - 18.4.2 Retention — 269
  - 18.4.3 Referrals — 270
  - 18.4.4 Related Sales — 272
  - 18.4.5 Lifetime Value of a Customer (LVC) — 273

19 FORECASTING I — 275

- 19.1 Introduction — 275
- 19.2 Assessment of Recent Trends — 275
- 19.3 A Comparison between British and Irish Rail Demand — 276
  - 19.3.1 Recent Trends — 276
  - 19.3.2 Differences in GDP — 278
  - 19.3.3 Differences in Motorway Networks — 278
  - 19.3.4 Vehicle Kilometres Travelled by Car — 279
- 19.4 Revenues — 280
  - 19.4.1 Introduction — 280
  - 19.4.2 Pricing Policy — 281
  - 19.4.3 Forecasting Using Elasticities — 281
- 19.5 Reactions of Competitors — 281
- 19.6 Scenario Planning — 283
  - 19.6.1 Internal Consistency — 283
  - 19.6.2 "States of the World" — 284
- 19.7 Forecasting Costs — 284
- 19.8 Demand Forecasting – PDFH and Alternatives — 285
  - 19.8.1 GB Rail – Passenger Demand Forecasting Handbook — 285
  - 19.8.2 Critique of the PDFH — 286
  - 19.8.3 Alternative Methodologies — 286
  - 19.8.4 WebTAG — 287
- 19.9 Forecasting Rail Demand in Ireland — 289
- 19.10 How Effective Is the AECOM Model? — 291
- 19.11 Forecasts for Non-existent Services /Infrastructure — 292
  - 19.11.1 Introduction — 292
  - 19.11.2 New Direct Air Service — 292
  - 19.11.3 Replacing Worn-Out Infrastructure — 292
- 19.12 Chapter 19 Exercises — 295

20 FORECASTING II — 297

- 20.1 Chapter Overview — 297
- 20.2 Seasonality — 297
- 20.3 Time Series Decomposition (TSD) — 297
  - 20.3.1 Multiplication or Addition? — 297
  - 20.3.2 Assessing Seasonality — 299
  - 20.3.3 How Effective is the Model? — 302
- 20.4 Exponential Smoothing (ES) — 303
  - 20.4.1 Principles of ES — 303
- 20.5 Holt Winters Exponential Smoothing (HWES) — 305
  - 20.5.1 Overview — 305
  - 20.5.2 The HWES Model — 306
  - 20.5.3 Absolute Deviation — 306
  - 20.5.4 Optimized HWES Output — 307
  - 20.5.5 MAD for TSD Method — 308
- 20.6 Forecasting Using TSD and HWES Methods — 308
- 20.7 Lessons Learned — 310
- 20.8 Seasonality at Terminals — 311
- 20.9 Chapter 20 Exercise — 313
- 20.10 Annex: Formulation of HWES Spreadsheet — 315

21 HOW TO UNDERTAKE AN INVESTMENT APPRAISAL — 317

- 21.1 Overview — 317
- 21.2 Introducing the Discount Rate — 317
  - 21.2.1 General Concepts — 317
  - 21.2.2 The Discount Rate in Practice — 318
- 21.3 Net Present Value (NPV) — 319
- 21.4 Internal Rate of Return (IRR) — 319
- 21.5 NPV Compared to IRR: Which is Better? — 320
  - 21.5.1 NPV — 320
  - 21.5.2 IRR — 321
- 21.6 Applying Investment Appraisal Techniques — 322
- 21.7 A More Complex NPV Example — 327
  - 21.7.1 The Problem — 327
  - 21.7.2 Summarising the Data — 328
  - 21.7.3 Preparing the NPV Calculation — 329
  - 21.7.4 Calculating the NPV — 329
  - 21.7.5 Reassessing the NPV Calculation — 330
  - 21.7.6 Lessons Learned — 330
- 21.8 Lease or Buy Decision — 331
- 21.9 Benefit: Cost Ratios – An Alternative Approach — 332
- 21.10 Mitigation of Risk — 333

21.10.1 Scenarios	333
21.10.2 Optimism Bias	334
21.10.3 What a Financial Appraisal Can Miss	334
21.11 Chapter 21 Exercises	335

22 FROM INVESTMENT APPRAISAL TO ECONOMIC APPRAISAL — 337

22.1 Introduction	337
22.2 Financial and Economic Appraisals Compared	337
22.3 Stakeholders	338
23.3.1 New Airport at St Helena	338
23.3.2 Level 1 Stakeholders	338
22.3.2 Level 2 Stakeholders	339
22.3.4 Economic Factors Improve Viability	339
22.4 Geographic Area	340
22.5 Stakeholders Revisited	341
22.6 More Assumptions for the New Railway	342
22.6.1 Labour Costs	343
22.6.2 Revenues	343
22.6.3 Other Benefits	343
22.7 How are Financial and Economic Appraisals Related?	344
22.8 Value of Time	344
22.9 Wider Economic Impacts	345
22.10 Ex-post evaluation	346
22.11 Barcelona-Zaragoza-Madrid AVE Line Revisited	347
22.12 Example: An Economic Appraisal in Britain	348
22.13 Bus Station, Puerto del Carmen (PdC), Lanzarote	349
22.13.1 Objectives of a Bus Station	349
22.13.2 Description of the PdC Bus Station	350
22.13.3 Assessment of the Bus Station	351
22.14 Further Reading – Isle of Skye Bridge	351

23 CASE STUDY ON PRICE DISTORTIONS — 353

23.1 Introduction	353
23.2 Tourism Demand	354
23.2.1 Tourism and the Economy	354
23.2.2 Foreign Tourists	354
23.2.3 Peninsula Tourists	354
23.3 Spanish Leisure Trips Abroad	355
23.4 Peninsula-Canarias Air Traffic	356
23.4.1 Fares	356
23.4.2 Load Factor	357
23.5 Inter-Island Traffic	358

23.6 Inter-Island Air Fares	361
23.6.1 Types of Route	361
23.6.2 Fares on Longer Routes	362
23.6.4 Fares on Shorter Routes	363
23.7 Inter-Island Ferry Fares	364
23.8 Operators in the Canaries	365
23.8.1 Airlines	365
23.8.2 Ferries	365
23.8.3 Spotlight on Fuerteventura to Gran Canaria	366
23.9 Subsidies to Residents	367
23.9.1 Inter-Island Air Trips	367
23.9.2 Air Trips to/from the Peninsula	370
23.9.3 Ferry Trips	370
23.9.4 Summary of Subsidies	370
23.10 Tourism Expenditure Losses	370
23.10.1 Quantified Costs – Peninsula Tourists	370
23.10.2 Wider Economic Benefits	372
23.11 Alternative Uses for Funds	373
23.11.1 What Funds Are Available?	373
23.11.2 Change from Unlimited Subsidy per Person	373
23.11.3 Abolition of Subsidy	374
24 ANSWERS TO EXERCISES	375
INDEX	412

TABLE OF FIGURES

Figure 2-1: Dataset used to demonstrate Data Presentation 31
Figure 2-2: A Useful Chart or a Piece of Modern Art? 32
Figure 2-3: Passengers by Mode 33
Figure 2-4: Stacked bar version of passenger journeys 33
Figure 2-5: Initial Plot of Trips against GDP 34
Figure 2-6: Trips and GDP using Two Axes 34
Figure 2-7: Index Version of Trips vs GDP 35
Figure 3-1: Demand Schedule for Return Tickets 39
Figure 3-2: Demand Curve with Prices and Quantities 39
Figure 3-3: Notional Supply Schedule for Return Tickets 40
Figure 3-4: Supply Curve with Prices and Quantities 40
Figure 3-5: Equilibrium Point for Supply and Demand 41
Figure 3-6: Demand Curve Shifts Downwards 42
Figure 3-7: Supply Curve Shifts Upwards 42
Figure 4-1: Differentiating Factors by Mode 46
Figure 4-2: Single fares Frankfurt-Palma on 31/08/2015 46
Figure 4-3: Airlines Operating between Bangkok and Singapore 47
Figure 4-4: Map of Surat Thani Province 53
Figure 4-5: Impact of Monopoly at Koh Samui 53
Figure 5-1: Demand and Individual Price for each Customer 57
Figure 5-2: Demand and Flat Rate Price for each Customer 58
Figure 5-3: Demand and Price Discrimination (market segmentation) 59
Figure 5-4: Generalised Journey Time Example 60
Figure 5-5: Demand Curve Elasticities 62
Figure 5-6: Demand Curve Elasticities – increasing 63
Figure 5-7: GJT of rail and bus between Luton airport and central London 65
Figure 6-1: Modal Split of Domestic Passenger-Kms (%) 70
Figure 6-2: Comparative Journey Cost 71
Figure 6-3: Distribution of Journey Lengths, England (%) 73
Figure 6-4: Modal Share by Distance (England, 2014) 73
Figure 6-5: Market Shares on Paris-Lyon 74
Figure 6-6: Air Traffic Volume between London and Scotland (000s) 75
Figure 6-7: Snapshot of Paris-Marseille fares 76
Figure 6-8: Demand (000s) on the English Channel Corridor 2005-15 78
Figure 6-9: Cross-Channel Market Share by Mode 79
Figure 6-10: Population of Major Towns and Growth 80
Figure 6-11: Barcelona-Zaragoza-Madrid Corridor 80
Figure 6-12: Air vs. Rail, Madrid-Barcelona 81
Figure 6-13: Road Traffic on Corridor (Average Daily Flow) 81
Figure 6-14: Zaragoza Rail Traffic 82
Figure 6-15: Reworked Modal Shares 83
Figure 6-16: Madrid-Seville Corridor 84
Figure 7-1: Terminology for Money Adjusted by Inflation 87
Figure 7-2: Inflation and Ticket Prices 88
Figure 7-3: Example of Current and Real Revenue (5% Inflation) 88
Figure 7-4: Current and Real Revenue and Costs 89
Figure 7-5: Italian Kerosene Prices 90
Figure 7-6: Three Versions of Kerosene Prices 91
Figure 7-7: Simple Measure for Measuring Price Volatility 91
Figure 7-8: Nominal and Real GDP, UK 92

Figure 7-9: Calculation of Real GDP figures (£bn) 93
Figure 7-10: Relationship between GDP and Trip Rates 93
Figure 7-11: Changes in Rail Demand in Great Britain & Real GDP 94
Figure 7-12: Changes in Transport Demand & Real GDP, Canary Islands 95
Figure 7-13: Expected Income and Population Impacts on Demand 96
Figure 8-1: Raw Data of Air Passengers from Mainland Spain and UK 99
Figure 8-2: Data Summary Tools 100
Figure 8-3: Outcome of Poisson Distribution 106
Figure 8-4: Selection of Individual Bus Journey Times (in minutes) 107
Figure 8-5: Count of Late and Early Journeys 107
Figure 8-6: T Distribution 110
Figure 8-7: Conversion of T value to Probability 111
Figure 8-8: Probability of Between 895 and 915 Trains On Time 112
Figure 8-9: Middle 95% of the T Distribution 113
Figure 8-10: T values 115
Figure 8-11: Ten Days of Passenger Counts 116
Figure 8-12: Confidence Intervals with Different Sample Sizes 117
Figure 8-13: Twenty Days of Passenger Counts 118
Figure 8-14: Summary of Results of Three Sample Sizes 119
Figure 8-15: Sample Size (Y axis) and Range 120
Figure 8-16: Tourism Volume Estimates for Lanzarote 122
Figure 8-17: UK-Lanzarote Flight Volumes 123
Figure 8-18: Punctuality on Gatwick-Malaga, April 2015 (in minutes) 124
Figure 8-19: Results of Airline Punctuality Example 125
Figure 8-20: Confidence Interval by Airline 125
Figure 9 1: Relationship between Trips and GDP from Figure 7-12 132
Figure 9-2: Three Versions of Correlation 133
Figure 9-3: Calculation of Correlation Coefficient 134
Figure 9-4: Line of Best Fit through the Data 136
Figure 9-5: Raw data to be used for analysis 137
Figure 9-6: Scatter diagram of rail demand and unemployment 138
Figure 9-7: Scatter diagram of rail demand and car ownership 138
Figure 9-8: Step 1 of undertaking a regression in Excel 140
Figure 9-9: Step 2 of undertaking a regression in Excel 141
Figure 9-10: Output from Regression Analysis - Unemployment only 142
Figure 9-11: Results using Unemployment and Car Ownership 142
Figure 9-12: Comparison of Results 144
Figure 9-13: Confidence Intervals of Variables 145
Figure 9-14: Modelled and Residual Values 146
Figure 9-15: Results of Model compared to Actual Data 146
Figure 9-16: Detection of Bias in the Model 147
Figure 10-1: Actual Performance over 52 periods (4 years) 151
Figure 10-2: Daily Performance (PPM) 152
Figure 10-3: AML Residuals over Time 153
Figure 10-4: AML Residuals Ordered by Size of Observed AML 154
Figure 10-5: No Outliers 154
Figure 10-6: One Outlier 155
Figure 10-7: Delay Minutes Attributable to a Railway Operator 155
Figure 10-8: Four Weeks of Daily Sales Data 157
Figure 10-9: Regression Input Using a Dummy Variable 157
Figure 10-10: Dummy Regression Output (Abridged) 158
Figure 10-11: Initial Residuals Analysis (Time) 159
Figure 10-13: Residuals by Observation Size Without and With Dummy 160
Figure 10-14: Regression with 39 periods 161

Figure 10-15: Regression with 52 Periods 162
Figure 10-16: Comparison of Errors 162
Figure 11-1: Average Waiting Time per Person by Arrival Rate 168
Figure 11-2: Probability Distributions for Arrivals and Service 169
Figure 11-3: First Six Rows of Simulation 170
Figure 11-4: Three Simulation Runs 171
Figure 11-5: Probability Distribution of Unserved Customers 172
Figure 11-6: Summary Results of Simulations 172
Figure 11-7: Improvement in Service Rate 173
Figure 11-8: Variation in Arrivals per Hour 174
Figure 11-9: Impact of Adding a Server 175
Figure 11-10: Reduced Waiting Time with Additional Server 175
Figure 11-11: Demand and Cost of Additional Server 175
Figure 11-12: Single vs Two Parallel Queues 176
Figure 11-13: Probability of X Events Occurring per Month 178
Figure 11-14: 12 Months' Simulation for Invoking "Plan B" 179
Figure 11-15: Incidence Occurrence Distribution 180
Figure 11-16: Length of Incident Distribution 181
Figure 11-17: Time of Day Distribution 182
Figure 11-18: Distribution of Causation of Incident 182
Figure 11-19: Results of the Simulation (Extract) 183
Figure 12-1: Sample Overview of Bus and Rail Costs 185
Figure 12-2: Levels of Average Fare on Bus and Train 186
Figure 12-3: Graphic demonstrating different Cost Structures 190
Figure 12-4: Examples of Marginal Cost in Transport and Travel 192
Figure 12-5: Demonstration of Average and Marginal Cost 193
Figure 12-6: Average and Marginal Cost Curves 193
Figure 12-7: Output, Revenue, Costs and Profits 194
Figure 12-8: Comparison of Marginal Revenue and Costs 194
Figure 12-9: Marginal Revenue Costs and Profits 195
Figure 12-10: Items to include in an Investment Appraisal 197
Figure 12-11: Performance Indicators for Balearic Islands Airports 198
Figure 12-12: Obstacles to Benchmarking Transport Businesses 199
Figure 12-13: Complete Journey Time Cycle for Aircraft 199
Figure 12-14: Stage length and cost per ASK 200
Figure 12-15: CASM Adjusted for Stage Length 201
Figure 12-16: Daily Seat Capacity by Class from Heathrow to Bahrain 202
Figure 12-17: Overall Cost Structure of GB Railway Operators (TOCs) 203
Figure 12-18: Operating Costs (expressed in pence per passenger-km) 204
Figure 13-1: Supply and Demand in the US Aviation Sector 211
Figure 13-2: Example of Scale Economies 212
Figure 13-3: Long Run Average Cost Curve 213
Figure 14-1: Data on Zurich Air's Fleet 218
Figure 14-2: Flight Distance and Demand by Route 218
Figure 14-3: List of Aircraft Allocation Constraints 220
Figure 14-4: Starting Point to Solve the Aircraft Allocation Problem 221
Figure 14-5: Solver Screenshot 222
Figure 14-6: Results from Solver 222
Figure 14-7: Removing the La Palma Restriction 223
Figure 14-8: Accra Converted to B787s Only 223
Figure 14-9: Only Nine Boeing 787s Available 224
Figure 15-1: Equilibrium with a Fixed Subsidy 226
Figure 15-2: Equilibrium with an Ad Valorem Subsidy 227
Figure 15-3: easyJet Annual Profit 2011-2015 229

Figure 15-4: Fares on First Great Western Services, Summer 2015 230
Figure 15-5: Cross-subsidy on Airline Fares 232
Figure 15-6: London to Dubai return, September 30th to October 8th 2015 232
Figure 15-7: Fares Summary on London-Dubai-Sydney (£) 233
Figure 15-8: Impact of Discriminatory and Subsidized Fares 234
Figure 15-9: Comparison of Fares in London and Madrid (2015) 236
Figure 16-1: Overview of Consumer Behaviour Influences 240
Figure 16-2: Punctuality between London and New York 243
Figure 16-3: Lanzarote Airport Check-In, January 2016 246
Figure 16-4: Benidorm Bus Station 249
Figure 16-5: Trade-Off between Journey Time and Price 250
Figure 16-6: Journey Time and Price, adjusted for GJT 251
Figure 17-1: Pricing Structure on Ryanair 253
Figure 17-2: Cost of One Night in Leeds, UK 254
Figure 17-3: Rail Fares between Manchester and London 255
Figure 17-4: Rail Fares between Valencia and Madrid 256
Figure 17-5: Valencia-Madrid Fares - Cheapest Fares 256
Figure 17-6: Sample of Prices Based on Time before Purchase 260
Figure 17-7: Screenshot from Lastminute.com 262
Figure 17-8: Fares for Two Types of Off-Peak passenger 263
Figure 18-1: Services as % of GDP in 2014 by Region 265
Figure 18-2: Impact of Increased Retention 270
Figure 18-3: Impact of Referrals 271
Figure 18-4: Details of Ancillary Revenue, 2013 272
Figure 18-5: LVC Example 273
Figure 19-1: Two Examples of Optimistic Forecasts 276
Figure 19-2: Passenger Journeys in GB (millions) 277
Figure 19-3: Passenger journeys in Ireland (thousands) 277
Figure 19-4: Percent changes in real GDP, Ireland and UK 278
Figure 19-5: Length of Motorway Networks in km 279
Figure 19-6: Vehicle-km by Car, GB and Ireland 279
Figure 19-7: Market Shares at Stansted Airport 282
Figure 19-8: Long Distance Car Journey Times from Greater London 288
Figure 19-9: AADT per Lane on the M1 289
Figure 19-10: Actual and Modelled Data for the Republic of Ireland 290
Figure 19-11: Author's calculation of the Error Term in the AECOM Model 290
Figure 19-12: Actual and Modelled Demand on Irish Railways 2010-2014 291
Figure 19-13: Master Plan Forecasts for TAZARA 293
Figure 20-1: Hourly Bus Service Demand 298
Figure 20-2: Air Traffic between UK and Turkey, Jan 2006- Dec 2009 299
Figure 20-3: Air Traffic between the UK and South Africa, 2006-2010 300
Figure 20-4: Turkish Data with Trend Line 300
Figure 20-5: Monthly Weights for Turkish Data 301
Figure 20-6: Calculation of Residuals - 2006 Data 302
Figure 20-7: Actual and Modelled Turkish Demand 302
Figure 20-8: Residual Terms of the Mode 303
Figure 20-9: Simple ES Example 304
Figure 20-10: Previous Table Showing Formulae 304
Figure 20-11: Actual and ES Data 305
Figure 20-12: HWES Model (Abridged) 306
Figure 20-13: LP Formulation to Solve Parameters 307
Figure 20-14: Optimised HWES Output 308
Figure 20-15: Outturn Demand Against Forecasts 309
Figure 20-16: Graph of Actual and Forecast Demand 309

Figure 20-17: Summer Demand to Turkish Resorts 310
Figure 20-18: Aircraft Movements at Bole Airport – Morning 312
Figure 21-1: Value of €1 Over Time 318
Figure 21-2: Current Value of a future €1 319
Figure 21-3: NPV Example 319
Figure 21-4: NPV and IRR Combined 320
Figure 21-5: Conflicting NPV and IRR Results 321
Figure 21-6: Guidelines for Discount Rates from the Green Book 323
Figure 21-7: Step 1 – Set out all costs and revenues 323
Figure 21-8: Step 2 – Add the annual summary of revenues and costs 324
Figure 21-9: Step 3 – Add a discount rate into your spreadsheet 324
Figure 21-10: Step 4 – Calculating the NPV 325
Figure 21-11: Step 5 – Calculating the Internal Rate of Return 326
Figure 21-12: Step 6 – Confirmation that the IRR is Correct 327
Figure 21-13: Summarised Data for New Route Problem 328
Figure 21-14: Net Profit Calculations by Route 329
Figure 21-15: NPV Calculation 329
Figure 21-16: Sensitivity of Total Demand to Annual Growth Rates 333
Figure 22-1: Urban Rail Service: Financial & Economic Appraisal Items 340
Figure 22-2: Transport Network for A, B and C 340
Figure 22-3: Benefits of New Rail Service 341
Figure 22-4: Benefits of Interested Parties 342
Figure 22-5: Relationship between Financial and Economic Appraisals 344
Figure 22-6: Changes in Value of Time per Hour (2010 prices) 345
Figure 22-7: Benefits of Madrid-Barcelona AVE Line 347
Figure 22-8: Annual Benefits and Costs for Rotherwas Rail Project 349
Figure 22-9: PdC Bus Station 350
Figure 23-1: Foreign Tourists by Island, 2007 and 2014 354
Figure 23-2: Peninsula and Total Tourists by Island, 2007 and 2014 355
Figure 23-3: Tourism Demand over Time 355
Figure 23-4: Spanish Leisure Trips Abroad 356
Figure 23-5: Minimum Single Air Fares from Tenerife, 2015 (€) 356
Figure 23-6: Flights in 2014 by Island to and from the Peninsula 357
Figure 23-7: 2014 Load Factors by Airline 358
Figure 23-8: Inter Island Traffic: Major Flows 359
Figure 23-9: Changes in Real GDP and Tourist Volumes 360
Figure 23-10: Top Six Flows Demand Changes, All Modes 360
Figure 23-11: Propensity of Tourists to "Island Hop" 361
Figure 23-12: Canarian and Balearic Air Fares 362
Figure 23-13: Fares on Shorter Routes 363
Figure 23-14: Ferry Fares Tenerife-Gran Canaria 364
Figure 23-15: Ferry Prices in the Canaries and Elsewhere 364
Figure 23-16: Market Shares by Route 366
Figure 23-17: Events of the FUE-GC Route 366
Figure 23-18: Demand by Mode on Fuerteventura-Gran Canaria 367
Figure 23-19: Total and Subsidized Air Trips 368
Figure 23-20: Seasonality of Demand January 2011– April 2015 369
Figure 23-21: Lost Expenditure from Peninsula Tourists 371
Figure: Euro: NKR Exchange rate 388

1 INTRODUCTION

1.1 For Whom This Book is Written

If you work in operations, finance or marketing in any part of the public transport sector, this book was written for you.

Business planning is a combination of many closely intertwined management disciplines, so chapters include advice on pricing and product strategy, marketing, linear programming, regression analysis, queuing theory and investment appraisal techniques as well as economics. All have impact on assessing changes in supply, demand, revenue and costs, so it is important to be aware of these techniques and understand how what they monitor affects the overall health of any business. The book demonstrates how they can be applied across the public transport industry.

Examples taken from all over the world show that the issues discussed are relevant to more than a single country, region or city and work for the whole industry, globally.

1.2 Why this Book?

The principal objective of this book is to provide people with a set of practical business planning tools that can be used to develop a business in the public transport sector. For the purposes of this book, public transport includes railways, ferry, long distance bus/coach and air transport services.

The book covers a wide range of subject areas, including economics, statistical and forecasting techniques, marketing and investment appraisal. Economics is a subject that many operators approach with trepidation, hoping to ignore it, or leave it to specialists. This is unwise, as no manager can go far without needing to make decisions based on customer prices and company costs and income (otherwise known as microeconomics), or on the more global and national effects of financial decisions (macroeconomics) that affect all our lives and, frankly, these decisions are too important to be left to economists!

Similarly, the book contains a considerable number of numerical techniques from the mundane (probability, for example) to the esoteric (Holt Winters Exponential Smoothing).

It is critical to bear in mind that businesses cannot be assessed or planned without numbers, be they concerning costs, demand, revenue capacity or seasonality, to name but some categories.

This book places a heavy emphasis on tools to enable the user to understand how a business can quantify many of the important issues it faces.

Forecasting tools are also a significant feature of this book.

These tools help us to quantify the three standard questions that business planning should undertake, namely, 'where have we been', 'where are we now' and 'where will we go'.

It is important to point out at the outset that these tools are a guide to decision-making and certainly do not replace it; a plumber, for example, not only needs the tools to do the job but also the expertise in knowing which tools to use in a given situation and how to use the tools appropriately.

Business planning is about more than supply and demand. Marketing strategy also plays a role in determining future demand, costs and revenues.

If, for example, we need to calculate market share, just how do we define the market in the first place? Long distance rail, for example, will compete with air and/or coach services sometimes and car journeys pretty much always. Finding air transport passenger volumes is straightforward; determining coach volumes on a particular route is well-nigh impossible in most countries whilst private cars' share of a corridor requires the use of traffic counts (known as secondary data) or undertaking your own primary research, which may be unfeasible and is certainly expensive. The book contains an example of market-share calculations for the corridor between Spain's two largest cities, which results in some messy calculations, but that is one of the objectives of this book – to reveal the reality of incomplete or incorrect data yet making the best of what we have available.

Messy calculations and results as well as uncertainty are very much the nature of the game. One of my abiding memories during a lecture was to be told, "you can't be right but you can be wrong." What (I believe) this lecturer meant was that if we were studying a market that has been declining by, say, 5% per annum for the last ten years and were presented with a forecast projecting annual growth of 20%, we would probably have very good cause to fire the forecaster on the spot!

Although we shall examine certain economic models, it is important to realise that these are only starting points on the long journey towards reality.

It is not so much that the economic models are faulty but more a matter of appreciating that they have their limits. Investment appraisal techniques address the question, "is it worth it?".

Nobody will want to sign off on a project that loses a company money but, particularly with transport projects, there are very often benefits and costs beyond the company's assessment of a specific project. So, as well as looking at its financial impact on a company, this book will also cover an assessment of costs and benefits on society, such as time-saving and the impact of employment. This wider assessment is known as economic appraisal.

Whilst it is neither the intention nor the objective of this book that you become expert in these techniques – there are plenty of good, detailed textbooks covering marketing, statistics, financial management and so on – you will nonetheless be guided, through using them, to appreciate how they function and to question how results of these techniques are interpreted.

Knowing what questions to ask when presented with analysis is an extremely valuable skill. Whether publicly-owned or in the private sector, whether providing a public service or run purely for profit, transport businesses cannot avoid being subject to the normal disciplines of business. This applies both to the industry as a whole and to its individual components and companies.

Questions of raising money, controlling costs, and maximising income apply as much to the transport sector as to any other. However, given the public sector's involvement in many areas of transport, such as ports, airports or major railway stations (to name but three), investment decisions take into account economic as well as financial considerations more than in many other sectors of the economy. You will find several case studies in the text, which show the application of some of the theory.

These studies come principally from Spain, where I have lived for the past seven years and the United Kingdom, where I was born and educated.

There are also many references to the Canary Islands, where I live now.

There are two reasons for using Canary Islands data, other than a local interest: first, data is much easier to come by in this market compared to the UK or mainland Spain public transport market and, second, there is a choice of only two modes for travel – air and ferry – which makes inter-island travel an excellent place to view how the theories turn out in practice.

1.3 About the Author

Up until 1988, I worked in two British transport companies, British Rail and London Transport. Since then, I have been involved in several franchising competitions for rail services in Great Britain.

I have also worked on the other side of the fence, particularly in auditing revenue and performance models for the Department of Transport and Network Rail.

On the international front, I have worked on major passenger, freight and infrastructure projects on all five continents.

I have been particularly involved in transport and corridor studies throughout Africa as well as the Caribbean, Southeast Asia and Europe and have also participated in studies concerning the political and structural aspects of transport infrastructure, demand forecasting and economic/ financial analysis (including cost-benefit analyses). In addition,

I have undertaken European aid projects on ex-post evaluation and institutional restructuring.

I am also employed by Warwick University as a Teaching Associate in Modelling for Management and by Birmingham University, in a similar role, for Service Operations Management and by the Institute of Railway Operators (UK) as a tutor in Railway Economics and Business Organization.

I have previously worked part-time as a lecturer at Westminster University Business School and as a freelance lecturer elsewhere in the London area on a wide array of subjects including quantitative analysis for marketing, services marketing, business strategy and financial management.

1.4 How this Book is Structured

First, we start with a Chapter on data presentation. This might seem like an odd topic to start the book but in the same way that 'a picture can paint a thousand words', a well-constructed graph or chart can provide much more insight into an issue that a sheet full of numbers. The data presentation techniques covered in Chapter 2 are employed throughout the book.

Chapters 3 and 4 introduce two core concepts for this book, which are the laws of supply and demand followed by discussion on how a particular transport industry is structured. The behaviour of firms in the market place will change considerably depending on whether there is cut-throat competition, a monopoly provider or something in between these two extremes.

Chapter 5 is the third Chapter on economics. In this Chapter, we focus on more transport-specific issues such as the generalised journey time (a door-to-door journey time will usually include getting to and from an airport, station or port, waiting times for the service and perhaps an interchange on the way) and elasticities, which examine how demand varies in relation to ticket price or income, for example.

Chapter 6 applies the concepts of the preceding Chapters with an examination of how modes compete with each other. The Chapter introduces the examples of the short sea Cross Channel market between the UK and France and the Madrid-Zaragoza-Barcelona corridor in Spain.

Chapter 7 is the final Chapter on applied economics and discusses the role of Gross Domestic Product (GDP) in the passenger transport sector and how to account for inflation and exchange rates when undertaking business planning. This book is very much about the application of theory and arriving at quantifiable solutions to issues in the transport sector, so the next three Chapters discuss various numerical techniques.

Chapter 8 looks at how we can summarise data, the broad issues we encounter when using samples of data (which arise in just about every economic evaluation that has ever been undertaken). This Chapter also introduces popular probability distributions, which are applied in later Chapters.

In Chapter 9, we will first look at ways of measuring relationships between variables and then meet a technique known as regression, which allows us to understand relationships between several variables at once and is also a valuable technique for forecasting.

Chapter 10 continues with regression, examining further topics. One factor prevalent in many transport terminals is queuing, either at machines or manned windows for tickets, for check-in or immigration control.

Chapter 11 provides an overview of how queues are modelled, the cost implications of queuing and the impacts of improving the queuing system to the customers' benefit.

Next, we define various types of costs in Chapter 12. To what extent are they fixed and what is the impact on overall costs of ramping up or reducing service? Understand the nature of costs in a transport business will have an impact on cost control and how prices for the service are set.

Costs and how businesses are best managed lead to questions over how a business with two or more brands or separate markets should be structured.

In Chapter 13, we will examine some important economic concepts, especially economies of scale and scope, and how these theories influence an organisation's structure.

Chapter 14 provides an extension of the assessment of transport costs through a brief introduction to linear programming.

Although this somewhat complex subject is generally perceived as belonging to the realms of operational research rather than business planning, the outputs from the technique are definitely of relevance to many business disciplines.

Subsidies are the main subject of Chapter 15. We will examine what types of subsidy are used in the transport sector and provide arguments for and against the use of subsidies. We will also discuss whether funds used to subsidise service can be put to better use elsewhere.

The issues of pricing and subsidies provide a segue into the next three Chapters, which provide an overview of marketing. In Chapter 16, we will discuss how consumers behave. Classical economic theory assumes that consumers are rational and have full access to information.

Whilst the latter is probably more true now than previously, thanks to the internet, consumers are guided as much by emotions and peer pressure as by rational choice.

Chapter 17 addresses the important distinction between products and services and how marketing strategy differs between these two concepts.

In Chapter 18, the last of the three principles of marketing Chapters, we will take a look at pricing and how this differs between different market segments. We will also look at how companies try to prevent 'leakage' between segments to improve the transport company's profitability. Forecasting is an essential element of business planning and we now return to this subject.

Chapter 19 applies the discussion on regression in Chapter 9 and takes a more in-depth look at forecasting and its pitfalls. When forecasting, it is important to assess various options/scenarios and to consider the reactions of competitors; the Chapter will provide some guidance on these topics.

In Chapter 20, we consider the role that time plays in short-term forecasting and examines particularly how we handle the problems of projecting demand-trends, taking account of seasonal variation.

The next two Chapters focus on the technique of investment appraisal, which we will examine from two quite different viewpoints. In Chapter 21, after a discussion of the tools used to appraise investments, we will assess an investment from the point of view of a company that wishes to invest in a new route, terminal or vehicles. The focus of this Chapter is very much on financial viability and profitability. By contrast, in Chapter 22, we switch the emphasis to society as a whole and examine economic appraisals, discussing the inherent difficulties and uncertainties in carrying out these appraisals.

The final core Chapter of the book is a brand-new case study written specifically for this text.

In Chapter 23, we assess how the distortions in the market caused by subsidies to transport prices both to and from mainland Spain and within the Canary Islands archipelago have detrimental economic consequences on the islands' tourism revenue.

You will see that there is a small number of exercises to attempt at the end of most Chapters. Some of these problems are quite lengthy and complicated, but then, problems sometimes can be vague, information is not always available and assumptions may need to be made.

In Chapter 24, you will find detailed solutions to these problems.

1.5 Excel

The book uses a wide variety of techniques from Excel and the reader is assumed to have a reasonable knowledge of how to use a spreadsheet. Although it is possible to go through the book without using Excel, it would be beneficial to go through the exercises to help you understand the concepts and calculations in this book.

For some of the more complex examples and exercises, sheets showing the formulae and cell references are presented.

Some quite large datasets are used in the book and these can all be downloaded in one file ("Data Sets") at

http://adamsimmons.biz/business-planning-in-transport/.

2 PRINCIPLES OF DATA PRESENTATION

2.1 Introduction

Acquiring data is important but how the information is presented is equally important. If you cannot get your message across, then much of your effort will simply have been wasted.

Figure 2-1 shows a table of data. Although such tables can provide precise numbers, they are not especially good at explaining trends and comparing one set of numbers with another. To illustrate the value and power of charts, we will use data from the Canary Islands. For now, do not be concerned with the 'real GDP' column, as this will be explained in detail in Section 7.3; we will just say that it is a measure of the total wealth generated by a country or, in this case, region.

Figure 2-1: Dataset used to demonstrate Data Presentation

	Trips Las Palmas - Tenerife	Air	Ferry	Real GDP (€m)
2002	1,719,073	463,719	1,255,354	36,800
2003	1,752,738	478,616	1,274,122	38,723
2004	1,759,606	580,642	1,178,964	39,942
2005	1,707,544	721,420	986,124	41,659
2006	1,888,450	799,905	1,088,545	43,591
2007	1,963,065	808,338	1,154,727	44,340
2008	1,855,284	802,164	1,053,120	44,442
2009	1,734,495	738,927	995,568	42,800
2010	1,728,062	701,703	1,026,359	42,526
2011	1,789,203	754,652	1,034,551	41,752
2012	1,612,298	667,701	944,597	39,997
2013	1,749,410	574,372	1,175,038	40,288
2014	1,755,457	615,482	1,139,975	41,523

2.2 Presentation of Data

The first rule of data presentation is to make sure that a chart is not cluttered. If a chart has too many lines or blocks, then the chart will be like a piece of modern art: nice to look at but useless for presenting a business case! I hope that Figure 2-2, taken from a professional publication, which shall remain nameless, illustrates the point.

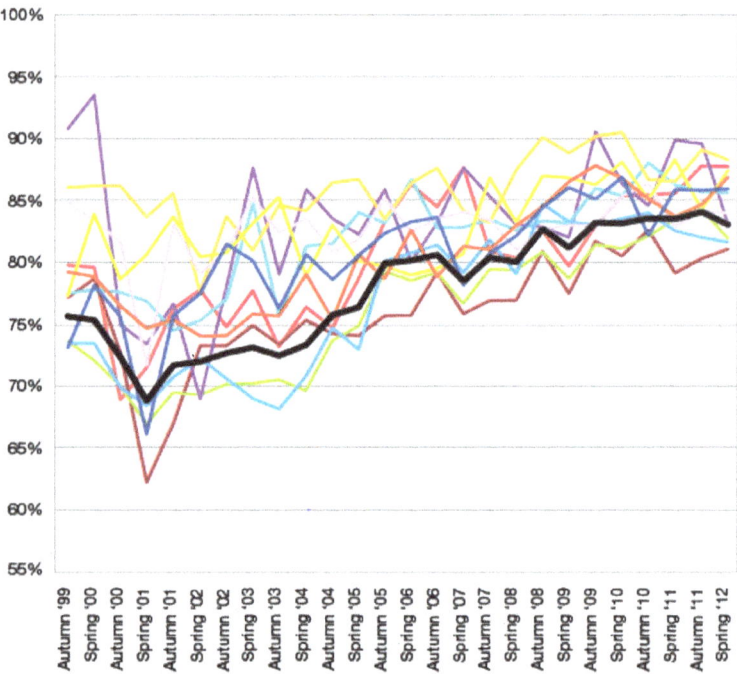

Figure 2-2: A Useful Chart or a Piece of Modern Art?

This figure shows eleven variables on a chart, which is simply too many.

The solution in this case would be to either delete variables which are less important or to split the graph into three separate ones, with three to four variables on each.

2.3 What is the Message?

Going back to our dataset, how we present the data will vary depending on what message we wish to convey to our audience and Figure 2-3 presents the same information but in different ways.

Figure 2-3: Passengers by Mode

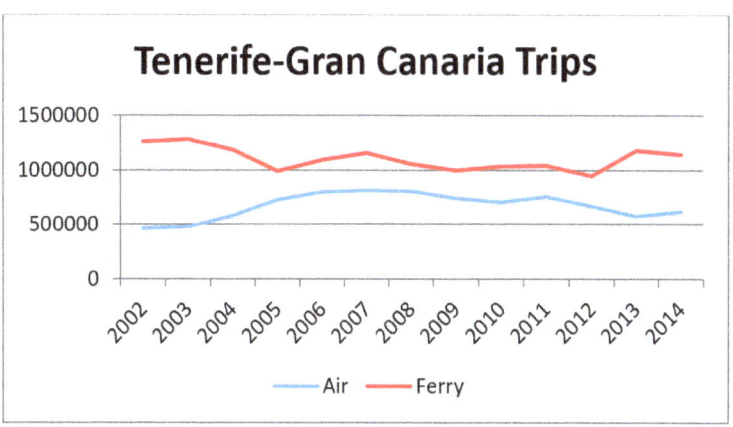

Figure 2-3 shows the number of trips by mode over the thirteen years studied. If you are trying to understand how the airlines are competing in this market, then this figure is helpful; it shows that, up until 2006, air travel increased whilst ferry travel declined but, in the last couple of years, ferry travel has increased its dominance in this market. What it does not really show us is the size of the overall market.

Figure 2-4: Stacked bar version of passenger journeys

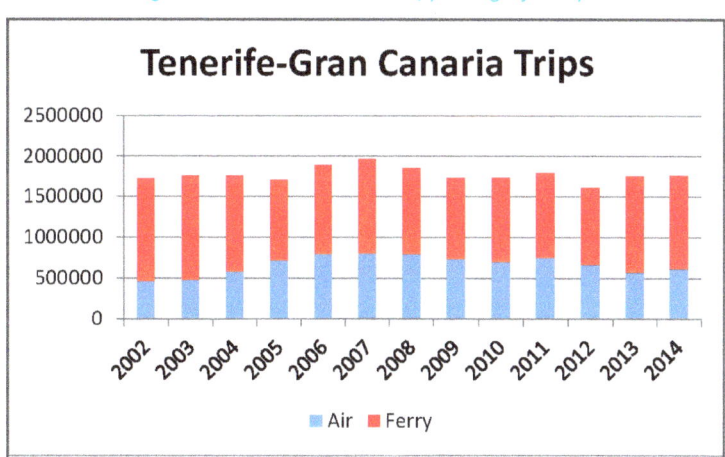

Figure 2-4 alleviates this problem by using a stacked bar chart. We can now see that the overall market for travel between Gran Canaria and Tenerife declined from 2007 but has been reasonably stable since 2009.

2.4 Plotting Data with Different Orders of Magnitude

Next, we will plot the total number of trips against GDP. Our first attempt, using the same axis, is unsatisfactory, as it does not show us the movements in GDP because the vertical axis cannot cope simultaneously with both numbers in the thousands (GDP in €m) and in millions (number of trips).

We can see the result in Figure 2-5.

Figure 2-5: Initial Plot of Trips against GDP

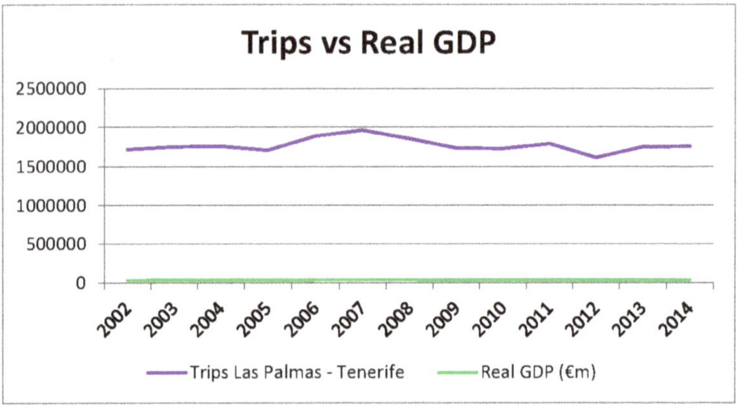

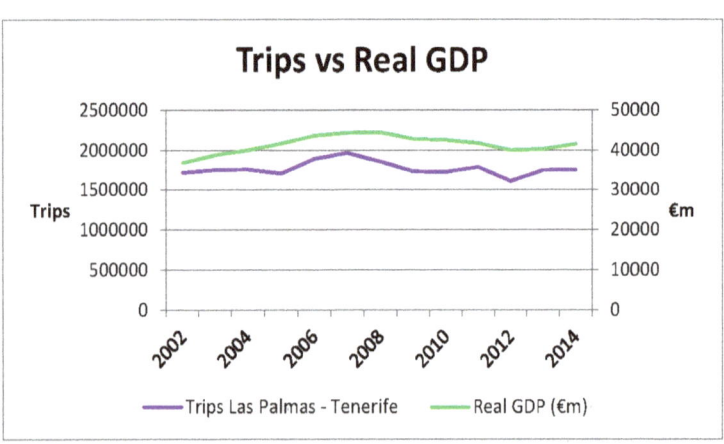

To get around this problem, Excel allows us to create a secondary axis. Now, let us draw a line graph of passenger journeys using these indices and we get Figure 2-6 as a result.

Figure 2-6: Trips and GDP using Two Axes

This chart is an improvement; in it we can see movement in both trips and GDP. However, using different vertical axes for the two sets of data can be somewhat confusing and Figure 2-6 also has the problem that most of the chart area is blank.

To overcome this problem, we can use a process of indexation. For both trips and GDP, we fix the base year as 100 and subsequent years show the changes in relation to 100.

We have also eliminated the blank space problem we encountered in Figure 2-6 by forcing the vertical axis to start at 90 rather than 0.

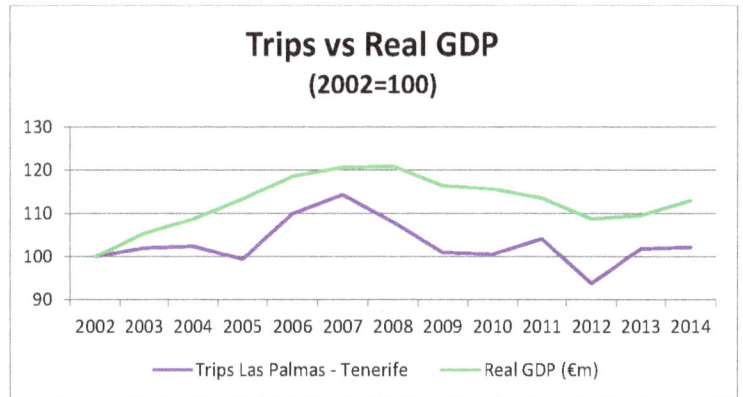

Figure 2-7: Index Version of Trips vs GDP

Although we no longer have the absolute values of the number of trips and GDP, this should not be a problem provided that, together with charts developed from the data, we also present the data from Figure 2-1.

One revealing point from 2-7 is that there seems to be a relationship between the number of trips and GDP over time, as they increase and decline in tandem, albeit at different rates.

It is easier to discern these trends if we use a metaphorical magnifying glass on the data, as we have done here by reducing the range of the vertical axis by removing the blank space at the bottom of Figure 2-6.

We will explore the extent of this relationship in Chapter 8.

2.5 Chapter 2 Exercises

Question 1 Suggest at least TWO ways in which the following data for the demand by various modes over a specific corridor can be presented graphically and then develop the charts. Which method do you prefer and why? What information do your charts provide?

	2012	2013	2014	2015
Car	21,592	21,464	22,287	20,864
Train	17,603	18,592	19,176	20,475
Bus	11,938	12,365	13,017	13,758

Question 2 The Table on the following page shows the number of tourists per month visiting the island of Tenerife from January 2011 to June 2015 from the United Kingdom and mainland Spain. Chart this data and discuss what trends and fluctuations you see in the data.

	UK	Spain		UK	Spain
Jan-11	100,888	57,951	Apr-13	140,557	43,755
Feb-11	125,162	47,633	May-13	135,190	50,213
Mar-11	139,560	50,073	Jun-13	133,600	58,783
Apr-11	145,417	59,788	Jul-13	144,048	73,691
May-11	121,317	52,153	Aug-13	148,225	76,460
Jun-11	106,890	57,282	Sep-13	136,739	62,557
Jul-11	148,156	72,138	Oct-13	162,945	58,243
Aug-11	146,684	86,534	Nov-13	135,803	49,393
Sep-11	144,433	76,177	Dec-13	140,249	62,261
Oct-11	163,311	68,841	Jan-14	130,537	44,438
Nov-11	132,974	58,243	Feb-14	127,675	36,679
Dec-11	136,865	67,558	Mar-14	148,517	38,074
Jan-12	115,148	52,238	Apr-14	162,088	50,704
Feb-12	124,463	48,946	May-14	146,408	42,175
Mar-12	147,395	45,542	Jun-14	136,609	39,596
Apr-12	136,309	64,247	Jul-14	144,506	65,739
May-12	122,613	60,406	Aug-14	168,431	78,275
Jun-12	135,139	60,176	Sep-14	158,895	62,015
Jul-12	136,723	75,028	Oct-14	184,783	51,684
Aug-12	139,207	73,055	Nov-14	135,795	41,020
Sep-12	132,529	57,817	Dec-14	140,327	51,353
Oct-12	162,087	48,928	Jan-15	136,212	45,038
Nov-12	134,860	37,229	Feb-15	129,295	46,946
Dec-12	129,054	55,797	Mar-15	162,060	40,827
Jan-13	113,149	46,438	Apr-15	143,447	47,810
Feb-13	122,094	39,563	May-15	142,013	49,691
Mar-13	148,313	45,715	Jun-15	139,344	53,063

Source of data: ISTAC (http://www.gobiernodecanarias.org/istac/)

3 MARKETS, SUPPLY AND DEMAND

3.1 Introduction

In these next three chapters, we will be going through some principles of economics that will be applied in later chapters. These include demand and supply, industry structure, generalised journey time, price setting and elasticity. We will also discuss precisely what we mean by cost later, in this book.

3.2 Markets

Much of economic theory and its application is about markets, but what do we mean by this? In the transport sector, defining a market can be challenging!

Let us examine the market between Malmö and Stockholm, approximately 610km apart. If we examine the suppliers of air transport between Malmö and Arlanda (Stockholm's principal airport, which is 40km from the centre), we would conclude that there was a duopoly, as only Norwegian and SAS offer service on this route.

Next, we can bring into play Bromma airport in Stockholm, which is much closer to central Stockholm (10km). A third airline, Malmö Aviation, flies several times a day between the Malmö and Bromma. Flights between the two cities take a little over one hour.

The route from Malmö has been used as an example because of the unusual nature of the city's relationship with its airport. Although Malmö airport is 30km from the centre of the city,

Copenhagen airport is just 2km farther and is much faster to reach by public transport from Malmö than the local airport.

Copenhagen has a somewhat higher frequency of flights provided by Norwegian and SAS but also a daily flight by Ryanair between Copenhagen and Skavsta airport, which is some 100km to the southwest of Stockholm.

It is acknowledged that the Ryanair flight does somewhat strain the definition of 'Stockholm', however!

Let us now expand the market still farther. There are hourly trains between Malmö and Stockholm which complete the journey in just under 4½ hours. Finally, we can add long distance buses (these are infrequent and take around 8 hours) and, of course, the private car, with an expected journey time of 5½ to 6 hours. So, even in this one corridor, we can see that defining the market is rarely straightforward. Also, bear in mind that not only have we expanded the size of the Malmö-Stockholm market, but its nature has changed from being a duopoly to one with quite intense competition, once competing airports and other modes are taken into account.

3.3 Demand

3.3.1 Definition

Economists have a very precise definition of demand, which is the relationship between the quantity of goods or service consumers will purchase and the prices charged for that commodity. Demand is not simply a quantity consumers wish to purchase such as '5 day returns' or '17 shares of Microsoft', because demand represents the entire relationship between quantity desired of a good and all possible prices charged for that good.

The specific quantity desired for a good at a given price is known as the quantity demanded. Typically, a time period is also given when describing quantity demanded.

For example, when the price of a railway ticket is £2.50, the expected quantity demanded is 100 tickets per day.

If the price of this ticket is cut to, say £2.25, we would expect that the quantity demanded will rise above 100 tickets. Therefore, price and demand should be inversely related and we will now explore this relationship further.

3.3.2 The Law of Demand

The law of demand states that, *ceteris paribus* (Latin for 'assuming all else is held constant'), the quantity demanded for a good rises as the price falls.
In other words, the quantity demanded and price are inversely related.
Demand curves are drawn as 'downward-sloping' due to this inverse relationship between price and quantity demanded.

We will illustrate this with a simple demand schedule that lists the possible prices for a good and service and the associated quantity demanded. Figure 3-1 shows how the demand schedule for day returns could look (in part):. Figure 3-1 shows how the demand schedule for day returns could look (in part):

Figure 3-1: Demand Schedule for Return Tickets

Price of Return Ticket	Demand per Day
£4.00	40
£3.50	50
£3.00	60
£2.50	70
£2.00	80

The combination of price and quantity demanded for the highest and lowest prices in the schedule is illustrated in Figure 3-2.

Figure 3-2: Demand Curve with Prices and Quantities

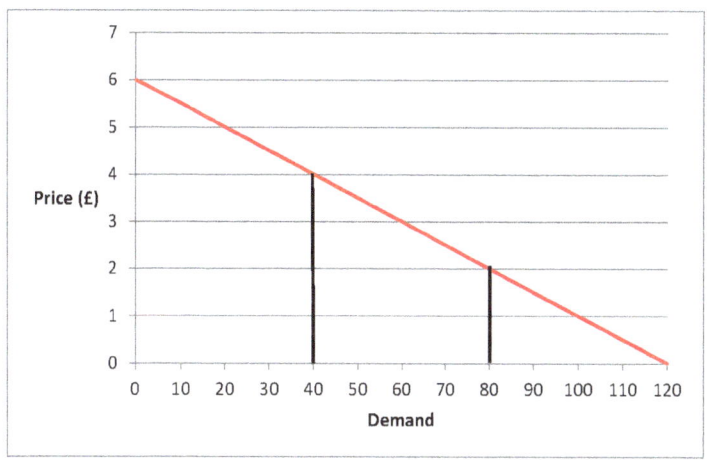

3.4 Supply

3.4.1 Introduction

A key objective of an operator is to make profits for its shareholders and, even if the operator is in the public sector, it is usually expected to behave commercially. If an operator is able to charge a higher price for its tickets, it will have an incentive to supply more seats and frequencies on routes where profitability can be increased.

We see this phenomenon in all sorts of business sectors as well as transport. For example, with agricultural or mining products, increased demand will induce the plantation of more crops or increase the number of shifts in the mine.

Note that in all these examples, there may be a time lag between wanting to increase supply and being able to do so; for train operating companies, for instance, there will be a gap between ordering and receiving new trains.

3.4.2 Supply Curve and Schedule

A producer will be willing to supply more quantity to the market as the price increases as profitability per unit of output increases.

Let us take the same price points as we saw in the demand schedule and we can observe the willingness of the supplier to increase production as prices increase.

Figure 3-3: Notional Supply Schedule for Return Tickets

Price of Return Ticket	Supply per Day
£4.00	80
£3.50	70
£3.00	60
£2.50	50
£2.00	40

The supply curve is shown below in Figure 3-4 with the same two quantities as we illustrated in the demand curve.

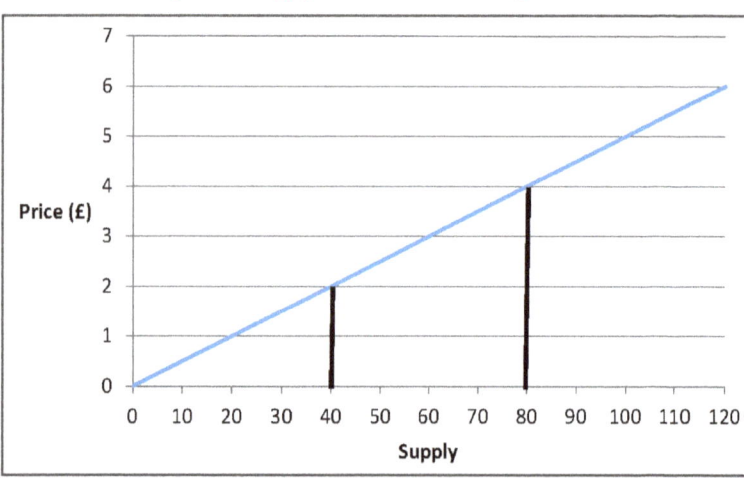

Figure 3-4: Supply Curve with Prices and Quantities

3.5 Equilibrium Point

So, the objective of the operator is, wherever possible to match supply with demand. Where the two lines cross is called the point of equilibrium – see Figure 3-5.

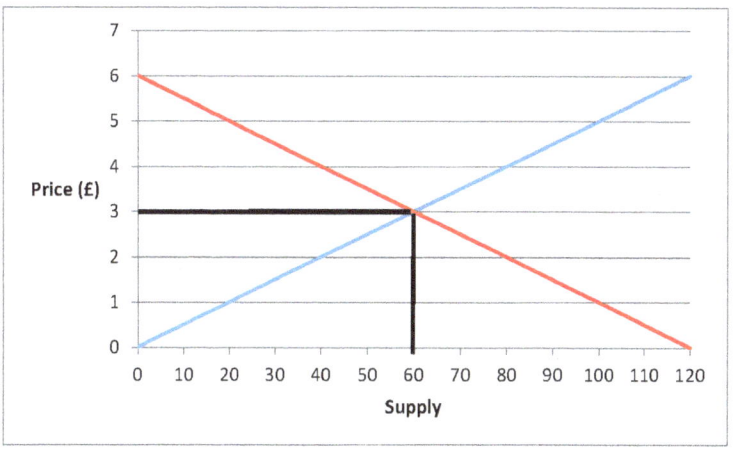

Figure 3-5: Equilibrium Point for Supply and Demand

In the example above, we can see that the capacity demanded and supplied are equal at a point where 60 tickets are made available at a price of £3. If the price is lower, there is a possibility of insufficient capacity as demand surges whereas if the price increases, the trains or buses could be carrying more air than passengers! Please note that the revenue in the above case is £180 (£3 * 60).

3.6 Changes in Demand

Let us now assume that demand is subject to an external 'shock'.

This shock, also known as an exogenous effect, could be a reduction in income, an increase or taxation or a fall in the price of a substitute product (for example, demand for a railway service will decline if a competing bus service slashes its fares).

We can see in Figure 3-6 that the entire demand curve shifts downwards (or to the left – both expressions are common). Revenue will now be approximately £2.75 * 55 = £151 (approx.). This is a significant change on the original revenue shown in Figure 3-5, as both quantity and demand are lower.

Figure 3-6: Demand Curve Shifts Downwards

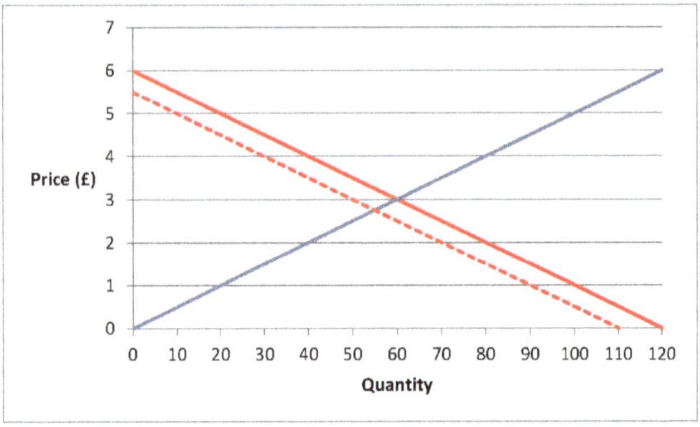

3.7 Changes in Supply

What happens when the supply curve shifts? Let us assume a negative shift, so that the producer's costs increase or subsidies are reduced. In other words, at any given level of supply, the producer will need more revenue to consider supplying a given quantity.

Please note that a supply line will only shift in this manner if there is an exogenous effect which impacts on the market, such as oil price changes. The entire supply curve shifts upwards because, for any given quantity that the operator is willing to supply, the price at which any quantity will be offered is higher than before. We can see how this affects supply by examining the dotted blue line in Figure 3-7.

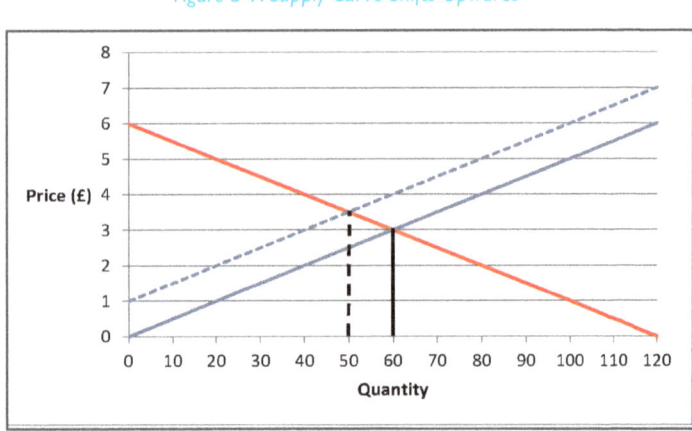

Figure 3-7: Supply Curve Shifts Upwards

The equilibrium point has now changed and the market is in balance when the supply is for 50 units at a price of £3.50 each. Before the revenue was £180 but is now a little lower (£3.50 * 50 = £175). Although demand is lower, the price per unit is higher, which offsets the reduced demand. Note, however, that this shift does not tell us anything about the operator's profitability; using the oil price example, all we know is that costs per unit output will be higher than before.

A similar analysis can be undertaken if, due to reductions in costs, the supply curve shifts downwards. Note that when the demand curve shifts, price and demand will move in the same direction, whereas when the supply curve moves up or down, price and demand will move in opposite ones. So, when the demand curve shifts, the range of outcomes is higher.

3.8 Luxury Goods

So far, we have described what happens to demand and supply for normal goods. However, luxury goods behave differently.

A return economy fare between London and New York costs between €500 and €600, whereas a First Class return ticket costs over €3,000. Now, imagine that a new entrant into the market sets a first-class price of under €2,000. One set of customers would undoubtedly be keen to try such a product, but others will be deterred by the low price.

The reason for the negative reaction from some parts of the market is because what is perceived as a luxury product will be considered as undervalued. For many people who buy luxury goods, what is important is image and cachet rather than price.

3.9 Chapter 3 Exercises

Exercise 1 In this Chapter, we discussed how demand curves can shift up or down. Supply curves are subject to similar shifts; what factors can induce these curve shifts?

Exercise 2 On a single chart, draw demand curves or lines for:
- A railway line, used principally for commuting;
- An airline route used principally by holidaymakers;
- First class travel on a long-haul airline route.

Comment on your results. Do not worry about units on the price or quantity scales

4 INDUSTRY STRUCTURE

4.1 Overview

In this Chapter, we are going to look at some theory and rather more practice on how different industries are organised. First, we will examine the four main structures of

- perfect competition;
- oligopoly;
- duopoly; and
- monopoly.

We will then see how well these structures apply to the transport sector using examples from various modes and regions throughout the world and then examine the role of economic regulation in the transport sector.

4.2 Perfect Competition

Much economic theory has been developed using the assumption of perfect competition.

Key features of perfect competition include:

- Each business in the sector offers an identical product;
- It is not possible to charge different prices to different segments of the markets;
- All firms charge the same price; and
- Entering and exiting the market is easy (there are few or no barriers to entry or exit).

Personally, I have only ever seen one example of perfect competition, which was in Jemaa-el-Fnaa Square in Marrakech. Within this square, there are over 50 vendors of freshly squeezed orange juice and all sell their product at the same price. If one vendor, say, tried to charge 11 dirham rather than 10 for a glass of juice, the theory says that demand for his product would fall to zero, because everybody else is selling the identical product for less.

The start-up costs of this orange juice business are small and, if the vendor wishes to leave, he can take his equipment out of the square and set up business elsewhere. We can also assume that there are too many vendors to establish a price cartel.

On any route, by any mode, the conditions of perfect competition rarely apply.

Figure 4-1 provides some examples of how transport operators differentiate their product to be able to charge prices which differ from their competitors.

Figure 4-1: Differentiating Factors by Mode

Mode	Differentiating factors
Train	Schedule, speed, frequency
Air	Schedule, aircraft type, frequency, loyalty programmes, service levels, brand/reputation
Ferry	Schedule, speed (ordinary or fast ferry)

We will use schedule as an example of a differentiated product. On Monday, August 31st 2015, there were 11 nonstop flights between Frankfurt and Palma de Mallorca. This route was selected at random and a date four weeks ahead was chosen.

Figure 4-2: Single fares Frankfurt-Palma on 31/08/2015

Departure Time	Airlines	Service Level	Fare
Before 0600hrs	Tuifly, Condor, Germania	Low	€115-€140
1600-1730	Lufthansa, Air Berlin	High	€157-€185
1005hrs	Lufthansa	High	€193
Before 0600hrs	Air Berlin	High	€215-€245
1150hrs	Air Berlin	High	€285

Source: www.skyscanner.es Fares reviewed on July 20th 2015

Although we would never expect to see a perfect match between fares and schedule, what Figure 4-2. does imply is that people are willing to pay less for the inconvenience of early morning flights and, similarly, people prefer not to arrive too late at their holiday destination.

In this one day sample, the most expensive departures are the most convenient, leaving Frankfurt mid- or late-morning.

Lufthansa and Air Berlin are full service carriers whilst Condor, Germania and Tuifly are charter/low cost operators, which goes some way to explaining the fare differentials.

We will explore these issues in more detail in the next Section.

4.3 Oligopoly

4.3.1 Bangkok-Singapore Air Market

For our purposes, we will define an oligopoly as a market in which three or more firms operate. We will use the air route between Bangkok and Singapore to demonstrate an oligopolistic market.

There were seven airlines operating the route on a non-stop basis at least once per day during the summer of 2015 with an average 29 flights per day each way between the two cities, which are just over 1,400km apart. Flight times were, unsurprisingly, very similar, between 2 hours 15 minutes and 2½ hours.

4.3.2 Perfect Competition or Oligopoly

To understand why this market is more oligopolistic than one exhibiting perfect competition, let us examine Figure 4-3.

Figure 4-3: Airlines Operating between Bangkok and Singapore

	Low Cost Carrier	Loyalty Programme	Frequency/week	Don Muang airport
Air Asia	✓	✓	42	✓
Cathay Pacific		✓	7	
Jetstar	✓	✓	39	
Scoot	✓		10	✓
Singapore Airlines		✓	37	
Thai Airways		✓	32	
Tiger Air	✓		35	

Note: schedules are from August 2015. Source: Skyscanner, airline schedules

Under perfect competition, the prices for a one-way trip on each of these airlines would be identical or at least similar. However, in the first week of August 2015, a one-way price ranged from €43 (Air Asia) to €280 (Singapore Airlines). This market breaches perfect competition in various ways:

- *Low cost carriers.* Four of the seven competitors offer high density seating and lower prices. Therefore, the products cannot be said to be identical;

- *Loyalty programme.* Frequent flyer rewards are a means of rewarding more loyal passengers but they also serve to 'lock in' customers who would not gain air miles if they switched to a competing airline;

- *Frequency*: an airline offering a higher frequency is providing a higher quality product and service than one offering a low frequency. We would normally expect a superior product to translate into higher prices, but Air Asia offers the highest frequency and lowest prices on the route;

- *Airport*. Two of the seven airlines operate from Don Muang airport, around 25km north of Bangkok, whereas the remainder uses Suvarnabhumi, 32km to the east. Don Muang is used exclusively by low cost carriers offering point to point traffic, so Bangkok provides a similar comparison with Heathrow versus Stansted in London.

It is worth pointing out that of the 202 weekly frequencies shown, 82 are flown by either Singapore Airlines, a full-owned subsidiary (Scoot) or an airline in which Singapore airlines is the largest shareholder (Tiger Air).

4.3.3 How Competitive is this Oligopoly

In the Bangkok-Singapore example above, the top three firms operate around 56% of the total frequency.

If, however, we include Scoot and Tiger Air in the Singapore Airlines grouping, the top three concentration ratio increases to 80%.

Whilst the concentration ratio can provide a useful indication of market power, the test is by no means conclusive. This is the case here, as it is unclear to what extent Tiger Air, for example, is an independent player, given its ownership by Singapore Airlines. What we can infer, from the range of prices on offer, is that there is no evidence of collusion.

Another test we could run is to benchmark this route against similarly competitive ones in the region. For example, Kuala Lumpur to Jakarta uses different countries and airports, with a route length of 1,140km.

4.3.4 Price Setting in an Oligopoly

As this Section is concerned with the impact of price changes, let us narrow down the market a little for this discussion to the LCCs operating in the Bangkok-Singapore market.

There are three players with a roughly equal share of weekly departures (Air Asia, Jetstar, Tiger Air) and one low frequency operator (Scoot). It is a fair assumption that passengers using these four carriers are somewhat more price-sensitive than those using full service carriers. Let us first assume that overt collusion via a cartel is illegal and that airlines would face severe penalties if they attempted to act in this manner. An overt cartel is not the only means of fixing price, however. If Jetstar, for example, were to raise its prices on the route by 10%, competing firms would have three broad options:

- *Raise prices by the same amount.* If the other firms respond to the price signal sent out by Jetstar, their market shares on the route should stay more or less the same, but the overall market size will be less, as the supply curve shifts upwards and demand would decline (recall that an upward shift means that prices are higher for all quantities offered);

- *Raise prices by less, say 5%.* The other firms will take some market share from Jetstar because their price increases are less severe. The market size will be a little smaller than before the price rises but larger than if all airlines raised their fares by 10%. The effect on Air Asia is a little more complicated to predict, as it uses a different airport in Bangkok; or

- *Competitors' prices remain unchanged.* Under the rules of perfect competition, Jetstar's position would be untenable and its market share would fall to zero. Such a scenario is unlikely because certain people will prefer Jetstar's schedule or service quality, or else there may be customers locked into Qantas' (Jetstar's owner) loyalty programme. *In extremis*, Jetstar may have to reverse its price increases if it lost sufficient market share so that the price increase meant a net loss of revenue to the company on this route.

Needless to say, this range of possible outcomes makes life much more complicated! To forecast a company's future revenue and profitability, we require a more complex method of forecasting and we will discuss one such tool, known as scenario planning, in Section 19.6.

4.4 Duopoly

4.4.1 Overview

The example in the previous Section had seven players in the market. As market size declines, the number of viable competitors declines and so having just two operators is quite commonplace. From an operator's or terminal owner's viewpoint, the range of outcomes is somewhat easier to predict as there is only one other competitor.

From the user's viewpoint, however, the risk of (tacit) collusion increases; a simple way to think of this is that it is easier for a committee of two to reach an agreement on something than a committee of seven.

There are many instances of duopolies (and indeed oligopolies) being subject to legal and economic regulation. As the number of players in a market declines, the need for regulation to protect consumers generally increases along with the likelihood of collusion.

4.4.2 Jersey - Gatwick Market

British Airways (six daily weekday flights) and easyJet (three) competed on the Jersey-London route using identical aircraft (Airbus A319) in 2015 and Gatwick accounted for around 90% of total demand.

The other operations included easyJet flights into Southend three times per week and Blue Islands Air, operating into London City three times per day but using smaller and slower aircraft.

Using their dominance of the market, two types of collusive behaviour are possible[1].

First, the two dominant operators could raise fares. As Blue Islands operates smaller aircraft into a different airport, BA and easyJet may be able to make these price rises stick.

Alternatively, if the dominant operators wish to drive out a small operator, they could tacitly collude to reduce fares in order to make business difficult for the smaller third operator (this is known as predatory pricing).

---
1 Please note that the discussion in this Section is purely hypothetical and that there is no suggestion on the part of the author of any collusion between BA and easyJet.

BA and easyJet, given their sizes (hundreds of aircraft), can clearly sustain a price war on a single route for much longer than a smaller operator with just five.

4.4.3 Tests for Collusion

How can we test to see whether a market is acting in a competitive manner? This is an extremely complex area but there are nonetheless some simple tests that can be carried out.

Using our Jersey-London example above, one test is to see how the price per kilometre compares to similar routes served by BA and easyJet, taking into account differences in airport charges, number of competitors, etc.

A second test would be to see how prices between the two airlines move over time. We would expect variations in fuel prices to have an impact on fares offered so, ideally, research should be undertaken over a period when crude oil prices are stable.

A final test is to test the sensitivity of prices to a new operator. Blue Islands started operations in March 2011 between Jersey and London City airport. To what extent, if any, did prices between Jersey and Gatwick fall because a third operator entered the London market?

However, it should be pointed out that it is very difficult to determine whether any price reductions were due to a functioning market or an attempt to put pressure on the new entrant through predatory pricing.

4.5 Monopoly

4.5.1 Occurrence of Monopolies

Monopolies, as defined in this Section are either pure, when there is only one operator, or *de facto*, when there are two or more operators but one has a dominant market share so that it is perceived to be in a situation of monopolistic supply.

Monopolies occur frequently in the provision of terminals; Dover, for example, had an effective monopoly on cross-Channel short sea routes until Eurotunnel was opened; the Port Authority of New York and New Jersey operates all three large New York airports (JFK, Newark, La Guardia) and Aéroports de Paris exerts similar control over Charles de Gaulle and Orly airports.

4.5.2 Reasons for the Occurrence of Monopolies

Monopolies can occur for many reasons, good and bad. In the United States, for example, the Essential Air Services Program provides support to individual airlines that serve small communities that might not otherwise receive services.

Within the EU, Public Service Obligation (PSO) routes are commonplace for many domestic air services which national governments consider would not be commercially viable and the successful operator is granted a monopoly on the route for a four-year period.

Terminals may be perceived also as natural monopolies, although it is critical to define the market in this case.

Heathrow airport, for example, may be considered as being in competition with Gatwick, Stansted, Luton and so on. However, for a wide range of long-haul and inter-connecting flights in southeast England, Heathrow has an effective monopoly, even though Gatwick and Stansted are now owned by separate entities after the breakup of the British Airports Authority.

The PSO cases above can be perceived to be the target of abuse, however. In 2011, easyJet was forced to withdraw its service between Paris Orly and Corsica because the French government refused to allow competition on a route serving over half a million passengers per annum[2].

By December 2014, the situation had changed somewhat; there are currently two operators on the route, with Air Corsica offering lead-in fares of a little over €70 (similar to the prices being offered by easyJet) and Air France offering a similar service for €180 or more. However, the airlines are still compensated for serving this route and Air France has a minority shareholding stake in Air Corsica.

In 2015, there were over 540,000 passengers between Ajaccio and Paris, an average of 5.5 flights per day each way and each flight carried on average 136 people[3] , so the route seems to be unusual in requiring funding from the government. The second route between Paris and Corsica (Bastia) was not much smaller, with 440,000 passengers during the year and an average of 126 passengers per flight.

---
2 http://corporate.easyjet.com/latest-news-archive/news-year-2006/16-03-06-en.aspx?sc_lang=en
3 http://www.developpement-durable.gouv.fr/IMG/pdf/Bulletin_statistique_2015_mise_en_ligne_maj-V2.pdf (page 6)

4.5.3 Monopoly in Thailand

Thailand provides one of the world's more unusual aspects of a monopoly; in air transport, airport operators and airlines rarely share common ownership, but the island of Koh Samui, in Thailand, is an exception.

The airport on the island is owned by Bangkok Airways and, unsurprisingly, the airline is the dominant customer of the airport. On the mainland, there is an airport a similar distance from Bangkok, called Surat Thani; this airport is owned by a public body, the Department of Aviation.

A map of the area known as Surat Thani province is shown in Figure 4-4.

Figure 4-4: Map of Surat Thani Province

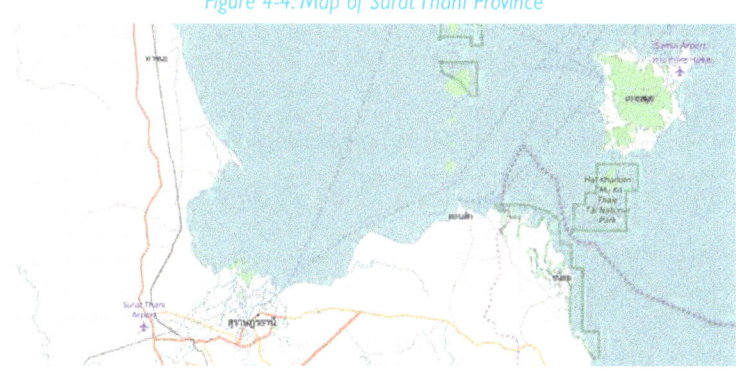

Source: www.openstreetmap.org

The impact of the unusual relationship between airport and airline operator at Koh Samui is immediately evident from the fares and frequency between Bangkok and the two airports, as shown in Figure 4-5, which shows a typical set of fares and frequencies from Bangkok.

Figure 4-5: Impact of Monopoly at Koh Samui

	Surat Thani	Koh Samui
Single Fare Range (€)	22-82	120-180
Daily Frequency (one way)	18	20

Source: www.skyscanner.net

The range of fares shown for Surat Thani, a distance of 640km from Bangkok, is what we would expect to find in a competitive market. On the same day (August 4th, 2016), Bangkok Airways was scheduled to operate seven flights from Bangkok to Chiang Mai, Thailand's second largest city and 690km away. The range of fares on this route was €60-€104 for Bangkok Airways only.

Koh Samui's monopoly is reinforced by its island status; the only alternative ways to reach the island are by air to Surat Thani, then bus to a port, followed by a 2 to 4 hour ferry journey. Buses also operate from Bangkok to the mainland port serving Koh Samui, taking around 12 hours for the bus journey alone.

4.6 Economic Regulation

4.6.1 Types of Regulation

When a market is likely to fail, such as in the case of a small market unattractive to several competitors, governments can use different sorts of regulation to correct market distortions and/or to protect the consumer. We can classify the types of regulation into three broad categories:

- Price;
- Rate of return; and
- Conditions of Service

4.6.1 Price Regulation

For British franchised railway companies, around 45% of all fares that are offered may only increase by inflation plus or minus one or two percent. The requirement for such controls is self-evident in certain types of fare but less so in others.

For example, railways often have an effective monopoly on commuting traffic, as other modes will be too slow or not exist in the first place.

So, fares may only be increased in January by the retail price index of inflation (RPI) from the previous July plus or minus a small number of percentage points ("RPI + X"). By contrast, the case for regulating longer distance flows, particularly when there is significant competition from other modes such as air, coach or private car, is less robust.

4.6.3 Rate of Return Regulation

Heathrow and Gatwick airports are both constrained by the amount of income they can receive, taking account of both aviation-related and commercial activities (this is called the "single till" approach).

This method of regulation of regulation encompasses three phases:

- Assessment of the Regulatory Asset Base (RAB). Let us take Heathrow as an example of how this works. Heathrow used to have five terminals but, in 2007, a total redesign and expansion of terminal 2 was approved, which cost around £2 billion. In addition, Terminal 1 and Terminal 3 are both slated for demolition within the next few years, allowing T2 to expand. This capital expenditure is then added to Heathrow's RAB;

- An expanded RAB will bring with it higher interest charges, deprecation and operating costs, which are quantified; and

- The regulator then calculates what revenue is required to a) cover these costs and b) provide an adequate rate of return for the owners.

Under the 'single till' mechanism, the Civil Aviation Authority will calculate the revenue projections from commercial activities such as car parks and revenue from retail businesses operating within the airport. The remaining regulated revenue is then determined and is allowed to change over time in a similar manner to the RPI plus or minus X described earlier.

4.6.1 Conditions of Service Regulation

For rail operators providing a monopoly service, conditions of service regulations can be very detailed, including requirements to operate rail services according to:

- Route;
- Stations at which calls must be made;
- Times of first and last services;
- Minimum frequency; and
- Maximum journey time between origin and destination.

These conditions are important, especially when the operator faces highly seasonal demand by time of day. In the absence of regulation, the operator could maximise revenue and profits by providing an even level of service throughout the day and would not acquire significant volumes of rolling stock that are idle for most of the week.

For example, Thameslink provides 14 trains arriving into Kings Cross in the peak hour but just six in an off-peak hour.

Airline operators will be required to provide a minimum number of seats in regulated markets according to season along with minimum frequencies, although larger aircraft may be used to reduce frequencies, so long as the minimum seat volume condition is met. A second sort of condition of service regulation concerns performance. In a free market, passengers are able to switch away from providers whose services are frequently late or cancelled but this is not the case where monopoly supply prevails.

Whilst franchised rail services are subject to performance targets and are penalised for missing them, performance contracts and systems for monitoring performance are surprisingly absent in the case of many monopoly suppliers of urban transport.

4.7 Chapter 4 Exercises

Question 1 An economics textbook suggests that grocery shopping, plumbing and dry cleaning are examples of perfect competition. Do you agree?

Question 2

In Britain, there are not many markets that have direct rail competition but two of these markets are:

- London to Yorkshire from Kings Cross (Virgin East Coast, Grand Central Rail, Hull Trains); and

- Liverpool to Manchester (Transpennine, East Midlands, Northern).

For each of these markets, assess the power of the dominant player (listed first) and how the smaller companies compete. You should also consider the role of coaches (National Express, Megabus) in these two markets.

5 CONSUMER SURPLUS & ELASTICITIES

5.1 Price Setting & Consumer Surplus

Costs are relatively straightforward to calculate. The price of labour, vehicles, fuel (if bought in advance at a fixed contract price) and track access/air navigation/port berth fees can either be determined quite quickly or are subject to regulation.

By contrast, pricing of railway services is vastly more complicated. When we briefly looked at price and revenue earlier in this book, we made the assumption that a rail journey was available at a single price at the time of purchase, what we could call the Tesco or 'take it or leave it' approach to pricing.

We will now make the discussion about pricing more realistic, as we know that, on any given train, there are people using the same service but paying many different prices. To make life even more complicated, a passenger faces a barrage of different fare options at the time of booking. Figure 5-1 shows a typical demand curve. We can imagine that there are thousands of combinations of price and demand and, theoretically, we would charge every single person a different fare based on his or her willingness to pay. Whilst this is unrealistic for passenger services, this is, however, what occurs between freight operators and their customers. Of course, there are far fewer freight customers than passengers, which makes the tailoring of price per freight customer feasible.

Figure 5-1: Demand and Individual Price for each Customer

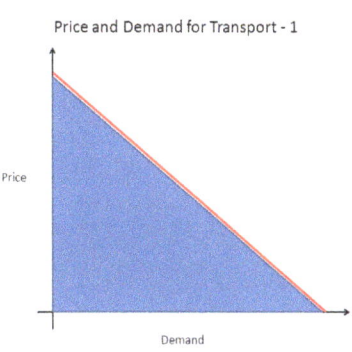

In this first case, the operator will be able to capture all the revenue under the demand line, shaded blue. At the far-left hand side of Figure 5-1 are business travellers who are willing to pay a high price whilst, as we move farther to the right, we can see that the willingness to pay declines until we come across people who are willing to pay virtually nothing.

Now let us look at the opposite extreme, where there is just one price available, as shown in Figure 5-2. In fact, this is how many European railways used to operate. It is also worth noting that, prior to 1976, airlines in the USA operated to a strict formula, setting fares as a function of distance, as laid down by the Civil Aeronautics Board. Whether the journey was on a rural route with a couple of services per day or a busy inter-city route, the price of, say, a 1,000km journey was fixed by this formula, with no variation for time of day, advance booking and so on.

With a fixed price P, the total demand will be fixed at Q, so total revenue in this case is P * Q. Clearly, this area is much smaller than the triangle in Figure 5-1.

Figure 5-2: Demand and Flat Rate Price for each Customer

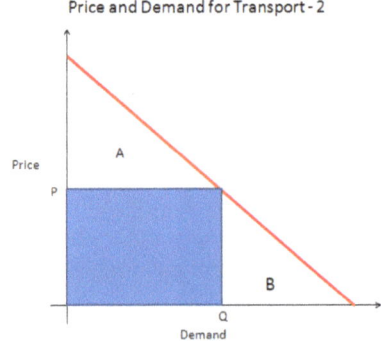

Let us look again at Figure 5-2 and examine why the revenue is less. First, area A contains a group of people (between 0 and Q) who are willing to pay more than P to travel, so these people consider that they are getting a bargain. In economics, area A is called the consumer surplus. Next, we have the group of people who do not travel in area B, as they consider the price too expensive.

What the operator therefore needs to do is to try and charge different groups of people different prices. First, the operator will wish to take onto its services as much of the consumer surplus as possible and attract, also, people willing to pay less.

Once a journey is scheduled, it costs very little to carry extra passengers, so the operator can afford to sell remaining seats at a 'giveaway' price. On the other hand, the operator will wish to avoid a situation where the fares structure is so complicated that hardly anybody understands it. Another aspect of pricing discrimination, to use the technical term, is to prevent people attaching a high value to the trip being able to get a cheap ticket.

Figure 5-3 below shows this compromise. Please note that, compared to Figure 5-2:

- Overall revenue (the blue shaded area) is higher; and therefore
- The total consumer surplus (A1 + A2 + A3) is smaller than A; and
- The volume of people who elect not to travel (B) is significantly lower.

Therefore, the operator becomes more profitable by having a range of fares rather than a single price. But there are also economic benefits as well: by having lower fares available, accessibility to the railway network has improved and this is an economic benefit to the region in which the service is being provided. We will return to the subject of economic benefits in Chapter 22.

Figure 5-3: Demand and Price Discrimination (market segmentation)

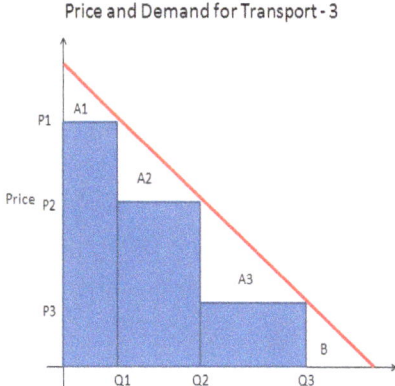

Figure 5-3 alludes to market segmentation, which effectively means offering a product or service to different groups and, in the case of transport, often at a different price for each group.

We will explore segmentation further in Section 17.3.

5.2 Generalised Journey Time (GJT)

5.2.1 Types of Regulation

One of the factors, other than price, which will influence a customer's willingness to travel is the journey time faced by this customer. When it comes to developing projects, which inevitably require some sort of forecast, the appraisal of the project will also need to consider how time influences demand. For example, if a new piece of infrastructure reduces rail journey time by 5 minutes, how will this affect demand? Before we answer this question, we need to define precisely what we mean by 'journey time'. What we have to consider here is that the public transport journey itself is just part of the passenger's overall trip. Using the example of rail, we can break down a passenger journey into several steps:

- Wait for bus to railway station (5 minutes, for example);
- Bus to railway station (10 minutes);
- Wait for train (5);
- Travel by train (35); and
- Walk to final destination (5).

With this journey, the total time required is 60 minutes.

However, research shows that a passenger's perception of waiting and in-bus time is less favourable than time spent on the train, typically by a penalty factor of 1.5 and 2 respectively, so we double the amount of time spent walking and waiting. We therefore have the following elements for the journey time in GJT terms:

Figure 5-4: Generalised Journey Time Example

Element	Physical time	GJT Multiplier	GJT
Wait for bus	5	2	10
Bus to railway station A	10	1.5	15
Wait for train	5	2	10
Travel by train to B	35	1	35
Walk to final destination	5	2	10
TOTAL	60		80

Therefore, the generalised journey time (GJT) is 80 minutes and so our 5 minute improvement in rail time brings down the GJT from 80 minutes to 75 minutes, which is a saving of around 6% (1-75/80). Compare this with the reduction in the rail journey time itself of 14% (1-30/35).

However, it is important to note that, Figure 5-4 only shows the GJT for one customer.

To assess the GJT for the total client base, it would ideally be necessary to undertake survey work to ascertain the catchment area for the station and calculate how far customers live from the originating railway station and which onwards modes are used between B and the final destination.

Whilst it is obviously impossible to calculate GJT for every customer, we can, however, use a survey to ask a sample of people where they live, how they arrive at the origin station (walk, car, etc.), at which railway station they alight and the postcode of their ultimate destination.

5.3 Elasticities

5.3.1 Principle of Elasticity

Elasticity is of central importance in the business planning process.

What we need to be able to identify is how much demand, and therefore revenue, will change as a result of either actions undertaken by the operator or exogenous factors beyond the operator's control.

Elasticity is often defined with respect to the following factors:

- Price (negative elasticity);
- GJT (negative);
- Income/GDP (positive); and
- Cross (other modes). These take positive values with respect to price, so an increase (reduction) in price of a competing mode will raise (decrease) demand on "our" mode.

Elasticity normally takes values between -2 and +2. A value of between 1 and 2 (or -1 and -2) means that demand is *elastic* with respect to the input factor (so a price reduction of X% will increase demand by more than X%) and values between -1 and +1 are referred to as *inelastic*.

5.3.2 Price Elasticity

Let us take another look at the demand schedule in Figure 3-1 and see how demand changes with respect to price.

The operator is considering reducing the price of the ticket from £3 to £2.50, a reduction of one sixth or 16.7%.

According to our demand schedule, we estimate that demand would increase by one sixth, from 60 to 70, which is also a change (this time positive) of 16.7%.

In general, we quote the elasticity as the percentage change in quantity divided by the percentage change in price So, the elasticity would be calculated as 16.7%/-16.7% or -1.

The complete set of hypothetical elasticities for the incremental changes are shown in Figure 5-5.

Figure 5-5: Demand Curve Elasticities

Price of Ticket	Demand per Day	% Demand Change	% Price Change	Elasticity
£4.00	40			
£3.50	42	5.0%	-12.5%	-0.62
£3.00	46	9.5%	-14.3%	-0.66
£2.50	54	16.7%	-16.7%	-1.00
£2.00	67	24.1%	-20.0%	-1.20

There are two issues which come to light when examining this figure. First, and obviously, the elasticity figure varies across the range of prices and quantities.

This is feasible because, as we discuss later in the book, passengers could well react differently to a large percentage change in a small price (say €0.50 to €0.60) compared to a smaller change in a larger price (€200 to €210).

So, although it is a useful starting point to suggest that the elasticity of demand for rail commuters is X, it is worth backing up this figure with survey work.

Second, and much less obviously, the calculation of elasticity as presented here is asymmetric.

To prove that this is the case, we will show the demand schedule in terms of an increasing price and recalculate the elasticities.

Figure 5-6: Demand Curve Elasticities – increasing

Price of Ticket	Demand per Day	% Demand Change	% Price Change	Elasticity
£2.00	67			
£2.50	54	-19.4%	25.0%	-0.78
£3.00	46	-14.8%	20.0%	-0.74
£3.50	42	-8.7%	16.7%	-0.52
£4.00	40	-4.8%	14.3%	-0.33

If we compare the £2.00 and £2.50 rows of the two figures, the elasticity shown for a price reduction is -1.20 but for an increase, the figure is -0.78. So, initial thoughts on the way we have calculated the elasticities is that the method is incorrect.

Whilst it is true that the method is indeed a simplification of the purist version, which involves a branch of mathematics known as calculus, might the method be wrong in the real world?

If an operator reduces prices, then it is likely that the price reduction will be accompanied by a promotional campaign that highlights the lower prices; ask yourself how often, if ever, have you seen an advertising campaign that starts with 'We have raised our prices'?

So, it is important to bear in mind both the absolute value of the price change as well as whether the fare is being increased or reduced when assessing the elasticity of demand.

For simplicity, we will stick with the simple calculation method in this book.

Let us examine different sorts of customers and consider what elasticities they are likely to face.

Rail commuters in the London area are likely to face a low elasticity, i.e. greater than -1 (i.e. between -1 and 0).

Why is this so? If there is a fare increase, most commuters will have no choice but to pay the fare increase if they want to retain their job, as switching to car or bus is not a realistic option for the majority of London's rail users. In this case, we say that demand is inelastic.

This inelastic demand is why commuter fares are regulated and so railway operators in Britain cannot just push up fares at will. Compare this with, say, leisure trips. If the price increases by, say, 10%, there is a possibility that demand may decline by more than this.

If a 10% increase leads to a drop of 12% in passenger demand, we have an elasticity of -1.2 (-12%/10%) and an operator pushing through this fare increase will be worse off than before, assuming that there is no cut in services to compensate for the lower demand resulting from the fare increase.

> ## Case Study 1 - Part 1
>
> It can often be difficult to isolate how a significant change in fares can impact on demand because other factors may be brought into play at the same time, such as frequency increases, new rolling stock and so on.
>
> In the Canary Islands, Fred Olsen Express (the main ferry operator between the two largest islands of Tenerife and Gran Canaria), announced a major restructuring of prices, effective mid-October 2012. This restructuring involved a simplification of tariffs and, overall, a significant price reduction. There was, however, no change in service frequency.
>
> The table below shows how passenger demand changed in the months before and after the price changes. As we can see, the impact on overall demand was highly significant.
>
> | Month | Change | Month | Change |
> |---|---|---|---|
> | Jan-12 | -12% | Nov-12 | 6% |
> | Feb-12 | -11% | Dec-12 | 23% |
> | Mar-12 | -36% | Jan-13 | 33% |
> | Apr-12 | -25% | Feb-13 | 62% |
> | May-12 | -9% | Mar-13 | 49% |
> | Jun-12 | -14% | Apr-13 | 19% |
> | Jul-12 | 1% | May-13 | 21% |
> | Aug-12 | -9% | Jun-13 | 45% |
> | Sep-12 | -3% | Jul-13 | 28% |
> | Oct-12 | 2% | Aug-13 | 33% |
> | | | Sep-13 | 28% |
>
> Source: http://www.puertosdetenerife.org/index.php/en/tf-statistics/tf-consultations?id=846

5.3.3 Journey Time Elasticity

We saw in the previous Section that a five-minute improvement in journey time decreased overall journey time by 6% in GJT terms, but how does this affect demand?

Assuming a journey time elasticity of -0.6 (again, the elasticity figure is negative as a decrease in time leads to an increase in demand), we would expect demand to improve by 6% (-10% * -0.6).

5.3.4 Income Elasticity

Income elasticity defines how increasing incomes impact on demand. In the case of surface transport, a figure of 0.7 – 0.8 has been stable for several decades in Europe[4], so a 1% increase in income has led to a 0.8% increase in transport demand. The income elasticity for air transport has been estimated to be a little higher than this, though.

5.4 Cross Elasticities

A passenger traveling by bus will often complete his or her journey exclusively using the one mode. By contrast, railway, ferry and air transport do not generally exist in isolation from other modes. For many rail commuter flows outside London, for example, there will often be competing bus services that may provide a slower but cheaper means of getting to work, whilst for longer distance, rail will compete with coach, air services and car. So, the introduction of a new motorway or a low-cost airline route between two points where rail has traditionally had a high share of the market will impact on demand for rail services. A value of 0.2 is a reasonable estimate for cross elasticities between rail and car, bus or coach[5].

However, it could be argued that cross-elasticities suffer from an inherent weakness, above all the inability to take into account competitor reactions. To explain this, here is an example of the bus and train options between Luton airport and central London in Figure 5-7.

Figure 5-7: GJT of rail and bus between Luton airport and central London

Expressed in GJT minutes	Bus-rail (Thameslink)	easyBus
Wait time (*2)	10	20
Bus Journey time (* 1.5)	15	90
Interchange at Luton Airport Parkway Station	19[6]	
Wait for train (*2)	15	
Train to central London	30	
Access to street (*2)	10	
TOTAL	99	110

Source: author's calculations. Note that the weight used for bus journey times is the key factor in comparing the two modes.

In 2010, rail was the market leader in public transport share with 17% of all passengers, whilst the bus and coach share was calculated at 15%[7].

---

[4] http://ideas.repec.org/p/hcc/wpaper/2012-01.html
[5] http://www.demandforpublictransport.co.uk/TRL593.pdf (Chapter 9)
[6] 30-mile value from www.networkrail.co.uk/5879_Demandforecastingtechnicalnote.pdf (table 4-4, page 52)
[7] http://www.london-luton.co.uk/en/content/8/242/surface-acces.html

As the buses and coaches serve a much wider range of destinations than rail, we may assume that rail was the market leader in the airport-central London corridor.

Now, assume that Thameslink raises the Luton Airport Parkway – London fare by 10%. There are three possible outcomes:

- easyBus does not react with any changes to price or frequency. In this case, we would assume an increase in bus demand of 2% (using the cross price elasticity of 0.2);

- as the market leader has raised prices, easyBus takes the opportunity to do the same, so there is no change in modal share; or

- on the back of the negative publicity caused by the rail fares price increases, easyBus reduces its fares, accompanied by a major publicity campaign. We would therefore expect a more significant demand change than +2% if easyBus' management selected this third option.

So, we can see that the cross elasticity between rail and bus will apply in only one of the three possible outcomes resulting from a price rise imposed on rail by Thameslink.

Therefore, these elasticities should be treated with caution.

Case Study 1 - Part 2

We saw, in Part 1 of this case study, how volumes on the leading ferry operator shot up as a result of tariff restructuring in October 2012. What happened to air traffic during this same period?

We can see that demand for air transport between the two islands was not in an especially healthy state before Fred Olsen Express announced its price cuts and, in the year following the announcement, air traffic continued its steady decline.

What is difficult to work out in this case is how much of the decline after October 2012 was due to Fred Olsen's pricing strategy and how much due to other factors.

Jan-12	12%
Feb-12	-1%
Mar-12	2%
Apr-12	-6%
May-12	-5%
Jun-12	-11%
Jul-12	-12%
Aug-12	-23%
Sep-12	-24%
Oct-12	-19%
Nov-12	-25%
Dec-12	-24%
Jan-13	-21%
Feb-13	-25%
Mar-13	-24%
Apr-13	-12%
May-13	-17%
Jun-13	-16%
Jul-13	-16%
Aug-13	-16%
Sep-13	-5%

Source: http://www.gobiernodecanarias.org/istac/jaxi-istac/tabla.do?uripx=urn:uuid:d97bef20-aa72-4fd7-9725-6bfd4083b01f&uripub=urn:uuid:5fce6935-21a5-4fea-a2e8-4298fa3d1096

5.5 Chapter 5 Exercises

Question 1 Consider a railway station which is a thirty-minute journey from the city centre terminus. The trains run every ten minutes from Monday to Saturday, so we may assume that passengers arrive randomly at the station.

The station is quite remote but serves two catchment areas: a residential development, which is ten minutes' walk away and a town four miles away but is served by a bus every fifteen minutes and a journey time of 15 minutes.

Assume that the following weights apply to generalised journey time.

Wait for bus, train	2.0
Walking	2.0
Time on bus	1.5
Time on train	1.0

- For each catchment area, calculate the raw and generalised journey times from the catchment area to the city centre terminus

- On Sundays, the train frequency is only every 30 minutes and the bus frequency is unchanged. Recalculate the GJT for each catchment area.

- Comment on the Sunday results. Are these likely to reflect actual behaviour?

Question 2 A rail service currently carries 1,000 passengers per day and the competing bus service carries a similar number. You have asked some consultants to undertake a study on the likely level of rail fares and competing modes and incomes in the railway service's catchment area in five years' time.

Assume no inflation.

You have just received the consultant's report which has the following key information. By the end of year 5:

- Rail fares are expected to increase by 10% (elasticity of -0.9);
- Incomes are expected to rise by 20% (elasticity of 0.8); and
- The competing bus service is expected to suffer an overall 5% fare rise (elasticity of 0.2).

You are required to calculate the individual and combined impact on rail demand of these three factors.

6 COMPETITION WITH OTHER MODES

6.1 Overview of How Modes Compare

In this Chapter, we will explore further cases of inter-modal competition. We shall assume that the issues of monopoly provision and collusion do not apply in these cases.

Traditionally, railways competed with road traffic, either private or public transport. The increase in car ownership, for example, led to a 30% decline in rail journeys in Great Britain between 1950 and 1980. However, in the last thirty years or so, the nature of road-rail competition has changed dramatically due to:

- Increases in road congestion and parking restrictions;
- Commercialisation of rail operators; and
- Technological advances in rail, particularly high speed travel.

Whilst rail used to be perceived as providing only limited competition to airlines in Europe, the growth of high speed rail networks has markedly changed rail's competitive scope.

However, rail remains under attack from coach services and Deutsche Bahn's long distance unit has shown a decline in volume (albeit small) since deregulation of coach services in Germany in 2013.

6.2 Private and Public Transport

6.2.1 Introduction

In developed countries, cars provide the dominant mode of transport for both short- and medium-distance journeys.

In Figure 6-1, we can observe the development of the car's share of total journeys for various EU Member States, along with Switzerland and Turkey.

Figure 6-1: Modal Split of Domestic Passenger-Kms (%)

Passenger cars	Car 1990	Rail 1990	Bus 1990	Car 2013	Rail 2013	Bus 2013
Belgium	83	6	11	77	7	15
Denmark	82	6	11	80	10	10
Germany	85	5	9	86	9	6
Greece	64	4	32	81	1	18
Hungary	61	15	25	68	10	22
Italy	80	7	13	80	6	13
Poland	41	31	28	80	6	14
Slovenia	63	7	31	86	2	11
Spain	78	7	15	81	6	13
Sweden	84	7	10	84	9	7
Switzerland	82	14	4	78	17	5
Turkey	28	5	67	64	1	35
United Kingdom	88	5	7	86	8	6

Source: http://ec.europa.eu/eurostat/web/transport/data/main-tables (tsdtr210)

By examining the earliest and latest available data 23 years apart, we can see certain trends:

- Countries which have gone through significant development (Hungary, Greece, Poland, Slovenia, Turkey), have witnessed considerable increases in the use of private vehicles and a consequent decline of public transport usage;

- Car's share of total passenger passenger-km seems to hit a peak at a little over 85%. This peak value occurs when disposable incomes have reached developed country levels, poor public transport networks or a combination of the two; and

- However, in certain developed countries, car's share of total transport volume has declined since 1990 (certainly in Belgium and Switzerland). This reduction is likely due to a combination of factors, including:

    o Lower car ownership, seen as less desirable than in the past in urban areas (cost, awareness of the environmental impacts);
    o The costs of owning and running a car compared to public transport alternatives; and/or
    o Improved public transport.

Before examining specific cases of inter-modal competition in a couple of corridors, we will examine why the car has been so successful and how public transport operators can compete.

6.3 Car's Perceived Competitive Advantages

6.3.1 No GJT Penalties

In general, those using a car are able to enter the vehicle at their point of origin and step out at their final destination. When car owners assess journey times by competing modes, there are no penalties for walking to a stop, waiting for a service or interchanging when using their own vehicle. However, although this is a reasonable representation of many car journeys, such a scenario is unlikely to be the case for people living in dense urban areas, thanks to restrictions on where a car can be parked.

6.3.2 Group Size

Although most car journeys are undertaken by one person (the average number per journey is a little over 1 per vehicle), a significant number of journeys, mainly leisure-based, have at least one passenger in addition to the driver. To illustrate the impact of group size on total journey cost, in Figure 6-2 there are five variations on the cost per person of undertaking a journey between Leeds and Manchester, a return journey of 86 miles or around 140km.

Figure 6-2: Comparative Journey Cost

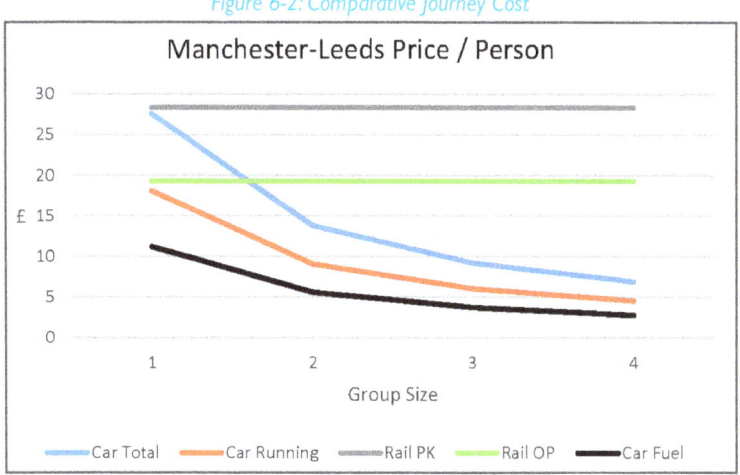

Sources: www.qjump.co.uk for rail fares; http://www.theaa.com/resources/Documents.pdf/motoring advice/running costs petrol2014.pdf (medium sized car, adjusted to 110p/litre for fuel)

For rail, the prices are quite straightforward: the cost per person does not normally vary, as each person needs to purchase a ticket (but see next page).

For car journeys, however, there are three levels of cost which may be perceived by car users:

- Fuel cost only. This is clearly the lowest variation and can be viewed (albeit incorrectly) as the marginal price of the journey;

- Running cost. In addition to fuel, we should take account of tyres, maintenance and parking. This figure is the true marginal cost of the journey; and

- Full cost. Even if a car sits in a garage and does nothing except one journey per annum, it still incurs costs. First, the car needs taxing and an MOT (certificate of roadworthiness in the UK) and also insurance. In addition, an older car will be perceived as less valuable to future buyers, so there is also a depreciation charge, independent of usage.

Moreover, because the journey costs of a car are per vehicle rather than per person, public transport begins to compare poorly in price terms once the group size per journey exceeds one person; we can see in Figure 6 2 that once two people are travelling together, the most expensive of the three car cost options is cheaper per person than the off-peak rail fare.

It was only recently (March 2014) that railways in Britain addressed this competitive disadvantage and introduced the "Two Together Railcard"[8] ; for £30 per annum, the card reduces most fares by around one third for two named adults (16 years old or over).

To what extent this card alleviates the disadvantage is a moot point. Ignoring the £30 upfront cost of the card, two people travelling off-peak from Manchester to Leeds will still pay £11.75 each for the return journey, whilst the full cost of using a car remains unchanged at just over £9.

6.3.3 Distance

When assessing the advantages of car over competing modes, we need to consider how journey lengths are distributed. Figure 6-3 shows the distribution of journey lengths for 2014.

---

8 http://www.twotogether-railcard.co.uk/

Figure 6-3: Distribution of Journey Lengths, England (%)

Under 1 mile	1-2 miles	2-5 miles	5-10 miles	10-25 miles	25-50 miles	50-100 miles	100 miles+
19	19	28	17	12	3	1	1

Source: National Travel Survey, table NTS0308

This figure shows that two thirds of all journeys undertaken were five miles or less and, for this distance, we would expect car to compete with walking, cycling and local bus. Indeed, in Figure 6-4, we can observe that the car is not generally the mode of choice for very short journeys (under 1 mile).

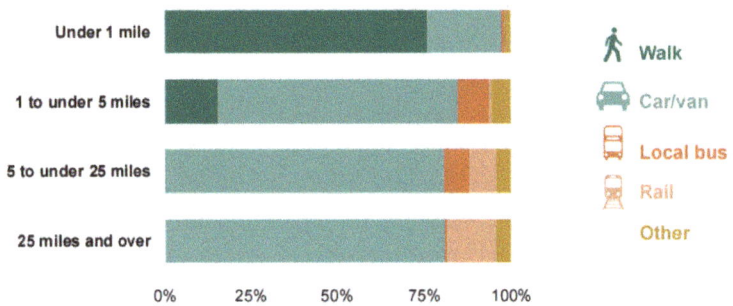

Figure 6-4: Modal Share by Distance (England, 2014)

Source: https://www.gov.uk/government/uploads/system/uploads/attachment_data/file/457752/nts2014-01.pdf (page 12)

As distance increases, both rail and car begin to dominate and, as distances increase, car's share is likely to decline, as rail's higher average speed on longer distance routes begins to erode the advantage of car travel and compensates for the higher price of rail.

6.3.4 Other Considerations on Comparative Cost

We suggested in Section 6.3.2 that many people do not take account of the fixed elements of car costs and therefore they will perceive a journey of, say, 100km as being twice as expensive as a 50km journey. A public transport operator, by contrast, needs to absorb its fixed costs in its pricing structure.

We would therefore expect to see a taper of fares, so that the cost per km declines for bus and rail fares as distance increases.

However, this relationship has broken down somewhat and, in many cases, the cost per mile or kilometre increases with distance; this phenomenon may be attributed to rail's increasing competitiveness over longer distances. We will examine this aspect of market-based pricing in more detail in Section 15.5.

6.4 Assessment of European Air-Rail Competition

6.4.1 Phase I (to 1983): Inauguration of High Speed Rail

Phase I is characterised by an absence of high speed rail and an airline route network which remained subject to regulation by national authorities.

In 1983, Europe's first high speed line between two major cities opened (Paris and Lyon). Not only were train speeds significantly higher than on the lines they replaced but the route was considerably shorter (425km between the two cities compared to 512km on the classic network).

Prior to the TGV service, the fastest time for the Paris-Lyon service was a little under four hours, but the TGV brought the journey time down to an average of two hours.

The impact on market share was dramatic, with rail passengers more than doubling in the five years up to 1985 and air travel between the two cities nearly halving.

Figure 6-5: Market Shares on Paris-Lyon

Paris-Lyon	1980	1985	Change
Rail Demand (million)	1.5	3.7	+151%
Air Demand (million)	1.4	0.8	-46%
Rail + Air Demand	2.9	4.5	+55%
Rail Share	52%	83%	
Air Share	48%	17%	

Source: Author's calculations, BonnaJous, A., 1987, "The regional impact of the TGV", Transportation 14 (2), 127-137

It is clear from Figure 6-5 that, for distances in the 400-500km range, rail can be seen to dominate the public transport market between two cities.

In the case of the new TGV service, rail prices were not increased to recoup the investment made in developing the service.

Much of the air market that remained in 1985 may have been attributable to customers making long-haul connections at Paris airports rather than point-to-point traffic, although there is no clear evidence to support or reject this assertion.

6.4.2 Phase 2 (1983 to the mid 1990s): Consolidation of High Speed Rail

The development of Europe's high speed rail network in the next fourteen years was principally in France, although Spain opened the Madrid-Seville line in 1992. By early 1997, just prior to liberalisation of air transport in Europe, European air fares were roughly twice as expensive as those in the USA, whose airlines had been deregulated twenty years previously[9].

6.4.3 Phase 3 (mid 1990s onwards): Air Service Deregulation

Deregulation in the UK started in 1995 with easyJet's first flights between Luton and Scotland. To gain an idea on how the airline sector was able to compete after deregulation, we can observe annual passenger volumes between the London area and Edinburgh and Glasgow/Prestwick for years prior to and after the event.

Figure 6-6: Air Traffic Volume between London and Scotland (000s)

	Edinburgh	Glasgow and Prestwick	Long Distance Rail (all UK routes)	GDP/head (£, real)
1994	1,791	1,728	54,300	19,376
1996	2,282	2,261	58,100	20,290
2000	3,017	2,864	69,700	22,772
2003	3,536	3,455	81,500	24,703

Sources: www.caa.co.uk/airportstatistics, https://dataportal.orr.gov.uk/ (rail), http://www.imf.org/external/pubs/ft/weo/2015/02/weodata/index.aspx (GDP data). Rail data by route is unavailable.

There is some evidence from Figure 6-6 that airline deregulation had a significant impact on air transport demand.

To control for other factors, we have added information on long distance rail demand over the period as well as information on GDP per capita. From this figure, we can see that, although rail journeys increased strongly by some 50% between 1994 and 2003 and GDP/head increased by almost 30% in real terms, both increases are dwarfed by the 100% increase in air transport demand between London and Edinburgh/Glasgow over the same period.

9 http://www.economist.com/node/146627

Please note that the neither of the two lines linking London and Scotland had any significant speed increases between 1994 and 2003.

6.4.4 Phase 4 (2013 on): Long Distance Bus Deregulation

This phase applies to France and Germany which, until very recently, had little or no competition on long distance routes from coach services. Germany liberalised its bus services in 2013 and France followed two years later. In terms of price, it is reasonable to suggest that new entrants into the German and French coach markets would target low yield rail travellers. The reaction of French railway operator SNCF provides an innovative strategy to protect market share. In 2013, SNCF developed a subsidiary called Ouigo[10] (pronounced "We Go"), which has many features very similar to the low-cost airlines against which it was originally set up to compete:

- Ticket purchase only via the internet;
- Higher density seating on Ouigo rolling stock;
- Use of Marne-La-Vallée station (Disneyland) outside Paris rather than a central terminal; and
- Reduced staffing per train and no buffet car.

However, it appears that SNCF has already started diluting the Ouigo brand. As Figure 6-7 demonstrates, not only are Ouigo tickets now available on the main SNCF website but the fares offered on Ouigo are not significantly different from those on standard SNCF services.

Figure 6-7: Snapshot of Paris-Marseille fares

Departure station	Paris	Marne La Vallee Disneyland Paris	Paris	Paris	Paris	Paris	Paris
Leaving at	09h16	09h48	09h55	10h32	11h32	12h02	12h32
From	29.80 €	25.00 €	55.00 €	25.00 €	37.00 €	54.00 €	37.00 €
Journey time	04h08 1 change	03h15 Direct	03h54 1 change	03h33 Direct	03h34 Direct	03h48 1 change	03h36 Direct
Travel with	TGV	OUIGO	TGV	TGV	TGV	TGV	TGV

Source: www.voyages-sncf.com Fares examined on November 25th, 2015

---

10   https://www.ouigo.mobi/MobileSearch.aspx?reference=0000000009

6.4.5 Lessons derived from Changes in Supply of Modes

High speed rail is often positioned as a competitor to airlines in terms of distance. For example, we saw in the Paris-Lyon example how a much faster rail service came to dominate the public transport market between Paris and Lyon.

However, what is crucial in discussing intermodal competition on this route is price. The public was offered a much superior service on the route with no change in price; this strategy contrasts sharply with the introduction of high speed rail travel in Spain, when prices were increased significantly once high speed services were introduced. Airline deregulation brought no change in speed but instead ushered in a much higher set of frequencies from a wider range of London's airports as well as significant reductions in price. So, for both the examples we have shown in this Section, the improvement was absolute (i.e. with no strings attached).

A Section on intermodal competition would not be complete without at least a mention of car-sharing, a market dominated in Europe by Blabla[11]. Statistics are somewhat hard to come by, but in 2014, the company's subscribers were reportedly making around one million journeys per month with an average journey length of some 350km.

Therefore, the car-sharing mode is in effect competing with both rail and coach services. In the following two Sections, we provide a more detailed assessment of inter-modal competition along two of Europe's busiest corridors: London-Paris and Madrid-Barcelona.

6.5 Rail, Ferry & Air: UK-France Cross Channel

6.5.1 Assessment of Modal Split

In this Section, we examine the state of inter-modal competition in the cross-channel market between UK and France.

It is important in this case to state up-front how the market is defined.

For the purposes of our analysis, we will assume that the market is northern France (centred on Paris and Beauvais) and Belgium (Ostend, Brussels, Antwerp, Liège).

---
11 https://www.blablacar.com

For the purposes of assessing inter-modal competition, we therefore include the following links and modes:

- Air travel between London and Paris or Brussels;

- Eurostar services over the same links as air. However, Eurostar does serve intermediate origin and destination points, such as Ebbsfleet and Lille respectively as well as occasional longer haul services to Avignon. The data to break down Eurostar is unavailable, but we will assume that the overwhelming majority of traffic travels between the capital cities and so all Eurostar demand is included;

- Channel Tunnel shuttle traffic; and

- Ferries on the routes between southeast England and France/Belgium.

The demand on the Cross-Channel market, as defined above, is shown, by mode, in Figure 6-8[12].

Figure 6-8: Demand (000s) on the English Channel Corridor 2005-15

	London-Belgium(air)	London-Paris(air)	Eurostar	Channel Shuttle	Ferry	TOTAL
2005	1,009	2,401	7,454	8,200	14,141	33,205
2006	949	2,400	7,858	7,800	14,217	33,224
2007	996	2,304	8,261	7,900	14,597	34,058
2008	826	2,019	9,113	7,000	14,149	33,107
2009	649	1,741	9,220	6,900	13,442	31,952
2010	568	1,625	9,529	7,500	13,330	32,552
2011	597	1,784	9,680	9,300	13,050	34,412
2012	620	1,741	9,912	10,000	12,065	34,338
2013	640	1,821	10,133	10,300	12,823	35,717
2014	740	2,031	10,398	10,600	13,296	37,065
2015	722	2,171	10,399	10,500	13,022	36,814

Source for aviation data: http://www.caa.co.uk/airportstatistics; Eurostar, Shuttle: http://www.eurotunnelgroup.com/uk/eurotunnel-group/operations/traffic-figures/; Ferry: author's calculation from GB Maritime Statistics

The overall cross-Channel market has followed a pattern similar to the UK economy, with growth up to 2007, contraction in 2008 and 2009 followed by recovery. Indeed, for a mature market, annual average growth since 2009 at 3% per annum could be considered impressive. If we summarise the data by mode, a picture of the different fortunes of each emerges in Figure 6-9.

[12] In 1993, the full year before the Tunnel opened, air passenger demand was 3.4 million between the London area and Paris.

Figure 6-9: Cross-Channel Market Share by Mode

	Air	Rail	Ferry
2005	10%	47%	43%
2006	10%	47%	43%
2007	10%	47%	43%
2008	9%	49%	43%
2009	7%	50%	42%
2010	7%	52%	41%
2011	7%	55%	38%
2012	7%	58%	35%
2013	7%	57%	36%
2014	7%	57%	36%
2015	8%	57%	35%

From this data, it appears that air has barely recovered from its reduction in share after the recession although, in absolute terms, air passenger volumes have grown since 2009.

The main mode switch over the ten years, however, has been between ferry and rail.

This phenomenon is somewhat surprising, as the Channel Tunnel had already been open for ten years in 2005.

However, it should also be noted that the first full year of operation for the high-speed link between London and the Channel Tunnel was 2008 (it opened in November 2007).

The reduced journey time explains the significant increase in demand for Eurostar in 2008 and the fact that passenger volumes still managed a small net increase in 2009 in spite of the recession; by contrast, demand on all other routes fell during that year.

6.6 Rail, Road & Air: Barcelona-Zaragoza-Madrid

6.6.1 Assessment of Modal Split

The high-speed railway linking Madrid and Barcelona was built in sections. The section between Madrid and Lleida (roughly halfway between Zaragoza and Barcelona) opened in October 2003 but did not reach Barcelona until February 2008.

There are only four cities of any significant size along the route and the population of each is presented in Figure 6-10.

Figure 6-10: Population of Major Towns and Growth

	2000	2005	2013	2000-05	2005-13
Barcelona	1,496,266	1,593,075	1,611,822	6%	1%
Lleida	112,194	124,709	139,809	11%	12%
Madrid	2,882,860	3,155,359	3,207,247	9%	2%
Zaragoza	604,631	647,373	682,004	7%	5%

Source: INE Demographic Statistics www.ine.es

Population growth in all four cities was significant up to 2005 but, with the exception of Lleida, population growth has slowed somewhat since then. The area under consideration in this Section is shown in Figure 6-11.

Figure 6-11: Barcelona-Zaragoza-Madrid Corridor

In Figure 6-12, we can see the impact of the Madrid-Barcelona high speed rail line, which opened in February 2008.

Prior to its opening, the Madrid-Barcelona air route was one of the world's busiest.

In 2004, for example, the route had an average of over 50 departures each way per day. By 2013, the number of daily flights had declined to 27[13].

The figure provides a snapshot of the market shares on the route in 2004 and 2013 (note that the rail figures are 'point to point' only, so comparable with air passenger volumes).

2013 is the latest year for which detailed rail data are available.

---

13 Update: in the first six months of 2016, there were 24 flights each way per day between the two cities.

Figure 6-12: Air vs. Rail, Madrid-Barcelona

	2004	2013
Air Operations	40,924	19,860
Air Passengers	4,176,000	2,213,000
Rail Passengers	448,000	3,117,000

Sources: http://www.ferropedia.es/wiki/Tr%C3%Aflicos_AVE_y_LD_corredor_Barcelona_Madrid (rail and air traffic), AENA Statistics (air operations).

The distance by road is almost identical to the railway (624km and 621 km respectively) and both road and rail are routed via Zaragoza.

There are also seventeen departures each way per day by bus taking between 7½ and 8 hours.

What the information in Figure 6-12 does not provide, is any impact on road traffic and consequently any information on travel demand by road. However, by examining traffic counts for the years 2005 (the closest year available to 2004) and 2013, we can observe a significant drop in average daily traffic in Figure 6-13.

The points listed in the figure have been chosen as much as possible to be between the middle of the major towns in order to avoid the impact of short distance commuting traffic.

Figure 6-13: Road Traffic on Corridor (Average Daily Flow)

		2000	2005	2013	2000-05	2005-13
Madrid-Zaragoza	Acolea del Pinar (GU 1/2)	14,838	16,561	14,250	12%	-14%
	Calatayud (Z-7/1)	14,693	17,410	16,874	18%	-3%
Zaragoza-Lleida	Point Z-503	14,138	15,448	10,573	9%	-32%
Lleida-Barcelona	Tarrega (E-178) + Montblanc (T-502)	37,051	45,737	38,579	23%	-16%

Sources: http://www.fomento.gob.es/...

For Zaragoza-Barcelona, there are two motorways east of Lleida towards Barcelona, so the figures for these two roads has been combined.

The drop on the Section between Zaragoza and Lleida is especially marked, with a fall of 32% between 2005 and 2013.

Even though the high-speed rail service was running between these points in 2005, we may infer that the bulk of the traffic on this section was to and from Barcelona, which is over ten times Lleida's size. By contrast, the fall between Lleida and Barcelona is not as dramatic. However, whilst the road section between Madrid and Zaragoza is toll-free, the Zaragoza-Barcelona section of road incurred a toll of around €30 in 2015 for cars from end to end. It is also noteworthy that between 2000 and 2005, the section of road without AVE competition (Tarrega and Montblanc) had the highest increase in road traffic. To complete the picture, we include rail traffic between Zaragoza and Madrid/Barcelona in Figure 6-14. Air traffic from Zaragoza is excluded from the analysis, as its market share is negligible.

Figure 6-14: Zaragoza Rail Traffic

		2003/04	2013
Madrid-Zaragoza	Rail Passengers	481,000	1,189,000
310km	Journey time (hours)	2.9	1.3
Zaragoza-Barcelona	Rail Passengers	140,000	488,000
308km	Journey time (hours)	4.1	1.8

Note: all "pre-AVE" rail journey times are sourced from http://www.forotren.The points listed in the figure have been chosen as much as possible to be between the middle of the major towns in order to avoid the impact of short distance commuting traffic.o/viewtopic.php?f=9&t=51686&start=60

6.6.2 Converting Average Daily Road Figures

In Figure 6-13, we saw that the average daily traffic count between Zaragoza and Lleida (point Z-503) was 10,573 vehicles. So, how do we convert this into passengers per annum?

First, we need to exclude vehicles other than cars (for the purposes of this analysis, we are excluding coach travel in the corridor). Data held elsewhere on the website of the Ministerio de Fomento indicates that 80% of vehicles on the motorways between Madrid and Barcelona are private rather than commercial vehicles.

We will also assume a rate of occupation of 1.2 vehicles per car.

This figure is similar to occupation rates found elsewhere in Europe. A mobility study undertaken in 2001 estimated that roughly 80% of the journeys between Madrid and the community of Catalonia were to or from Barcelona. Therefore, the annual passenger count by road between Zaragoza and Lleida may now be calculated as:

$$10{,}573 * 365 * 0.8 * 1.2 * 0.8$$

This works out at roughly 3 million journeys per annum. We can now recalculate market shares using the information provided and calculated.

Figure 6-15: Reworked Modal Shares

Mode	2005 Volume	2005 Modal Share	2013 Volume	2013 Modal Share
Rail	448,000	5%	3,117,000	37%
Air	4,176,000	47%	2,213,000	27%
Car	4,330,000	48%	3,014,000	36%
TOTAL	8,954,000		8,344,000	

Note: the 2005 car volume used the identical methodology as 2013, starting with a base traffic figure of 15,448 vehicles per day.

We now need to ask how reasonable these market shares appear. In 2007 (a year which predates the opening of the high-speed line to Barcelona), a national mobility study[14] assessed market shares for air and rail to be almost identical, and we have reached a similar conclusion here for the 2005 data.

There has been no further mobility study undertaken since 2007; however, as our 2005 figure seems reasonably robust, we can employ the same methodology for 2013 data with a degree of confidence.

6.6.3 Coach Travel on the Madrid-Zaragoza-Barcelona Corridor

Thus far, we have glossed over the issue of coach travel due to the difficulties of acquiring data in most countries. However, we will now say a few words about this thorny issue. For Spain as a whole, long distance bus travel accounted for roughly half as many passengers as rail. As long distance is defined as anything in excess of 300km, both Madrid-Zaragoza and Zaragoza-Barcelona are covered within this definition as well as Madrid-Barcelona. Unusually, some long-distance bus service data is available online[15].

Throughout the entire Madrid-Barcelona corridor, 994,000 passengers were recorded in 2013, an increase from the 962,000 passengers recorded in 2010. No further information is provided, however, on the origins and destinations of these passengers.

---

14 http://www.fomento.gob.es/BE2/?nivel=2&orden=27000000 Section 82-10

15 http://www.fomento.gob.es/MFOM/LANG_CASTELLANO/DIRECCIONES_GENERALES/TRANSPORTE_TERRESTRE/AphL/DVSP/TVUG/

6.6.4 Conclusions from Modal Split Analysis

What conclusions may we draw from the foregoing assessment of the Barcelona-Madrid corridor?

- The public transport (air plus rail) market increased between 2004 and 2013, by 12 percentage points, with rail's market share of public transport increasing from 10% (5%/(5%+47%)) to nearly 60%;

- Due to its shorter distance, the Zaragoza-Madrid market is probably dominated by car traffic but rail still managed to more than double its volume as a result of high speed services cutting journey times from nearly 3 hours to less than 90 minutes; and

- Road's share of the market has fallen significantly but not as much as the air market.

We have assumed that the increase in demand has been due to the introduction of the high-speed rail service, but other factors will also be at play, such as economic growth, changes in population and so on. What we should therefore do is find other routes that have not undergone significant changes between 2004 and 2013. For Spain, however, this is somewhat difficult, given the volume of lines built over the last 12 years. However, we will undertake a comparison with Seville-Madrid, whose high-speed line has been operational since 1992. Figure 6-16 shows data for 2005, as 2004 rail demand was not available.

Figure 6-16: Madrid-Seville Corridor

	2004-05	2013	change
Air Operations	4,929	2,794	-43%
Air Passengers	455,000	242,000	-47%
Rail Passengers	2,282,000	2,165,000	-5%
Air plus Rail	2,737,000	2,407,000	-12%
Road Traffic Count	26,936	26,532	-1%

Sources: http://www.ferropedia.es/wiki/Tr%C3%Alfico_corredores_Andaluc%C3%ADa_Larga_Distancia, AENA Statistics

We can see from that public transport demand on this corridor has fallen by 12%, so the 12% increase on the Madrid-Barcelona corridor infers that the high-speed rail network has been responsible for considerable traffic generation on the route.

It is noteworthy that air demand has shown a considerable fall in market share over the eight years, even though the high-speed rail service had been running for over ten years before 2005.

There are two motorways linking Seville to Madrid and there has been negligible change in demand between 2005 and 2013.

On the basis of these figures, therefore, we would conclude that public transport lost a small proportion of market share to road traffic during the period.

6.6.5 Lessons Learned

What the foregoing exercise analysing the Madrid-Barcelona makes clear is that assessing a full set of market shares, including road traffic, is a complex business.

We have gathered data which is neither totally up-to-date or complete, but it has still been possible to infer the impact of high speed rail services.

It is also of critical importance to use a control flow (i.e. a corridor where there have been no significant changes in infrastructure or service provision) to add a measure of confidence to the analysis.

6.7 Chapter 6 Exercises

Exercise 1 Hamburg-Köln Express (HKX)[16] started daily operations in July 2012 as an open access rail operator between these two large German conurbations, calling at Düsseldorf and Duisburg en route. During 2015, HKX operated one train each way per day between Köln and Hamburg five days per week (excluding Tuesday and Wednesday). In December 2015, two of the five weekly services were extended to Frankfurt, with a journey time of slightly under 2½ hours between Köln and Frankfurt. However, from September 2016, HKX reduced services significantly by removing the Frankfurt extension and serving the core Köln-Hamburg route just four times per week. The trains start their day in Köln and, with a 90 minute turnaround, return from Hamburg on the same day.

Deutsche Bundesbahn operates between Köln and Hamburg with a very similar journey time to HKX but with several services per day. Between Köln and Frankfurt, DB uses a high speed line with journey times under 60 minutes. Germanwings also offers several flights a day between the Köln and Hamburg.

Flixbus is one of the new operators in the recently deregulated long distance bus market (2013). Between Köln and Hamburg, the fastest coach time is around 6 hours and 15 minutes, whilst between Köln and Frankfurt, the coach is often faster than HKX, with many of the journeys scheduled to last 2 hours and 15 minutes.

What is your opinion of HKX's strategy to date? Consider price, journey time and frequency in your answer (www.bahn.de, www.flixbus.de, www.skyscanner.net for competing operators).

Exercise 2 For the 12 months between July 2015 and June 2016, the following passenger volumes were recorded between the islands of Gran Canaria and Tenerife.

Company	Mode	Passengers	Website
Armas	Ferry	404,215	http://www.navieraarmas.com/
Binter	Air	660,618	https://www.bintercanarias.com/
Canary Fly	Air	26,318	www.canaryfly.es
Fred Olsen	Ferry	824,611	https://www.fredolsen.es/en

Using the data above and the websites provided, what do you think of the degree of competition in this market? For prices, use a date approximately one month ahead of the day you undertake this exercise.

---

[16] *https://www.hkx.de/ (in German only)*

7 INFLATION AND GROSS DOMESTIC PRODUCT

7.1 Inflation

Much of economics is concerned with assessing an industry over time and, when we consider costs or revenues, it is critical that we are able to compare one year's figures with those of other years.

We'll start the Chapter with a simple example. Imagine we are told that sales of a company last year were £100 but this year the figure was £105. Superficially, sales have increased by 5%. But what if inflation over the year was 10%?

To compare like with like, we need to reduce this year's figure to take account of inflation. To do this, we use the following formula:

$$[\text{This Year's Sales}] / [1 + \text{Inflation rate}]$$

Plugging in the figures above, this year's sales, after stripping out inflation, come to 105/ (1+10%) which is £95.45. In other words, compared to last year, sales have actually fallen by almost 5%.

The terminology for expressing this calculation is messy and various authors use different words to describe it.

Figure 7-1 shows some of the terminology used for unadjusted and adjusted money.

Figure 7-1: Terminology for Money Adjusted by Inflation

Unadjusted Money Values	Adjusted Money Values
Nominal, money-of-the-day, current	Real, constant

In this book, we will use 'nominal' for unadjusted money values and 'real' for those which have been adjusted for inflation.

Let's work through an example (in Figure 7-2), with a ticket between two points that costs £10 in 2011.

We will assume that inflation for the three subsequent years is 5% but the price of the ticket increases by 7% in 2012, 2013 and 2014.

Figure 7-2: Inflation and Ticket Prices

	2011	2012	2013	2014
Inflation Index (2011=100)	100.0	105.0	110.3	115.8
Ticket (£)	10.00	10.70	11.45	12.25

So if, in 2011, we are examining how much a ticket will cost in 2014, there are two possible answers:

- £12.25. This figure is nominal price; or

- £10.58 ((£12.25/1.158). This is the real price, expressed in 2011 terms. In this case, the ticket in 2014 will cost £10.58 at 2011 price levels and so has increased by almost 6% over and above inflation.

Let us now bring demand into the calculations in Figure 7-3. We will assume that there were 100,000 passengers in 2011 and 90,000 in 2014.

Figure 7-3: Example of Current and Real Revenue (5% Inflation)

	2011	2014: nominal prices	2014: real prices
Passengers	100,000	90,000	90,000
Revenue per passenger	£10	£12.25	£10.58
Total Revenue (£m)	£1.00m	£1.10m	£0.95m

We can see, using just this single example, how revenue has in fact deteriorated compared to the current year (i.e. 2011), although the headline figure of £1.10 million, announced in 2014, would seem to show an improvement. Similarly, costs should also take account of inflation to allow a year-on-year comparison. Revenue and cost increases are often assumed to be the same so we can deflate future costs and future revenues by the same amount. However, if ticket prices change at a different rate to general inflation (as has been the case for rail fares in Britain for many years) and/ or a change in costs is envisaged through lower wages, higher productivity or redundancies, it is critical to show the different bases being used for future revenues and costs.

To demonstrate the importance of this concept, we will expand Figure 7-3 to include costs running at 5% per annum and also 10%.

Figure 7-4: Current and Real Revenue and Costs

	2011	2014: nominal prices	2014: real prices
Total Revenue from Figure 7-3 (£m)	£1.00m	£1.100m	£0.950m
Costs – 5%	£0.80m	£0.93m	£0.80m
Costs – 10%	£0.80m	£1.07m	£0.92m
Profit (Costs 5% inflation)	£0.20m	£0.17m	£0.15m
Profit (Costs 10% inflation)	£0.20m	£0.035m	£0.030m

In Figure 7-4, if costs are rising at the same rate as general inflation (i.e. 5%), there is no change in real costs in 2014 compared to 2011.

However, a cost inflation rate of 10% has a significant impact on the profitability of the business and wipes out 80% of the £150,000 profit that was calculated if costs rise at a rate no different to general inflation (5%).

So, we can now summarise the profitability of the company using Figure 7-4. Although ticket prices rose in real terms between 2011 and 2014, real revenue declined due to a reduction in demand.

If the costs incurred by the company rose at the same rate as general inflation, there would be a reduction in profits of £0.05 million compared to 2011.

However, if the company suffered specific price pressures which meant that its costs increased by 10% rather than 5% per annum, profit is reduced from £0.20 million in 2011 to £0.03 million in 2014.

7.2 Fuel Costs

Fuel is one of the more challenging feature of costs, since the prices fluctuates wildly and independently of domestic inflation and, to add to the complexity, fuel inputs are priced in US Dollars.

For this example, we will assume that an airline in Italy wishes to assess its fuel cost over time.

The raw data used in the calculation is shown in Figure 7-5, on the next page.

Figure 7-5: Italian Kerosene Prices

	US cents/l	€1 = $	€ cents/l	Inflation (Italy)	2014 € cents/l
2000	22.4	0.9236	24.3	100.0	32.3
2001	19.1	0.8956	21.3	102.8	27.6
2002	18.1	0.9456	19.1	105.3	24.2
2003	21.8	1.1312	19.3	108.1	23.7
2004	30.4	1.2439	24.4	110.5	29.4
2005	45.2	1.2441	36.3	112.7	42.9
2006	50.7	1.2556	40.4	115.1	46.8
2007	56.3	1.3705	41.1	117.2	46.6
2008	78.2	1.4708	53.2	121.1	58.5
2009	43.8	1.3948	31.4	122.0	34.3
2010	56.7	1.3257	42.8	123.9	46.0
2011	79.1	1.392	56.9	127.3	59.4
2012	80.7	1.2848	62.8	131.2	63.8
2013	77.2	1.3281	58.1	132.8	58.3
2014	71.2	1.3285	53.6	133.1	53.6

The first column of inputs for the price of kerosene per litre on the spot market (we will assume that our operator does not engage in hedging or similar tactics and simply buys fuel as and when necessary).

Our next task is to convert the US$ to € prices to remove exchange rate volatility.

Our Italian airline will need to purchase Dollars to buy the fuel so the price it faces in its local currency is provided for each year in column 4.

The fuel costs presented in column 4 are still in nominal terms, albeit now in local currency.

We can see from column 5 that inflation in Italy has been around 33% since 2000, so we now convert all annual fuel prices to 2014 Euros.

The results of this conversion are in column 6.

We can summarise the calculations using a chart which shows the nominal price in US$ and € and the '2014' price, as presented in Figure 7-6.

Figure 7-6: Three Versions of Kerosene Prices

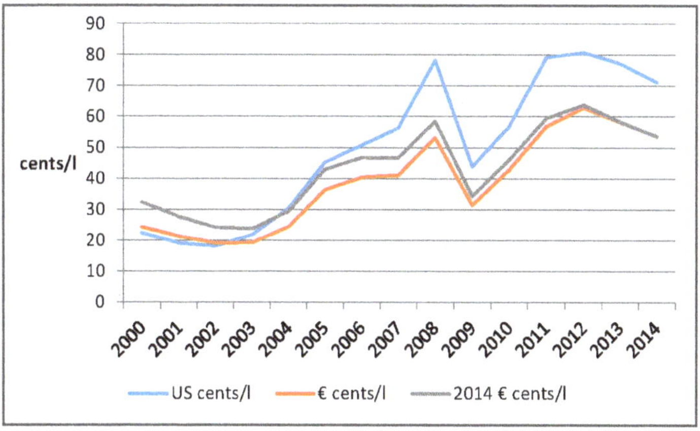

[Chart showing kerosene prices in US cents/l, € cents/l, and 2014 € cents/l from 2000 to 2014]

A simple measure of volatility is to divide the maximum by the minimum prices in each column. We can see the results of this exercise in Figure 7-7.

Figure 7-7: Simple Measure for Measuring Price Volatility

Fuel Price	Maximum value / minimum value
US cents per litre (nominal)	4.46
€ cents per litre (nominal)	3.28
€ cents per litre (real)	2.69

We can see both from the preceding chart and table that price volatility declined when using nominal Euros and then declined further when converting to 2014 € prices.

It should be pointed out however, that a country using a different currency and a different inflation profile might show quite a different level of volatility from that shown in Figure 7-6.

7.3 Real Economic Growth

7.3.1 Calculating Real GDP

As the issue of inflation is important, we present here a second example looking at a country's whole economy rather than the price of a single item. Why is it important to examine economic growth in real terms? In order to say compare money values in different years, we need to be able to make a direct comparison between £1 this year and £1 five years hence, which is the identical argument we employed with our Italian airline in the previous Section.

Once we have worked through the calculations for real GDP, we will then examine the relationship between real economic growth and transport demand for two separate systems and compare the results.

The UK Office of National Statistics (ONS) provides GDP/head in nominal values and the ONS also provides inflation indices.

The data for the years 2002 to 2014 inclusive are shown in Figure 7-8 below. The factor which we will use here is Gross Domestic Product (GDP), which measures the total value of economic activity. As we will be looking at values of GDP over time, we need two sets of data to calculate GDP:

- GDP, measured in £ billions; and
- Inflation[17].

Before proceeding to the numbers, it is worth explaining the purpose behind using GDP. For our purposes, we can define GDP as the wealth per person multiplied by the size of the population.

So, if population doubled and there was no change in wealth per person, we would expect twice as many people to use the transport system. Similarly, if the population got wealthier but there was no change in its size, we would again expect to see an increase in the number of journeys made. So, the GDP measure takes into account both average wealth and population.

Figure 7-8: Nominal and Real GDP, UK

	GDP (£ bn)	Inflation (2005=100)	Real GDP (2002)	Real GDP (2014)
2002	693	95.4	693	930
2003	730	96.7	720	966
2004	771	98.0	751	1,007
2005	813	100.0	775	1,040
2006	851	102.3	793	1,065
2007	898	104.7	818	1,098
2008	927	108.5	815	1,093
2009	908	110.8	782	1,049
2010	953	114.5	794	1,066
2011	986	119.6	786	1,055
2012	1,022	123.0	793	1,064
2013	1,060	126.1	802	1,076
2014	1,104	128.0	823	1,104
change	59.3%	34.2%	18.7%	18.7%

---

17 *Ideally, we should use a measure known as the GDP Deflator. However, as this statistic is less available in certain countries than inflation, we will stick to the overall consumer price index for the purposes of this book.*

Before we examine this impact, however, we will demonstrate, using Figure 7-9, how the results in Figure 7-8 were calculated.

Figure 7-9: Calculation of Real GDP figures (£bn)

Year	GDP (2002)	GDP (2014)
2002	£693 * 95.4/95.4	£693 *128.0/95.4
2003	£730 * 95.4/96.7	£730 * 128.0/96.7
2004	£771 * 95.4/98.0	£771 * 128.0/98.0

If we look back at Figure 7-8, we can see that the growth in real GDP is 18.7% over the twelve years shown, irrespective of which date is used.

What matters is that, when calculating real values, you are consistent in your approach; in other words, we should consistently use 2002 or 2014 values in the above example.

As a final check, we can see that growth in nominal GDP/head was 59.3% over the twelve years and inflation increased by 34.2%.

So, the real growth was

$$(1+59.3\%)/(1+34.2\%)-1 \text{ or } 1.593/1.342-1$$

which is the same as the 18.7%, which we calculated earlier.

7.3.2 Real GDP and Transport Demand

In this Section, we will examine the impact of GDP on transport demand.

Figure 7-10 below shows two key important factors which pull in opposite directions as GDP goes up or down.

We will assume no change in population for now.

Figure 7-10: Relationship between GDP and Trip Rates

	Increase in GDP	Reduction in GDP
Car usage	Higher disposable income, higher propensity to acquire and use private transport	Lower disposable income, people more likely to switch to (cheaper) public transport
Economic Activity	Increase in trips made, including by rail, air and bus	Decrease in trips made, including by rail, air and bus

There are, of course, other factors which affect public transport demand (service quality and frequency, for example) but the above summary table shows that passenger demand forecasting is no simple task!

However, in this Section, we will limit ourselves to comparing transport demand and GDP. Figure 7-11 shows the changes in Britain's rail demand and the UK's GDP. Note that Northern Ireland is excluded from the rail figures but the resulting error will be slight.

Figure 7-11: Changes in Rail Demand in Great Britain & Real GDP

Financial year	Total passenger journeys	Change	GDP (£bn)	Change
2002-03	976		930	
2003-04	1,012	3.7%	966	3.9%
2004-05	1,040	2.7%	1,007	4.2%
2005-06	1,076	3.6%	1,040	3.2%
2006-07	1,145	6.4%	1,065	2.4%
2007-08	1,218	6.4%	1,098	3.1%
2008-09	1,266	4.0%	1,093	-0.4%
2009-10	1,258	-0.7%	1,049	-4.0%
2010-11	1,354	7.6%	1,066	1.6%
2011-12	1,460	7.8%	1,055	-1.0%
2012-13	1,501	2.8%	1,064	0.8%
2013-14	1,586	5.7%	1,076	1.1%
2014-15	1,654	4.2%	1,104	2.6%
Total		69.5%		18.7%

Rail data is from http://dataportal.orr.gov.uk

For background information, the population of the UK rose by approximately 9% between 2002 and 2014.

There are two noteworthy issues from this table:

- Up until 2005/06, rail demand and GDP growth changed at roughly similar levels of magnitude but, from 2006/07, rail demand consistently showed stronger growth; and
- Rail demand has proved itself impervious to the recession, so we may assume that there are other factors at work which are driving rail demand.

7.3.3 Real GDP and Inter-Island Transport

As a contrast, we may compare trips between the two largest Canary Islands (Gran Canaria and Tenerife) over the same period. The number of trips and the GDP for the Canary Islands as a whole were originally shown in Figure 2-1 and are repeated in Figure 7-12.

The GDP is shown for the entire chain of seven islands whereas we will be looking here at movements between just two of them. However, as the two biggest islands make up over 80% of the population and GDP by island is not published, the island-wide GDP should be adequate for our purposes.

Figure 7-12: Changes in Transport Demand & Real GDP, Canary Islands

	Trips Las Palmas - Tenerife		Real GDP (€m)	
2002	1,719,073		36,800	
2003	1,752,738	2.0%	38,723	5.2%
2004	1,759,606	0.4%	39,942	3.1%
2005	1,707,544	-3.0%	41,659	4.3%
2006	1,888,450	10.6%	43,591	4.6%
2007	1,963,065	4.0%	44,340	1.7%
2008	1,855,284	-5.5%	44,442	0.2%
2009	1,734,495	-6.5%	42,800	-3.7%
2010	1,728,062	-0.4%	42,526	-0.6%
2011	1,789,203	3.5%	41,752	-1.8%
2012	1,612,298	-9.9%	39,997	-4.2%
2013	1,749,410	8.5%	40,288	0.7%
2014	1,755,457	0.3%	41,523	3.1%
2015	1,842,032	4.9%	42,317	1.9%
	change:	7.2%		15.0%

Data sources: http://www.puertosdetenerife.org/index.php/en/tf-statistics-tf-consultations?id=846 for ferry data; http://www.aena.es/csee/Satellite?pagename=Estadisticas/Home for air passengers; http://www.gobiernodecanarias.org/istac/temas_estadisticos/economiageneral/ for GDP data.

What we observe here is a very different picture to rail travel in Britain. Real GDP has increased twice as fast as the number of trips between the two major islands. Unlike with railways in Britain, there are no other modes of transport, so the number of trips shown in Figure 7-12 by air and ferry, is not subject to any distortion by private vehicles; there are no bridges or tunnels linking the two islands.

However, over the same period of time, the population of these two islands increased by 12.4% and for the Canary Islands as a whole by 14.2%. So, (assuming that the GDP growth applies just to the two biggest islands and using the population changes of Tenerife and Gran Canaria combined) we can estimate that the change in real income per person over the twelve years since 2002, has been between +0.4% and -1.2% (applying Canarian GDP and Canarian population growth).

Whichever estimate is used, the issue is that real income growth was, in effect, static over these twelve years.

In Section 5.3.4, we saw that changes in demand due to income had an elasticity of roughly 0.7 and, earlier in this Section, that any change in population would feed through directly to transport demand (hence an elasticity with respect to population of l).

So, let us now examine how we would expect demand to change. We will assume that the real income per head on the two islands declined by 1.2% and the population growth figure is that for the two islands (12.4%). Applying an elasticity of 0.7 to the income effect and 1 to the population effect, the expected increase in demand was 11.5% as detailed in Figure 7-13.

Figure 7-13: Expected Income and Population Impacts on Demand

	GDP	Income	Population
Demand Change %		-1.2%	12.4%
Elasticity of Demand		0.7	1
Demand Change * Elasticity		-0.0084	0.1240
Add 1		0.9916	1.1240
Multiply Impacts	1.1146		
Convert to % change	11.5%		

In brief, the formula is (1+ change) * (1+change) * (1+change), etc., for however many factors are in play. We then deduct 1 to see the actual compound change and convert this to a percentage so the figure is easier to understand. It is evident that the change in demand (7.2%) was actually less than this figure and we will investigate this problem further in later Chapters.

7.4 Chapter 7 Exercises

Exercise 1 A transport operator wishes to make a high-level forecast of its profitability for the next five years and has brought you in to undertake the calculations. The operator has provided you with data for 2015 and wishes all figures to be presented in 2015 € so that the Board of Directors can compare like with like.

2015 Passengers	500,000
Average ticket price	€10
Total costs	€4,000,000
General Inflation	3%
Operator Cost Inflation	5%
Ticket Price Inflation	2%
Elasticity of Demand	-1.1

The table above indicates that the operator has decided on a strategy of increasing volume at the expense of average revenue per passenger, as there is spare capacity on most of its services. However, the operator believes that costs will increase as a result of the extra passenger volumes, which is reflected in the operator cost inflation figure.

For each of the five years 2016 to 2020, calculate the profitability of the company in 2015 €. Based on your analysis, what advice would you give the Board of Directors?

Exercise 2 What follows is potentially an extremely complicated exercise. The good news is that you are not required to undertake it but just to highlight the issues involved.

http://www.norwegian.com/globalassets/documents/annual-report/nas_annualreport_2015.pdf shows the profit and loss accounts for the airline Norwegian between 2005 and 2015. As well as running domestic services within Norway, the airline not only has many routes between Scandinavian cities and the rest of the world but also several routes which pass nowhere near Norway. For this exercise, you are required to highlight the issues involved in:

- Compiling a single year's accounts for Norwegian; and
- Comparing the airline's financial performance over time.

8. SUMMARISING DATA, PROBABILITY & SAMPLING

8.1 Summarising Data

8.1.1. Why Summarise?

When faced with a set of data, it is useful to be able to summarise a set of raw numbers using a small number of measures that can convey a message much better than raw data. In Figure 8 1, we present the number of passengers between mainland Spain and the UK to the Canary Islands for fourteen years.

Figure 8-1: Raw Data of Air Passengers from Mainland Spain and UK

	Mainland	UK
2002	2,556,259	3,958,355
2003	2,851,482	4,061,229
2004	3,226,314	3,880,576
2005	3,474,452	3,631,588
2006	3,631,648	3,641,634
2007	3,894,694	3,475,772
2008	3,860,860	3,355,973
2009	3,491,335	2,831,689
2010	3,600,580	3,187,891
2011	3,562,402	3,625,403
2012	3,133,210	3,509,983
2013	2,942,434	3,667,380
2014	2,975,143	4,102,141
2015	3,169,369	4,277,020

All that we can tell from a quick examination of these numbers is that there are usually more UK than Mainland passengers, except for the years 2007 to 2010 inclusive.

But what else can we say about this data?

8.1.2 Tools to Summarise Data

There is a large number of measures that can be used to describe a set of data but we will limit ourselves to four here. The four measures are shown in Figure 8-2 and discussed thereafter.

Figure 8-2: Data Summary Tools

	Mainland	UK
Range	1,338,435	1,445,331
Mean	3,312,156	3,657,617
Standard Deviation	381,764	371,775
Coefficient of Variation	0.12	0.10

Range

This is the easiest measure and is the maximum value minus the minimum. It provides a crude measure of dispersion (i.e. how 'spread out' the data is).

However, it tells us nothing about the distribution of data within the range; all we can tell from Figure 8-2 is that the difference between extreme values is slightly higher for UK than for Mainland passengers.

To illustrate why the range has limited appeal, consider the two datasets (l, l, l, l, 99) and (l, 99, 99, 99, 99).

These have the identical range of 98 but the two sets are clearly very different.

Mean

There are three standard ways to calculate the average of a dataset but the most common is the arithmetic mean, which we will just call the mean from now on.

This is calculated by adding all the values and dividing by the number of observations (fourteen, in this case).

So far, then, we can conclude that the mean number of UK air passengers is a little higher.

Standard Deviation (SD)

The SD is a more sophisticated measure of how dispersed the data is; the mean, by itself, does not really give us adequate information on what a dataset looks like.

To illustrate this point, we will take two more simple datasets:

- 1,1,1,1,1; and

- 0,0,0,0,5;

Both have a mean of one but the SD of the first set is 0 (no dispersion at all) whereas the second has an SD of 2.

The formula used to derive a standard deviation is somewhat complicated but in Excel, we can derive the SD by invoking the formula STDEVP (Data Range).

For our dataset in Figure 8-1, we can conclude that UK passenger demand has less variation than that for mainland Spain;

Coefficient of Variation (CV)

The CV is very useful when comparing datasets with very different means and is calculated by dividing the SD by the mean.

To illustrate this point, we will examine two small but extreme dataset summaries as follows.

- Set 1 has a mean of 100 and a SD of 10; and

- Set 2 has a mean of 500 and a SD of 20.

It is not immediately obvious which dataset is more dispersed but the CV gives us the answer.

The CV for set 1 is 10/100=0.1 whilst for set 2, the CV is 0.04.

So, we would conclude that the data in set 1 is more dispersed.

We may say from the summary of the data on Canarian air traffic that not only has UK-based traffic been higher during the period 2002-2015 (higher mean), the year-on-year fluctuation in demand has been a little smaller, as its CV is lower.

8.2 Probability Distributions

8.2.1. How Probability Distributions Work

We are probably all familiar with certain types of probability distribution, even if the terminology as such is unfamiliar. For example, an individual toss of a coin has a 50% chance of being head or tails and a single die is thrown, the probability of any value of between 1 and 6 turning up is equally likely.

These are both examples of a uniform distribution, i.e. any possible outcome is equally likely.

From a transport perspective, probabilities have a multitude of uses and applications.

Here are just some questions which can be answered by use of probability techniques:

- What is the likelihood of an individual train arriving at its destination five minutes late or more?

- How frequently will a flight have a load factor of between 70% and 90%?

- What proportion of the population will be willing to pay at least €4 for a bus journey?

To answer questions such as these, we will first look at a little bit of probability theory and then examine some of the more common probability distributions used.

8.2.2 Basic Probability Theory

The first two important aspects of probability which we will discuss here are the sum of all possible outcomes and the concept of mutual exclusivity.

First, when discussing probability, it is necessary to realise that the sum of all possible outcomes must equal 1. Using the coin example, let's say that we are interested in the probability that, if a fair coin is tossed ten times, a head will turn up on at least seven occasions. For now, we will simply call this probability X. If we are then interested in the likelihood of six heads or less turning up, the answer is Y or 1-X. This is because these two events are mutually exclusive and they cover all possible outcomes: a head on 0-6 occasions OR a head on 7-10 occasions.

So, in summary:
- Prob (X) + Prob (Y) = 1; and
- X and Y are mutually exclusive events.

Another concept which we will introduce in this Section is the weighted average or expected value. Imagine that we have calculated three possible outcomes with attached probabilities as follows:

- Profit of €100 million, with a probability of 20% of this outcome occurring;
- €120 million (50%); and
- €150 million (30%).

We have made the assumption here that these are the only three possible outcomes (and so the probability of any of the three events occurring must equal 1) and so they are mutually exclusive.

What is the expected value of the range of outcomes? The calculation is quite straightforward:

$$€ (100 * 0.2) + (120 * 0.5) + (150 * 0.3).$$

So, based on the three possible outcomes, the expected value is €130 million. Note, however, that this value is not one of our three original options.

How we calculate these probabilities will form the remainder of this Chapter. We will explore some of the distributions used on a regular basis. As the focus of this book is very much on the application of theory, we will avoid the bulk of the algebra involved in generating these distributions and instead focus on how they can be applied.

8.3 Binomial Distribution

A binomial distribution contains only two possible outcomes and the distribution allows us to calculate how often one event occurs in a given number of observations. This distribution is discrete, in that it is used for a fixed number of outcomes (i.e. the probability of, 1,2,3 etc. events occurring). If the event in question is the punctuality of a bus service which arrives on time/early or otherwise is late, our two outcomes are p (on time/early) or q (late), where q = 1-p.

If we have good data for a particular service and an on-time arrival is expected on 90% of all occasions that the service runs, so p = 0.9 and q = 0.1. We will also assume that the performance of the bus on any specific day is independent of its performance on previous days.[18]

As long as we have these two conditions in place (only two possible outcomes, independent observations), we may use the binomial distribution. We will now invoke the Excel formula for the binomial distribution to show how it works in practice.

= **BINOMDIST** (number of 'successes', total observations, probability of one 'success', TRUE)[19]

We will now populate this formula using some numbers. Let's say that we wish to calculate the probability of the bus arriving on time on no more than 16 days (number of successes) out of 20 (number of observations). We have the probability of one success, which is 0.9.

The TRUE function at the end of the argument will provide us with the cumulative probability of the bus being on time on 0, 1, 2, etc. days all the way up to 16 days.

So, in Excel, if we plug in =BINOMDIST(16,20,0.9,TRUE), we obtain a probability of 0.133. What, then, is the probability of a bus arriving at its destination on time on at least 17 of the 20 days?

Because "16 or less" and "17 or more" are the only two possible outcomes for this trial, we can confidently say that the likelihood of an on-time arrival during at least 17 of the 20 days is 1-0.133 or 0.867. For this type of distribution, we can easily derive the mean and SD, which we will state without proof. The mean number of on-time arrivals is simply N*p or, in this case, 20*0.9, which is 18. The SD is slightly more complicated and is $\sqrt{(N*p*(1-p))}$. Sticking with the same example, the SD is $\sqrt{1.8}$ or 1.34.

8.4 Poisson Distribution

The Poisson distribution is also discrete and is perhaps the most "low maintenance" distribution in the world of probability (or the cheapest date, if you prefer) because it requires only one variable to generate an entire probability distribution.

---
[18] Here is the formula, in all its gory detail: if r is the number of successes and n is the number of observations/trials, then the probability of r successes out of n trials is $p^r * q^{n-r} * r!/(n! * (n-r)!)$
[19] Please note that from Excel 2010 onwards, slightly different formulae are used.

All we need to generate a Poisson distribution is the number of occasions on which we expect an event to occur during a certain period.

We will stick with bus routes and the operator expects that, as a town has become more popular for jobs, shopping, and so on, road congestion has increased. This increased congestion affects its ability to operate its full schedule, so when road congestion is especially heavy, the operator will need to run a revised schedule ('Plan B') with fewer bus-kilometres to ensure that its schedule is maintained. It is expected that this event will occur roughly once every two months.

For ease of demonstration, we will assume that all months have 30 days and that the likelihood of congestion is the same on weekdays or weekends. Finally, the likelihood of congestion occurring on any one day is independent of any other day.

First, we need to calculate the mean number of days per month that congestion is expected to occur. In our case, this mean is the probability 1/60 (once every 60 days) times the number of days per month (30), hence 0.5 days per month on average. We will call this mean µ.[20]

The only other input we need is the engineering constant "e", which is roughly 2.71828. With just the two inputs, µ and "e", we can generate the distribution. The probability of X events occurring per month is

$$e^{-\mu} * \mu^X / X!$$ (equation 1)

where X is the number of occurrences and X! is the factorial of X (for example, 5! is 5*4*3*2*1). As ever, we will rely on Excel to undertake the heavy lifting in calculating the probability for each number of events occurring and we can recast equation 1 into Excel as follows.

$$=EXP(-\mu) * \mu^{\wedge}X / FACT(X)$$ (equation 2)

We now have sufficient information to use equation 2 to generate the likelihood of the number of events per month. The results are shown in Figure 8-3 and we will now discuss this output in detail.

---

[20] *The standard deviation of the Poisson is similarly 'low maintenance' and is just the square root of the mean.*

Figure 8-3: Outcome of Poisson Distribution

Events	Probability	Cum Prob
0	0.6065	0.6065
1	0.3033	0.9098
2	0.0758	0.9856
3	0.0126	0.9982
4	0.0016	0.9998
5 or more	0.0002	1.0000

The probabilities of the zero to four events per month were calculated using equation 2 directly.

The likelihood of 5 or more must be 1 minus the probability of 4 events or less, as discussed earlier, and so is just 1 minus the sum of the other probabilities.

We can see in the final column of Figure 8-3 that the sum of all possible outcomes thus equals 1.

The 'cum prob' column shows the probability of the number of disruptions or less, so we can say that the probability of no more than two disruptions (for example) is 0.9856.

8.5 Sampling of Data

8.5.1 Introduction

Most data that we come across – revenue per week, performance data, market share estimates – is based on samples. If we are fortunate, our sample will be so large that it is not necessary to make adjustments, to take account of the size of our sample. Otherwise, we need to infer information from a limited set of data.

Later in this Section, we will briefly examine how the T distribution allows us to take account of sample size and show the limits of our sampled data.

One of the most difficult concepts that people encounter when studying statistics is knowing when to apply methods for a population and when to use sampling methods. In this Section, we will try to explain the difference between these two.

Generally, when we have a set of data from which we are trying to determine whether there is any change from the norm, we will use sampling methods.

As usual, we'll dive straight into an example.

A local authority has data on the journey time for a bus route which runs five times per day, on weekdays only and has 100 days of data (so 500 journeys).

The contract between the authority and the bus company is that the average journey time for the bus is 30 minutes and runs in practice with a mean of 30 minutes and a standard deviation of three.

The contract states that no more than 20% of services should run more than 3 minutes early or late – this is our norm.

The first ten days of data are shown in Figure 8-4.

Figure 8-4: Selection of Individual Bus Journey Times (in minutes)

Day	Service 1	Service 2	Service 3	Service 4	Service 5	Group Average
1	37.11	30.77	31.17	29.03	29.53	31.52
2	31.92	29.61	27.97	30.70	26.88	29.42
3	31.43	28.12	33.47	34.92	32.13	32.01
4	27.17	31.08	31.37	26.17	27.30	28.62
5	27.15	25.36	35.16	25.99	29.16	28.57
6	26.50	22.49	27.58	29.24	32.61	27.68
7	29.24	31.79	30.63	26.41	31.90	29.99
8	25.83	33.16	34.00	32.21	28.73	30.79
9	27.63	25.14	28.29	36.05	30.01	29.42
10	35.60	29.62	27.69	34.48	28.92	31.26

We can see the individual journey times for each of the five services and the column highlighted in yellow shows the average journey time for the day. Whenever a service completes its journey in under 27 minutes or takes longer than 33 minutes, this journey is flagged as a contract failure and a '1' appears, as in Figure 8-5.

Figure 8-5: Count of Late and Early Journeys

Day	Failure 1	Failure 2	Failure 3	Failure 4	Failure 5	Group Failure
1	1					
2					1	
3			1	1		
4				1		
5		1	1	1		
6	1	1				
7				1		
8	1	1	1			
9		1		1		
10	1			1		

We can now ask what is the probability that an individual journey runs more than 10% late or early. To answer this question, we are going to look, very briefly, at the normal distribution, which is a special form of the T distribution, which we will introduce in the next Section. Without proof, we will state here that we would expect slightly under one third of all bus journey times to fall outside the range 27-33 minutes.

In the case of our 500 individual journey times, 31.6% breach the target, so the data being used pretty much agrees with the normal distribution.

The bus company, armed with this information, points out that an 80% success rate is simple infeasible: traffic congestion causes too many journeys to be late and the road layout does not allow the bus to wait if it is running early.

Instead, the bus company proposes looking at the average journey time for the day, over all five daily services. One thing immediately apparent from the group average column in Figure 8-4 is that the failure rate is much lower; for the first 10 days, all averages are within the 27-33 minute limit and, in the long term, we would expect a failure rate of a little below 1.4%.

Before proving this 1.4% figure, it is worth stepping back and understanding why the variation is much lower.

Here is the data from day 5.

| 27.15 | 25.36 | 35.16 | 25.99 | 29.16 | 28.57 |

There are three individual failures on this day, namely services 2, 3 and 4. But, once they are averaged out, the early buses are, to some extent, cancelled out by the late running service 3, so the average masks a good deal of the variability of the individual services on the day in question.

The standard deviation of groups such as this (i.e. the yellow column in Figure 8-4) goes by the name of the "standard error of the mean" or SEM for short.

The relationship between the standard deviation of individual services and the SEM of the daily averages is as follows:

$$SEM = SD / \sqrt{n}$$

where n is the number of individual observations included in the average. In our case, n=5.

So, the SEM for this example covering 100 days was $3/\sqrt{5} = 1.34$. Each group of 100 averages will have a slightly different SEM but, in the long run, the SEM will be equal to 1.34.

So, what we now have is a set of 100 observations, which are the daily average journey times.

The mean of this group of 100 data points is 29.98 minutes (effectively 30) with variation fluctuating around this mean of 1.34 minutes.

Again, without delving into the calculations for now, the probability of a daily average journey time being above 33 minutes or below 27 is around 2½%, so the bus company would be very keen to see its performance measured by the daily average rather than the individual services.

8.5.2 Introduction to the T Distribution

The last probability distribution which we will cover is called the T distribution, on which will we draw heavily to use confidence intervals later in this Chapter.

Unlike the previous two distributions we have looked at so far, the T-distribution is continuous.

A good example of what this means is working out the probability of someone being, say, 182cm tall or more, as there is an infinite range of outcomes between 182cm and 183cm alone.

In Figure 8-6, on the next page, we can see a set of curves, all of which have a probability of 1 underneath each curve (and so satisfying the general condition that the probability of all likely outcomes must equal 1).

In the case of the blue curve, we have a very tall and thin distribution which means that most of the area under the curve is clustered around 0 and so the area in the tails is quite small.

This distribution therefore has a small standard deviation. By contrast, the green curve is relatively short and squat and so a higher proportion of the total distribution is found in the extremes.

The X axis represents distance from the mean and, as the standard deviation increases, the curves becomes flatter.

Figure 8-6: T Distribution

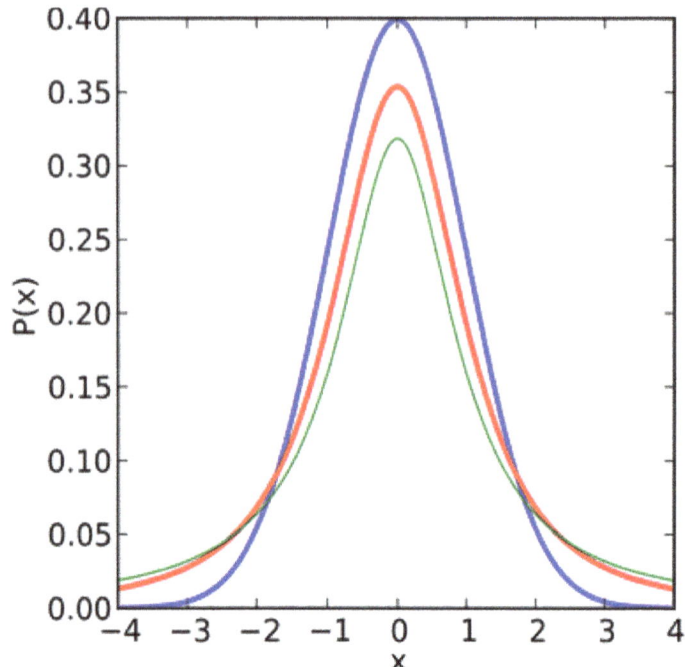

8.5.3 Use of T Distribution for Probability

We generally use the T Distribution when the numbers involved become quite large.

If, say, a train company runs 1,000 services per week and has a long-term average of 90% arriving on time, what is the probability of the company falling short of this target with no more than 890 trains per week arriving on time?

Now, before we continue, it is worth considering what we are trying to achieve.

We have a bell-shaped, symmetrical distribution and we know that the mean value is 900.

In other words, the distribution is symmetrical around the value of 900, so the probability of 900 or less is exactly 0.5. If this is the case, the probability of 890 or less must be below 0.5, so we are interested in that part of the distribution in just one of the tails of the distribution.

We will use a standard deviation of 7 trains in the initial calculation, so what we need to work out is:

T = (Target − Mean) / Standard Deviation (Equation 1)

or (890−900)/7, which is −1.429[21]

The final stage in the old days was to refer to physical tables, but there are easier methods nowadays. If we go to https://surfstat.anu.edu.au/surfstat-home/tables/t.php for example and select the option second from the left, showing one tail highlighted, we can see what value the figure of −1.429 represents. According to Figure 8-7, the likelihood of 890 trains or less arriving on time is 0.0767.

Figure 8-7: Conversion of T value to Probability

SurfStat *t-distribution calculator*

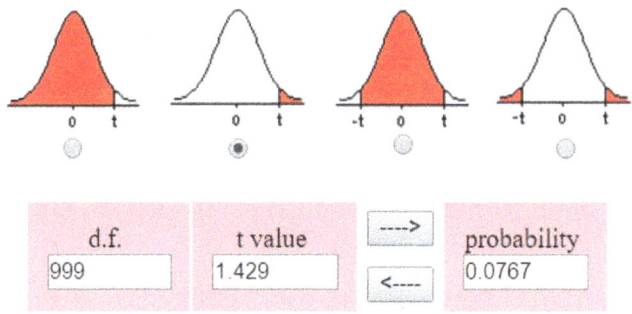

Source: https://surfstat.anu.edu.au/surfstat-home/tables/t.php

The number of degrees of freedom is generally just the number of observations minus one, so 999 in this case.

Now remember that this distribution is symmetrical, so the probability of 890 or less is the same as 910 or more (both figures being 10 away from the mean.

Once we appreciate this fact, we can select the second option from the Surfstat page. The probability value is well below 0.5, so we can be confident we have the correct answer.

If we stay on this site and repeat the calculation but, this time, with SD = 12 (so the distribution is a little flatter and more dispersed), the calculated T value is −0.8333 (from 890−900)/12).

---

21 There is a slight inaccuracy built in here. Unlike the Binomial and Poisson distributions, the T distribution is continuous, so '890' in fact covers the range '889.5 to 890.5'. However, we will ignore this point.

The likelihood of a day occurring when 890 trains or less arriving on time has increased significantly now, to 0.2024.

We'll just do one more query from this example. We would now like to know what is the probability of between 895 and 915 trains arriving on time, assuming that SD of 7 once more. This query may induce a bit of head-scratching at first, but we can rewrite the problem as follows:

$$p(895 \leq X \leq 915) = p(X \leq 915) - p(X \leq 895)$$

In other words, we need to undertake 2 separate calculations here: one for 915 trains or less and another for 895 trains or less. We then subtract the smaller probability from the larger.

The first T value is (915-900)/7 which is 2.143 and the second is (895-900)/7 or 0.714. The T values and the probabilities associated with them are shown in Figure 8-8.

Figure 8-8: Probability of Between 895 and 915 Trains On Time

	915 trains or less	895 trains or less
T value	2.143	-0.714
Probability	0.984	0.238

Now look carefully at the probability values we obtained from Surfstat. We know that the probability of 915 on time arrivals or less must be well over 0.5, as it covers 900 or less (we know that this value is 0.5) plus a further area to the right of the mean value. We also know that the probability of 895 trains or less being on time must be less than 0.5, as the area covered by the T distribution is under half. So, we can now say that the probability of between 895 and 915 trains arriving on time is 0.984 minus 0.238, which is 0.746.

8.5.4 T Distribution for Confidence Intervals

Our starting point for this Section is to explain what we mean by a confidence interval. We have a set of data with a sample mean and standard deviation and we need to know whether the sample mean, M, is significantly different from a population mean. The confidence interval forms a range around the sample mean XM and looks like this:

$$M +/- SEM * T\text{-}VALUE$$

So, the range of the interval is driven by the values of SEM and the T value and both of these in turn are influenced by the number of observations in the sample.

Let us now look again at the blue and the green curves in Figure 8-6. We can also use this distribution to determine what proportion of possible outcomes lie in the middle 95%[22] of the distribution.

To do this, we will need to lop off the 'tails' of the distribution, each of which contain 2½% of the total distribution. Precisely where we make the cuts will depend on the shape of the distribution.

If we retain our train punctuality example and we wish to find out the range of values which cover the middle 95% of the distribution, we just write 95% in the right hand box, use 999 degrees of freedom and press the left arrow in Figure 8-9, we attain a T value of 1.962.

Figure 8-9: Middle 95% of the T Distribution

d.f.	t value	---->	probability
999	1.962	<----	0.95

Source: https://surfstat.anu.edu.au/surfstat-home/tables/t.php

You can see that we have selected the third option from the left, so that each white tail covers 2½% of the total distribution. Alternatively, we could have input 0.05 and clicked the fourth option; if you do this, the resulting T value is identical.

How do we convert this T value into something useful for us?

Recall that what we are trying to do is to find the range of punctual trains that covers 95% of all possible outcomes.

We will keep the standard deviation at 7 trains.

---

[22] 95% is the usual measure, but there is nothing to prevent us using a 90% or 99% interval, for example

All we need to do now is to rework equation 1 slightly: we know the mean (900), the standard deviation (7) and the T value (1.962), so we have just one unknown value, which is the target.

$$(\text{Target} - 900) / 7 = 1.962 \text{ (Equation 2)}$$
$$(\text{Target} - 900) = 13.734$$

Therefore, the target figure is 913.734.

So, the right-hand tail represents values of 914 trains or more.

To work out the left-hand tail, we can either substitute -1.962 into equation 2 or, realising that the distribution is symmetrical, simply state that the lower bound is 900 - 13.734 or 886 trains.

So, the 95% range in this example is 886 to 914.

To put this another way, if the mean is 900 on time arrivals per day and the SD is 7, we would not expect to see values lower than 886 or higher than 914 more than 5% of the time or 1 day in 20.

If the operator is penalised for poor performance below a certain level, this technique enables us to assess the expected penalties that would have to be paid per month.

8.5.5 Confidence and Degrees of Freedom

We would consider ourselves very fortunate to have 1,000 observations when assessing confidence intervals; very often, we only have a relatively small number of observations available.

In this Section, we will examine samples of data and determine whether our sample conforms to the population. We will work with a set of passenger counts and use our samples to determine whether or not there has been any change from previously reported information.

If you are presented with two surveys with 50 and 500 respondents, the natural inclination is to have more faith in the one with the larger sample size. The T distribution takes this into account as the T value increases as the number of observations declines.

We shall demonstrate in this Section how a smaller sample increases the uncertainty in any answer we calculate. There are two ways to see how the T value changes. We can use the 'Surfstat' link above or, alternatively, we can invoke the TINV function in Excel.

The TINV function requires two pieces of information, which are the proportion of the distribution to shave off – in our case, 5%, or 0.05 – and the degrees of freedom. The degree of freedom value is simply one less than the number of observations.

The results for a number of observations is shown in Figure 8-10.

Figure 8-10: T values

Observations	Degrees of Freedom	T Value
5	4	2.776
10	9	2.262
15	14	2.145
20	19	2.093
25	24	2.064
30	29	2.045
35	34	2.032
40	39	2.023
50	49	2.010
60	59	2.001
70	69	1.995
80	79	1.990
90	89	1.987
100	99	1.984
200	199	1.972

We can see in Figure 8-10 that the T value declines but at a decelerating rate. As we increase the number of observations, T will tend towards its lowest value of 1.96 (which those with a statistical background will recognise as the 95% value for the Normal distribution, which is just a special version of the T distribution).

Also, notice that as the number of observations in the sample increases and the T-value (TINV) declines, so our confidence interval becomes smaller as the sample size increases.

8.5.6 Sampling of Passenger Counts

We will now look at a simple example to apply these concepts.

Assume that we are able to physically count all passengers boarding at a station or stop during the morning peak over ten weekdays and previous information available suggests that the average number of daily passengers is 10,000.

The results are shown in Figure 8-11: Ten Days of Passenger Counts.

Figure 8-11: Ten Days of Passenger Counts

Day 1	9,012
Day 2	7,056
Day 3	7,198
Day 4	13,042
Day 5	12,781
Day 6	3,330
Day 7	9,557
Day 8	12,579
Day 9	12,135
Day 10	8,041

From Section 8.1 we can determine that the mean of this data is 9,473 and that the standard deviation (SD) is 3,024. However, what we wish to do is determine from this sample whether there is any evidence that the average of 10,000 has changed or can we still assume that our old assumption is correct.

Before we delve into the mathematics (which will not be too painful!), let us recall that, as a sample size increases, the size of the confidence interval will decline and therefore we would expect to have more faith in the result. So, we will now return to the Standard Error of the Mean (SEM) that we first saw in Section 8.5.1. From our sample of 10 counts, the SEM is $3,024/(\sqrt{10}) = 956$ (approx.). This is one of the two statistics which we require to answer our question.

8.5.7 How Sample Size Affects the Size of Confidence Intervals

To illustrate the importance of sample size, we will use a hypothetical dataset which is drawn from a population with a mean of 5 and a standard deviation of 1.

Next, we will look at two examples of the size of the confidence interval with 10 observations in the sample and 100.

Figure 8-12: Confidence Intervals with Different Sample Sizes

Sample Size	Degrees of Freedom	T Value	Standard Error	Confidence Interval (T*SE)
10	9	2.262	0.316 (1/√10)	± 0.715
100	99	1.984	0.100 (1/√100)	± 0.198

We can see from Figure 8-12 that the confidence interval that will be applied to the mean is less than a third of the size once we increase the sample size from 10 to 100.

8.5.8 Probability Method

We are going to employ two different methods to evaluate whether or not the data we collected by sampling passenger counts leads us to believe that the average daily demand is still 10,000. In this Section, we will use a method of probabilities and, in the following Section, we will use confidence intervals to achieve the same result.

To use the probability method, we need to ask the question as follows: 'what is the probability, based upon our data, that the true average demand is 10,000?'

To answer this question, we require four pieces of information. The first three are:

- Our target value, which we will call X (10,000 in this case);
- Our sample mean M (9,473); and
- The SEM (956, which is 3024/√10).

First, we need to calculate the following value:

$$(X - M)/SEM$$

So, for our specific data, this figure is (10,000-9,473)/956 or 0.55. Now we introduce our fourth statistic, which is the critical value for the T-distribution against which we will measure our result.

If our calculated figure of 0.55 is less than the critical value, we will conclude that there is no evidence that our sampled data is significantly different from average daily demand of 10,000 and, conversely, if it is higher, we would reject the hypothesis that mean demand was still 10,000.

In this case, the T value is 2.262 (9 degrees of freedom) is higher than 0.55. Therefore, we accept the hypothesis that daily demand is still around the 10,000 per day mark. Let us now carry out a similar exercise but with an extra 10 days of data, as shown in Figure 8-13.

Figure 8-13: Twenty Days of Passenger Counts

Day 1	9,012	Day 11	6,418
Day 2	7,056	Day 12	5,170
Day 3	7,198	Day 13	11,676
Day 4	13,042	Day 14	10,568
Day 5	12,781	Day 15	8,637
Day 6	3,330	Day 16	7,787
Day 7	9,557	Day 17	9,441
Day 8	12,579	Day 18	11,974
Day 9	12,135	Day 19	8,244
Day 10	8,041	Day 20	9,653

If we undertake similar calculations on the mean and standard deviation, we find that the mean has changed to 9,215 and the SD has gone down a little to 2,601. We can now recalculate our statistic (X-M)/SEM, which is now $(10,000-9,215)/(2,601/\sqrt{20})$ or 1.350.

We compare this with our new critical value from the T-distribution which is 2.093. Please note that the statistic we have calculated (1.350) is still lower than the critical value and therefore we would continue to accept the hypothesis that average daily demand was still 10,000 per day.

Finally, we can examine a set of 100 observations, which is not shown here, but is available in the 'Data Sets' download mentioned in Chapter 1.

The mean of the set is 9,472 and the SD is 2,541. So, the SEM is $2,541/\sqrt{100}$ or 254 approximately. Our final calculation in this Section is (10,000-9,472)/254 or 2.08.

Obtaining the critical value for 100 observations, we can see that the appropriate value is 1.984. The calculated value is now higher than the critical value and so, in this case, we would reject the hypothesis that the mean daily demand was still 10,000 passengers per day.

We can summarise the three results in Figure 8-14.

Figure 8-14: Summary of Results of Three Sample Sizes

Sample Size	Sample Mean (SM)	SEM	(10,000-SM)/SEM	Critical Value	Hypothesis: True Mean is not significantly different from 10,000
10	9,473	956	0.551	2.262	ACCEPT
20	9,215	582	1.350	2.093	ACCEPT
100	9,472	254	2.079	1.984	REJECT

So, the lesson we may draw from this Section is that sample size is of critical importance and that a small sample can lead to erroneous results.

8.5.9 Confidence Interval Method

Our objective here is to define a range of values in which we can say, with 95% confidence, that the true value of the mean is expected to fall. By definition, the T distribution is a probability function with values ranging from $-\infty$ to $+\infty$.

What we are aiming for is a range of values within which we are 95% confident that our true value lies. With our 95% confidence interval, what we are in effect saying is that we wish to chop off 2½% from each of the tails so that we are left with a rump of area which covers 95% of the total.

We are now in a position to construct our confidence interval for 10 observations using the sample mean passenger count (9,473), the SEM (956) and the T value (2.262).

The lower bound for our confidence interval (CILB) is

$$\text{Sample Mean} - T * SEM$$

Plugging in the figures, this lower bound 9,473 − 2.262 * 956 or 9,473 − 2,162 or 7,311. Similarly, the upper bound (CIUB) is

$$\text{Sample Mean} + T * SEM$$

In this case, the upper bound, based on our sample of 10 days' counts, is 9,473+2,162 or 11,635. So, in summary, the range of our confidence interval is 7,311 to 11,635. As the figure of 10,000 is included within this range, we can state with 95% confidence that the average demand of 10,000 per day still applies.

However, the size of the range is quite large here (4,314), so let us reduce the size of the range by increasing the sample size.

Let us now extend the survey period to 20 days, as in Figure 8-13,, and rework the confidence interval; to do this, we will need to adjust the SEM and T statistics. The standard deviation from the sample is now 2,601 so the SEM is 2,601/√20 or 582. The T value we require is 2.093 (see Figure 8-14). So, our range is determined by T*SEM, which is now 1,212.

In our new confidence interval, we will use the sample mean of 9,215, which is based on 20 rather than 10 observations. The lower bound of the interval is now 7,998 (9,215-1,217) and the upper bound is 10,432 (9,215+1,217).

Note that the 10,000 is still in the confidence interval, so the conclusion we would draw is that we still have insufficient evidence that passenger volumes are no longer as high as 10,000.

Finally, using 100 observations, the mean of the set is 9,372 and the SD is 2,579. So, the SEM is 2,579/√100 or 258 approximately. The T value for 100 observations is 1.984, as before. If we undertake the calculations for the confidence interval, we will get

$$9,372 +/- 512$$

The upper bound of this interval is 9,884 which does not cover the value of 10,000. We would therefore conclude that passenger demand was not that high. Also, note that the range of the interval is now only 1,024 (512 * 2) which is much smaller than the range of 4,314 which is the range we calculated when we only had 10 observations available. We can now summarise the three confidence intervals on one chart; the range of each of the three confidence intervals is shown in Figure 8-15.

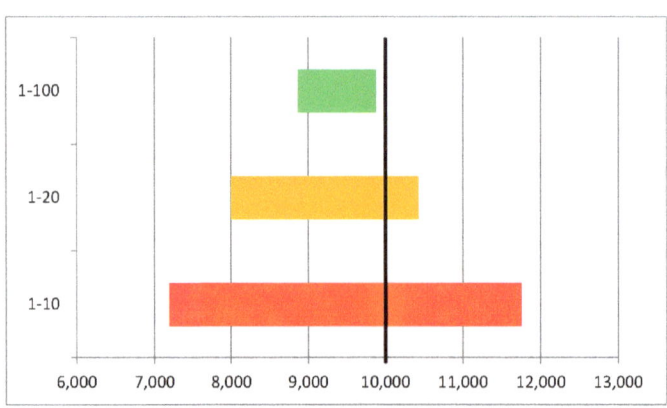

Figure 8-15: Sample Size (Y axis) and Range

8.5.10 Probability And Confidence Interval Methods Compared

If we compare Figure 8-14 and Figure 8-15, it should be apparent that we have undertaken the identical analysis but expressed in two different ways.

The two smaller samples both indicate that the mean count of 10,000 based on our samples, is still feasible, whilst the largest sample provides a definitive rejection of the hypothesis that average daily demand remains at 10,000.

8.5.11 Trade-off between Sample Size and Cost

So, the good news is that the more we are able to observe and sample, the narrower our range will be of our estimate of the true mean value of the number of passengers in Figure 8 13.
The bad news is that the more we sample, the more it will usually cost.

8.5.12 Case Study: Measuring Tourism Demand

In this mini case study, we are going to examine a situation in which an organisation has a large dataset at its disposal but seemingly ignores it and uses sampling methods instead.

The Canary Islands are highly dependent on tourism to survive and so, understandably, the local government goes to great lengths to measure how many tourists come to the islands, how long they stay and how much they spend. In this post, we will discuss what should arguably be the easiest of the three, which is passenger volume.

Early in 2016, the tool used to calculate tourist volumes, FRONTUR, underwent a significant change in methodology to calculate tourist volumes.

We will call these the 2009 and 2016 methods, named after the year in which they were introduced.

However, there was some overlap between the two methods, and so the number of foreign tourists was available using both the 2009 and 2016 methods for much of 2015 on the Canarian government's website.

The results for Lanzarote are posted next in Figure 8-16.

Figure 8-16: Tourism Volume Estimates for Lanzarote

	Tourists 2016	Tourists 2009	Intl Pax
Feb-15	196,328	170,608	167,902
Mar-15	217,927	198,026	195,030
Apr-15	208,027	177,742	182,898
May-15	163,338	174,911	171,868
Jun-15	171,768	175,592	172,936
Jul-15	180,083	200,163	191,917
Aug-15	195,777	200,823	204,745
Sep-15	189,754	175,171	175,214
Total	1,523,002	1,473,036	1,462,510

Sources: Instituto Canario de Estad'stica (ISTAC), AENA. Note that the 2016 data has since been removed from the ISTAC website

The final column is critical: this number shows the number of passengers ("Intl Pax") arriving off international flights at Lanzarote for the months in question.

The arrivals data, from AENA, should provide a pure and simple count of all passengers, as passenger volumes form a significant revenue stream for airports.

By contrast, the ISTAC figures in the first two columns are based on a sampling procedure.

But now, we run into a major and intractable problem.

If a full aircraft flies from, say, Gatwick airport to Lanzarote, then there are broadly two types of passenger on the flight:

- Passengers starting their journey in Britain. For simplicity, we will refer to this group as 'tourists'; and

- Passengers who live in Lanzarote and are undertaking the return leg of their flight back home. We will call this second group 'residents'. Based on an analysis of outbound travel[23], this group is small, at under 5% of the total.

So, we have a simple bit of algebra, which is:

$$\text{RESIDENTS} + \text{TOURISTS} = \text{INTL PAX or}$$
$$\text{TOURISTS} \leq \text{INTL PAX}$$

---

[23] *FAMILITUR assesses the number of trips by Spanish residents. In 2012, under 400,000 trips originated in the Canary Islands out of some 10 million departures to foreign airports.*

In other words, the number of tourists can never be greater than the number of international passengers passing through the airport.

If we run down the two tourist columns of Figure 8-16, we can see a good number of red cells that violate this basic condition. Moreover, the new methodology appeared to be worse than the old one. February, March, April and September show tourist volumes much higher than the number of international arrivals and, although the old methodology also had errors, the gap between international arrivals and tourists got worse under the new methodology. The old methodology overestimated tourist volumes by under 13,000 whereas the new method had at least 62,000 too many tourists.

To check just how reliable the international arrivals figures are, we can compare passenger volumes to and from the UK using Spanish data (AENA) and UK data (CAA).

Figure 8-17: UK-Lanzarote Flight Volumes

	CAA	AENA	AENA 'Error'
Feb-15	77,474	78,151	0.9%
Mar-15	94,872	95,588	0.8%
Apr-15	95,128	96,297	1.2%
May-15	94,714	96,877	2.3%
Jun-15	98,087	98,691	0.6%
Jul-15	106,500	107,543	1.0%
Aug-15	113,628	114,736	1.0%
Sep-15	99,468	100,298	0.8%
Total	779,871	788,181	1.1%

Sources: AENA, CAA

Ideally, these numbers should be identical, but we can see that the AENA numbers are very slightly higher throughout (except May, for some reason, which has a larger gap).

Nonetheless, the two datasets are reasonably consistent. So, given that we have, unusually, a 100% sample with 99% accuracy, what would be an alternative method to calculate tourism volumes?

ISTAC could ask airlines what proportion of their seats are sold in the Canary Islands to calculate the volume of residents. Alternatively, the National Police holds a database of Advance Passenger Information (API) that includes the nationality of all arrivals by air into Spain.

With these extra inputs, ISTAC could calculate tourism arrivals by nationality, age, journey purpose and so on, knowing that the overall totals were accurate. The 2016 methodology was withdrawn earlier in the year and was then updated and republished

8.5.13 More Complicated Example – Airline Punctuality

Airlines like to discuss their punctuality, so in this example, we will take a closer look at the route between Gatwick and Malaga. By examining one route, we are able to neutralize the effect of Gatwick being more or less congested to other UK airports and the same comments apply to Malaga.

For April 2015, we can see in Figure 8-18 that the mean delay of easyJet on the route was significantly higher than the other airlines and Monarch was comfortably the lowest. What we will do in this example is check whether there is any significant difference in the average delays between easyJet and Monarch in general, rather than just this specific month.

Figure 8-18: Punctuality on Gatwick-Malaga, April 2015 (in minutes)

Delay Category	Early-15	16-30	31-60	61-180	181-360	360+	Calculated Average	Actual Average
Delay per Class								
- BA	1.5	19.0	35.0	75.0	200.0	360.0		
- easyJet	0.2	17.0	33.0	70.0	185.0	360.0		
- Monarch	1.5	24.0	40.0	80.0	200.0	360.0		
- Norwegian	1.0	21.0	35.0	75.0	200.0	360.0		
British Airways	158	20	6	8	3	0	12.8	12.8
easyJet	195	48	38	13	1	1	18.3	18.3
Monarch	53	4	0	1	0	0	4.8	4.8
Norwegian	47	7	6	0	0	0	8.6	8.6

Source: CAA punctuality data, author's calculations

What we need to do first is to make certain assumptions. First, the data only tells us the number of flights which were between 0 and 15 minutes late or 16-30, etc., so for the purposes of calculating the standard deviation (and hence the SEM), we assign average delays for each category individually to each airline so that the calculated and actual average delay, which is shown in the final column of Figure 8-18, are identical. The average delay value, in minutes, by class and by airline, is shown in the top half of Figure 8-18. Readers may respond that there are several ways to manipulate the delays per class for each airline to arrive at the correct calculated average and, of course, they would be correct.

What this exercise demonstrates, however, is that data is rarely perfect and, from time to time, we need to make some assumptions. The calculation of the standard deviation is messy for this example and so the calculations are presented in an annex at the end of this Chapter. We now present the sample means and standard deviations for each airline in Figure 8-19.

Figure 8-19: Results of Airline Punctuality Example

	Flights Volume	Mean minutes	STDEV minutes	SEM minutes	T Value minutes	Lower minutes	Upper minutes
British Airways	195	12.8	28.7	2.06	1.972	8.8	16.9
easyJet	296	18.3	29.5	1.72	1.968	14.9	21.7
Monarch	58	4.8	10.5	1.38	2.002	2.1	7.6
Norwegian	60	8.6	11.1	1.44	2.001	5.7	11.5

What is immediately apparent from this figure is that the standard deviations are very high compared to the means and, in the case of BA and Monarch, nearly triple. Norwegian's SD, by contrast, is relatively small in comparison to the mean delay.

As before, we calculate the standard error of the mean (SEM) by taking the sample standard deviation and dividing by the square route of the number of flights (observations). The T values were derived using the TINV function described earlier; note that all the values are very close to the minimum of 1.96 (the Normal distribution value) because the number of observations in each airline are quite high. The lower and upper bounds of the range of the true (population) mean delay for each airline are calculated as before, namely sample mean − SEM*T for the lower bound and +SEM*T for the upper bound. The confidence intervals for each airline are presented graphically in Figure 8-20.

Figure 8-20: Confidence Interval by Airline

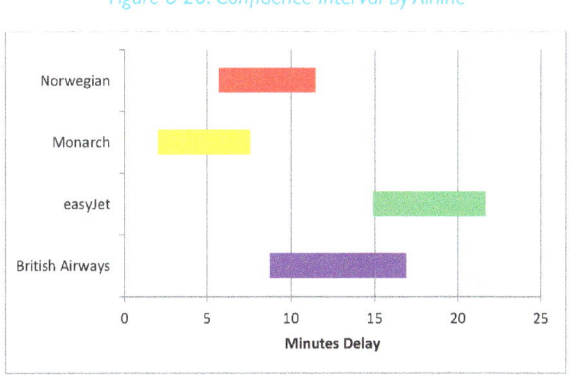

What may we conclude from this exercise? If we were asked to assess the punctuality performance of the four airlines on the Gatwick-Malaga route based only on April 2015 data, we would conclude that:

- The average delay for Monarch is significantly lower than that for easyJet (with 95% confidence) whilst the chances of Monarch's delay being similar to BA is also highly unlikely, as there is no overlap in the ranges;

- Norwegian's average delay is significantly below easyJet's but not below BA's (note that there is significant overlap in the ranges for BA and Norwegian); and

- Norwegian's and Monarch's average delays are not significantly different at the 95% confidence level, again due to the overlap of ranges. The difference may be due to chance or random events.

8.5.14 Confidence Intervals for Proportions

Sometimes we need to deal with proportions rather than absolute numbers. The methodology is the same but the SEM is a little different. If we wish to test whether, for example, in a sample of 100 aircraft arrivals, that 72% of on-time arrivals was consistent with our objective of a 75% on time rate, we would undertake the following calculation.

Let p be the observed proportion, so in this case, it is 72%.

The SEP (Standard error of the proportion) is $\sqrt{[p*(1-p)/N]}$ or $\sqrt{[0.72 * 0.28 / 100]}$ or 0.0449

So, our confidence interval, in this case, is 0.72 +/- 0.0449*1.984 or 0.72 +/- 0.089.

We can see, therefore, that the upper bound of this confidence interval is 0.809, which comfortably exceeds the 75% criterion and we would therefore state that, based on our sample, our aircraft have attained their 75% target.

8.5.15 Samples Should Be Representative

If our sample size is very large, then we may not need be too concerned about sample bias. If our sample is small, however, due to data collection cost or the availability of historic data, we need to bear certain factors in mind to ensure that the sample dataset we are using is as representative as possible of the real world.

Although sampling techniques alone could fill a book, it is worth bearing in mind certain factors that can distort a sample:

- Are there seasonal factors at work? For example, weekend demand may differ significantly from that on weekdays and summer may have a different demand profile to winter (we explore how to deal with seasonality in some detail in Chapter 20);

- Does weather affect demand? If one value in the sample is rather higher or lower than the others, it could be useful to check if weather conditions that day were not out of the ordinary[24]; and

- Other events to consider when compiling the sample are significant or rare events such as strikes, major sporting events and days of extreme disruption to the transport network.

However, this last point is contentious. The sample needs to satisfy two requirements, both to be representative but also not to present a picture best described as 'everything is rosy in the garden'. However, we will defer discussion how to handle this problem until Section 11.6, which discusses how to model unusual and rare events that disrupt the smooth running of the operation.

---

24 www.wunderground.com is an excellent source for historical weather data.

8.6 Chapter 8 Exercises

Exercise 1 In this exercise, we'll look at when you should use the standard deviation and when the SEM. So, for each part, the answer just needs to be SD or SEM.

a) You have recently purchased 10 vehicles and wish to find out the mean and variation in fuel efficiency of your new fleet;

b) You wish compare the results from a) with the manufacturer's stated fuel efficiency;

c) The Board of Directors of a ferry company wishes to know how many vehicles are loaded per crossing during May. There are 30 sailings in all;

d) The Board then asks whether demand during May was significantly different from the long-term average demand.

Exercise 2 You have been asked to carry out a survey for a long-distance bus company, the subject of which is satisfaction with fares, frequency and journey time. Due to budget constraints, the survey will be limited to 40 people.

The company has just one route, with several daily departures, and there is no obvious seasonality in demand by day of week or month. The average end-to-end journey time is two hours.

- Which factors should you consider when deciding how people should be selected to take part in the survey?

- Your initial reaction is to undertake surveys of passengers on the buses. What problems arise with limiting the survey to passengers on board?

Exercise 3 The bus company has set a target that 90% of its passengers are satisfied with the service overall. The results of the survey show, however, that just 30 of the 40 respondents eventually chosen (so 75%) stated that they were satisfied.

- Does this mean that we should be concerned about satisfaction levels? Use 95% confidence intervals to support your answer.

- The CEO is not happy with this result and suggests that another 40 people be surveyed. How many people from this second batch are required to give a satisfactory response?

(Hint: if you set up a spreadsheet which adds together the satisfactory responses from the original group of 40 with the second group and then allow the total proportion satisfied to vary, along with the SEP, you can arrive at the correct answer that way. Alternatively, this question can be solved using very complex algebra!)

8.7 Annex – Standard Deviation in Airline Punctuality Example

When data is presented as frequencies, as with the airline punctuality example, the calculation of the standard deviation is somewhat complicated. First, let us reproduce the original data from Figure 8-18.

Delay Category	Early-15	16-30	31-60	61-180	181-360	360+	Calculated Average	Actual Average
Delay per Class - -								
- BA	1.5	19.0	35.0	75.0	200.0	360.0		
- easyJet	0.2	17.0	33.0	70.0	185.0	360.0		
- Monarch	1.5	24.0	40.0	80.0	200.0	360.0		
- Norwegian	1.0	21.0	35.0	75.0	200.0	360.0		
British Airways	158	20	6	8	3	0	12.8	12.8
easyJet	195	48	38	13	1	1	18.3	18.3
Monarch	53	4	0	1	0	0	4.8	4.8
Norwegian	47	7	6	0	0	0	8.6	8.6

For each cell in the chart, we need to calculate the variance (which is the square of the standard deviation) using the following formula:

$$\text{Frequency} * (\text{mean} - \text{delay})^2$$

Let us look at the first line (BA) and we derive the figure of 20,729 by multiplying 158 by $(12.8-1.5)^2$. The figure of 762 is $20*(12.8-19.0)^2$, and so on. When we perform a similar calculation for the remaining columns, add them up add divide by the total number of BA flights (195, the sum of the cells in the table above shaded in green), we obtain the variance, which is the square of SDEV.

							Variance	STDEV
British Airways	20,279	762	2,949	30,922	105,099	-	820.6	28.7
easyJet	54,886	25	10,627	41,828	33,023	116,775	868.8	29.5
Monarch	584	804	-	4,925	-	-	108.9	10.5
Norwegian	2,366	758	4,183	-	-	-	121.8	11.1

We then add up the individual cells to produce the variance for each airline. The final step, to reach the sample standard deviation, is to take the square route of the variance and divide it by the total number of flights minus 1. So, the sample standard deviation for Monarch, say, is

$$\sqrt{[6,314 / (58-1)]}$$

which is 10.5.

9 CORRELATION & REGRESSION

9.1 Introduction

We will start this Chapter with an assessment of how variables are related to each other both through simple plots of data and, also, by using a more formal measure known as correlation.

We will then take this issue of relationships somewhat further and use several variables to show how, for example, demand can be modelled by GDP, population (POP) and car ownership (COW).

What we will end up with is a model that looks like:

$$\text{Demand} = a * GDP + b * POP + c * COW$$

We will follow the procedure for undertaking a regression from start to finish. This topic is also known as econometrics, which is a complex subject, to say the least (I have a textbook called "Basic Econometrics" and it is clear that the author of this book has a sense of humour, as this 'basic' textbook runs to over 900 pages!).

As well as carrying out the technique from scratch, the objective of this Chapter is to give you an appreciation of what is required and to be able to ask informed questions when you come across business models involving regression.

One of the assumptions of the regression technique is that we are able to assume that future behaviour will be influenced by the same factors as we have seen in the past. This is a reasonable assumption in most cases, as people will travel more if prices decline, a faster service will attract more trips than a slower one at the same price, and so on.

Intuitively, the more observations we have, to play with – be they weeks, months or years, the more likely it is that we can develop an understanding of how demand fluctuates, and why. Please note that, although we are will be using regression in a business or economic context, the procedure is valid in any other part of the transport industry where we are trying to explain the behaviour of one variable by others.

9.2 Relationships between Variables

This Section will examine two methods of determining relationships between variables:

- Graphical method; and
- Correlation.

The graphical method is useful for seeing if there is any clear evidence for any relationship between two variables, whilst correlation will be used to quantify the strength of the relationship.

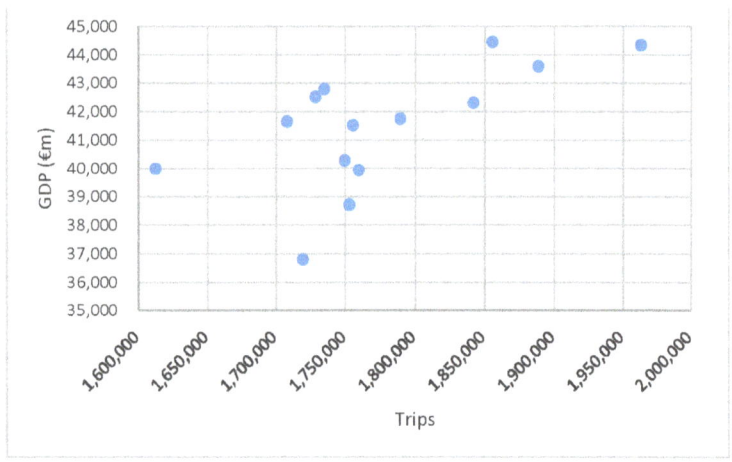

Figure 9 1: Relationship between Trips and GDP from Figure 7-12

Figure 9-1 looks at how GDP and trip volumes are related and it appears that there is a significant relationship: as GDP increases, so does the number of trips, which is not unexpected. However, Excel's initial scatter diagramme certainly needed a tidy up: if both axes start from 0, all the data is scrunched into one part of the graph area.

Take note, however, that we do not have a straight line, so the relationship is not perfect (and, frankly, we should be worried if it were!).

Although there is clear evidence of correlation between these two variables, we CANNOT assume causality (in this case, we are not providing evidence that an increase in GDP causes higher demand for inter-island trips).

We will address causation when we come to discuss regression later in this Chapter.

9.3 Correlation

9.3.1 Description of Correlation

To answer the question, "How strong is the relationship between the GDP and trip variables?", we need to use a technique known as correlation. Figure 9-2 shows the range of correlation values, from perfect to none.

Figure 9-2: Three Versions of Correlation

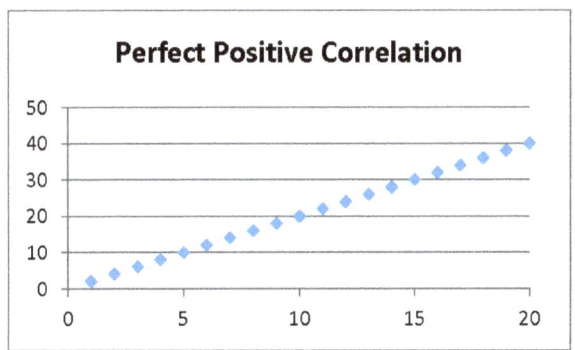

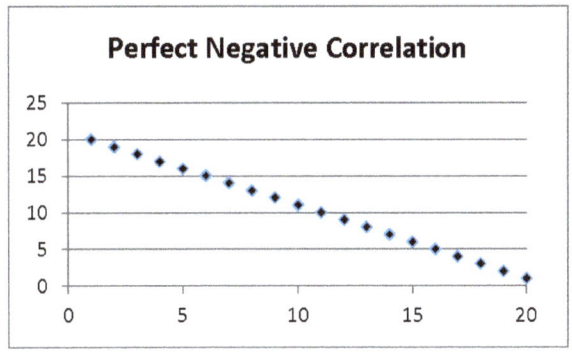

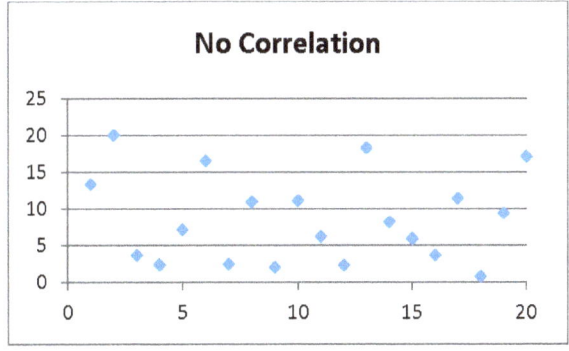

Perfect positive correlation occurs when an increase of, say, 10% is seen in one variable, the other variable will also increase by 10%. So, in other words, the relationship between the two variables is perfectly predictable and the correlation coefficient takes a value of 1. Perfect negative correlation also has a totally predictable relationship between the two variables: as one variable increases, the other declines and this demonstrates a correlation coefficient of -1. By contrast, the third panel shows no relationship at all between the two sets of data and the correlation coefficient is close to 0.

In the real world, coefficients of +1, -1 and 0 are effectively impossible. Even the example in the third panel has a correlation of -0.07, so the question we next need to ask ourselves is whether a correlation coefficient is actually meaningful, i.e. significantly different from 0.

9.3.2 Significance of the Correlation Coefficient

If we look back at Figure 7-12 and calculate the correlation coefficient between the number of trips and GDP, the correlation coefficient between the two is 0.64. In Excel, calculating a correlation coefficient is fairly straightforward. A simple example is presented in Figure 9-3.

Figure 9-3: Calculation of Correlation Coefficient

	Column B	Column C
	Variable 1	Variable 2
Row 4	0.7	5
Row 5	1.6	7
Row 6	0.9	8
Row 7	2.1	10
Row 8	3.7	12
Row 9	3.5	13
Row 10	4.1	15
		=CORREL(B4:B10,C4:C10)

The value of 0.64 looks reasonable but we have taken only a small sample of thirteen observations. Intuitively, if we had, say, 100 observations in our sample and got a similar figure, we would have more confidence of a relationship between the two variables.

There is a simple statistical test to determine whether a correlation coefficient is significantly different from zero; in other words, whether we can infer that there is in fact a relationship between two variables.

If N is the number of observations and R is the correlation coefficient, we can calculate the following significance statistic, which we will call SIG:

$$SIG = R * \sqrt{[(N-2) / (1-R^2)]}$$

For our specific example with thirteen observations, the calculation is

$$0.64 * \sqrt{(11/(1-0.64^2))}$$

which is approximately 2.76. If SIG is greater than 2.18[25], we may infer that there is evidence of a relationship between the two, as in this case. In other words, we may infer that there is indeed a relationship between the wealth of the islands, as expressed by GDP, and the number of trips made, which seems reasonable.

9.3.3 Correlation is not Necessarily Causation

Although there may indeed be a case for arguing that causation can occur when we see a significant level of correlation between two variables, this cannot be assumed. Looking back at Figure 7-12, we have said that we would expect higher GDP in general and particularly in disposable income to cause higher volumes of travel to occur.

So, in this case, we would say that the GDP variable is driving the one for travel demand. In this case, it is (hopefully!) self-evident which way the causality flows; in other words, nobody is likely to suggest that greater demand for travel drives GDP. It is also possible to find correlations between completely unrelated variables, such as rainfall in Uzbekistan and the proportion of students entering university education in Australia[26].

If we were to find any significant correlation (either positive or negative) between these two datasets, it would be very hard work indeed to prove that one causes the other!

---

[25] This statistic also uses the T distribution, so we need the critical value, which is TINV(0.05,12), or 2.18.

[26] There are a few websites devoted to 'crazy correlations'. See, for example, http://twentytwowords.com/funny-graphs-show-correlation-between-completely-unrelated-stats-9-pictures/

9.4 Regression

9.4.1 Regression Method Outcome

The regression method aims to find a straight line that best fits all the points in a set of data. Imagine we have the following small data set and we wish to achieve a line of best fit.

Rail Passengers	Car Ownership
1,201,357	0.440
1,306,977	0.561
1,375,340	0.442
1,408,567	0.395
1,521,812	0.412

A scatter diagram and an indicative line of best fit are shown in Figure 9-4 below.

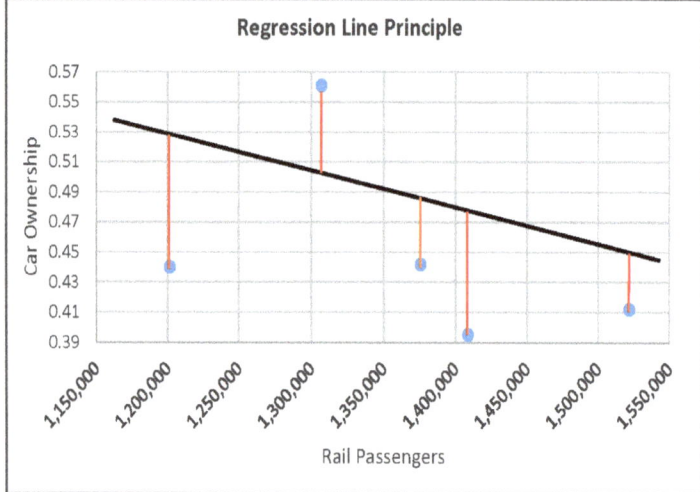

Figure 9-4: Line of Best Fit through the Data

So, what do we mean by 'best fit'? The method used in calculating this line is to take the sum of all the squared distances between the observations and the line which minimizes the sum of these squared distances (marked in red). The reasons we use the squares of the distance are that:

- Negative and positive errors do not cancel each other out; and
- Points which are farther away from the line of best fit get more heavily penalized.

The good news is that, in the method which we discuss in the following paragraphs, we do not need to worry about calculating this line, as Excel will do this for us and automatically provide us with the line of best fit. Once we have generated our model, we will undertake some tests to check it for accuracy, bias and usefulness of the model.

9.4.2 The Problem

We will use a larger dataset to illustrate the technique and assume that a railway operator has services on 15 non-overlapping routes. The operator wishes to find out what drives demand for rail services on the corridors that it serves and has been able to gather information on the proportion of adults owning cars (proportion) and levels of unemployment (%) in each corridor.

We will assume that populations for each corridor are roughly the same, so population is not a factor driving demand in this case. The data results for the year 2014 are shown in Figure 9-5. Please note that the data in this Section is entirely fictitious and has been developed solely to demonstrate the regression technique.

Figure 9-5: Raw data to be used for analysis

	Rail Pax	Unemployment	Car Ownership
Corridor 1	1,362,041	6.5	0.493
Corridor 2	1,851,464	6.3	0.457
Corridor 3	2,074,879	4.6	0.479
Corridor 4	1,111,785	6.8	0.612
Corridor 5	1,653,818	5.9	0.585
Corridor 6	1,970,312	6.1	0.430
Corridor 7	780,655	9.7	0.519
Corridor 8	1,075,750	8.1	0.426
Corridor 9	1,797,126	6.9	0.408
Corridor 10	2,039,137	5.2	0.394
Corridor 11	1,668,402	7.1	0.376
Corridor 12	544,972	10.4	0.684
Corridor 13	1,873,964	5.1	0.449
Corridor 14	1,338,315	7.2	0.651
Corridor 15	1,318,122	7.3	0.417

First, let us have a look at the data using scatter diagrams. To do this, just highlight, for example, the rail passengers and car ownership columns in Excel and then click Insert, Scatter. Figure 9-6 and Figure 9-7 show the results of this after they have been tidied up. Rail demand is shown on the horizontal (X) axis.

Figure 9-6: Scatter diagram of rail demand and unemployment

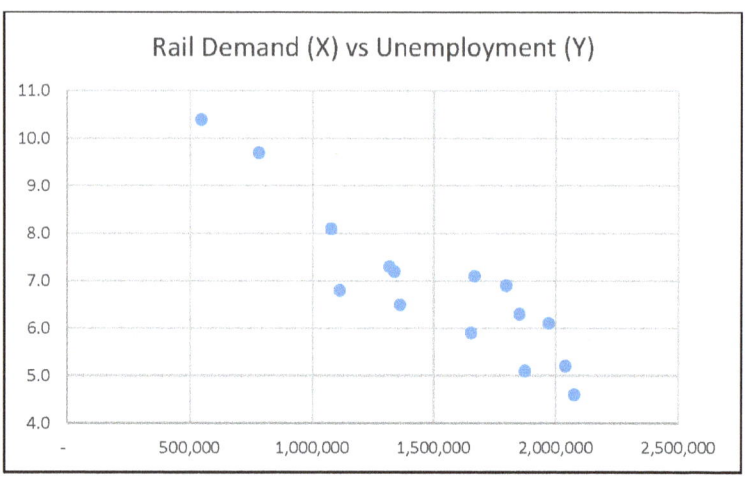

Figure 9-7: Scatter diagram of rail demand and car ownership

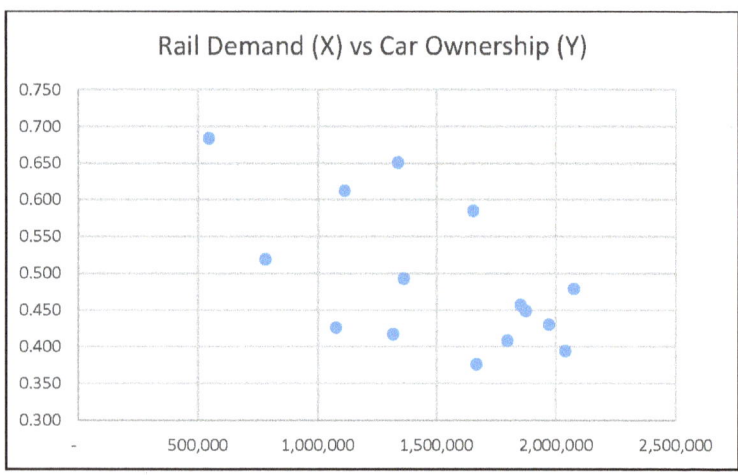

It appears that as unemployment and car ownership decline, we would expect in both cases that demand for rail increases and this is confirmed by the two scatter diagrams above.

Clearly, the relationship between car ownership and rail demand is less clear than in the case of unemployment, as drawing a straight line through the data is not so straightforward.

However, a downward sloping function is still discernible.

We should note, though, that both correlations are significant, using the test we introduced in Section 9.3.2.

There is one further test we should undertake before proceeding to the regression itself and that is to determine if there is a significant relationship between the input/independent variables, i.e. car ownership and unemployment.

The reason for doing this is as follows.

As we add variables to model the factor in which we are interested (in this case rail demand), each independent variable should, as much as possible, be unrelated to the other independent variables.

To see why this is so, imagine that we wished to model house prices on the number of rooms and the floor area of each property in our sample.

But, before we even start to build such a model, we would expect the number of rooms to increase as floor area increases and vice versa. This phenomenon is known by the unpleasant name of multicollinearity. So, in the ideal world, independent variables should show as little correlation as possible with each other.

In the case of our own model, the correlations from the data are as follows:

- Pax vs unemployment: −0.91;
- Pax vs car ownership: −0.60; and
- Unemployment vs cars: 0.42

So, we can see that there is correlation between our two independent variables, albeit fairly weak (use the test in Section 9.3.2 to prove that this is the case). Realistically, it can be very difficult to find totally unrelated independent variables.

9.4.3 Undertaking the Regression

This Section will show how to undertake the regression in Excel, once the Analysis ToolPak has been installed. These instructions are for Excel 2016 but should not be that different in other versions.

In this Section, we will first develop a model using demand and unemployment only. We will then include car ownership in the model and compare the results of the two models.

First, click Data, then Data Analysis and pick Regression from the drop-down box that appears. You should see a screen like Figure 9-8.

Figure 9-8: Step 1 of undertaking a regression in Excel

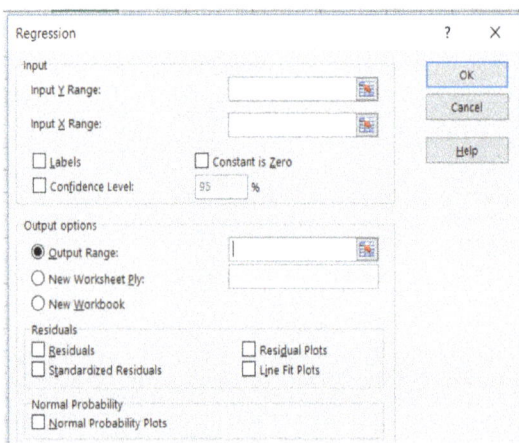

Next, highlight the column for rail pax (including the label). This is the Y variable, which is what we are investigating. The X variables are those that we believe influence our Y variable, so our X range is the column headed Unemployment (again, including the label). Make sure that the box 'Labels' is checked and select an empty space on the spreadsheet to display the regression results. Once you have done this, the Regression screen should look like Figure 9-9.

Figure 9-9: Step 2 of undertaking a regression in Excel

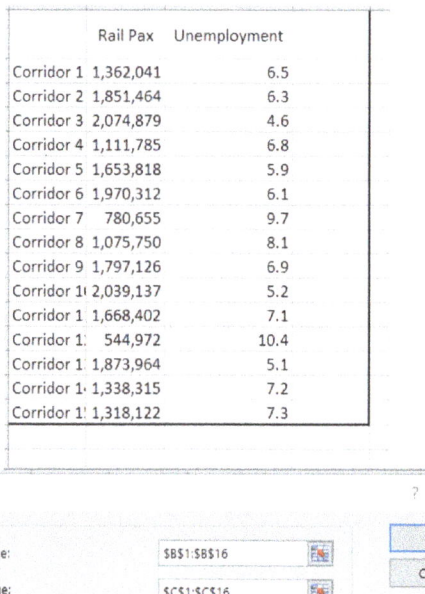

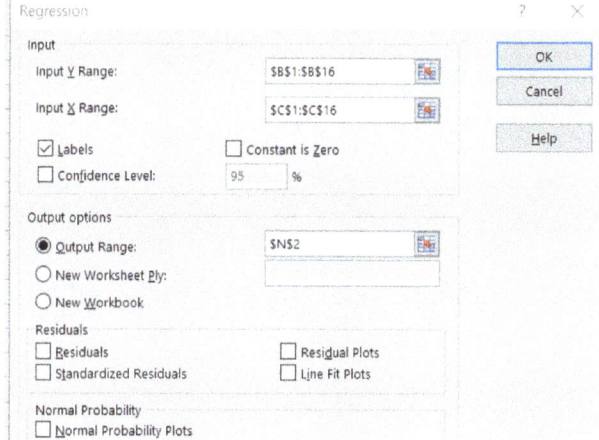

Just hit 'OK' and the results will appear starting in the cell you have designated as the output range.

Next, repeat the exercise, but this time, include car ownership in the input X range and select an output range 20 rows below the previous output range.

Once you have rerun the regression, a second set of regression outputs will appear.

Allow at least 20 rows between sets of regression outputs to avoid overlap.

Figure 9-10 and Figure 9-11 show the output; next we will interpret this output.

Figure 9-10: Output from Regression Analysis — Unemployment only[27]

SUMMARY OUTPUT
unemployment only

Regression Statistics	
Multiple R	0.9103
R Square	0.8287
Adjusted R Square	0.8156
Standard Error	201,581
Observations	15

ANOVA

	df	SS	MS	F	Significance F
Regression	1	2.5562E+12	2.56E+12[27]	62.90537	2.4573E-06
Residual	13	5.2825E+11	4.06E+10		
Total	14	3.0844E+12			

	Coefficients	Standard Error	t Stat	P-value	Lower 95%	Upper 95%
Intercept	3,346,039	238,824	14.0105	3.19E-09	2,830,090	3,861,988
Unemployment	- 268,700	33,878	-7.9313	2.46E-06	- 341,890	- 195,510

Figure 9-11: Results using Unemployment and Car Ownership

SUMMARY OUTPUT

unemployment and car ownership

Regression Statistics	
Multiple R	0.9412
R Square	0.8858
Adjusted R Square	0.8668
Standard Error	171,317
Observations	15

ANOVA

	df	SS	MS	F	Significance F
Regression	2	2.732E+12	1.37E+12	46.54612	2.2165E-06
Residual	12	3.522E+11	2.93E+10		
Total	14	3.084E+12			

	Coefficients	Standard Error	t Stat	P-value	Lower 95%	Upper 95%
Intercept	3,746,462	260,625	14.3749	6.32E-09	3,178,609	4,314,315
Unemployment	-236,491	31,653	-7.4713	7.52E-06	-305,457	-167,524
Car Ownership	-1,264,295	516,202	-2.4492	0.030637	-2,389,002	-139,587

---

27 *Excel uses engineering notation to save space, so a number like 2.56E+12 is equal to 2,560,000,000,000*

9.4.4 Developing the Model - Unemployment only

The procedure below will give us an equation in the following form:

Rail demand = A + (B * Unemployment)

First, the model tells us that almost 82% (the adjusted R square number in Figure 9-10) of the changes seen in rail demand may be attributed to changes in unemployment levels and therefore 18% of the variation is due to factors we have not yet modelled or else are due to chance.

We will not go into the theory here, but it is better to use the adjusted R Square figure rather than the one immediately above it. The second part of the output gives us the equation itself, which is:

Demand = 3,346,039 - 268,700 * Unemployment

So, how does this equation work? Let's assume that we forecast a drop in unemployment of one percentage point.

The model tells us that if this occurred, we would expect rail demand to increase by 268,700 passengers.

9.4.5 How Useful is our Model?

Next to the coefficients themselves, we have statistics which tell us how robust our model is.

For now, we will just say that the equation is satisfactory and we have confidence in all the coefficients our model has produced; the coefficients for the intercept and unemployment have a P value of less than 0.05, and therefore we can be confident that these coefficients are unlikely to be zero.

The model also produces two further columns, 'Lower 95%' and 'Upper 95%'.

If the range includes 0, we cannot be confident that the coefficient takes a non-zero value.

If the range between 'upper' and 'lower' does include 0, then T will be less than 2 (approximately) and p will be greater than 0.05; in other words, the confidence interval is providing the same message as the 'p' and 'T' values.

However, you may recall from the discussion in the previous Chapter that the critical T value varies according to the number of observations, so the recommendation here is to assess just the P-value and the confidence intervals.

Looking back at Figure 9-10, the middle section labelled ANOVA, provides an F value and, immediately to the right of the F value is a significance figure. In brief, F indicates how well the model fits the data overall and the higher the value of F, the better. We also require the significance of this F to be below 0.05, which it clearly is in this example.

9.4.6 Bringing in the Car Unemployment Variable

Although more sophisticated statistical packages will automatically select the line of best fit by testing combinations of independent variables, Excel does not do this. So, in this Section, we have brought together the key statistics from both regression outputs in Figure 9-12 and we will undertake a comparison manually.

Figure 9-12: Comparison of Results

	Unemployment Only	Unemployment and Car Ownership
Adjusted R^2	0.8156	0.8668
Significance F	2.457E-06[28]	2.217E-06
P Value Intercept	3.194E-09	6.320E-09
P Value Unemployment	2.457E-06	7.520E-06
P Value Car Ownership	N/A	0.0306

First, we can see that we have improved the proportion of the variation in rail demand explained by the model by over five percentage points if we include car ownership.

At this point, however, a word of warning is needed: as the number of variables included in the model increases, R^2 can only increase or stay the same. Therefore, we need to examine the output further to ensure that the model is valid.

The significance of F and the P value of both the intercept and unemployment have changed a little, but the values are clearly still extremely low and well below the 0.05 threshold.

The important change is the inclusion of car ownership itself. When we examined the scatter diagram of rail demand against car ownership (Figure 9-7), the relationship was clearly weaker

---

28 *The F statistic is particularly useful when there are two or more independent variables present. The significance of F should be less than or equal to 0.05.*

than that between demand and unemployment. We can confirm that this is the case with the regression output, as the P value is much higher, at around 0.03. Ideally, we would prefer the P value to be as small as possible but, since 0.03 is less than 0.05, we would conclude that the car ownership variable makes a significant contribution to our understanding of how rail demand varies and therefore it should be included in the model.

We can confirm that the performance of the car ownership variable is 'good' rather than 'superb' by examining the confidence intervals in Figure 9-13, which have been extracted from Figure 9-11.

Figure 9-13: Confidence Intervals of Variables

	Coefficients	P-value	Lower 95%	Upper 95%
Intercept	3,746,462	6.32E-09	3,178,609	4,314,315
Unemployment	-236,491	7.52E-06	-305,457	-167,524
Car Ownership	-1,264,295	0.030637	-2,389,002	-139,587

The confidence interval for car ownership is quite large in comparison to the other two variables but, crucially, it does not include zero.

We can therefore conclude that the coefficient for car ownership is indeed significantly different from zero and therefore should be included in the model, as we stated earlier.

9.4.7 Comparing Modelled & Actual Rail Demand

We will now add two further columns to the data in Figure 9-5: Raw data to be used for analysis.

Using the regression model including both unemployment and car ownership, we may now calculate the modelled demand value for each rail corridor and also the residual value (actual − modelled), which will inform us how far away we are from the recorded demand.

The results are presented in Figure 9-14.

The data has been ordered from the smallest to the largest flows so we can see how well the model performs over flows of different sizes.

Figure 9-14: Modelled and Residual Values

	Rail Pax	Unemployment	Car Own.	Modelled	Residual
Corridor 12	544,972	10.4	0.684	422,178	122,794
Corridor 7	780,655	9.7	0.519	796,330	- 15,675
Corridor 8	1,075,750	8.1	0.426	1,292,295	- 216,545
Corridor 4	1,111,785	6.8	0.612	1,364,575	- 252,790
Corridor 15	1,318,122	7.3	0.417	1,492,867	- 174,745
Corridor 14	1,338,315	7.2	0.651	1,220,671	117,644
Corridor 1	1,362,041	6.5	0.493	1,585,973	- 223,932
Corridor 5	1,653,818	5.9	0.585	1,611,553	42,265
Corridor 11	1,668,402	7.1	0.376	1,592,001	76,401
Corridor 9	1,797,126	6.9	0.408	1,598,842	198,284
Corridor 2	1,851,464	6.3	0.457	1,678,786	172,678
Corridor 13	1,873,964	5.1	0.449	1,972,689	- 98,725
Corridor 6	1,970,312	6.1	0.43	1,760,220	210,092
Corridor 10	2,039,137	5.2	0.394	2,018,577	20,560
Corridor 3	2,074,879	4.6	0.479	2,053,006	21,873

Before we delve into an assessment of the residuals in the next Section, it is worth plotting how closely or otherwise the modelled data fits the actual data recorded, which we show in Figure 9-15:

Figure 9-15: Results of Model compared to Actual Data

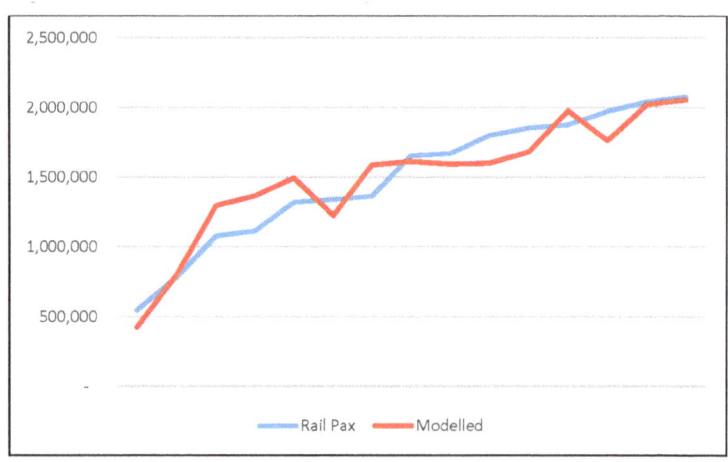

Overall, the fit between the actual and modelled values looks reasonable but what we will now do is run some simple tests to ensure that the model is appropriate for use. We will do this by checking for bias.

9.4.8 Checking for Bias

As we saw in the previous Section, the model is not a perfect match for the data, so it is important to see if these errors have any specific bias.

What we hope to see are the errors over time following a fairly random path, including both positive and negative values for the term [actual value – modelled value] and we do not want to see the errors increasing as the actual number of rail passengers increases over time.

There are several complex econometric tests to detect bias, but for now, all we will do is to take a look at the errors in a chart (see Figure 9-16). This chart is just a plot of actual minus modelled values.

Figure 9-16: Detection of Bias in the Model

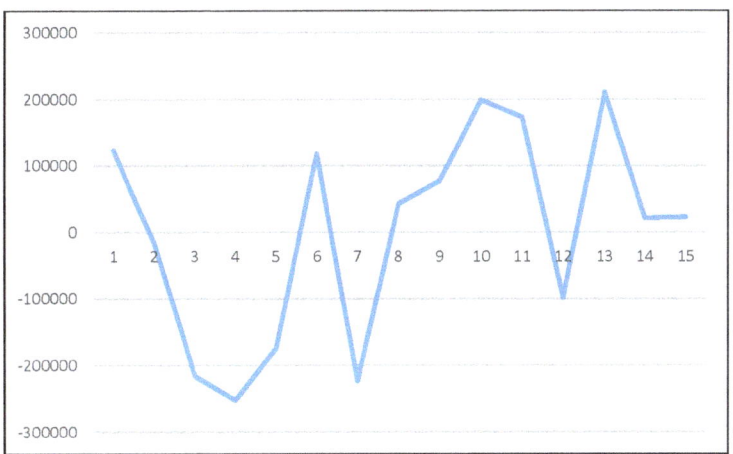

The error term crosses the X axis frequently (fulfilling the positive and negative error requirement).

However, the error term is quite large when expressed as a proportion of actual values for some of the corridors and there is some evidence that there is an upward drift in the residuals, rather than being oscillating around zero, as we would like.

To overcome this problem, we might need to split demand by ticket type (we would expect unemployment to be related to commuter and business travel rather than leisure trips) and also investigate the car ownership variable further.

For example, levels of car ownership may be attributable to either disposable income or a decision by well-to-do urban households which choose not to own a car through a lifestyle choice rather than lack of funds.

9.4.9 Relevant Range

We need to bear in mind that regressions are often undertaken not just to understand the relationships between variables but also to forecast future values.

Let us look back at the range of demand figures which we have in Figure 9-5.

The range of the sample is quite small, between 545,000 to 2.1 million passengers. The range of employment values is 4.6% to 10.4% and for car ownership between 38% and 68%.

So, it is critical to bear the limitations of the regression model in mind. Now, say that we wished to test the impact of an unemployment level of 13% and a car ownership level of 30%. If we plug these values into the equation in Section 4, we would get

$$\text{Rail Demand} = 3{,}746{,}461 - 236{,}491 * 13 - 1{,}264{,}295 * 0.3$$

So, our rail demand figure would be 292,795.

But how much confidence would we have in this figure?

We have used input variables which are well beyond the range of those provided in the sample data, so we should be uncomfortable about using our equation in this way.

Whilst we can step a little way outside the range of the sample data, it would be unwise to stray too far from the range of values used in developing the regression equation in the first place.

There are no hard and fast rules about the flexibility of the relevant range, so judgement needs to be exercised when using values of input variables outside the range available from the regression.

9.5 Chapter 9 Exercise

The following dataset shows the number of passengers on a branch line. In order to understand how demand on this line is influenced by competing bus services and the number of passengers alighting at the junction of the main and branch lines, the regional manager acquires the following information.

	Branch line pax	Bus Pax	Main Line
2010 Q1	864,031	1,182,984	807,745
2010 Q2	930,151	1,169,896	947,402
2010 Q3	922,372	1,561,935	1,308,203
2010 Q4	827,558	1,092,939	797,510
2011 Q1	722,910	920,011	630,824
2011 Q2	828,355	1,120,776	819,028
2011 Q3	836,469	1,533,662	1,198,652
2011 Q4	796,725	1,150,468	842,831
2012 Q1	715,597	1,053,130	752,451
2012 Q2	806,215	1,129,826	852,695
2012 Q3	814,155	1,591,128	1,135,171
2012 Q4	777,260	1,158,193	860,263
2013 Q1	753,786	1,110,943	732,647
2013 Q2	875,615	1,228,990	848,159
2013 Q3	941,882	1,603,132	1,133,207
2013 Q4	824,963	1,207,629	848,389
2014 Q1	761,770	1,117,326	653,368
2014 Q2	768,039	1,160,811	775,452
2014 Q3	733,279	1,488,885	1,007,681
2014 Q4	639,330	1,176,423	696,709
2015 Q1	590,254	1,354,106	612,418
2015 Q2	644,761	1,333,624	691,075

Required:

- Undertake a regression of branch line passengers as a function of bus and main line passengers;

- What is the equation, which the table shows, for the volume of branch line passengers? Does the equation make sense? Using your equation, show how 1,000 extra main line pax and 1,000 more bus passengers will affect demand on the rail branch;

- What other observations do you have about the equation? To what extent is the variation in rail branch line passengers attributable to bus and main line volumes? Also, do we have confidence in the values of the coefficients?

- Develop a line chart with the actual and modelled versions of branch line passengers. What comments can you make about the fit of the model compared with the actual data?

- What other data would you look for to improve the quality of the regression equation and how much variation in branch line demand is explained by other factors? Bear in mind when answering this question that we are looking at a small geographical area.

10. REGRESSION ANALYSIS: FURTHER CONSIDERATIONS

10.1 Chapter Overview

This Chapter includes an eclectic list of topics which arise frequently in regression analysis. The data used in the following Sections is real and the topics covered have all been addressed for a client for whom the author was retained to audit regression models.

10.2 Time as an Independent Variable

The example we have just used looked at a cross-section of data for one year, so time was not a variable. Very often, however, we encounter data that is presented over time. We will examine some data from a British rail operator's performance. Performance is measured for every train on every day and, at the end of each period (13 periods per year), a figure known as Average Minutes Lateness (AML) is calculated for each principal line of route used by the operator. The AML for 52 periods is shown in Figure 10-1.

Figure 10-1: Actual Performance over 52 periods (4 years)

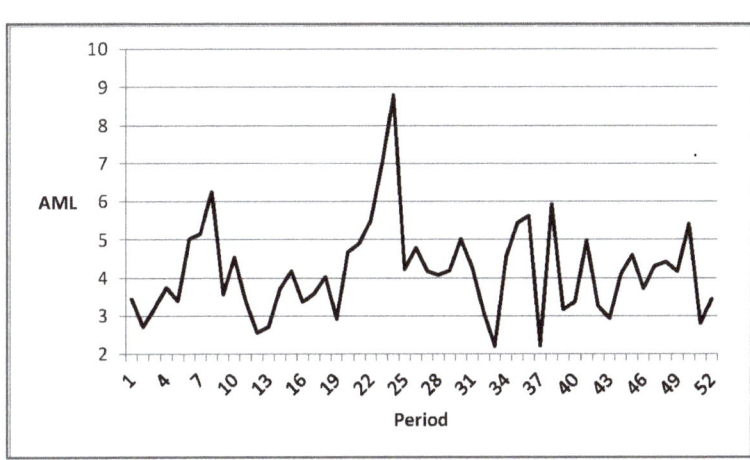

We can see from Figure 10-1 that performance has been remarkably stable, with performance hovering around a level of 4 units of AML, albeit with several peaks and troughs. But it is important to bear in mind that, even though the X axis is time, this is not a time series; rather, it is a set of 52 independent observations. So, there is no suggestion that performance in period 7, for example, is dependent in any way on period 6. To provide further evidence that time is not a dependent variable, we will examine two weeks of daily performance data selected at random. The data is from June 2016 and is shown in Figure 10-2.

Figure 10-2: Daily Performance (PPM)

Date	Day of Week	"Today"	"Yesterday"
13-Jun	Monday	82%	99%
14-Jun	Tuesday	98%	82%
15-Jun	Wednesday	97%	98%
16-Jun	Thursday	73%	97%
17-Jun	Friday	88%	73%
18-Jun	Saturday	99%	88%
19-Jun	Sunday	96%	99%
20-Jun	Monday	98%	96%
21-Jun	Tuesday	100%	98%
22-Jun	Wednesday	97%	100%
23-Jun	Thursday	4%	97%
24-Jun	Friday	56%	4%
25-Jun	Saturday	94%	56%
26-Jun	Sunday	100%	94%

Source: www.uktra.in

The data is for TfL rail, which comprises the stopping services between Shenfield and London Liverpool Street. The PPM measures the proportion of trains arriving within 5 minutes of the timetabled arrival at the train's destination. If 'today's' performance is dependent to some extent on 'yesterday's' we can set up a regression to test this. The regression equation is:

$$PPM_{today} = A*PPM_{yesterday} + B$$

However, if this regression is carried out, we find that little, if any, of the variation in daily performance is attributable to performance on the previous day.

Therefore, if daily performance does not include time as a variable, we can say with confidence that performance measured over one four-week period is independent of previous periods.

10.3 The Illusion of Time

The means used to forecast AML is a variable called delay minutes. The regression performed well (with all coefficients significant and a high value of R^2). The set of residuals, based on periods, is shown in Figure 10-3 below.

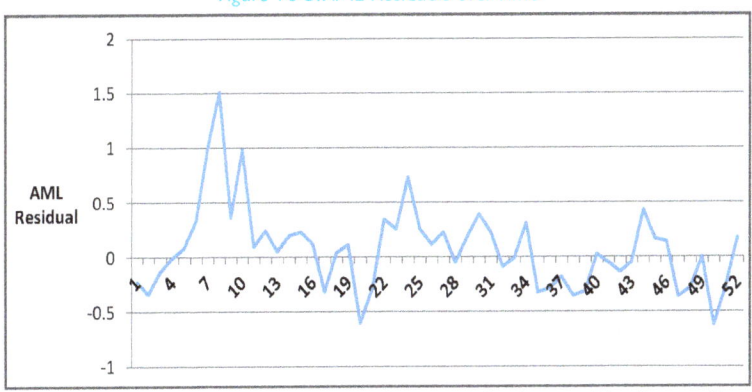

Figure 10-3: AML Residuals over Time

This pattern looks reasonably robust, with the residuals settling down from around period 20.

But, we now have to ask ourselves whether this result makes any sense?

The answer is no, as we have concluded that the data is not a time series as such but a selection of 52 independent observations.

What we are in fact interested in seeing here is whether the pattern of residuals works as well for both large and small values of AML.

To do this, we just need to reorder the AMLs by size, as with Figure 9-16, rather than the period over which they occurred; the resulting residuals chart is presented in Figure 10-4.

Figure 10-4: AML Residuals Ordered by Size of Observed AML

[Chart: AML Residual values ranging roughly from -1 to 2, ordered by size of observed AML]

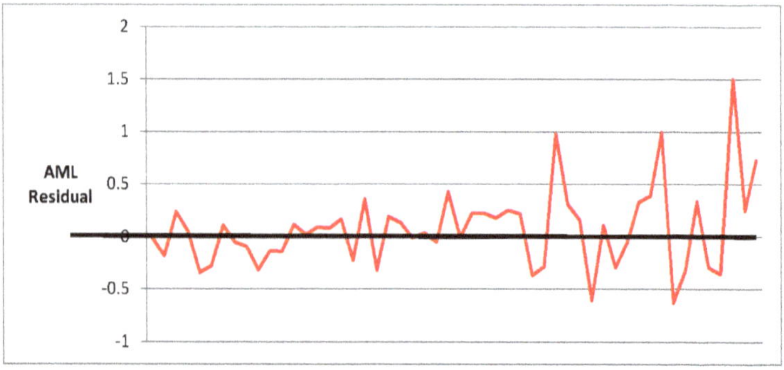

What we have now is a very different picture. We can see from Figure 10-4 that the model works well for smaller values of AML but once AML values are greater than 5 (approximately), we begin to see some significantly sized residuals. We should therefore be concerned about using this model for any occurrences of AML higher than 5.

10.4 How to Deal with Outlying Values

10.4.1 What is an Outlier?

An outlier is a data point which does not fit with the rest of the dataset. It is also important to be clear, however, on what an outlier is not. Figure 10-5 shows a data series, all of whose points lie on, or close to, the line of best fit.

Figure 10-5: No Outliers

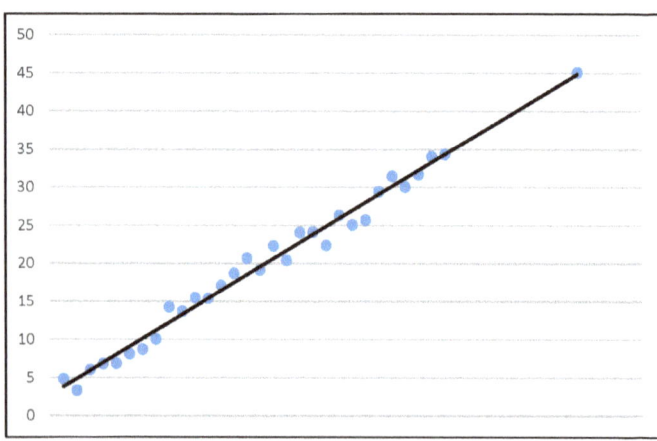

Note the point with a value of around 45 in the top right hand corner: although this point is some way removed from the others, it has the same pattern as the other points and so is NOT an outlier. Now contrast this figure with Figure 10-6, where one data point has been replaced.

Figure 10-6: One Outlier

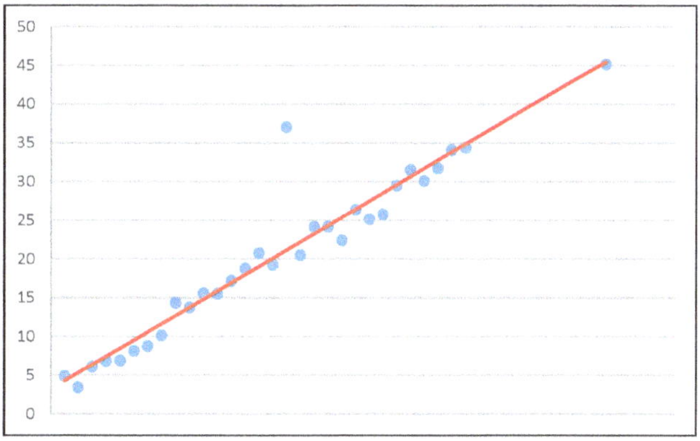

The line of best fit will have changed slightly to take account of this point. But the isolated point with a value of roughly 37 clearly does not fit the pattern of the others. Now that we have defined what an outlier is, we can move on to how to deal with them.

10.4.2 Dealing with Outliers

Let us now look at a hypothetical set series of delay minutes to illustrate the problem of outlying values. Assume that we are looking at several years of delay data but, in one particular year (see Figure 10-7), we observe one high and one very low value.

Figure 10-7: Delay Minutes Attributable to a Railway Operator

Period 1	45,812
Period 2	49,619
Period 3	42,917
Period 4	31,388
Period 5	47,082
Period 6	44,663
Period 7	45,901
Period 8	43,743
Period 9	48,804
Period 10	67,911
Period 11	46,395
Period 12	45,896
Period 13	44,623

It is simpler to explain what not to do under these circumstances, which is just to remove the two data points because they do not fit the smooth pattern. Indeed, the skill behind any sort of analysis is not in undertaking the calculation – Excel does this, after all – but in explaining the results.

First, we need to investigate if the data is simply an error. If there has been a mistake in data input, then there is a good case for excluding these two data points if we cannot get the correct values.

If, however, the data are correct, then we need to investigate why we observe these outlying values.

For period 4, was the number of trains or train-kms run significantly lower than other periods? If so, why?

In period 10, we would want to investigate if there were extra trains run or whether there was any severe weather affecting performance.

Were there one or major incidents at a key point of the network which had a major impact on the operator's punctuality?

In summary, rather than just deleting odd-looking data points, it is important to investigate why the data looks the way it does and this may help us gain further actual insight into how the data works.

10.5 Dummy Variables

10.5.1 What is a Dummy Variable?

A dummy variable is a very useful mechanism in regression analysis and is used to describe a state of the world with only two possible outcomes.

For example, an ice cream vendor wonders whether it is worth his or her while selling ice cream on a cloudy day.

So, the vendor – or one of the vendor's more statistically-minded friends – can look at daily sales and introduce a variable for each day, such as "mainly sunny".

If the day is indeed mainly sunny, the variable will take a value of 1. If, however, the day in question was cloudy, the variable would take a value of 0.

10.5.2 Dummy Variables in Transportation

Now we will see an example of a dummy variable when assessing demand. A transport operator is generally aware that demand is higher on Fridays and Sundays than on other days of the week.

The operator decides to examine four weeks of ticket sales by day of week and this data is shown in Figure 10-8.

Figure 10-8: Four Weeks of Daily Sales Data

Friday	32,382	Sunday	32,938
Friday	26,852	Sunday	34,278
Friday	28,443	Thursday	24,176
Friday	28,018	Thursday	24,698
Monday	23,994	Thursday	21,416
Monday	24,498	Thursday	22,664
Monday	24,851	Tuesday	23,087
Monday	20,078	Tuesday	24,673
Saturday	23,626	Tuesday	24,720
Saturday	24,130	Tuesday	20,842
Saturday	21,460	Wednesday	22,922
Saturday	20,708	Wednesday	24,167
Sunday	30,688	Wednesday	22,025
Sunday	23,634	Wednesday	23,932

All the operator wishes to know at this stage is whether demand is significantly higher on Fridays and Sundays and by roughly how much compared to other days of the week. So, we have our two outcomes: Sunday or Friday, to which we will assign a value of 1 and other days, which will have a value of 0.

We can now set up a simple regression in which the dependent variable is the daily demand and the independent variable is the dummy. A sample of the regression input is presented in Figure 10-9.

Figure 10-9: Regression Input Using a Dummy Variable

	Demand	Dummy
Friday	32,382	1
Friday	26,852	1
Friday	28,443	1
Friday	28,018	1
Monday	23,994	0
Monday	24,498	0
Monday	24,851	0
Monday	20,078	0

If we run the regression in the same way as previously, we can examine the output which is shown in Figure 10-10.

Figure 10-10: Dummy Regression Output (Abridged)

Regression Statistics	
Multiple R	0.803
R Square	0.645

	Coefficients	P-value	Lower 95%	Upper 95%
Intercept	23,133	2.36E-26	22,092	24,175
Dummy	6,521	2.66E-07	4,572	8,470

From this output, we can see that almost two thirds of the variation in demand was accounted for by whether the dummy variable takes the value 1 or 0.

In other words, 64% of the variation in demand was attributable to the day of the week being Friday or Sunday rather than Monday to Thursday or Saturday.

What the output also tells us is that the average demand for a non-peak day is around 23,100 but for Fridays and Sundays, it is significantly higher at 29,700 (23,133+6,521, rounded to the nearest 100).

The 6,521 supplementary demand volume calculated is very significant, given that the P value is almost 0.

Next, we will look at how a dummy variable is used in addition to standard independent variables.

10.5.3 Application of a Dummy Variable to Performance Data

Take a look at Figure 10-11, which is a set of residuals of a regression analysis showing the relationship between a dependent (Y) and an independent variable (X) over 52 railway periods.

The details of this regression cannot be discussed further due to client confidentiality but the discussion illustrates how to avoid one of the major mistakes in regression analysis, which is to immediately discard data that does not "fit".

Figure 10-11: Initial Residuals Analysis (Time)

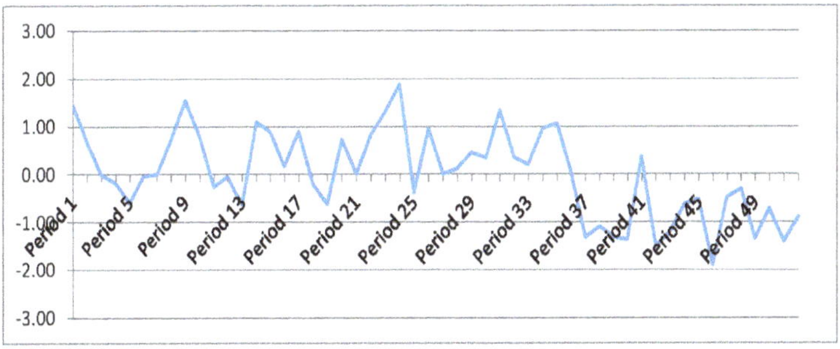

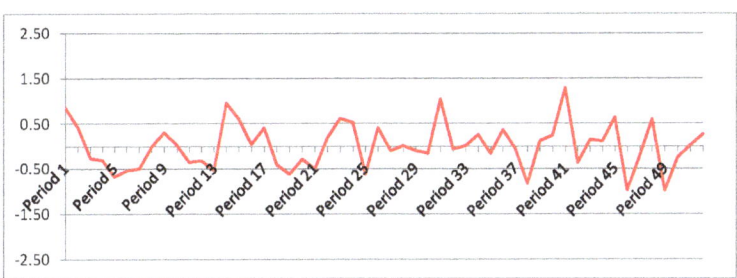

It is apparent that something changed in the relationship between Y and X at around period 36[29], so we are faced with two broad options:

- Ignore the first 36 periods of data. This option is certainly not recommended! As we discussed in Section 8.5, sampled data is precious and we should not discard it for no good reason; or
- Acknowledge the step change in period 36 through the use of a dummy variable. The dummy variable for this case will be assigned the value 0 for periods 1 to 35 and 1 for periods 36 to 52.

In this example, we have one dependent variable, a standard independent variable (X) and now a dummy variable.

10.5.4 Results from Using the Dummy Variable

In Figure 10-12, we can see the impact of the dummy variable in our regression. For ease of comparison, the same scale has been used for this figure as for Figure 10-11.

Figure 10-12: Residuals Analysis (Time) after Inclusion of Dummy Variable

---

[29] *The event in question was a major timetable change which altered the relationship between AML and delay minutes.*

We can see, immediately, that the pattern of residuals has improved markedly. Not only have we modelled all 52 data points but we have also increased the range of data used to build the regression model and thus improved the relevant range, a concept which we encountered in Section 9.4.9.

How does the inclusion of a dummy variable affect the pattern of residuals if we rearrange the observed AML values by size? We can see the results in Figure 10-13.

Figure 10-13: Residuals by Observation Size Without and With Dummy

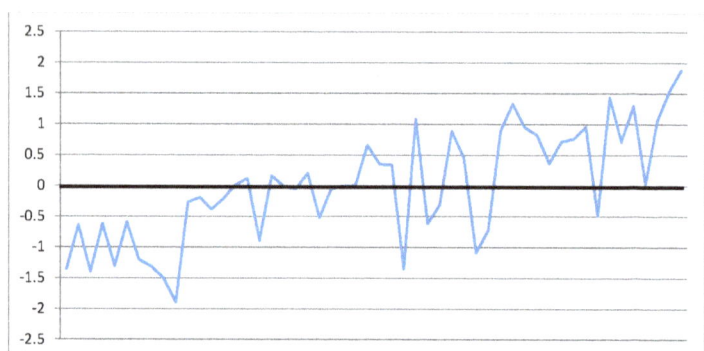

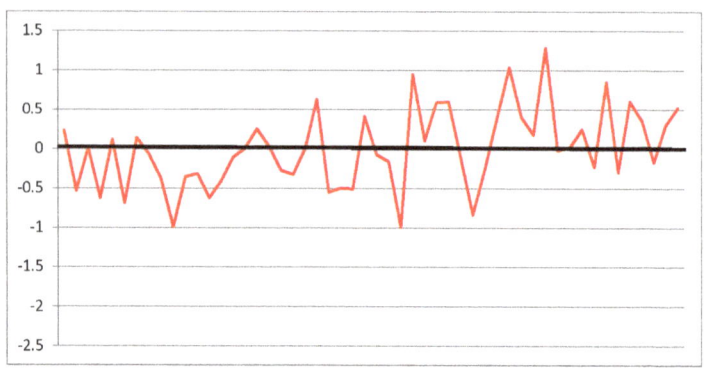

In the top of half the figure (without a dummy), the residuals show a clear upward drift, which violates one of the requirements of residuals for a robust regression model, namely stable and random residuals.

By contrast, this upward drift largely disappears once the residuals are displayed for the model which includes the dummy variable.

10.5.5 Closing Notes on Dummy Variables

We have already discussed the fact that, when we are undertaking a regression analysis, it is important to base any model on reality, rather than nonsensical models such as the example of rainfall in Uzbekistan that we encountered in the previous Chapter.

The same logic also applies to dummy variables: if there is a break or discontinuity in the data, then the dummy variable needs to be defined so that it is compatible with what has happened in the real world.

If the cause of the discontinuity cannot be identified, then the dummy loses much of its value, as its importance cannot be explained to a wider audience.

10.6 Updating Forecasts

A forecast should not be a one-off exercise but ideally something which is revisited and improved upon as new data becomes available.

An initial forecast was undertaken with 39 periods and the results are shown in Figure 10-14. The regression in question shows the proportion of trains arriving within five minutes of scheduled arrival time (PPM, or public performance measure) as a function of average delay per train.

Figure 10-14: Regression with 39 periods

SUMMARY OUTPUT

Regression Statistics	
Multiple R	0.976
R Square	0.952
Adjusted R Square	0.951
Standard Error	0.010
Observations	39

	Coefficients	Standard Error	t Stat	P-value
Intercept	1.018	0.006	177.944	7.2E-56
DpT	-0.034	0.001	-27.16679	4.83E-26

As we can see, the regression is a good fit with high values of R^2 and both the intercept and coefficient of DpT are significant at the 5% level.

One year later, a further 13 periods of data are available, so it is logical to rerun the regression with all 52 periods of data. The results of regression with the enlarged dataset are presented in Figure 10-15.

Figure 10-15: Regression with 52 Periods

SUMMARY OUTPUT – 52 periods

Regression Statistics	
Multiple R	0.973
R Square	0.947
Adjusted R Square	0.945
Standard Error	0.010
Observations	52

	Coefficients	Standard Error	t Stat	P-value
Intercept	1.022	0.005	192.119	2.15E-73
DpT	-0.035	0.001	-29.761	1.81E-33

There is little to choose between these two models, so if we are going to adopt the new model, it is worth comparing the models to see how well each version performs on:

- The original 39 periods;
- The new data (periods 40 to 52); and
- The new, enlarged dataset of 52 periods.

The results of the tests are shown in Figure 10-16 with the explanation of the numbers following the table.

Figure 10-16: Comparison of Errors

	Old Model	New Model	Improvement
P01-39	0.779%	0.797%	-2.3%
P40-52	0.830%	0.707%	17.4%
P01-52	0.792%	0.775%	2.2%

The method used to compare the models is to calculate the difference between the actual and modelled PPM for each period.

This error term was converted into an 'absolute deviation' (i.e. all errors being positive) so that negative and positive errors did not cancel out.

The figures shown in Figure 10-16 are the mean average errors for both the old (39 period) and new (52 period) models. This table demonstrates that:

- For the original 39 periods, the old model provides a slightly better fit. This is unsurprising, as the old model used the line of best fit in the first place;

- For the new periods introduced (P40-P52), the new model provides a significant improvement compared to the earlier version; and

- For all 52 periods, the new model is an improvement. Again, this is unsurprising, as Excel has provided the line of best fit for the enlarged dataset.

So, although this exercise in comparing errors may be perceived as stating the obvious, it is nonetheless useful to be able to quantify how much the model has improved if we are going to change from the old model to the new one.

11 QUEUING AND SIMULATION

11.1 Introduction

In this Chapter, we will address the issue of queuing. We are all familiar with queues but perhaps not so familiar with their operational or monetary impact.

We will start with examining queue behaviour from the viewpoint of both the customer and the service provider. We will then proceed to demonstrate the mathematics of simple, single server queues and then queues with more than one server.

This branch of mathematics will inform us, for a given arrival rate of customers and the rate at which an employee or machine can serve people, how long people can expect to wait to be served, what is the probability of a certain number of people being in the queue, and so on.

It is almost impossible to predict how many people will arrive at a railway station in a 5-minute period wanting to buy a ticket, how many will go through airport security over the same period or how many passengers will join passport control queues.

To tackle this uncertainty, we will use a process called simulation.

How long people are forced to queue affects the business in several ways.

An airport with a poor reputation for queuing time will not only increase passengers' perceived journey time (recall the discussion on generalised journey time in Section 5.2) but will reduce the competitiveness of the business.

London City Airport, for example, has a 15-minute cut-off for passengers checking in with hand baggage only, which is attributable to the efficiency of its operations as well as the compact nature of the terminal.

Queuing also impacts on other areas of business planning, such as the layout of the service facility and personnel costs. Queuing theory also plays a vital part in determining the capacity of a terminal.

In an airport terminal, for example, passengers will usually encounter queues at check-in, followed by security and passport control. Meanwhile, the airport operator or air traffic control needs to manage runway capacity and the allocation of gates for arriving aircraft.

11.2 Queuing Behaviour

11.2.1 Fairness and Equity

For our purposes, there are various types of behaviour which need to be taken into consideration when considering the design of the customer/provider interface system. Certainly, we would be keen to develop a view of the length of time it is acceptable to allow customers to wait in line.

A queue is normally served on a FIFO (first in, first out) basis. This works well for single queues with only one server available or a single queue with several servers but can be a problem if there are several parallel lines each served by a single server. As we shall demonstrate later in this Chapter, having a single queue with several servers is more efficient than the use of several single server queues.

11.2.2 Baulking and Reneging

Baulking and reneging are different versions of leaving the system.

First, we will consider baulking, which occurs when a customer sees a queue length and decides not to enter the system. Reneging happens when a customer does actually join the system but decides that the queue is moving too slowly and quits the system.

Of course, it could be argued that many customers will have no choice but to wait, whatever the length of the queue.

Whilst this may be true in the short term (for example, checking in a bag for a flight) such customers may decide to use other providers in future which process their customers more efficiently.

If baulking or reneging is a significant proportion of people queuing, there are revenue implications for the business which should be addressed.

This is most often the case when queues occur at the beginning of the process (such as buying a ticket or using a company's website to search for fares) when the potential customer has the option to drop out and go elsewhere.

11.3 Single Server Queue

11.3.1 Mathematics of a Single Queue

We will briefly go through the concepts and mathematics of a single server queue, where:

- λ (lambda) is the arrival rate per time period; and
- μ (mu) is the rate of service.

Using just these two variables, we are able to build up a wealth of information about a queue.

Let us assume for our example that λ is 24 per hour and μ is 30 per hour. The first statistic is queue intensity or λ / μ. For our example, queue intensity is 0.8.

The maximum value for the intensity statistic must be below 1; if it is 1 or higher, arrivals will be greater than service rate and the queue will never clear. Other very useful information we can derive from the two variables are:

- The probability that there is nobody queuing or being served is $1 - \lambda / \mu = 0.2$;
- Average number in the queue is $\lambda * \lambda / [\mu *(\mu-\lambda)]$ or 24*24/ [30 *(30-24)] or 3.2;
- Average number in the system is $\lambda / (\mu -\lambda)$ or 4.0;
- Average time in the queue is $\lambda/ [\mu *(\mu -\lambda)]$ or 24/ [30*(30-24)] or 24/180 hours or 8 minutes; and
- Average time in the system is $1 / (\mu -\lambda) = 1/6$ hour or 10 minutes.

Some of these results can be derived by logic.

We know from the queue intensity of 0.8 that this is the average number of people being served.

So, the number of people in the system is the number in the queue (3.2) and the number being served (0.8) which, together, add up to 4.0.

Similarly, we know that the average time in the queue is 8 minutes and the average time to be served is two minutes (from μ) so the average time spent in the system is 8+2 = 10 minutes.

11.3.2 Varying the Rate of Arrivals

Let us start with a relatively simple, single server queue.

We will assume that the server (which could be human or a machine) can process an arrival every two minutes or 30 per hour.

Note that once the arrival rate reaches and then exceeds 30 per hour, the queue will continue to increase and the system effectively breaks down.

If we vary the arrival rate for a service rate of 30 per hour, we can see from Figure 11-1 how the waiting time degenerates considerably.

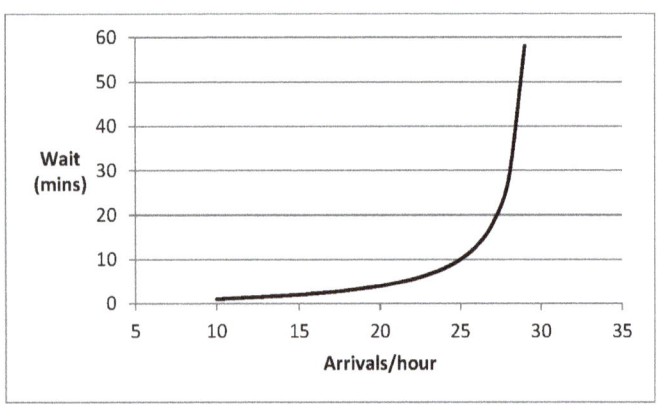

Figure 11-1: Average Waiting Time per Person by Arrival Rate

11.4 Single Server Queue Simulation

11.4.1 Developing Probability Distributions

We will now try and see how a single queue would actually work in practice. We will take as our starting point that one person arrives every 2.5 minutes on average (24 per hour) and the server can process one person every 2 minutes, or an average of 30 per hour.

We will break down a day into 10 minute intervals, starting at 0600hrs and finishing at 2200hrs. Using 10 minute intervals, the average number of arrivals is 4 per 10-minute period (24/6) and the service rate is 5. We would expect to see an average queue length of 3.2 people, as we saw in the previous Section. However, the arrival of customers is not so predictable! We will therefore assign simple probability distributions to arrivals and service rates as shown in Figure 11-2.

Figure 11-2: Probability Distributions for Arrivals and Service

Probability	Cum Prob.	Arrivals	Probability	Cum Prob.	Service Rate
0.1	0.1	0	0.3	0.3	4
0.2	0.3	2	0.4	0.7	5
0.4	0.7	4	0.3	1.0	6
0.2	0.9	6			
0.1	1.0	8			
Expected Per 10 minutes[30]		4	Expected Per 10 minutes		5

There is also variability in the service rate, as some customers will be served quite quickly whilst others engage in more complicated (and time-consuming) transactions.

So, we have retained the averages of 24 arrivals and 30 people served per hour but we have introduced uncertainty into the system. Using arrivals as an example, we are now saying that there is a 10% chance of nobody arriving during a 10-minute period but also a 10% likelihood of 8 people showing up.

11.4.2 Random Numbers

To show how the table of probabilities in Figure 11-2 is used in the simulation, we need to examine the 'cum prob' (cumulative probability) columns. Let us assume that for arrivals, we have a randomly generated number of 0.9594 (random numbers for our purposes are between 0 and 1). We can see from column 2 that 0.9594 is greater than 0.9 but less than 1.0, so that the simulation will return a value of 8 arrivals for this period.

In the same ten-minute period, a number of 0.5733 is generated for service rate, so the service rate for this period will be 5. Note that for arrivals and service rate, we need to generate two separate random numbers.

---

[30] The calculation here uses the expected value function which we met in Section 8.2.2.

The ticket clerk, for example, could be faced with 8 arrivals, all of whom are 'easy' customers, or just two, both of which make several enquiries and slow down the service rate. So, in other words, we must assume that arrivals rate and service rate are independent during any ten-minute period. So, if the counter is empty, eight people will turn up but only five will be processed during this ten-minute period. Before the next batch of arrivals turns up, three people are left waiting to be served.

11.4.3 Simulation Results

In Figure II-3:, we present the first six rows of the simulation covering the first hour of the day.

Figure 11-3: First Six Rows of Simulation

RAND 1	Time	Arrivals	Queuing	RAND 2	Service Rate	Number Served	Unserved
0.214251	06:00	2	0	0.376823	5	2	0
0.361979	06:10	4	0	0.219857	4	4	0
0.882994	06:20	6	0	0.439039	5	5	1
0.760098	06:30	6	1	0.096868	4	4	3
0.271028	06:40	2	3	0.904708	6	5	0
0.171427	06:50	2	0	0.768368	6	2	0

We can see that the unserved people are still in the queue when the next arrivals show up at 06:30 and 06:40.

Between 6:30 and 6:40, there are seven people now waiting to be served but only four people receive service during this ten-minute period. However, between 6:40 and 6:50, only two new arrivals turn up, leaving five people to be served. Fortunately, the transactions are all quite quick and so, by 6:50, there is no backlog.

11.4.4 Full Simulation Results

Because we have introduced variation into arrivals and service rates, it should come as no surprise that simulation results for three consecutive days can look very different. In Figure II-4, day one performed well, with the queue reaching no more than seven people, whilst on the subsequent day, the queue length spiked for one ten-minute period at 11 people. By contrast, day three saw significant people queuing for much of the afternoon.

Figure 11-4: Three Simulation Runs

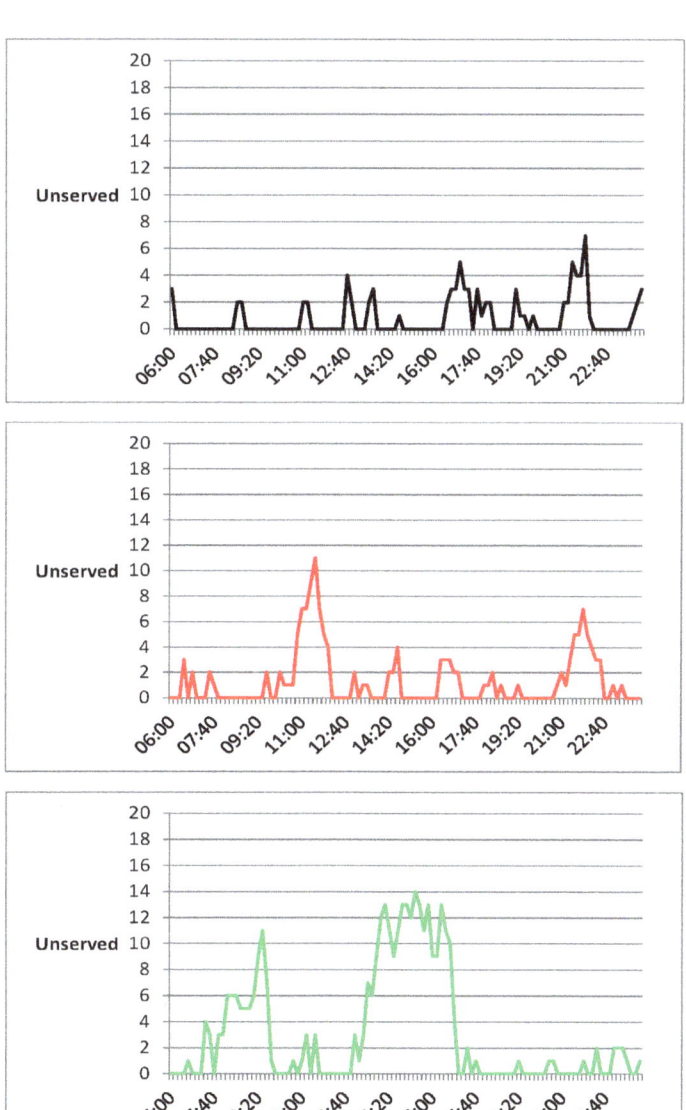

As the three quite different results above show, we need to run the simulation many times so that we can derive meaningful results, ideally the more the better. For illustration, we have shown the results of the simulation when limited to 50 days and when the analysis was expanded to 125 days. The results are shown in Figure 11-5.

Figure 11-5: Probability Distribution of Unserved Customers

Simulations: 50 days				Simulations: 125 days			
Unserved	Frequency	Probability	Cumulative	Unserved	Frequency	Probability	Cumulative
0	3082	0.5655	0.5655	0	7180	0.5270	0.5270
1	554	0.1017	0.6672	1	1362	0.1000	0.6269
2	573	0.1051	0.7723	2	1268	0.0931	0.7200
3	366	0.0672	0.8394	3	896	0.0658	0.7858
4	297	0.0545	0.8939	4	845	0.0620	0.8478
5	175	0.0321	0.9261	5	515	0.0378	0.8856
6	125	0.0229	0.9490	6	388	0.0285	0.9141
7	83	0.0152	0.9642	7	274	0.0201	0.9342
8	56	0.0103	0.9745	8	265	0.0194	0.9536
9	44	0.0081	0.9826	9	233	0.0171	0.9707
10	27	0.0050	0.9875	10	84	0.0062	0.9769
11	68	0.0057	0.9932	11	89	0.0065	0.9834
12+		0.0068	1.0000	12	94	0.0069	0.9903
				13+	70	0.0097	1.0000

Over 50 and 125 runs, the maximum number unserved in any ten-minute period was 19. We can use the data presented in Figure 11-5 to address certain questions regarding the performance of the queue, as shown in Figure 11-6.

Figure 11-6: Summary Results of Simulations

	50 days	125 days
Probability 5 people or less	92.6%	88.6%
Probability of 12 people or more	0.68%	1.66%

If we have a target whereby no more than 5 people should remain unserved at least 90% of the time, then an examination of just 50 simulations would show that we have satisfied this criterion, whereas using the larger sample of 125 days, we breach this requirement.

Similarly, if the likelihood of 12 or more unserved people was fixed at 1%, we would state that this criterion was satisfied using the smaller set of simulations but we are clearly in breach of the requirement when we look at observations covering 125 days, when the probability of 12 or more waiting was 1.66%.

The lesson from this Section is that undertaking the simulation over 50 days is insufficient and presented an over-optimistic picture of the queue's performance.

The situation is similar to the one we encountered in sampling, where a larger sample will provide more robust results than a smaller one. However, as there are no costs involved in increasing the number of simulations (except the analyst's time), we should undertake as many simulations as necessary until the frequency distribution of unserved arrivals stabilises.

11.5 Business Impact of Simulations

11.5.1 Available Options

We saw in the previous Section that, based upon the larger set of simulation results, the queue did not conform to performance requirements.

It is fair to say that, although we cannot control the rate of arrivals, we do have options available to improve service delivery which will, however, require investment.

The two options are:

- Improve the service rate either through training, better use of technology or simplifying procedures; or
- Adding a server.

11.5.2 Improve the Service Rate

When a system is especially intense (recall that our 24/30 system has an intensity of 0.8), a very small change in server capacity can make a major difference.

Using some of the formulae we encountered in Section 11.3.1, we can observe the overall improvements in the queuing system in Figure 11-7.

Figure 11-7: Improvement in Service Rate

	31 per hour	30 per hour	Improvement
Queue length	2.7	3.2	17%
Mean no. in system	3.4	4.0	14%
Time spent in system (mins)	8.6	10.0	14%
Mean waiting time (mins)	6.6	8.0	17%

We can see from the figures above that a 3% improvement in productivity (increasing the service rate from 30 to 31 people per hour) produces major benefits of 14% to 17% in the queue statistics.

We can see further improvements if we overlay the variation in arrival rate, first encountered in Figure 11-1, with the new higher service rate, as shown in Figure 11-8.

Figure 11-8: Variation in Arrivals per Hour

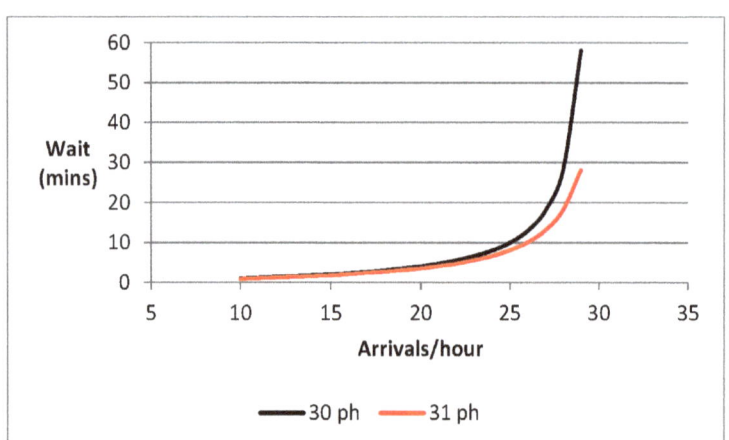

The difference in waiting time between a service rate of 30 and 31 per hour is significant once we exceed the average arrival rate of 24 per hour. With an arrival rate of 25 per hour, the difference is two minutes per person on average and 30 minutes if the arrival rate increases to 29 per hour. The key question we need to ask is what are the costs and benefits of this change? The costs might involve personnel training, new IT support systems or replacing personnel with machines (as has occurred over the London Underground network). The benefits include:

- Reductions in baulking and reneging; and
- Savings in time.

The savings in time can be expressed in both time and money; as we shall see in Chapter 22, time savings can provide an important stream of benefits when undertaking an economic appraisal of a project. In addition, a business can promote a more streamlined and efficient process and use the improvements to generate more demand and hence revenue.

11.5.3 Add a Server

If, instead, we elect to add a server to the current one available, we can observe dramatic reductions in the single queue's performance. We will not produce any of the equations here for multiple server queues as the mathematics is quite daunting.

We will now introduce a second server and, instead of requiring the server to process a transaction every 2 minutes, we allow an average process time of 2½ minutes instead, so 24 per hour. The changes are immediately apparent in Figure II-9 and Figure II-10, using the equations in Section II.3.

Figure 11-9: Impact of Adding a Server

	2*24 per hour	30 per hour	Improvement
Queue length	0.8	3.2	75%
Mean no. in system	2.1	4.0	49%
Time spent in system (mins)	4.1	10.0	59%
Mean waiting time (mins)	1.6	8.0	80%

Figure 11-10: Reduced Waiting Time with Additional Server

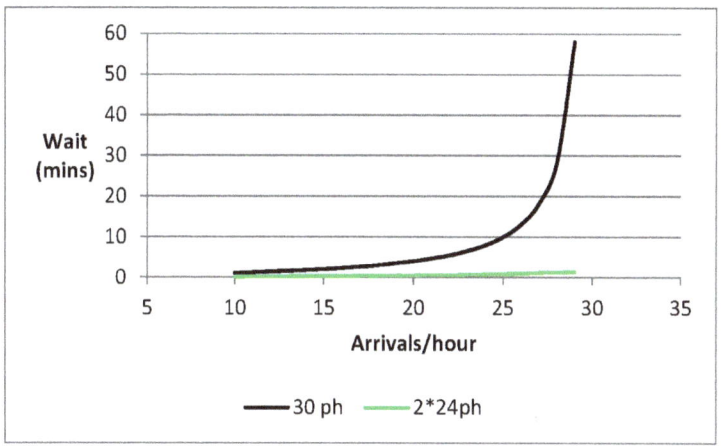

If we consider adding a second server in this way from an investment appraisal viewpoint, the initial costs are significantly higher than just improving the productivity of a single server but the benefits are also much greater.

Now, let us add some justification to adding a second server. We will make some assumptions about demand and the cost of an additional server, which are shown in II-11.

Figure 11-11: Demand and Cost of Additional Server

Assume		16.0	hours service per day
		350.0	days per annum
		£20,000	per annum for extra server
Time savings		134,400	annual arrivals
		14,336	hours

In the above example, our customers will save over 14,000 hours per annum in waiting time, so the cost to the company is £1.38 per hour saved (20,000/14,336).

According to guidance issued by the Department for Transport, the lowest value of time which could be used (for non-working time) is over £5 per hour, so adding an extra server should comfortably pay for itself in economic terms. The financial case may be harder to justify but may be viable if the extra demand generated more than covers the marginal costs of £20,000.

Alternatively, customers may be willing to pay a little more to benefit from an improved service quality.

11.5.4 One Queue or Two?

As an aside to the discussion on queues, let us now demonstrate the benefits of single queuing compares to having multiple, parallel queues.

Let two systems have the same intensity of 0.625 (30/48 or 15/24):

- A single queue manned by two servers. Arrivals average 30 per hour and the two servers can manage 24 transactions per hour each; and

- Two separate queues with an arrival rate of 15 per hour each and one server per queue with a service rate of 24 per hour.

We would expect that arrivals will pick the shorter line when they enter the system. The average results in queue performance can be seen in Figure 11-12.

Figure 11-12: Single vs Two Parallel Queues

	2*24 per hour	24 per hour	Improvement
Arrival rate	30	15	
Number of queues	1	2	
Queue length(s)	0.8	2.1	62%
Mean no. in system (total)	2.1	3.3	38%
Time spent in system (mins)	4.1	6.7	39%
Mean waiting time (mins)	1.6	4.2	62%

Having a single queue only has one disadvantage, and it is a perceived rather than actual one: the customer entering the system might be faced with one long queue rather than two shorter ones.

The results from Figure 11-12 demonstrate, however, that the average time elapsed between entering and leaving the system will be significantly shorter.

Other benefits of the single queue include:

- Easier management of the queue: it is easier to add servers to the single queue system to reduce the time spent in the system for everybody;

- The single queue may be longer but it moves faster, as the queue feeds into two servers rather than one; and

- There can be no allegations of unfairness if people at the end of the queue queue-jump to reach a server who has just opened a new service point.

Although many businesses now use the single queue, there remains a surprising number which do not.

If for example, ticket machines at a railway station are dispersed in several parts of the station's area, customers are first required to make a judgement to guess which queue will have the shorter waiting time and then endure a slower service than the single queue system.

The ticket offices at Gatwick (single queue) and Frankfurt (multiple queues) airport railway stations are excellent examples of this problem.

Supermarkets usually bundle their self-scanning machines together using a single queue but retain the several queues/single server approach for manned tills. Even here, however, Carrefour, in Spain, has converted to a single queue for manual checkouts (as witnessed by the author in Gandía, Spain).

11.6 Simulations for Significant Events

11.6.1 Taking Account of Significant Events

In Section 8.5.15, we mentioned the difficulty of modelling such events, so we will use a simulation technique to show how this works. But first, we need to recall the Poisson distribution, which was discussed in detail in Section 8.4. We will also continue with the example of the bus company, introduced in the same Section, which needs to run a reduced schedule ('Plan B') during days of heavy traffic congestion.

First, let us recall Figure 8-3, which we will adjust slightly to use for simulation[31]. The adjusted table is shown in Figure 11-13.

Figure 11-13: Probability of X Events Occurring per Month

Events	Probability	Cum Prob	Events
		0	0
0	0.6065	0.6065	1
1	0.3033	0.9098	2
2	0.0758	0.9856	3
3	0.0126	0.9982	4
4	0.0016	0.9998	5
5+	0.0002	1	

Let us now turn our attention to the last two columns of Figure 11 13. This tells us that the probability of no more than 1 event occurring – the cumulative probability – is 90.98%, no more than 2 events occurring is 98.56% and so on.

The final figure in this column must be 1, which says that the probability of any number of events occurring, including 0, must be 100%.

We will use random number generation (RAND() in Excel) to inform us how many events to assign to a month.

Let us say for the sake of simplicity that random numbers have just 4 decimal places and these range from 0.0000 to 0.9999, which means we have 1,000 possible values.

If a random number of 0.6064 or less is generated, we will assign 0 events to the month; if the number is between 0.6065 and 0.9097, then we will use this number to state that one event occurred, and so on.

---

[31] *The figures in red form an array which is used to drive the simulation via Excel's LOOKUP function, so a generated random number provides the number of events occurring each month.*

Using the random numbers, we are then able to see over the course of a year how often the operator would need to invoke 'Plan B'.

A small sample of the output can be seen in Figure 11-14. We would ideally run this simulation hundreds or even thousands of times to ensure that the simulation was typical; as we are using random numbers, we will get different results each time.

Figure 11-14: 12 Months' Simulation for Invoking "Plan B"

	Random Number	Events
Month 1	0.7841	1
Month 2	0.7942	1
Month 3	0.6452	1
Month 4	0.8891	1
Month 5	0.4212	0
Month 6	0.3929	0
Month 7	0.9627	2
Month 8	0.5522	0
Month 9	0.4236	0
Month 10	0.4693	0
Month 11	0.3521	0
Month 12	0.9558	2

So, from Figure 11-14, we would not need to invoke 'plan B' for six months of the year and in two months, we would be required to operate the limited service on two occasions during the month.

11.7 Lessons Learned

In Section 8.5.15, we raised the question asking what is meant by a representative sample.

Based on the simulation in Figure 11-14, it would be incorrect to ignore major disruptions to traffic if our sample contained only days when traffic ran smoothly.

Disrupted days will have a positive impact on operating costs, particularly fuel and depreciation but also a negative impact on demand, revenue and possibly the company's reputation.

With the simulation, the company can take into account in its forecasts these changes.

11.8 Rare Incidents – An Advanced Example

11.8.1 Introduction

The following example is based upon work undertaken recently by the author. The simulation was required to assess likely performance penalties on a light rail system and the performance regime was extremely complicated. The penalties incurred for any incident lasting over 30 minutes depended on:

- Time of day;
- Day of week (weekday or weekend);
- Duration of an incident; and
- Whether the incident resulted from operator actions or the local authority (a road closure, for instance).

The location of the incident was also an issue, but we will avoid this unnecessary complication here.

The unit of penalty in this example is a 'customer delay minute', which had a fixed monetary value. Each of the four variables above needed to be modelled for the proposed light rail system; in the following Section, we will show how this was done.

11.8.2 Modelling the Simulation Variables

First, before determining what type of incident was likely to occur, it was necessary to assess the likelihood of an incident occurring in the first place.

Using data from light rail networks elsewhere, the average number of incidents per day was estimated at 0.095. To simulate the number of incidents likely to occur in a given day, we once again use the Poisson distribution in the same way as in Section ; the results are shown in Figure 11-15.

Figure 11-15: Incidence Occurrence Distribution

	Expected number of events per day	0.095
Cumulative	Number of Incidents	Prob of Occurrence
0.000	0	0.909
0.909	1	0.086
0.995	2	0.004
1.000	3	0.000

As a recap of the Poisson distribution, the probability of no incidents occurring on a certain day is

$$e^{-0.095} * 0.095^0 / 0! = \text{EXP}(-0.095) * 1 / 1 = 0.909$$

How long an incident is likely to last is clearly impossible to determine for a railway which has yet to be built. However, there was access to incident data for two other light rail systems.

These were counted and categorised by incident length and the distribution which came out of this analysis was used for the proposed railway. In Figure 11-1, for example, a short incident of 31-60 minutes occurred 2,329 times out of 3,211 recorded, which is 72.5% of the total.

The likelihood of four or more incidents occurs in a day was estimated at 31 in one million, so the model was set up to handle between zero and three incidents per day only.

Figure 11-16: Length of Incident Distribution

Cumulative	Duration	Interval	Count
0	45	31-60	2,329
0.725	75	61-90	480
0.875	105	91-120	137
0.917	135	121-150	90
0.945	165	151-180	41
0.958	330	330	134
			3,211

Please note that the average duration of an incident per class was assumed to be the middle value of the range in each case.

For extreme incidents, a value of 330 minutes (6½ hours) was estimated.

To determine the time of day that an incident occurred, we assumed 20 hours of operation per day and that an incident was likely to occur as much in one hour as in another.

This assumption could be perceived as simplistic, but no data was available to apply more robust weights to time of day.

This uniform distribution became the third variable which was going to be simulated and the probabilities, based simply on the duration of the length of the periods in question, is presented in Figure 11-17.

Figure 11-17: Time of Day Distribution

Cumulative	Service Period	Duration (hours)	Probability (Uniform)
0	AM Peak	2	0.1
0.100	Early Morning	2.5	0.125
0.225	Evening	3	0.15
0.375	Inter-peak	7	0.35
0.725	Night	3	0.15
0.875	PM Peak	2.5	0.125
		20	

The final variable was whether the incident could be attributed to the operator (Opco) or the Government. Based on datasets from elsewhere, the operator was likely to be penalised for an incident around 91% of the time, as shown in Figure 11-18: Distribution of Causation of Incident.

Figure 11-18: Distribution of Causation of Incident

Cumulative	Attribution	Probability	Assign Value
0	OpCo	0.9075	1
0.9075	Government	0.0925	0

If the simulation showed that the Government was likely to be the perpetrator of the incident, the calculation of CDMs was to be multiplied by zero, so that the operator would show zero CDM's for a Government-perpetrated incident; otherwise, the number of CDM's was multiplied by one and the full number of CDMs attributed to the incident would be allocated to the operator.

11.8.3 Output from the Simulation

Separate random numbers were used for each day to determine the number, length, time and attribution of incidents.

It is important to use different random numbers for each of the variables so that, for example, a random number which yields one incident can occur at any time of day (subject to a separate random number).

An extract of the simulation results is shown in Figure 11-19.

Figure 11-19: Results of the Simulation (Extract)

	No. of Incidents	Incident time 1	Incident time 2	Incident time 3	Duration 1	Duration 2	Duration 3	Delay Minutes
05-Jan	1	AM Peak			45			38,688
12-Jan	2	Inter-Peak	PM Peak		45	330		275,871
14-Jan	1	PM Peak			45			63,640
22-Jan	1	Inter-Peak			75			66,295
25-Jan	1	Evening			45			25,327
11-Feb	1	Inter-Peak			45			37,471
17-Feb	1	Inter-Peak			45			37,471
23-Feb	1	Night			45			8,510
09-Mar	2	Night	Inter-Peak		45	45		45,981
10-Mar	1	Night			45			8,510
12-Mar	2	Evening	Early Morning		45	45		33,540
07-Apr	1	PM Peak			45			63,640
08-Apr	1	Night			45			8,510
28-Apr	2	AM Peak	Inter-Peak		45	45		76,159
10-May	1	Night			45			8,510
02-Jun	1	Inter-Peak			45			37,471
07-Jun	1	Early Morning			45			8,213
21-Jun	3	Inter-Peak	Evening	Early Morning	45	45	45	71,011
28-Jun	1	Night			45			8,510

In this extract, all weekdays on which no operator-caused incidents occurred have been omitted. Because weekends use separate periods of the day, a separate simulation was run for weekends and holidays, but this is not shown here.

The extract above shows how many incidents occurred on which day, what time of day and how long they lasted.

The calculation of CDM's was undertaken in a separate sheet, but we can see from the extract that a 45-minute incident occurring at night (February 23rd) or early in the morning (June 7th) is penalised much less heavily than one occurring in the PM peak (January 14th). By running this simulation many times, the average number of delay minutes attributable to major incidents was shown to be between 97,000 and 101,000.

11.9 Chapter Exercises

Exercise 1 A ticket office opens at 6am and, based upon previous experience, the number of people arriving at the ticket window is 3 every 5 minutes. People arrive at the window at random and the number arriving in any five-minute period can be modelled using the Poisson distribution. There is just one server in this small ticket office and the person serving customers can handle four customers every five minutes. Using the equations we examined earlier in this Chapter, calculate:

- The average number of customers in the system (waiting plus being served);
- The mean time that a customer spends in the system; and
- The average number of customers waiting to be served (to one decimal place).

Exercise 2 The server's ability to serve an average of four customers every five-minute period varies, depending on the complexity of each customer transaction. The probability distribution for the number served is as follows.

Using this information and the Poisson distribution for arrivals, develop a simulation model for every five-minute period from 0600 until 1200.

Served	Probability
2	0.1
3	0.1
4	0.5
5	0.3

Hint: set up two sets of random numbers (one for arrival, one for service) for the 72 five-minute periods on one sheet of an Excel workbook. On another, use the following column headings:

| Time | Queue | Potential Service | Actual Service | Unserved |

The times are 0600, 0605, 0610 and so on. The queue is the value 'Unserved' from the previous five-minute period; 'arrivals' is the number who join the queue based on the Poisson distribution; 'Potential Service' is the number who are capable of being served based on the server's probability distribution; 'Actual Service' is the minimum of Arrivals and Potential service; 'Unserved' is Queued + Arrivals – Actual Service.

12 COSTS

12.1 The Importance of Costs

12.1.1 How Costs Influence Price

Understanding costs is as critical to business development as demand and affects the economics of the business, since the structure of costs faced by the business will determine how flexible it can be on price.

We have already seen in previous Chapters that the price an operator can charge is a function of supply and demand and an operator's ability to segment the market. But this ability is further constrained by the underlying structure of costs. Let us use a very simple example to illustrate how cost structure can influence and constrain pricing.

Figure 12-1: Sample Overview of Bus and Rail Costs

	Bus	Train
Operating cost per passenger-km (pence)	17	11
Operating Costs proportion of Total Costs	80%	44%
Total cost per passenger-km (pence)	21	25

If bus and rail compete over a certain route and the cost structure of the two modes is shown in Figure 12-1, we can make some observations about pricing in general here:

- To make a profit, an operator must cover not only its operating costs but also its fixed and therefore total costs (operating plus fixed);
- At a minimum, an operator's fares must be higher than its operating cost to survive; and
- Although rail's total costs are higher – unsurprising, given the requirement for a dedicated right of way (track, signals) – its operating costs are lower.

So, a fare of, say, 13 pence per kilometre would cover rail's operating costs and make some inroads into paying the operator's fixed costs, the bus operator cannot afford to price its services as low as this. Figure 12-2 provides a summary of the fare constraints which each operator faces.

Figure 12-2: Levels of Average Fare on Bus and Train

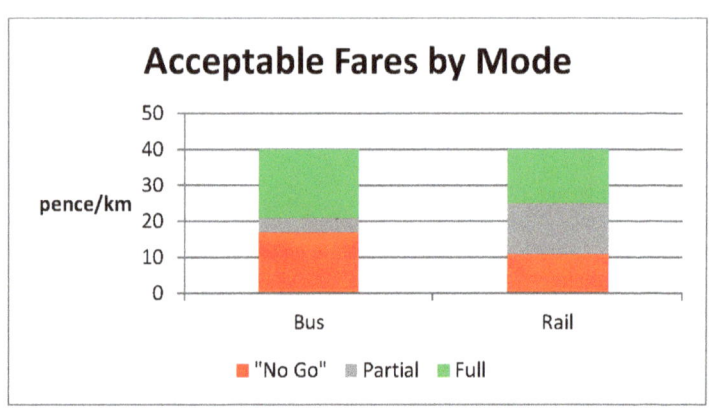

The red area in Figure 12-2 is classified as "no-go" because the cost of carrying the passenger is greater than the fare. The grey area of each bar represents some contribution towards fixed costs and this sort of price level can be used to fill up spare capacity off-peak or for last-minute sales. It is only when we reach the green areas that the operators are able to make a full profit, taking account of both variable and fixed costs.

12.1.2 How Costs Influence Investment Decisions

If we examine an investment that will last fifty years (as in the case of Terminal 1 at Heathrow airport, which closed in June 2015), we are able to assess the investment by understanding three types of costs:

- Sunk costs. Once these are spent, the money is irrecoverable. These costs apply mainly to infrastructure such as terminals, tunnels, runways and roads. Even if they are closed down early – Ciudad Real airport to the south of Madrid cost over €1 billion to build by some reports and was closed down after just three years – the assets have no alternative value and are in effect worthless[32];

---

[32] Or very little – see http://www.theolivepress.es/spain-news/2016/04/20/ciudad-real-ghost-airport-finally-sold-for-e56-2-million/

- Fixed Costs. Lighting and heating the terminal needs to be done irrespective of how many passengers use the facility. Similarly, any business taxes attributable to the building will be paid independently of passenger volume as well; and

- Variable Costs. For a terminal we would need to take into account the number of security staff employed, cleaning and information desk employees.

We will explore the implications of these types of costs in the rest of the Chapter.

12.2 Sunk, Fixed and Variable Costs

12.2.1. Which Type of Cost?

We need to ask various questions about the nature of the costs incurred by a business:

- If we incur costs on a project, are we able to sell the asset and use the money elsewhere if the project does not meet expectations?

- Which costs remain unchanged irrespective of how much output we have?

- To what extent do costs vary with output and what proportion of costs are variable?

- Are any of our costs "lumpy" and fall between the last two types of cost? Examples include the acquisition of new rolling stock when all our trains are full or a new airport terminal is required as the current facility is operating above capacity.

12.2.2. Sunk Costs

Sunk costs are those which, once spent, can never be recovered or sold on. Tunnels are perhaps the best example, such as Crossrail or the Channel Tunnel Rail Link.

These tunnels have no realistic alternative use and so, once the money has been spent in their construction, this money is no longer included in a business case (although tunnel maintenance would certainly be included).

The concept of sunk costs is best considered through an example. Before a tunnel is built, the estimated costs of the tunnel are £6 billion and the present value of the benefits has been estimated at £10 billion (the concept of 'present value' will be explored in much more detail in Chapter 20). So, at the beginning of the project, the net benefits are £4 billion. Construction is estimated to take five years.

Now let us consider two scenarios. First, after £3 billion has been spent on the tunnel, the estimated costs have increased to £11 billion.

The tunnel is three years away from completion and benefits are still assumed to be £10 billion. So, during this mid-term review, we are in the position that future benefits outweigh future costs by £2 billion (£10 billion of benefits minus £8 billion of future expenditure). On this basis, we would argue that the project should continue, despite the total cost of £11 billion exceeding the benefits.

For the second scenario, the future cost estimates of the mid-term review still stand at £8 billion but projected benefits have been cut to £7 billion, due to increased competition from other modes (such as low cost airlines or a new motorway close to the alignment of the proposed tunnel). At the time of the mid-term review, projected costs now outweigh the forecasts benefits by £1 billion and therefore the economic argument would be to abandon all work on the tunnel.

Please note that in neither scenario have we considered the £3 billion which has already been spent. We cannot ever recover what has already been expended and so previous costs are not relevant to our decision on whether to continue with or abandon the project. Although this might be counter-intuitive, consider that, for the second scenario, the choices are losing the £3 billion already spent (abandon) or losing £4 billion (continue).

12.2.3 Fixed, Semi-fixed and Variable Costs

The usual definition for fixed costs are those which are incurred regardless of the volume of activity. An example would be the costs of maintenance of major structures.

A tunnel or viaduct must be maintained in a safe condition even if no vehicles run through it at all, and the change in maintenance triggered by a change in the number of vehicles is relatively small.

Similarly, a port's channel needs to be dredged irrespective of how many vessels use the port.

The difference between sunk and fixed costs is that sunk costs are associated with building infrastructure whereas fixed costs are an annual recurrence – in other words, the difference between building the aforementioned tunnel and maintaining it.

Variable costs are those that move directly in proportion to the volume of service provided. Fuel, be it oil-based or electric, is about as variable as a cost can be. Similarly, air traffic control fees are payable when a flight occurs and vary in accordance with the length of the flight.

For a franchised passenger rail operator in Britain, track access charges present a clear example of both fixed and variable costs. A franchised operator will pay a large fixed sum to Network Rail each year for the right of access to the network, regardless of how many trains are actually run. In essence, the total of these charges covers the cost of providing and renewing the network.

Each train that runs then incurs a small variable charge per kilometre per vehicle, whether it is part of the planned service or an extra. This relates to the cost of extra wear and tear attributable to each train.

There are however, other sorts of variable costs which are not quite so clear-cut.

In a large organisation, with hundreds or thousands of employees, there is a constant movement in human resources, with people being recruited, fired or resigning/retiring.

If such a large organisation decides to reduce its activities, it can institute a recruitment freeze, offer early retirement or make redundancies. In such a case, labour costs can be assumed to be variable. But what about smaller organisations?

For a new entrant with few resources, assets such as labour or a locomotive are much "lumpier".

If an operator has 500 drivers, for example, then the loss or addition of 1 driver has only a slight impact. However, for a small company with just five drivers, the loss of one driver has major consequences on the operations of the company.

Or, if this small operator wishes to increase operations by 5%, it may have to recruit another driver and so add 20% to its crew costs. In such cases, labour is described as a 'semi-fixed' or 'semi-variable' cost.

Similar considerations apply to locomotives, rolling stock, aircraft and ferries. An operator is able to increase operations using a fixed volume of capacity but will reach a point at which it will need to invest in new vehicles. For a company that has a large fleet from which to draw, the impact of adding one locomotive, for example, will be much smaller for a larger operator than for a small one. Other cost items are rather easier to pinpoint, such as the cost of fuel for running trains and the variable element of track access fees.

When a cost is in two parts, such as track access, there is a general consensus that the fixed element of the fee should contribute towards the fixed costs of the charging organisation (Railtrack/Network Rail) whilst the variable element compensates the infrastructure provider for increased wear and tear on the network due to high train volume and weights. However, the imbalance of pricing toward the fixed element has had some perverse effects. In the early years of privatisation, train operators took the opportunity to increase their services, but Railtrack received very little income in exchange. So, whilst the train service pushed usage towards the limits of capacity and punctuality deteriorated as a result, income to justify investment was not generated.

The additional track access income Network Rail receives from a network enhancement compensates for no more than wear and tear of the asset after completion of the project, so that the investment element itself still depends on external funding. We can compare the tariff structure of Network Rail with that of AENA, the world's largest airport operator but whose business is predominantly in Spain.

Figure 12-3: Graphic demonstrating different Cost Structures

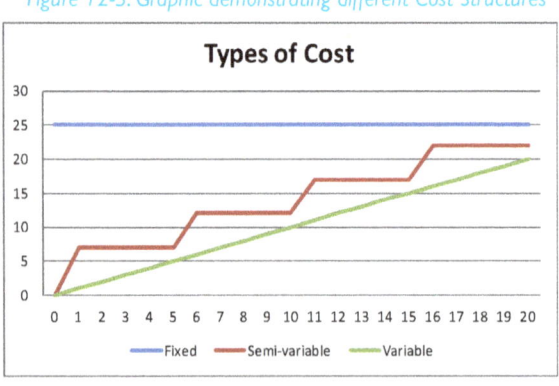

The tariffs for a provider of airport infrastructure are all variable, based on per aircraft or per passenger charges[33]. In brief, it is not always clear whether a cost is variable or semi-variable, so an element of judgement is required on the part of the people undertaking an appraisal. The variability of labour costs, for example, depends on the flexibility of labour laws in an individual country and the ability to 'hire and fire' quickly and cheaply.

12.2.4 More Considerations on Labour Costs

We just previously asserted that when there is a significant downturn in demand, one option is to shed labour and hence to treat labour as much as possible as a variable cost. Leaving aside any political considerations of contributing to higher unemployment, an employer should also consider alternatives to the outright shedding of staff, such as reducing labour hours per person rather than headcount. There are three principal reasons to evaluate this option:

- When demand increases after a recession, the workforce will already be in place to meet this demand;

- There are costs involved both in redundancy payments and recruiting new staff; and

- Reducing headcount may also mean reducing the knowledge pool of the workforce. We can reasonably assume that an employee with 10 years or more experience will know much more about the business than a new or recent hire.

The first two points just raised are relatively easy to evaluate and cost whilst the third is somewhat more complicated. Nonetheless, retaining the pool of knowledge is real, albeit difficult to quantify.

12.3 Marginal Costs and Revenues

12.3.1 Overview of the Marginal Concept

Marginal cost and revenue (following later in this Section) provide a theoretical framework for determining the level of capacity a transport operator should provide and at what price(s) in order to maximise profitability.

---

[33] http://www.aena.es/csee/ccurl/861-788/Guia%20tarifas%20aena%20aeropuertos%202015%20ingles_ed%20marzo.pdf

It is debatable just how useful a marginal analysis is in practice, given that pricing and quantity supplied are often distorted from optimal levels by competitors, regulation and external shocks.

However, as with supply and demand analysis earlier in this book, it does provide a useful starting point for considering supply and pricing decisions.

12.3.2 Marginal Costs per Journey

Marginal costs can be one of the more complex concepts for non-economists, so it is best to illustrate these with some examples.

At its most simplistic, the marginal cost is that involved in producing one extra unit. In transport terms, this is the cost of carrying one extra passenger.

Figure 12-4: Examples of Marginal Cost in Transport and Travel

	Marginal Cost
Aircraft with spare seats	Cost of processing the ticket, slightly higher fuel cost to account for the increased take-off weight, airport passenger charge
Full aircraft	One aircraft including fuel, cabin crew, flight crew, air navigation fees, etc. in addition to the costs identified in the previous row
Train	Cost of processing the ticket, slightly higher fuel cost to account for the increased weight of the train
Airport terminal or railway station	Negligible
Hotel	Housekeeping costs for the room, energy and water used by the guest

Figure 12-4 provides a rather simplistic assessment of marginal cost, so now we will see how marginal cost varies over an organisation.

12.3.3 Marginal Costs by Company

To illustrate the generic development of marginal cost as a company increases in size, we will use this simple dataset.

Figure 12-5 shows a company which has fixed costs of €10, as these are the costs incurred when there is no output.

Figure 12-5: Demonstration of Average and Marginal Cost

Output	Total Costs	Average Cost	Marginal Cost
0	10		
1	25	25.0	15
2	36	18.0	11
3	44	14.7	8
4	51	12.8	7
5	59	11.8	8
6	69	11.5	10
7	82	11.7	13
8	98	12.3	16
9	117	13.0	19
10	139	13.9	22

Between 1 and 4 units, the rate of total costs decreases. The easiest way to explain this is to imagine a train company that performs only two 30-minute journeys per day.

This is obviously quite an expensive exercise, as the company is not utilising the assets very efficiently, either the train or the crew. So, the first journey has a marginal cost of €15 (€25-€10), the second is cheaper at €11 (€36-€25), and so on. Once output exceeds six units, we observe that average costs start increasing. We can relate this to the transport business by considering a rail network that becomes congested and delays start accruing, or an airport terminal, which operates above optimal capacity and queues of people need to be managed on a regular basis. We can examine the relationship between average and marginal cost by plotting the two lines together on Figure 12-6.

Figure 12-6: Average and Marginal Cost Curves

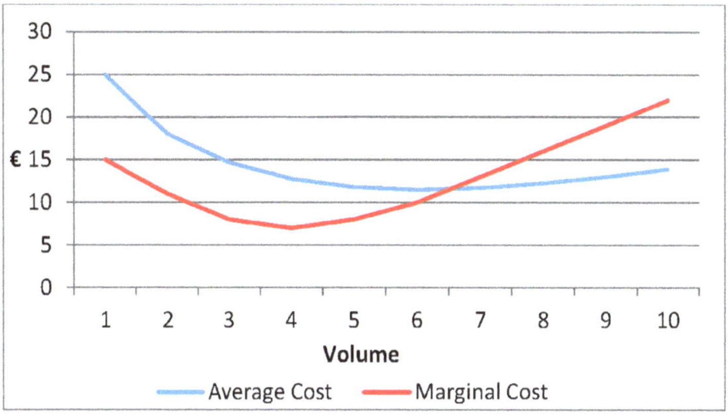

It is straightforward to prove that the MC line will cross the average total cost line at its minimum point – if you have studied calculus! As most people have not done so, we shall take this as a given and focus instead on what the implications are of Figure 12-6. If we look back at Figure 12-5, we can see that the lowest average cost occurs somewhere between six and seven units. Figure 12-6 confirms that this level of output coincides with a matching of average and marginal costs. Let us now expand our dataset to include revenue and profit, as shown in Figure 12-7.

Figure 12-7: Output, Revenue, Costs and Profits

Output	Total Costs	Average Cost	Marginal Cost	Total Revenues	Marginal Revenue	Profit
0	10			0		
1	25	25.0	15	21.0	21.0	-4.0
2	36	18.0	11	40.4	19.4	4.4
3	44	14.7	8	58.2	17.8	14.2
4	51	12.8	7	74.4	16.2	23.4
5	59	11.8	8	89.0	14.6	30.0
6	69	11.5	10	102.0	13.0	33.0
7	82	11.7	13	113.4	11.4	31.4
8	98	12.3	16	123.2	9.8	25.2
9	117	13.0	19	131.4	8.2	14.4
10	139	13.9	22	138.0	6.6	-1.0

The revenue stream shown in Figure 12-7 is typical of that found in a transport operator, with the same product being sold at several different prices, similar to the charts presented previously on price discrimination. If we plot marginal revenue and marginal costs, we can see that, once again, the two lines coincide at an output level of between 6 and 7, as shown in Figure 12-8.

Figure 12-8: Comparison of Marginal Revenue and Costs

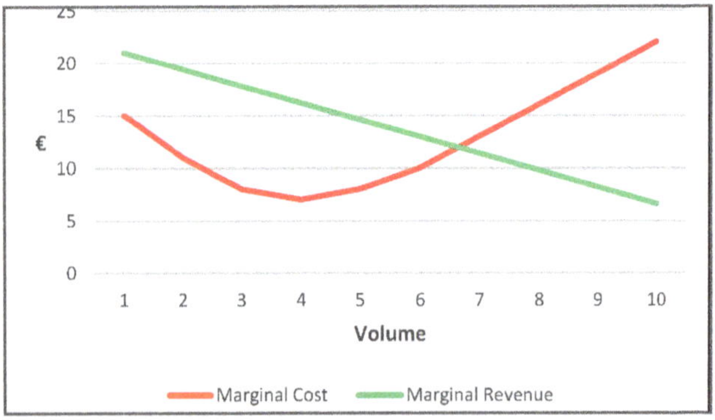

The objective of this exercise is to determine what is the optimal price and quantity from the operator's viewpoint, i.e. the level of supply and price that optimises profit. What is the significance of the point at which marginal revenue and marginal cost meet?

We saw back in Section 5.1 and Figure 12-2 that it was worth reducing prices to service the more price-sensitive segments so long as they contributed to fixed costs. Figure 12-8 is telling us the same thing; as long as the price of the trip is above the marginal cost of providing it, then the operator should accept the traffic. In Figure 12-9, we put together the cost revenue and profit calculations. We can see that the highest profitability for the firm occurs when marginal revenue and marginal cost coincide[34].

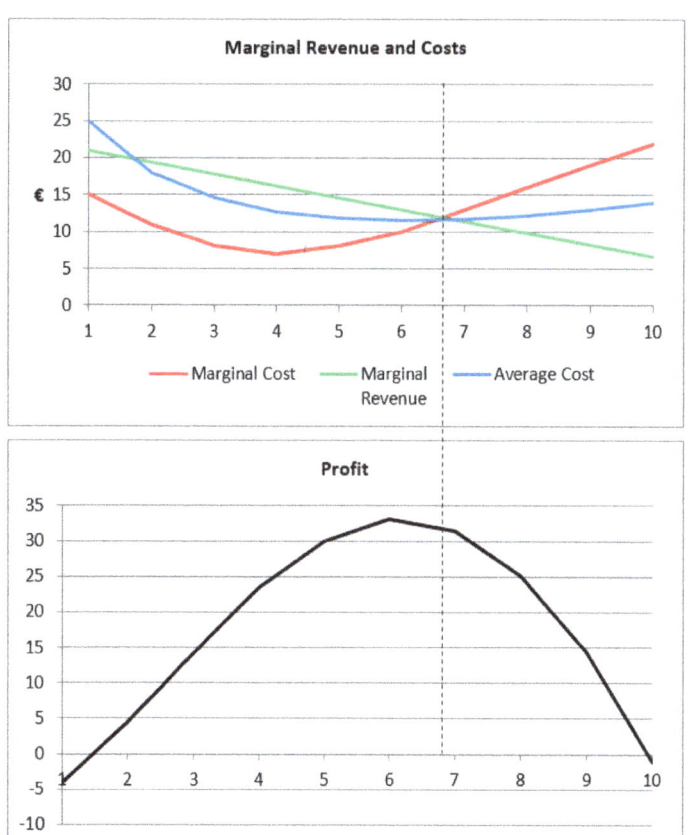

Figure 12-9: Marginal Revenue Costs and Profits

---

[34] Please note that, because we are not dealing here with pure and continuous curves, the dotted line does not meet exactly at the point of highest profit. An algebraical version, which proves that this does in fact happen, is provided in the annex to this Chapter for interested readers.

Note that the point of maximum profit is not exact, as the charts above deal only with ten units of volume. The marginal revenue, marginal cost and maximum profit points would coincide if volumes were in hundreds or thousands.

It is worth reiterating that the point of maximum profit is a theoretical construct that gets distorted in the real world.

If we look at 'last minute' sales of aircraft or train seats, revenue for which will be completely lost forever once the aircraft or train has departed, should such seats be sold to high-yield business travellers or potential customers on a very low budget?

An operator may also consider that their reputation is vulnerable if their 'product' is sold too cheaply, irrespective of the rationale for increasing revenue and profitability.

12.4 Costs for Investment Appraisal

As economists are generally interested in the cost of undertaking additional activity, such as buying new trains, renewing a railway line, replacing signalling, etc. the focus is on marginal costs.

In other words, we are interested in the specific costs and revenues associated with the activity and nothing else.

Consider the following example.

A freight operating company (FOC) has just won a new contract and needs to consider what costs to include in its business plan.

Let us assume that the plan calls for five sets of locomotives and wagons and 20 train crew. The rolling stock will require maintenance and the company will need to undertake marketing activity to retain its customer.

The FOC currently has two spare sets of rolling stock which could be used for the new service and their maintenance depot is operating significantly below capacity.

Similarly, the FOC has five crew members who are currently surplus to requirements but the FOC made the decision not to make them redundant in case new business came their way.

In order to determine what costs the new service will incur, we need to compare the total costs of providing the new service with the current situation, i.e. without the new contract.

To illustrate the process, we will go through each item in Figure 12-10 in turn.

Figure 12-10: Items to include in an Investment Appraisal

Item	Assumptions	Inclusion in Investment Appraisal
Five units of locos and rolling stock	FOC did not intend to sell its spare sets	Three new sets only to be included in the investment appraisal
Train crew	No redundancy for idle crew	Only the cost of 15 new crew should be accounted for
	Redundancy of the train crew was imminent	All 20 crew members should be counted as a cost for the new service
Maintenance	Spare capacity of both labour and the maintenance depot	There are no extra costs incurred as a result of the new contract, except for spare parts.
Marketing	Full time customer liaison manager required	All costs accruing to employing this new manager should be included in the appraisal.
Fuel and track access fees	These costs are incurred as a result of the new business	The difference between current and higher fuel bills and track access fees should be included.

What we have done in the above table is only include marginal costs in the calculation. These are costs which are incurred as a direct result of winning the contract and nothing else.

Similarly, if a company decides to withdraw from an activity, we should only consider those costs which can be avoided as a result of reducing business levels.

For a rail passenger operator in Britain, for example, the fixed element of track access does not change, whilst the variable element of the fees which will be avoided needs to be considered.

These 'negative marginal' costs are usually referred to as avoidable.

12.5 Benchmarking

12.5.1 Introduction to Benchmarking

As well as costs, the focus of this Chapter, benchmarking is a valuable tool for comparing the performance of one organisation or division with another or to compare current with previous performance in the same organisation. Benchmarking can be undertaken as a snapshot at any moment in time or over a lengthier period. To illustrate these concepts, we will imagine that the management of Palma de Mallorca airport wishes to evaluate its performance. In 2009, the most recent year with a major recession, demand fell by 7% but in 2015, demand increased by 4% compared to 2008.

However, this does not really help us to understand Majorca's performance. A more detailed set of indicators is provided in Figure 12-11

Figure 12-11: Performance Indicators for Balearic Islands Airports

	2008	2015	change 2008-09	change 2014-15	change 2008-15
Majorca	22,832,857	23,745,131	-7.1%	2.7%	4.0%
Ibiza	4,647,360	6,477,283	4.3%	4.3%	39.4%
Menorca	2,605,932	2,867,482	-6.6%	8.9%	10.0%
SPAIN	203,862,028	207,404,141	-8.0%	5.9%	1.7%

What this figure tells us is that, compared to Spain as a whole, a loss of 7% of traffic in 2009 was similar to the nationwide decline but was the weakest performing of the three Balearic airports.

Also, in 2015, although the change in demand was positive, the growth figure was less than half the average for Spain.

When considering just the Balearic Island airports, the picture is in fact worse: over the seven years, Palma de Mallorca grew by just 4%, which is a fraction of the rate of its two neighbours and competitors.

So, this Section illustrates how benchmarking is dependent both on the comparators used and the timeframe over which the benchmarking exercise takes place.

12.5.2 Obstacles to Benchmarking

Before we proceed to the following Sections which compare costs across the rail and airline sectors, it is important to make some observations about benchmarking.

If company A wishes to compare its cost performance with that of company B, how does it going about doing so?

No two businesses are exactly the same and there are all sorts of factors we would expect to make 'our' cost per train-km or available seat mile different from 'theirs'.

Figure 12-12 presents a list of factors which need to be considered when undertaking a benchmarking exercise.

Figure 12-12: Obstacles to Benchmarking Transport Businesses

	Airline	Bus	Ferry	Rail	Terminal
Intensity of Asset Use	✓	✓	✓	✓	✓
Seasonality	✓	✓	✓	✓	✓
Average Trip Length	✓	✓	✓	✓	
Vehicle/Building Size	✓	✓	✓	✓	✓
Seating Density	✓	✓			
Proportion of Retail Space					✓

We shall add some detail to these points in the following Sections.

12.5.3 Intensity of Asset Use

There are two aspects of asset use, namely speed and the number of hours that an operator uses an asset. We can illustrate the speed argument with a jet compared to propeller-driven aircraft.

Figure 12-13: Complete Journey Time Cycle for Aircraft

	Leave ACE	Arrive LPA	Depart LPA	Arrive ACE	Depart ACE
Jet	0700	0730	0800	0830	0900
Propeller	0700	0745	0815	0900	0930

Figure 12-13 shows that a full cycle by jet between Lanzarote (ACE) and Las Palmas (LPA) takes 2 hours whilst the equivalent cycle time by a turboprop takes 30 minutes longer.

If we assume that the flying day lasts 14 hours (in other words, there is viable demand between, say, 0700hrs and 2100hrs), the jet can fit in seven cycles and 14 journeys whilst the turboprop aircraft can only manage 12 journeys. Assuming that the two aircraft have the same capacity, there is a trade-off between speed and the higher initial cost of the more expensive jet aircraft.

Similar considerations apply to fast ferries (catamarans) and high speed trains. Buses, by contrast, can run express services but the vehicles are generally no different from those used in standard, all stops service.

12.5.4 Seasonality

A terminal which exhibits significant seasonality in demand will have very different cost and operating characteristics from another whose demand is level throughout the year.

By contrast, an airline can buy in extra capacity when needed or lease out spare aircraft when supply exceeds demand.

The seasonality of terminals is discussed in more detail in Section 20.8.

12.5.5 Average Trip Length

Whenever a plane, train, etc. arrives at a terminal, it requires time to unload passengers and then for a new set of passengers to embark.

This turnaround time is clearly unproductive, since an aircraft sitting on the ground or a train standing at a terminus platform generate no revenue.

In Figure 12-14, we can see that there is a large spread between different airlines operating in the USA. The twelve airlines shown in the chart include low cost operators such as Spirit and full service carriers such as American.

We can see, however, that Virgin America's stage length is more than double that of Hawaiian.

So how can we compare like with like?

Figure 12-14: Stage length and cost per ASK

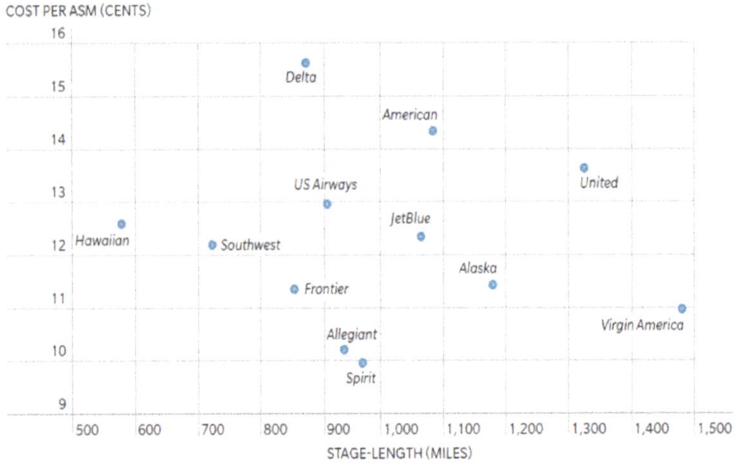

Source: "Airline Economic Analysis", Oliver Wyman (November 2014)

The solution to this problem is to standardize the average stage length to make a like-for-like comparison feasible. For the airlines above, the adjustment factor used is approximately

$$(\text{Average Stage Length}/1{,}000 \text{ miles})^{0.5}$$

The square root acknowledges the fact that whilst doubling stage length (for example) certainly reduces costs per mile, the fixed element at each end of the route means that the reduction in costs will be less than 50% of the total. See Figure 12-15 for the results of the adjusted unit costs.

Figure 12-15: CASM Adjusted for Stage Length

12.5.6 Vehicle/Building Size

An airline is able to provide various levels of service for a given level demand using different strategies such as:

- A lower frequency service with large aircraft;
- A higher frequency serviced with small aircraft;
- Offer a combination of classes very different from a competitor.

A route chosen at random illustrates this third point *in extremis*. The route in question is Heathrow to Bahrain and there are two competitors on the route, namely Gulf Air (GF) and British Airways (BA).

GF flies the route twice daily and BA once per day.

Figure 12-16: Daily Seat Capacity by Class from Heathrow to Bahrain

	First	Business	Premium Economy	Economy
Gulf Air (GF)	0	64	0	512
British Airways (BA)	14	48	40	122

Exactly 800 seats are offered on the route per day with GF offering 72% of total capacity (576 seats).

But what we are benchmarking here is the profitability of the route.

GF will clearly incur significantly higher operating costs operating their double-daily frequency but BA has a much higher proportion of premium seats, with almost twice as many First and Business Class seats per flight per flight as GF.

However, the differences do not stop there.

A Business class seat on BA ('Club World') can cost nearly double the GF equivalent ('Falcon Gold') and economy class prices are also much higher on BA.

So, in addition to examining differences in operating costs, frequency and aircraft size when benchmarking, we will also need to consider the yield per seat and the volume of passengers.

12.6 Breakdown of Costs – GB Rail

12.6.1 Overall Cost Structure

In this Section, we will examine the cost structure of railways in Great Britain, which is a very different case form the airline industry previously discussed earlier in this Chapter.

We will also use this Section to demonstrate a range of cost performance indicators, which can signal to management how well costs are being controlled.

Figure 12-17 shows the aggregate cost structure over all GB railway operators from 2009-10, when Allen & Co. wrote their report 'Costs of Railway Outputs'.

The costs exclude transfer payments to and from Network Rail for performance-related issues and track access fees.

Figure 12-17: Overall Cost Structure of GB Railway Operators (TOCs)

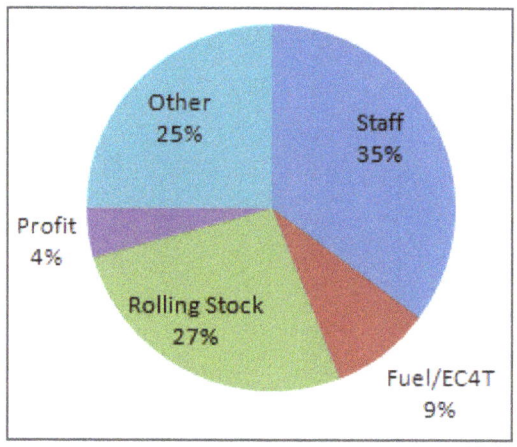

Source: http://www.rail-reg.gov.uk/upload/pdf/rvfm-booz-outputs-cost-081010.pdf, p18

According to this report, variable elements comprised around 44% of the total (staff, fuel) and rolling stock, which is classed as semi-variable, accounted for 27% of the total.

The 'other' category, a quarter of the total, is associated with the TOCs' management of their organisations, including headquarters and administration costs. This last category may be regarded as fixed.

12.6.2 Drivers of TOC Costs

We would expect operating costs to vary by the type of TOC. For example, Northern manages almost ten times as many stations as Thameslink, even though the latter carried more passengers.

Service frequency and types of operation (high speed or urban stopping services) will also clearly have a bearing on differences in operating costs between TOCs. Figure 12-18 is derived from the ORR report "Costs and Revenues of Franchised Passenger Train Operators in the UK"[35], published in November 2012 and compares operating costs under the TOC's control.

These controllable costs, which exclude fixed access fees and performance regime payments, average around 75% of the TOCs' total operating costs.

---

[35] http://orr.gov.uk/publications/reports/costs-and-revenues-of-franchised-passenger-train-operators-in-the-uk

Figure 12-18: Operating Costs (expressed in pence per passenger-km)

	Total Cost p/p-km	£/veh-km	£/train-hr	Speed (km/h)	m Pax-km	Pax-km (000)/staff	Stations
East Coast	8.09	1.96	2,320	132	4,772	1,700	12
Stagecoach South Western	8.14	1.80	646	54	5,524	1,247	185
First Great Western	8.79	2.26	811	80	5,520	1,246	211
First Capital Connect	8.94	1.85	750	64	3,223	1,391	55
C2C	9.21	2.25	760	57	958	1,634	24
National Express East Anglia	9.28	1.73	691	64	3,887	1,355	167
Virgin Trains	9.32	1.81	1,991	134	5,699	1,956	17
First Transpennine Express	10.09	3.20	736	75	1,058	1,038	30
East Midlands Trains	10.10	2.27	764	92	2,085	1,021	89
Cross Country	10.27	2.41	895	91	3,079	1,912	-
Chiltern Railways	10.49	3.01	679	74	925	1,172	30
Southern	10.93	2.44	677	53	4,133	1,021	157
Southeastern	11.06	1.98	674	53	3,985	1,067	173
London Midland	13.45	2.57	634	65	1,852	792	147
First ScotRail	15.22	2.93	580	60	2,642	602	346
Arriva Trains Wales	16.51	3.16	433	56	1,101	553	244
MerseyRail	18.61	4.92	610	37	545	454	66
Northern	19.10	3.58	449	52	2,026	423	462
Correlations		0.83	-0.46	-0.51	-0.56	-0.83	0.60

Source: http://www.rail-reg.gov.uk/server/show/ConWebDoc.11052

Beneath the table, there is a row which gives the correlation between each variable and the operating *Cost per passenger-km*. We can see that the correlation figure gives us an indication of how strong the relationship is between two variables.

The variables which influence operating costs are given in columns 3 to 8 of the table and we will go through each of these factors in turn.

Cost per vehicle-km: as a TOC's major expense is the running of trains, we would expect this cost to be highly correlated with operating Cost per passenger-km. The relationship assumes that the TOCs use their capacity efficiently and do not run eight coach trains, say, when only two are required. If there were a major mismatch between capacity and demand, we would not expect to see the high correlation between these two variables. What this figure does not tell us is the extent to which operating costs are driven by differences in rolling stock. Although the average age of rolling stock is available on the ORR Data Portal website, there was no significant evidence of a correlation between operating Costs per vehicle-km and the average age of each TOC's fleet (correlation of 0.28).

Cost per train-hour/speed: this figure is calculated as the total operating costs divided by the total annual timetabled train hours for each TOC. The higher values in the table are attached to the 'pure' inter-city operators, which incur significantly higher costs due to relatively large numbers of on-board staff, including catering and cleaning that are not offered on service that offer shorter journeys. It is worth noting that cost per train-hour and speed are very highly correlated, at 90%.

Passenger-km per staff member: although the absolute number of staff per TOC shows no relationship whatsoever with operating costs (correlation of 0%), it is possible to compare the staffing efficiency of TOCs by examining how many units of output (in this case passenger-km) are generated on average by each staff member. This does not imply that Northern, which ranks bottom on this measure, is inefficient, because comparing Virgin to Northern is hardly comparing like with like! A more reasonable comparison is between the three TOCs operating south of the Thames, where it is interesting to observe that SWT's efficiency, as measured in passenger-kilometres per member of staff, is 20% higher than Southern or Southeastern. The last column shows how many stations are managed by each TOC and this will clearly have a bearing on costs; for example, we would expect Northern's staff bill for station staff to be much higher than, say Cross-Country's! Overall, though, the number of stations managed by a TOC does appear to have a bearing on operating costs, with a correlation of 0.6.

12.7 Airline Costs

Whilst passenger volumes by train are not limited to the number of seats, this is certainly the case for airlines, in spite of efforts by Ryanair and others to change this[36]! Similar considerations apply to long-distance bus or coach operators, where a seat is required for the journey. Airline operating costs comprise a range of categories, including:

- Labour;
- Fuel;
- Aircraft lease/depreciation costs;
- Landing and navigation fees; and
- Miscellaneous other costs.

---

36 See, for example, http://edition.cnn.com/2014/07/10/travel/standing-cabin-plane-study

Benchmarking cost performance against competitors is complicated by a host of factors beyond the control of an individual airline operator:

- *Age and type of aircraft operated.* The Airbus A340 was first flown in 1993, so is not old compared to other long range aircraft. However, many are being scrapped, stored or sold as more modern and fuel-efficient replacements come onto the market;

- *Aircraft fleet composition.* One of the key factors for maintaining lower operating costs is to have as narrow a range of aircraft as possible. Ryanair, for example, has over 300 aircraft in operation but just one aircraft type (Boeing 737-800). So any pilot, for example, can be used on any route the airline offers with no training costs associated with familiarising crew or maintenance staff with other aircraft types;

- *Route Network.* If we retain the Ryanair example, the downside of having just one aircraft type is reflected in the type of network an airline operates. The 737 is limited to flights of around seven hours and is not very efficient on very short routes. So, in practice, it can be complicated to compare one airline focussing on short- and medium-haul routes with one whose main focus is on long haul, such as Emirates;

- *Service proposition.* Continuing the Boeing 737-800 example, comparing the offerings of Ryanair with another European airline, KLM, Ryanair is strictly one class and fits as many seats into the aircraft as regulations permit (189). In contrast, KLM offers a three-class service so the same aircraft accommodates only 170 people. Many airlines fly identical aircraft with under 160 seats. Premium seats require significantly higher fares to offset the loss of seats compared to an all-economy layout.

So, a key metric in assessing cost performance is cost per available seat mile or kilometre (CASM or CASK). An individual airline will have access to sufficient internal information to calculate this statistic over time by aircraft type or by region served, but, for benchmarking against competitors, the two factors which can be controlled for are average flight length (also known as stage length) and whether the comparator is a full-service airline or a low-cost carrier.

MIT's Airline Data Project[37] undertakes this analysis for eleven of the largest airlines operating in the USA.

Elsewhere in the world, however, this analysis is not freely accessible or it is necessary to examine the individual financial reports of comparable airlines or the reports of share brokers who will often undertake the comparison work.

12.8 Depreciation

So far, we have not addressed the issue of depreciation in costs.

When an operator invests in vehicles or infrastructure, these will last a certain number of years, after which they will need to be replaced.

When considering the life of assets, buses probably have one of the shortest lives (say 5-10 years) whilst a terminal can last much longer: Heathrow's Terminal 1 closed in June 2015 after 47 years of service.

As these assets wear out over time, a depreciation expense needs to be taken into consideration.

Although there are various methods which accountants use to quantify deprecation, we will just discuss one here, which is the 'straight line' method.

An airline buys a new aircraft for $104 million and, after 20 years, the airline expects to be able to sell this aircraft for $4 million.

So, over 20 years, the aircraft will show a depreciation of $5 million per annum or approximately $13,700 per day.

How onerous this cost is in practice depends on how well the asset is utilised, as aircraft only generate revenue whilst they are in the air.

So, if the airline only schedules this aircraft to fly for 7 hours per day, for example, the depreciation charge per flying hour will be double that of an airline that sweats its assets more intensively and flies its aircraft for 14 hours per day.

---

[37] http://web.mit.edu/airlinedata/www/default.html

12.9 Chapter 12 Exercises

Exercise 1 A bus company operates a fleet of 10 buses, costing €100,000 each. On average, each bus operates 500km per day over 360 days of the year.

Each bus has a full service once a year, which costs €1,200 in spare parts. A bus is expected to stay in service for five years, after which its value is written down to zero.

The company employs 15 drivers and 6 mechanics for maintenance, at a cost of €20,000 per employee. Fuel costs are 20 cents per bus kilometre and the company incurs head office costs of €80,000 per annum.

Finally, each bus requires licenses and operating certificates which cost €1,000 per vehicle, irrespective of the distance covered. For this company, calculate for each bus-km run:

- The marginal cost;
- The operating cost; and
- The full cost.

Exercise 2 You have been asked by a ferry company to compare the costs of two of the routes, which the company operates.

Each route runs with just one dedicated foot passenger only ferry per route.

The frequency of each route is such that maintenance can be undertaken on the ferries whilst the ferries are either in port or are idle for one day of the week.

How will you proceed to compare the costs of the two routes? Assume that any information you ask for will be available.

12.10 Annex: Proof of Profit Maximisation

Let P = Profit, R = Revenue and C = Cost. Therefore,

$$P = R - C \text{ (equation 1)}$$

We require a value for so that the last unit sold makes a negligible, but still positive, profit. We express this marginal profit function by $\delta P/\delta q$, which represents the change in profit as the quantity sold (q) increases.

If we convert profit to the marginal profit with respect to quantity (or the first derivative, as it is known in calculus) on the left-hand side of the equation, then we must do the same for the right-hand side.

We can see the result in equation 2.

$$\delta P/\delta q = \delta R/\delta q - \delta C/\delta q \text{ (equation 2)}$$

We stated earlier that we are seeking the point at which total profit is (almost) unchanged when the last unit is produced or ticket is sold, so we can say that both sides of the equation are equal to 0, as in equation (3).

$$\delta P/\delta q = \delta R/\delta q - \delta C/\delta q = 0 \text{ (equation 3)}$$

Now, $\delta R/\delta q$ is the marginal revenue with respect to quantity sold and $\delta C/\delta q$ is the marginal cost, so let us now re-label equation (3)

$$MR - MC = 0 \text{ (equation 4)}$$

Adding marginal costs to both sides we get

$$MR = MC \text{ (equation 5)}$$

This proves that the optimal level of output occurs when marginal revenue equals marginal cost.

13 COMPANY SIZE AND STRUCTURE

13.1 Introduction

In this Chapter, we will take a brief look at company size and structure. We will examine issues such as how a firm grows and the benefits and costs of this growth.

As a firm grows its markets, what sort of business structures do we see and why? We will examine some of the advantages and disadvantages of these different business structures.

13.2 Company Size

In Chapter 4, we looked at individual states of industry such as perfect competition and duopoly. What we will now investigate are the forces which change the industry structure over time.

Consider Figure 13-1, which shows the number of players in the aviation market in the USA from before deregulation occurred in 1978 to the present day.

Figure 13-1: Supply and Demand in the US Aviation Sector

	Air carriers	Major air carriers[38]	Other air carriers	Passenger miles (m)
1975	36	N/A	N/A	119,591
1980	63	N/A	N/A	190,766
1985	102	13	89	275,864
1990	70	14	56	345,873
1995	96	11	85	403,912
2000	91	15	76	515,598
2005	85	17	68	583,771
2010	77	21	56	564,695
2016	64	18	46	618,657

The table above includes a small number of all-freight carriers but the picture is clear nonetheless. In the years after deregulation, the number of new entrants into the market boomed and almost tripled the number of carriers operating in the market.

---
[38] A major air carrier is defined as having over $1 billion of revenue. This threshold was fixed nearly 20 years ago.

Many of the new entrants went bankrupt or merged, in part due to the recession, which afflicted much of the global economy in the early 1990s.

Since 1995, however, when the number of carriers hit another peak, the trend has been unmistakably downwards, with around one third of all carriers having disappeared in the last twenty years. What is also noticeable from Figure 13-1 is that demand has continually increased since deregulation, with the exception of the recession from 2009-2010.

So, we have a smaller number of carriers serving an ever-larger market. In this Section, we will explore this phenomenon and seek to understand why the number of suppliers has been shrinking. Although some of the carriers will have gone bankrupt due to a poor quality of product of service, many have merged to become extremely large suppliers of air transport.

13.3 Economies of Scale

The principle behind economies of scale is reasonably straightforward. If you have a bus company with a total of five buses in the fleet, you will need to have various head office functions such as maintenance and marketing.

The size of these head office operations is unlikely to double, say, if the number of buses in the fleet increased to ten.

Moreover, if you are in the market to buy a larger number of items, be it office furniture, computers, buses or aircraft, it is usually possible to bargain with the supplier to get a higher discount per item due to the large number of items being purchased. We can illustrate how this works using a simple example as illustrated in Figure 13-2.

Figure 13-2: Example of Scale Economies

Buses purchased	Head Office Costs	Purchase Cost	Total Costs	Costs per Bus
5	300,000	2,000,000	2,300,000	460,000
10	350,000	3,900,000	4,250,000	425,000
15	400,000	5,700,000	6,100,000	406,667
20	450,000	7,400,000	7,850,000	392,500
25	500,000	9,000,000	9,500,000	380,000
30	550,000	10,500,000	11,050,000	368,333

We can see how the average cost per bus declines as the volume operated increases, although, as expected, total costs obviously increase.

13.4 Long Run Average Cost

In many economics textbooks, a typical long-run average cost curve is presented as shown in Figure 13-3.

Figure 13-3: Long Run Average Cost Curve

When the company produces Q1 units of output, the average cost per unit, C1, is at its lowest.

We can compare this position to the smaller volume of output in Q2, which comes with higher average costs, as we demonstrated in Figure 13-2.

But how do we explain the fact that, as we increase output from Q1 to Q3, average costs start rising again?

From point Q1 to Q3, the company starts suffering what are called diseconomies of scale and this phenomenon can be explained as follows:

- In a small to medium-sized company, the CEO will have a relatively large amount of power and be in a position to oversee day to day operations. However, as the company increases in size, the CEO will need to delegate and, in effect, hand over power to a new tier of management. If these divisional chiefs starting acting in the interests of their division, rather than the company as a whole, then the efficiency with which the company operates will decrease;

- Similarly, a divisional manager will be appraised and promoted (or demoted) based on how well he/she has performed aginst set targets. For example, one target may be to increase a region's market share. However, if the manager reduces fares significantly, the target may well be reached, but what would be the impact on the company's overall profitability; and

- As a company increases in size, the cost and complexity of communication betweern different divisions, spread over various time zones and locations will increase. Another aspect of larger companies is the 'principal-agent' problem, whereby a divisional manager may appoint staff who are more loyal to the person appointing them than on the criterion of whatis best for the firm as a whole.

Although it is difficult to observe a long-run average cost curve such as Figure 13-3, it is important to be aware that economies of scale not only has its limits but also that, as a company grows, the costs of this growth may well outweigh the benefits at some point.

13.5 Company Structure

13.5.1 Outright Takeover

If a company decides to expand and to take over the assets, operations and branding of another company, there are several possible outcomes to the way the enlarged firm will look.

The simplest of these is the outright takeover.

Originally established as a low-cost operator by KLM, the Dutch national airline, Buzz was one of the earlier low cost operators in the UK.

In 2003, Ryanair bought Buzz and, within a year, the brand, many routes and all the aircraft that Ryanair had inherited had disappeared.

Once Buzz's personnel and remaining routes (Ryanair shut down many of the ones it inherited) had been absorbed into Ryanair, Buzz ceased to exist.

13.5.2 Wholly Owned Subsidiary

Unlike the outright takeover, a wholly owned subsidiary (WOS) will retain its brand and significant management control independent of the parent company.

A WOS can be developed in-house or can be acquired as the result of a takeover. Ted Airlines started operations in 2004 as a wholly-owned subsidiary of United Airlines in the USA. Its objective was to compete in the low-cost airline sector.

Delta Airlines promoted a similar strategy with its Song subsidiary, which started operations in 2003.

Both Ted and Song were kept separate from the main company, as both United and Delta were, and remain, full service carriers. Therefore, to avoid confusion in the market place, separate subsidiaries were developed so that the core, full service business was unaffected by the battle for market share in the low-cost segment of the USA domestic air travel market.

Many airlines have tried and failed to make this strategy work and these low-cost brands lasted less than five years before staff and aircraft were absorbed back into the parent companies and the brands shut down.

An alternative means of owning a subsidiary is to acquire one. In 2003, First Group acquired 80% of the shares of Hull Trains (HT) and the remaining 20% in 2014.

As its name implies, HT's key objective was, and remains, to serve the Hull rail market, particularly to and from London, with five to seven trains per day each way.

As well as having a specific market niche, HT runs under very different conditions to First Group's two other large main line rail businesses, which are franchises[39].

HT is not subject to any control on its fares, maximum journey time requirements or minimum frequency like a standard rail franchise.

However, HT enjoys synergies with the parent, especially in the areas of fleet acquisition and heavy maintenance, so HT is able to acquire and maintain its fleet at a lower cost than an independent operator which only had four train sets in its fleet.

---

[39] These are Great Western and Transpennine Express.

13.5.3 Conglomerate

Stagecoach Group, based in Scotland, is an example of a conglomerate. Apart from its rail operations, Stagecoach has 19 regional local bus operations and often more than one brand within each region. Stagecoach also operates express buses between Oxford and London (Oxford Tube) and Megabus, which operates long distance buses throughout the UK and beyond.

Bus demand is very much a local matter, so decisions on routes and frequency would be delegated down to regional level. However, the corporate headquarters maintains an important monitoring role and will direct the regional subsidiaries as necessary.

The following statement appears in Stagecoach's annual report[40]:

"The key features of [their] business model are:

* *A decentralised management structure enabling local management to identify quickly and respond to developments in each local market;*

* *An emphasis on lightly regulated bus operations enabling management to vary prices, operating schedules and timetables in response to developments in each local market without significant hindrance from regulation; and*

* *A flexible cost base whereby operating mileage and operating costs can be flexed in response to changes in demand."*

Before, we came across economies of scale, whilst Stagecoach is a good example of *economies of scope*.

Scope economies occur when a business diversifies into separate but related businesses rather than growing an individual segment (i.e. economies of scale). In this case, Stagecoach not only operates local and regional bus networks but also two express coach brands.

---

[40] https://www.stagecoachbus.com/about/national (page 5 of the 2014-15 annual report)

14 LINEAR PROGRAMMING

14.1 Introduction

In the previous Chapter, we discussed the nature of costs incurred by transport companies. In reality, operators of all modes have a fixed number of vehicles, in the short term, of varying sizes that are assigned to routes to both meet demand (and hence maximise revenue) but also to minimise costs. This Chapter provides a brief overview of a technique known as linear programming.

Before we go into any detail of what the technique is and how it works, consider the following problem. An airline will have several types of aircraft and needs to allocate its fleet to a daily schedule of flights which best meets demand for each route the airline flies.

We will assume for this simple example that short-term demand is known and we know what the average revenue per passenger is likely to be (and therefore we will assume that revenue is fixed).

Therefore, the objective here is to use the fleet at the airline's disposal to minimise the cost of the daily flight plan required to meet demand and hence maximise the airline's profitability.

However, in developing the flight plan, the airline will need to take account of a large number of constraints, including:

- Runway length. Not all airports can accept the largest aircraft, so certain parts of the fleet cannot be deployed on various routes;

- Flight crew are legally allowed to work only a certain number of hours and these constraints need to be considered when allocating airline employees to the day's flight plan;

- Certain airports are subject to limited opening hours. These restrictions normally apply to night-time arrivals and departures.

To give an indication of the size of the problem, Turkish Airlines was recently using a linear programming model with 2,160 variables and 1,588 constraints[41].

---
41 http://ac.els-cdn.com/S1877042812035847.1-s2.0-S1877042812035847-main.pdf?_tid=2cd4ec08-9cf4-11e5-83ca-00000aacb35d&acdnat=1449501004_b9231ac3e97356418af74194ce17eb46

So, whilst this Chapter will present a highly simplistic view of the means whereby transport operators assign their fleet to routes, the objective in this Chapter is to provide an awareness of the method, how it works and its relevance to understanding an important aspect of managing costs in the transport sector.

14.2 A Simple Example of Linear Programming

Zurich Air, a fictional airline based (unsurprisingly!) in Zurich, Switzerland, operates a mixed fleet of Boeing 737s and 787s. Information about each of the two aircraft types is provided in Figure 14-1.

Figure 14-1: Data on Zurich Air's Fleet

	Capacity	Operating Cost / km	Op cost per ASK	Available Fleet
Boeing 737	170	7.10 €	0.0418 €	8
Boeing 787	290	9.00 €	0.0310 €	10

The larger aircraft has lower operating costs when measured in cents per available seat kilometre (ASK).

The airline has 8 Boeing 737s and 10 787s available for deployment on the day in question and Zurich Air plans to operate five routes.

Figure 14-2 shows the details of each route and the expected demand.

We will assume that each aircraft performs one return journey per day and that the demand on the return leg is the same or lower than on the outward leg (in other words, if we can allocate aircraft to the outbound legs of each route, there will be sufficient capacity for the return journey).

Figure 14-2: Flight Distance and Demand by Route

Distance/Demand Table		
Distance Table (from Zurich Hub)	km	Demand
Dubai	4,773	1,410
Luxor	3,212	540
Tenerife	3,063	660
Accra	4,713	730
La Palma	3,087	250
		3,590

We'll now add a couple of complications to this problem. Zurich Air's marketing strategy requires that the Dubai route only be flown by 787s. This is the company's flagship route with the longest haul and the highest demand.

In addition, La Palma airport has a short runway and so can only accommodate Boeing 737s. So, to summarise this Section, our objective is to minimise operating costs whilst satisfying the demand on each of the five routes and also certain constraints.

We will now go into some detail on how these constraints are formulated.

14.3 Constraints

14.3.1 Aircraft Variables

First, it is important to understand how many variables we have in this problem. We have two aircraft types which can be flown – for now – over five routes. So, on the Zurich-Accra route, our variables can be labelled as Accra_737 and Accra_787. The same applies to the other four routes. Our task is to determine how many aircraft to deploy on each of these ten aircraft-route combinations.

14.3.2 Integers and Non-Negative Responses

With many linear programming problems, we are able to find a solution which may or may not be a whole number. For example, the optimal mix for an alcoholic beverage may be 28.347 grammes of ingredient X, 17.981 grammes of ingredient Y and so on. In the fleet allocation problem, however, the answers must be integers. Similarly, the method used to solve this problem can produce negative answers, so a further constraint is that the number of aircraft allocated to a route must be greater than or equal to zero.

14.3.3 Demand

The problem requires that all demand on that day is satisfied (leaving behind a booked passenger does nothing for an operator's reputation![42]). So, the capacity supplied for each route must be greater than or equal to demand.

---

42 *This happened recently at Lanzarote with Vueling: http://www.lavozdelanzarote.com/articulo/sociedad/mas-180-pasajeros-vueling-afrontaron-varias-horas-retraso-avion-demasiado-pequenho/20160711175905108471.html (in Spanish only)*

14.3.4 Aircraft Supply

In Figure 14-1, we were told how many of each aircraft were available for the day's flight plan. Therefore, the solution requires that no more than 8 Boeing 737s and 10 Boeing 787s be used to determine the least cost of running the day's flight plan.

14.3.5 Route-specific Constraints

We have been advised that Boeing 737s must not be used on the Dubai route and 787s cannot fly to La Palma. Therefore, Dubai_737 and LaPalma_787 should both be set to zero.

14.3.6 Summary of Constraints

In Figure 14-3, we bring together all the constraints described above. To make the problem more comprehensible, all the cells used in defining constraints have been named in the Excel spreadsheet.

Figure 14-3: List of Aircraft Allocation Constraints

	Variable	Operation	Value
Non-Negativity	Allocated_737s	>=	0
	Allocated_787s	>=	0
Integers	Allocated_737s		Integers
	Allocated_787s		Integers
Satisfy Demand	Accra_Capacity	>=	Accra_Volume
	Dubai_Capacity	>=	Dubai_Volume
	LaPalma_Capacity	>=	LaPalma_Volume
	Luxor_Capacity	>=	Luxor_Volume
	Tenerife_Capacity	>=	Tenerife_Volume
Maximum	Total_737s_Used	<=	Available_737s
Availability	Total_787s_Used	<=	Available_787s
Route-Specific	Dubai_737	=	0
	LaPalma_787	=	0

14.4 Defining the Objective Function

We mentioned earlier that the objective of the problem was to minimise operating costs. Let us now be a little more specific about how we express these costs.

For each route, there will be a number of 737s (X) and 787s (Y) being employed. We know the distance and cost per km on each route, so the cost of the Accra route (for example) can be stated as:

$$4{,}713 \text{ (km)} * €7.10 \text{ (cost/km)} * X + 4{,}713 * €9.00 * Y$$

In Figure 14-4, we show the starting point for the allocation of aircraft to routes by manually inserting 1 into each of the changing cells. The reader can check that the costs for one of each aircraft per route is as shown in the final column, using the equation above.

Figure 14-4: Starting Point to Solve the Aircraft Allocation Problem

Distance Table (from Zurich Hub)	km	Volume Required	Boeing 737	Boeing 737 Cap	Boeing 787	Boeing 787 Cap	Total Aircraft Capacity	% of Capacity Utilised	Operating Cost
Dubai	4,773	1,410	1	170	1	290	460	307%	€ 76,845
Luxor	3,212	540	1	170	1	290	460	117%	€ 51,713
Tenerife	3,063	660	1	170	1	290	460	143%	€ 49,314
Accra	4,713	730	1	170	1	290	460	159%	€ 75,879
La Palma	3,087	250	1	170	1	290	460	54%	€ 49,701
		3,590	5	850	5	1,450	2,300	156%	€ 303,453

14.5 Excel's Solver

Solver is an add-in provided by Microsoft to solve linear programming problems. In Figure 14-5, we can see that our objective function needs to be minimised by altering the cells (shaded in grey and green in Figure 14-4) to provide us with the allocation of the number of each aircraft type to each route whilst satisfying all the constraints.

The traditional method of solving linear programming problems is the Simplex method, which we will not discuss here; just ensure that the Simplex option is selected.

Next, we will examine the solution by pressing 'Solve'.

Figure 14-5: Solver Screenshot

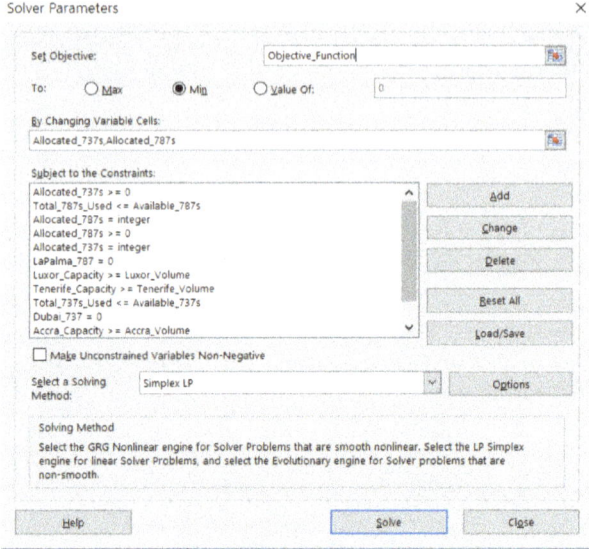

14.6 Solution

With the solved problem, we can see in Figure 14-6 that all the constraints are satisfied.

Figure 14-6: Results from Solver

Distance Table (from Zurich Hub)	km	Volume Required	Boeing 737	Boeing 737 Cap	Boeing 787	Boeing 787 Cap	Total Aircraft Capacity	% of Capacity Utilised	Operating Cost
Dubai	4,773	1,410	0	0	5	1,450	1,450	97%	€ 214,785
Luxor	3,212	540	0	0	2	580	580	93%	€ 57,816
Tenerife	3,063	660	4	680	0	0	680	97%	€ 86,989
Accra	4,713	730	1	170	2	580	750	97%	€ 118,296
La Palma	3,087	250	2	340	0	0	340	74%	€ 43,835
		3,590	7	1,190	9	1,450	3,800	94%	€ 521,722

Notice especially that supply always exceeds demand, so the load factor (% of capacity utilised) is less than or equal to 100%. Dubai is a Boeing 787-only route and La Palma uses only Boeing 737s. So, the daily cost of this operation is €521,722.

14.7 Sensitivities

The previous solution shows that there is a little bit of slack in the flight plan, with one 737 and one 787 remaining unused. We can see that the load factor for the La Palma route looks poorer than most, as it is only 74% (we need to use two 737s to satisfy demand rather than one Boeing 787). The impact of this restriction is evident by changing the LaPalma_787 constraint to >=0. If the runway could accommodate 787s, then the operating cost would decline from €521,700 to €505,700, as shown in Figure 14-7.

Figure 14-7: Removing the La Palma Restriction

Distance Table (from Zurich Hub)	km	Volume Required	Boeing 737	Boeing 737 Cap	Boeing 787	Boeing 787 Cap	Total Aircraft Capacity	% of Capacity Utilised	Operating Cost
Dubai	4,773	1,410	0	0	5	1,450	1,450	97%	€ 214,785
Luxor	3,212	540	0	0	2	580	580	93%	€ 57,816
Tenerife	3,063	660	4	680	0	0	680	97%	€ 86,989
Accra	4,713	730	1	170	2	580	750	97%	€ 118,296
La Palma	3,087	250	0	0	1	290	290	86%	€ 27,783
		3,590	5	1,190	10	2,610	3,750	96%	**€ 505,670**

We can also see that if the restriction were removed, all the 787s would be deployed but three 737s would remain unused on this day.

A more feasible alternative would be to examine what would be the impact of converting Zurich Air's other longer haul route (Accra) to exclusively Boeing 787 operation. In Figure 14-8, a new constraint was added (Accra_B737 = 0) and Solver was re-run. La Palma has been reset to use Boeing 737s only.

Figure 14-8: Accra Converted to B787s Only

Distance Table (from Zurich Hub)	km	Volume Required	Boeing 737	Boeing 737 Cap	Boeing 787	Boeing 787 Cap	Total Aircraft Capacity	% of Capacity Utilised	Operating Cost
Dubai	4,773	1,410	0	0	5	1,450	1,450	97%	€ 214,785
Luxor	3,212	540	0	0	2	580	580	93%	€ 57,816
Tenerife	3,063	660	4	680	0	0	680	97%	€ 86,989
Accra	4,713	730	0	0	3	870	750	84%	€ 127,251
La Palma	3,087	250	2	340	0	0	290	74%	€ 43,835
		3,590	6	1,020	10	2,900	3,750	92%	**€ 530,677**

Operating costs are around €9,000 higher than the base case and the load factor on the Accra route has dropped.

If Zurich Air were to pursue this strategy, the airline would presumably be hoping that having more attractive aircraft on the route would increase demand. As a final test, we will retain the assumptions of exclusive 787 operations to Dubai and Accra but now also assume that one of the Boeing 787s becomes unavailable.

Can we still meet the demands of the flight plan with just 9 Boeing 787s rather than 10? We can see from Figure 14-9 that the answer is 'Yes'.

We have had to substitute Boeing 737s onto the Luxor route so that the demands of Dubai and Accra being run exclusively with Boeing 787s can be met. The load factor and operating costs of the Luxor route have changed significantly. Most importantly, we now have no slack remaining in the supply of aircraft.

Figure 14-9: Only Nine Boeing 787s Available

Distance Table (from Zurich Hub)	km	Volume Required	Boeing 737	Boeing 737 Cap	Boeing 787	Boeing 787 Cap	Total Aircraft Capacity	% of Capacity Utilised	Operating Cost
Dubai	4,773	1,410	0	0	5	1,450	1,450	97%	€ 214,785
Luxor	3,212	540	2	340	1	290	630	86%	€ 74,518
Tenerife	3,063	660	4	680	0	0	680	97%	€ 86,989
Accra	4,713	730	0	0	3	870	870	84%	€ 127,251
La Palma	3,087	250	2	340	0	0	340	74%	€ 43,835
		3,590	8	1,360	9	2,610	3,970	90%	€ 547,379

Operating costs have also increased by some €16,700 compared to but this is hardly surprising, as we have tightened the constraints.

14.8 Conclusion

In the Zurich Air example above, we can observe how operating costs showed significant variation, depending on the constraints imposed on the operator's ability to assign its fleet to satisfy the demand for its services. Even a small operator can benefit from the application of linear programming to determine whether it is deploying its fleet efficiently.

Although this example only examined costs, the method could also be employed to assess the revenue impacts of alternative fleet allocation options.

15 SUBSIDIES

15.1 Introduction

For many transport operators, revenues are insufficient to provide funds to cover either operating costs, to service debts which have been assumed to pay for the original investment in the transport system or possibly both. As a result, operators require subsidies to maintain the service.

As we shall see later on in this book, there are various social reasons why a subsidy may be justified. A non-exhaustive list includes:

- Providing service to small, isolated communities which would otherwise be cut off;
- Increasing job opportunities;
- Reducing time spent travelling;
- Reducing road congestion and pollution; and
- Reducing accidents and fatalities.

One of the major challenges in transport economics is to place monetary values on these social benefits.

Time savings, for example, have been extensively researched over many years and we will come back to this topic in Section 22.8. The impacts of a reduction in pollution are, by contrast, somewhat more complicated to calculate!

15.2 Types of Subsidy

Subsidies or grants can come in various forms. In the UK, for example, local bus operators receive a rebate on the fuel duty of around £0.34 per litre.

The GB rail industry similarly receives subsidies, payable both to Network Rail and certain franchised operators and local authorities, in excess of £5 billion per annum[43].

---

[43] http://orr.gov.uk/__data/assets/pdf_file/0007/14497/rail-finance-statistical-release-2013-14.pdf

For the purposes of our discussion on this complicated subject, we will limit ourselves to three types of subsidy:

- Fares reduced for all passengers;
- Fares reduced for certain groups of passenger only; and
- Cross-subsidy.

Ferries and airlines within Europe provide examples of all three subsidy types, so we will use such ferries to illustrate the issue.

15.3 Fixed Subsidy

In Figure 3-5, we saw how there was an equilibrium price that matched supply and demand. Here, we will see how subsidies affect this equilibrium point. In Figure 15-1, the original equilibrium point without subsidies is 100 seats sold at a price of £25.

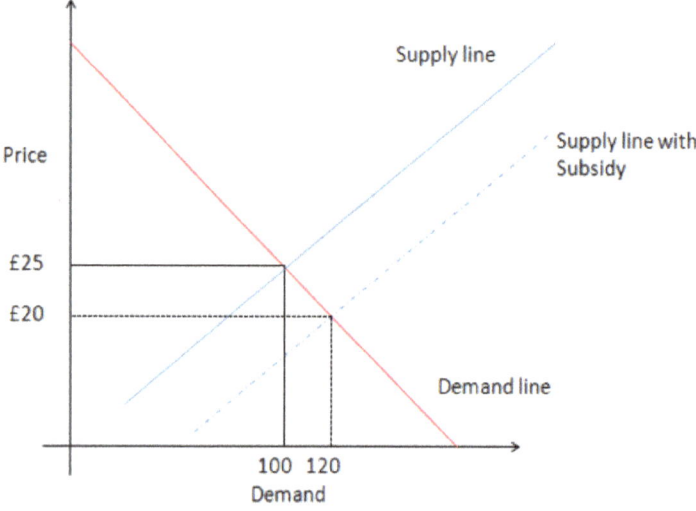

Figure 15-1: Equilibrium with a Fixed Subsidy

If we now introduce a subsidy of £5 per passenger, irrespective of the fare, the supply line shifts downwards and the new clearing point is £20, with 120 seats sold. Using this simplistic analysis, the operator will receive £3,000 (£25 * 120). Of this total, £2,400 is received from passengers (120 * £20) and £600 in subsidies.

An example of this subsidy type is the ferry which operates in the Straits of Messina linking mainland Italy and Sicily.

The fare in 2015 was €5 return for a total of 16km, or €0.31 per km. The operator is only able to offer this fare as a result of subsidies provided by Government. This fare applies to both residents and visitors alike, without discrimination. The Gozo ferry between Malta and the island of Gozo provides an example of a fixed but discriminatory tariff. The one-way fare on this ferry was €4.65 in 2015 for tourists and residents of the island of Malta, whilst residents of Gozo paid €1.15 for the same journey. The difference in fares is met by the Government of Malta.

15.4 Variable/Ad Valorem Subsidies

The picture gets more complicated when we deal with both variable subsidies (or 'ad valorem' subsidies, to give them their formal name) and discrimination between different types of passenger. Flights between mainland Spain and the Balearic and Canary Islands, for example, have variable fares, as we would expect in the airline sector. Therefore, flying between Madrid and Mallorca, for example, is much cheaper in February than in August, when tourist demand is at its peak. Residents of the islands, however, receive a 50% discount on fares and there is no limit on the price of the fare or the frequency with which the passenger chooses to fly. Figure 15-2 shows how this subsidy works.

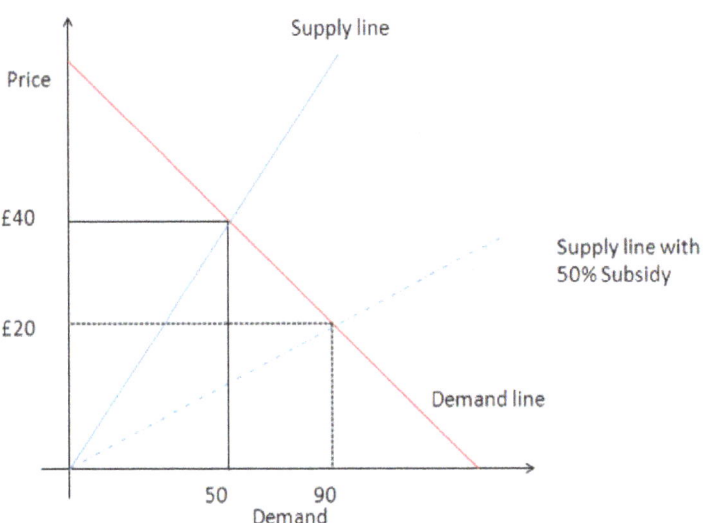

Figure 15-2: Equilibrium with an Ad Valorem Subsidy

In Figure 15-2, we have two equilibrium points, one each for residents and non-residents. The revenue from non-residents in this figure is £2,000 (£40 * 50) whilst for residents, total revenue is £1,800 (£20 * 90).

In Section 5.3, we discussed the price elasticity of demand. In the case of the Gozo ferry, the price difference between residents and non-residents return fares is around €7 (€9.30 and €2.30), so we would expect to see less demand from non-residents due to the higher fare they face.

That said, a return fare of €9.30 is unlikely to be a make-or-break decision in determining whether to make the trip, as the transport cost for this day excursion for tourists is low.

For flights, however, the price differences are of a very different order of magnitude.

In the second half of 2015, the difference in price for a return fare between Madrid and the Canary Islands ranged from €40 to €250 return.

It is important to note that whilst price elasticities may be used with confidence for small percentage or absolute changes in price, what we have in the case of large differences is two separate market segments.

15.5 Cross Subsidy

15.5.1 Time of Year

European holiday routes show levels of high demand in summer months and much lower demand outside the summer peak; routes to Turkish resorts are an extreme example of this problem, as we shall see in Chapter 20.

Although operators can and do adjust prices to try and reduce seasonality (be it month, hour of day or day of week), the fundamental problem remains that, in Northern Europe, people will generally want to take their beach holidays in summer and start weekend trips on Friday.

To give an example of the problem faced by many operators, we can examine easyJet, which divides the year into summer (April to September inclusive) and winter.

In Figure 15-3, we can see a case of cross-subsidy. easyJet has traditionally made all its profits in just six months of the year, although 2014/15 saw its first ever winter profit, of £7 million.

This still means, however, that the airline made 99% of its operating profit in six months of the year.

Figure 15-3: easyJet Annual Profit 2011-2015

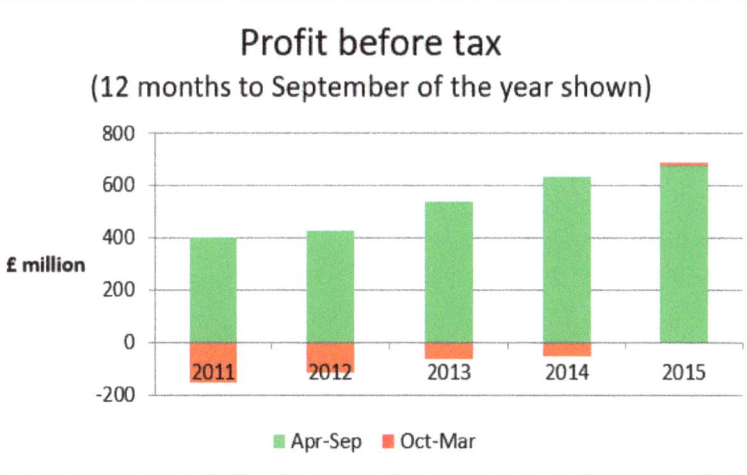

Although many operators are able to shift capacity during off-peak periods (for example, a European airline might lease aircraft to south American carriers in winter, which is their summer, or a cruise company will shift operations from Europe in summer to the Caribbean in winter), this option is not always available.

Commuter-focused rail operators, for example, will keep much of their rolling stock in sidings for much of the day or hotels may close off certain floors to reduce energy and housekeeping bills during quiet periods.

However, debt repayments still have to be made and it is unfeasible in many industries and countries to fire staff in October and rehire them in April.

15.5.2 Subsidies between Short & Long-Haul Routes

The example above shows cross-subsidy by time but cross-subsidy by route is also widespread.

Consider, for example, two routes selected at random from First Great Western's network, shown in Figure 15-4 on the next page.

Figure 15-4: Fares on First Great Western Services, Summer 2015

	Exmouth to Exeter St Davids	Exeter St Davids to London
Distance (miles)	11.3	173.8
Peak single fare (£)	4.50	109.00
Standard off-peak single (£)	4.10	63.00
Super off-peak single	N/A	47.10
pence/mile (peak)	40.0	62.7
pence/mile (off-peak)	36.4	36.3
pence/mile (super off-peak)	N/A	27.1

We would expect, given the much longer distance of Exeter to London, that the price per mile would be lower, but this is not the case; only the cheapest single fare between Exeter and London offers savings per mile over the short route.

There are two principal reasons why an operator would choose to operate in this manner.

First, the operator is obliged to run services on what is probably the loss-making route between Exmouth and Exeter and its pricing strategy is constrained by potential customers being able to use a car for such a relatively short journey (moreover, the average speed of the trains along this line is less than 30 mph).

The prices it charges, therefore, will reflect this; irrespective of how many passengers join the train, the services still need to run.

By contrast, the route between Exeter and London has an average speed in excess of 80 mph and the road corridor with which the train competes (the M4 motorway) is severely congested at many times of day.

So, we can argue that the long-haul route faces less competitive pressures than the short haul one, which allows the operator to charge the higher fares.

Second, there is a network effect to consider.

FGW wishes to encourage people to use the trunk route, which has higher profitability and, to do this, it will suppress fares on the branch line.

It is interesting to note that the operator in this case charges the same prices in many cases from Exmouth to London as from Exeter; in other words, for passengers to London, travel on the connecting service from Exmouth is effectively free.

15.5.3 Pricing Strategies for Different Markets

Long-haul airlines are particularly adept at this type of pricing strategy.

If we examine the route from London to Sydney, a customer is offered a wide array of choices, all of which involve one or more stops.

Airlines will often have one or several hubs, be it Heathrow for British Airways, Paris for Air France, and so on.

For flights to and from the hubs, the main operator will be able to charge a premium reflecting both its dominance of flights at the hub and also the convenience of a non-stop flight.

By contrast, if a passenger is faced with a journey (usually long-haul), which offers an array of one-stop options, there are often significant savings to be made if a passenger's journey flies through a hub rather than to or from hubs.

We will now look at the London-Sydney market in more detail.

The only airlines offering through flights between the two cities are British Airways (hub at Heathrow) and Qantas (hub at Sydney).

If, however, a passenger is willing to change aircraft enroute, the competition multiplies sharply, with Chinese, Middle East and southeast Asian operators becoming viable alternatives.

Emirates, for example, had eight flights per day between London and Dubai during April-October 2015 (out of 15, with four competitors responsible for the remaining seven) and two daily flights between Dubai and Sydney, with a third flight operated by Qantas.

For a passenger whose journey starts or ends in Dubai (Emirates' hub) the fare is significantly higher for passengers than for those who use Dubai as just a transit point.

First, we will examine Dubai-Sydney and London-Sydney. In Figure 15-5, we can see that Emirates is effectively paying a passenger €226 (€1,892 - €2,118) to fly between London and Dubai on the way to Sydney.

Although this pricing policy may seem bizarre at first glance, it is important to bear in mind that Emirates faces much greater competition in the London-Sydney market than it does in the Dubai-Sydney one.

Figure 15-5: Cross-subsidy on Airline Fares

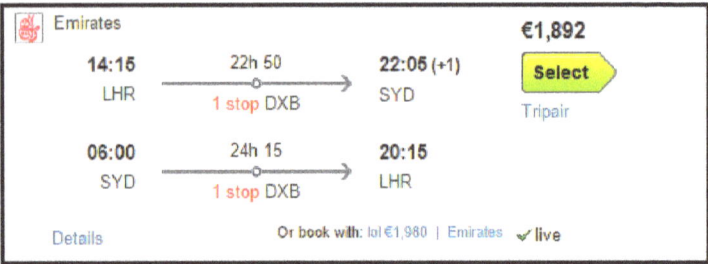

Source: Skyscanner, fares examined on June 27th 2015

Now, we will examine the price on the same flight, on the same day, for a passenger who was travelling between London and Dubai only.

We can see in Figure 15-6 that the fare would be €563.

Figure 15-6: London to Dubai return, September 30th to October 8th 2015

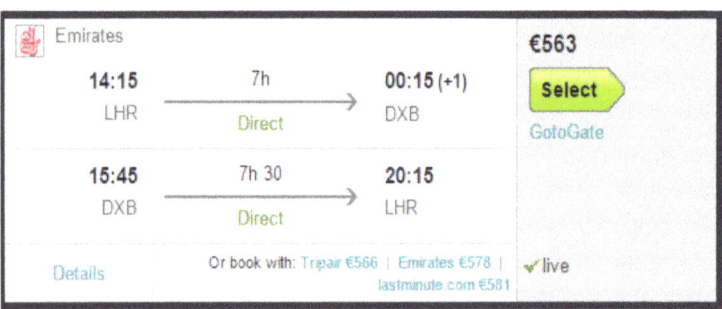

Source: Skyscanner, fares examined on June 27th 2015

Note that in the two figures immediately above, the flights employed are identical.

So Emirates is, in effect, subsidising London-Sydney passengers on the London-Dubai segment of the journey to the tune of €789 (€563 plus €226) by being able to charge higher fares in the London-Dubai and Dubai-Sydney markets, both of which Emirates dominates.

In summary, Figure 15-7 demonstrates how much incentive Emirates is offering London-Sydney passengers to fly via Dubai rather than Singapore, Bangkok, Abu Dhabi and so on.

Figure 15-7: Fares Summary on London-Dubai-Sydney (€)

Route	Economy Return Fare
London-Sydney	1,892
Dubai-Sydney	2,118
London-Dubai	563
London-Dubai-Sydney (bought as separate tickets)	2,681
Through ticket subsidy	789

15.6 Arguments against Subsidies

In Section 15.1, we mentioned some of the reasons for providing subsidies. Here, we shall examine some arguments against them.

15.6.1 Market Distortion

In the case where the fare is an *ad valorem* subsidy, which is payable only to certain market segments, it is likely that fares are higher than in a case where no subsidies are paid.

We can illustrate this best using an example, bringing together the arguments we saw in Figure 15-1 and Figure 15-2.

Let us imagine that the operator charges a single price of £25 between points A and B. Therefore, the revenue is just the fare multiplied by the number of passengers, say 100 passengers per day. The local government then decides that it will subsidise the residents of point A by 50%.

The operator takes this opportunity to raise the unsubsidised fare to £40, knowing that it will be reimbursed £20 per subsidised passenger (i.e. 50% of the new fare). Meanwhile, the demand for travel for passengers from point B will decline, as the fare has increased from £25 to £40. By contrast, those originating in point A see a fare reduction of 20%, from £25 to £20, and so we would expect demand to increase.

We will now make two further assumptions: half of the original 100 passengers lived in point A and half in point B and, for the purposes of this argument, the elasticity of demand, with respect to price, is -0.5. Figure 15-8 shows the changes in revenue derived from passengers when a subsidy is introduced for a segment of the market.

Figure 15-8: Impact of Discriminatory and Subsidized Fares

Segment	Old fare	New Fare	Demand change	New Passenger Numbers	Old Revenue	New Revenue
Living in A (50)	£25	£20	+ 10%	55	£1,250	£1,100
Living in B (50)	£25	£40	- 30%	35	£1,250	£1,400
Subsidy	£0	£20		55	£0	£1,100
Totals				90	£2,500	£3,600

So, we can see from Figure 15-8 that revenue from passengers is unchanged at £2,500. But we also need to bear in mind that the government will give the operator £20 for each trip undertaken by residents of A.

So, in addition to the £2,500 received from passengers, the operator also will receive a further £1,100 (55 passengers, £20 per passenger) in subsidy payments, making total revenue £3,600.

Note that the higher revenue is in spite of a drop in volume, from 100 to 90 passengers.

15.6.2 Who Benefits from Subsidies?

It is generally assumed that subsidies are designed to assist the poorer members of society to reduce their expenditure on the newly subsidized good and thus allow them to use their income elsewhere. Let us again return to Figure 15-8 and assess the benefits and costs of the subsidy. Clearly, the non-residents living in B are worse off, as they either need to pay more for the same journey or they choose not to travel. Those people who are deterred from travelling will presumably either save the money or divert it to other expenditure that will have a less desirable outcome. So, both subgroups living in B incur a loss in welfare.

Superficially, residents of A are better off, because they now enjoy lower air fares than before.

However, in 2014, the subsidies paid come from general taxation and, by way of example, the government of Spain paid out €447 million in residency subsidies to the ferry and air operators[44].

This use of taxation revenue may have produced greater benefits elsewhere; a blanket subsidy with no limit on the number of subsidized goods purchased usually benefits the wealthier members of society who are in a position to buy more of the good in the first place.

Subsidies on fuel are another example of this phenomenon and there is widespread evidence that the main beneficiaries are not those whom the subsidy was intended to help. Fuel subsidies in Indonesia, for example, flowed mainly to the wealthier sections of society[45] these subsidies were abolished in January 2015.

15.6.3 Flat Fares by Distance

A common tariff on many bus and some metro systems in Europe and the USA is a flat fare that is valid for a ride of one stop or twenty.

Although this system has the benefit of being easy to understand and is easier to patrol (nobody can be penalised for riding too far, as the fare is the same for everybody), it also carries certain disadvantages.

You may recall the argument about consumer surplus in Section 5.1. It is reasonable to assume that somebody travelling 5km would be willing to pay more than a passenger travelling, say, 1km. So, with a flat fare, longer distance travellers are being subsidized by short distance trips.

A flat fare of €1.50 may therefore act as a deterrent for travellers wishing to undertake a short hop, whereas those on longer trips are getting very good value for their money. In Britain, up to the 1970s, it was commonplace for bus rides to be charged in stages (a group of stops).

Although this system could be construed as equitable – the farther you travel, the more you pay – the system was not easy to communicate to the travelling public.[46]

---

44 http://www.sepg.pap.minhap.gob.es/Presup/PGE2016Proyecto/MaestroTomos/PGE-ROM/doc/L_16_A_G7.PDF (pages 132 and 140)
45 http://www.iisd.org/gsi/sites/default/files/indonesia_czguide_eng_update_2012.pdf
46 A similar system continues to operate in Lanzarote. The minimum fare is €1.40 for trips outside Arrecife and the maximum fare is €3.60. In between, there are at least 20 price points.

The compromise adopted in most places is a zonal system. So, even by moving to a simple two-zone system (say 'inner' and 'outer'), the transport company extracts more money from longer distance travellers going to the centre whilst also encouraging the generation of shorter trips. Even on a network the size of London's, the average trip length by bus was only 3.5km in 2013/14[47] with the length of most routes being between 10 and 20 km[48].

15.6.4 Fares by Time of Day

Similar considerations apply to the situation in which the fare does not change according to the time of day. As we saw in Section 15.5, much of the cost of providing services is due to the requirement to service peak periods, so a fare that does not vary by time of day implies that off-peak passengers are subsidizing peak period customers. Whilst Transport for London has lower off-peak single fares, for example, the railways and buses in Madrid do not. It is also interesting to note that the policy of fare-recovery differs between the two cities, as shown in Figure 15-9.

Figure 15-9: Comparison of Fares in London and Madrid (2015)

	London Zones 1-5	Madrid A-C2
Single Peak	£4.70	€4.05
Single Off Peak	£3.10	€4.05
Monthly Season	£210.10	€99.30
Ratio Monthly: Single Peak	45	25
Ratio Monthly: Single Off-Peak	68	25

So, in London, at least 45 single journeys during the peak are required before any discount for season tickets comes into force whereas, in Madrid, a season ticket is much greater value for money compared to single fares (the savings kick in after 25 single trips). There is evidence of a clear difference in policy between the two cities regarding how much commuters should be subsidised by customers who travel less regularly. However, it is worth bearing in mind that more regular users of transport, especially rail, are generally among the better-off members of society.[49]

---

47 https://tfl.gov.uk/cdn/static/cms/documents/travel-in-london-report-7.pdf
48 http://www.londonbusroutes.net/details.htm
49 See, for example, http://content.tfl.gov.uk/london-travel-demand-survey-report.pdf

15.7 Chapter 15 Exercise

A bus company currently operates a flat fare system of €2 per trip. With 4 million passengers per annum, revenues are €8 million and operating costs are €9 million. The local authority currently pays the operator €1 million per annum to cover the gap between these two figures.

The operator is interested to see if demand for shorter distance services can be increased and the local authority would also like to see longer distance passengers pay more of the fair cost of operations (and hence reduce subsidies).

The company has assessed the distance that its passengers travel and has also undertaken extensive survey work on current passengers as well as members of the public who do not use the service. The results of the analysis of distance travelled as well as the elasticity of demand for each group are shown in the following table.

Miles	Passengers	Old Fare	New Fare	Elasticity
0-1	400,000	2.00	1.50	-0.7
1-2	900,000	2.00	2.00	-0.5
2-3	1,600,000	2.00	2.00	-0.3
3-4	600,000	2.00	2.50	-0.3
4-5	300,000	2.00	2.50	-0.2
5+	200,000	2.00	3.00	-0.2
	4,000,000			

- You will notice that the elasticity of demand differs significantly by the length of the journey travelled. Why do you consider this to be so?
- Using the information given, provide the expected passenger volumes and the new fares.
- Do you consider this to be a fair solution to the welfare of the people served by the bus company or not? Give your reasons, referring to the new levels of demand, revenue and subsidy.

The operator has also decided to test a lower set of fares, based on the data provided on the following page.

Miles	Passengers	Old Fare	New Fare	Elasticity
0-1	400,000	2.00	1.20	-0.7
1-2	900,000	2.00	1.50	-0.5
2-3	1,600,000	2.00	2.00	-0.3
3-4	600,000	2.00	2.00	-0.3
4-5	300,000	2.00	2.50	-0.2
5+	200,000	2.00	2.50	-0.2
	4,000,000			

- Follow steps 2 and 3 from before and calculate the volumes and revenue from this lower set of fares.

- What are the benefits and unbeneficial elements of this lower fare structure compared with both the flat fare and the previous set of proposed new fares?

16 PRINCIPLES OF MARKETING I

16.1 Introduction

If you were to board any train outside rush hour, where the majority of passengers have the sole objective of getting to work or back, and asked ten people selected at random for interview to discuss their journeys, you would most likely get several different answers.

For example, those on business trips would have different expectations of the railway from an older couple who are off for a few days to see relatives and the business traveller would probably have paid a different (higher) fare.

Clearly, it is impossible to subject all passengers to on-board interviews in this way and so, to get a better understanding of the customer base, we need to divide them into groups.

One of the major objectives of this segmentation process is to determine what these groups are willing to pay, as we discussed in Section 5.1.

In this Chapter, we will start with a brief overview of consumer behaviour, focussing on how a purchasing decision is made.

The focus is clearly on purchases with a 'significant' monetary value, as buying a bus ticket for £2 or €2 does not require too much research or thought!

By contrast, a family that budgets £3,000 or more for a family of four to take long-haul flights will take the decision more seriously and carefully.

We will then have a look at the two techniques known as stated and revealed preference, techniques used to determine how people say they would choose a product and how, actually, they did.

The Chapter will then look at what may seem an obvious question: "What is a product?"

Defining what goes into a product or service, however, is vital for determining in what market a business operates in fact.

16.2 Consumer Behaviour

16.2.1 Dynamics of Consumer Behaviour

In this Section, we provide a brief overview of consumer behaviour. Classic economic theory dictates that decisions are based on an assessment of price, supply and demand. The reality, however, is rather more complex than this. Figure 16-1 provides a high-level summary diagram, which explains the dynamics of customer purchase decisions.

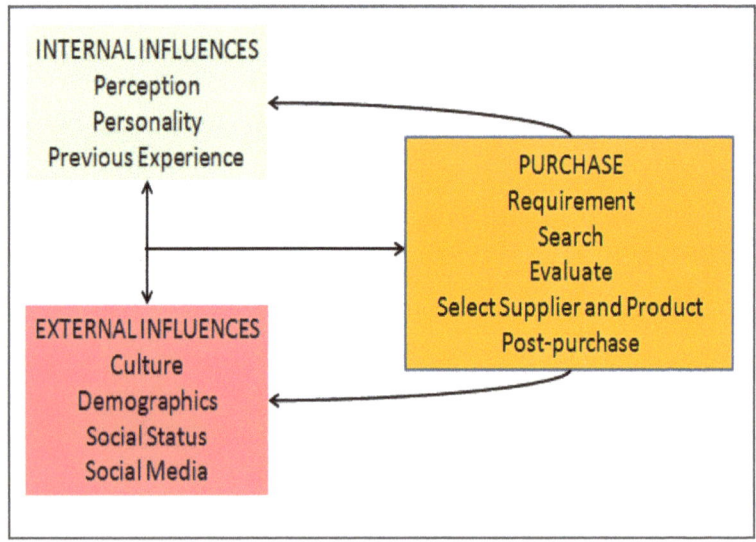

Figure 16-1: Overview of Consumer Behaviour Influences

We shall go through the main elements of the diagram above, which will demonstrate the importance of 'knowing your customer'.

For many users of public transport, however, irrespective of mode, there is often little choice but to use the monopoly provider; this applies to commuter services more than other journey purposes.

Most transportation is in effect derived demand: it is not a good or service desirable in itself but is a means to an end (cruises are the obvious exception).

For many people, therefore, transport can be considered a tax rather than the exchange of money for goods or services for which the consumer receives benefits.

16.2.2 Culture, Demographics, Social Status

We can group these external influences together because, ostensibly, they are 'pre-programmed' and beyond the control of the consumer.

A simple example of cultural difference is evidenced by the way McDonalds varies its product range by country to take account of local tastes and customs, such as using halal meat in Muslim countries, a McFalafel in Egypt, the lack of beef products sold in India and so on.

Subcultures include dimensions such as age and gender. Marketers have recognised for a long time that different features of a car, for example, would appeal more to males than females and vice versa.

Similarly, a Twitter campaign is more likely to generate sales among people in their twenties than those in their seventies.

Social status is correlated with income so a price-based product and promotional strategy is more likely to succeed with lower income households whereas a campaign and product with more focus on quality and product features has a higher probability of success with households with a higher disposable income.

One of the challenges faced by terrestrial public transport, particularly bus operators, is that public transport is perceived by many people as a 'method of last resort' but this perception will vary from region to region.

These perceptions can also be changed, as the bus operator in Reykjavik managed to do.[50]

16.2.3 Influencers

Traditional influencers include friends and family members to whom a potential consumer may turn for advice before purchasing a product. To a significant extent, however, newer influencers have come to dominate.

TripAdvisor, Facebook and Twitter have supplemented a small number of family members and friends as influencers with a much larger quantity of strangers.

Ryanair's "Getting Better" programme was launched in 2014 after a series of profit warnings and reduced loads on its flights.

50 http://www.trapezegroup.co.uk/case_study/straeto-reykjavik

The perception of poor quality service and strict adherence to petty rules was driven by word being spread on social networks and review sites as well as more traditional channels such as newspapers.

There seem to be many smaller businesses, which are unaware just how much damage can be done from a series of poor reviews, whether these reviews were justified or not.

A railway example worthy of mention is the website "First Crapital Connect"[51] that, as the name implies, was most uncomplimentary about the rail service offered by First Group between Bedford and Brighton in England.

However scurrilous and inaccurate the allegations on this website may have been, the website was clearly unwelcome publicity for First Group, who ran the service up from 2006 until 2014.

16.2.4 Internal Influencers

As well as being influenced by outsiders (see the previous paragraph), people will develop their own perceptions based on their experience of the product or service.

Discretionary travellers or those in competitive markets may foreswear an certain operator after a poor experience, whereas others will build up a series of positive experiences and become 'brand ambassadors' for the transport service or terminal operator (and thus become an influencer).

16.2.5 Purchase Decision

The purchase decision has five main stages as shown in Figure 16-1. The stage in which influencers play a key role is 'evaluation'. Let us assume that part of the evaluation for a consumer buying a ticket is the likelihood of delay.

There are essentially two ways in which we can evaluate punctuality: a quantitative method (examining each airline's punctuality performance) and qualitative (how well each airline copes with complaints and attempts to recover the service). The website "flightontime.info" is one of the early such results from Google using the search term 'airline punctuality' and the results for the first six months of 2015 are shown in Figure 16-2.

51 At the time of writing, the site was still available at http://www.firstcrapitalconnect.co.uk/

Figure 16-2: Punctuality between London and New York

2015 (Jan-Jun)

Rank	Airline	Operating airports LHR LGW LCY STN LTN	Operating months J F M A M J J A S O N D	Average delay (mins)	Operated within 15 mins (%)	Over 1 hour late (%)	Over 3 hours late (%)	Total flights analysed
1	Delta Air Lines	●	● ● ● ● ● ●	12.31	82.80	5.05	1.24	1,209
2	Virgin Atlantic Airways	●	● ● ● ● ● ●	13.37	78.54	5.62	0.96	2,083
3	British Airways	● ●	● ● ● ● ● ●	13.94	78.75	4.88	0.98	4,198
4	American Airlines	●	● ● ● ● ● ●	16.00	77.01	6.80	1.63	1,044
5	United Airlines	●	● ● ● ● ● ●	16.30	79.45	7.60	1.44	1,737
6	Kuwait Airways	●	● ● ● ● ● ●	29.83	56.86	14.38	2.61	153
7	Norwegian Air Shuttle	●	● ● ● ● ● ●	30.51	59.90	15.46	3.38	207
	ROUTE AVERAGE			14.78	78.43	6.02	1.21	10,631

Looking at these figures, there appears to be a significant difference in performance between the top 5 and bottom 2 airlines when looking at average delay and the likelihood of a flight incurring a delay of more than one hour.

To undertake a qualitative evaluation, potential customers have plenty of choice.

There is received wisdom that customers are more likely to share a bad experience on social media than a good one, so many companies are now much more proactive regarding response to customer complaints and recovering the service, for example by offering monetary compensation or discounts on future purchases.

16.2.6 Revealed & Stated Preference Techniques

In a sense, an examination of how demand has changed with the introduction of a new service or terminal/station can be termed 'revealed preference'.

If, say, a new station has generated passenger flows and the line on which the new station lies has shown an increase in volume of 5% whilst lines in the control group (lines with similar characteristics that have not had a new station) have shown a lower increase or a decline, we may infer from the data conclusions about how people's travel patterns have changed due to the new station.

Alternatively, or in addition to revealed preference, we can ask people what they would do under certain circumstances.

For example, if a new light rail line is going to be built parallel to an existing bus service (journey time 30 minutes, £3 single fare), we can develop a list of options to which people can respond, such as:

- 20-minute journey time, £4;
- 20-minute journey time, £4.50; or
- 20-minute journey time, £5.

Similar questions could be asked about the frequency of the new light rail service in order to determine what fare we could charge and how frequently the service would need to run to attract the necessary demand.

Of course, there is a danger with surveys that people will say one thing to a pollster and then act quite differently in reality. Therefore, as a tool, stated preference should not be used in isolation of other demand forecasting techniques.

16.2.7 "In the factory we make cosmetics. In the drugstore we sell hope."

This classic marketing saying comes from Charles Revson, who founded the Revlon perfume brand. Put simply, although a transport operator is in the business of selling seats between two points on a network, this is quite different from what the customer wants, which is to get from one point to another on his or her personal network (home, office, friends, holiday destination, etc.) as quickly and as comfortably as possible at a price the customer is willing to pay. However, these two 'products' do not always coincide. In the following Section, we examine ways in which customers' requirements and the service offered can be brought more into line with each other.

16.3 Core and Augmented Product

16.3.1 Core Product

The core product for most transport operators is the sale of trips between two points. On airline routes, especially those facing competition, there is very little, if any, difference in the core product offered by individual airlines – journey time, seat pitch (distance between one row of seats and the next) and width are all very similar on short haul. Other modes, including ferry, train and bus, can sometimes offer different journey times by using higher speed vehicles (ferry) or limited stop/express services (rail, bus).

16.3.2 Features are a Competitive Battleground

For many people and journeys, the journey itself is just a small part of the process, especially for longer distance travel. The augmented product includes many other features such as:

- Reservation and ticket purchase;
- Procedures prior to the journey;
- Baggage allowance;
- On board catering; and
- Helpfulness and friendliness of the staff.

We will examine each of these in turn and use examples to illustrate how the augmented product can be used to segment the market as well as to develop competitive advantage.

16.3.3 Reservation and Ticket Purchase

The processes of buying and reserving a ticket are those areas that have seen the greatest changes in the 21st Century, thanks mainly to advances in technology and the internet. The airline industry has gone farthest along this route, so we will focus on air travel to illustrate the changes:

- *Seeking*. Price comparison websites allow customers to choose from a range of options, including desired departure date and time, non-stop flights or one-stop flights (the latter are usually cheaper, reflecting the inconvenience and longer journey time). One point to highlight is that the seeking stage of the reservation process is often beyond the control of carriers, as Skyscanner, Expedia and so on are not owned by the airlines;

- *Booking*. Carriers in competitive markets have invested heavily in their websites and online booking is now the overwhelming choice, in the UK at least, for booking flights and holidays. In 2014, Ryanair, for example, completed a major overhaul of its website to facilitate the ease of booking flights on its site; it competitors are likely, in due course, to try and improve their booking experiences to the benefit of consumers; and

- *Tickets/boarding passes.* With a few exceptions, mobile boarding passes are available for use on low cost carriers (LCCs) in Europe and their use is growing on full service airlines such as British Airways.

16.3.4 Features at the Terminal

For passengers without luggage, the need for checking in has been eliminated.

However, even though many airlines now require their passengers to check in online, the time required to drop bags once they arrive at the airport is not materially different from old-fashioned check-in.

Figure 16-3 illustrates the congestion at check-in at Lanzarote airport. Although the airport authority (AENA) spent significant amounts of money in 2015 reconfiguring the duty-free shopping area so that all passengers had to pass through the shop between security (also improved) and the departures area, investment in the check-in part of the journey process has been zero to date.

Moreover, as Lanzarote is principally a holiday and leisure route, most customers are likely to need to check in baggage.

Figure 16-3: Lanzarote Airport Check-In, January 2016

Source: Author

Whilst LCCs have generally led the way in improving the booking and reservation experience, it is the full-service airlines, in Europe at least, that have worked most to reduce check-in and baggage drop queues. By substituting machines for baggage drop desks, passengers can print out their own luggage labels and this technology significantly reduces the waiting time necessary before proceeding to security[52].

16.4 Product Augmented by Geography

16.4.1 Bringing the Core Product Closer to Home

The product augmented by geography applies to transport more than most other sectors.

If, for example, you wish to send a package by private courier, the package will often be picked up from your home or office and be delivered to your final destination.

Although the transportation of people can never be quite as painless, there are many examples of operators adding value to their core product by extending the reach of their service from terminal to terminal.

In essence, geographic augmentation comes in various forms of integration. Destination integration is the most straightforward, namely that the public transport network should serve places that people want to go.

This may seem self-evident, yet in Spain, for example, there are several instances in which the urban network does not pass key attractions such as markets, law courts, shopping streets or hospitals.

Schedule integration occurs when the arrival of one mode is timed to meet the departure of another. This form of integration works well when frequencies are low, since it is unnecessary when a bus or train departs, say, every five minutes.

The third and most complex form of integration concerns tariffs. Although integrated tariffs and tickets are available in most large European cities, these are by no means as widespread in areas with less dense populations.

Next are several examples of how this works.

---

52 *The author has flown twice recently with Ryanair from Edinburgh. In both cases, the total check-in process time was under 3 minutes using self-service check-in technology.*

16.4.2 Getting to the Port

Fred Olsen Express (FO) is one of the two large ferry operators in the Canary Islands. On Gran Canaria, it uses the port of Agaete, which is quite distant from the capital of Las Palmas.

Similarly, on Tenerife, many ferries run from Los Cristianos, on the southern coast of the island, whilst the capital, Santa Cruz, is in the north.

To improve connectivity of its services, FO runs free buses between the capital cities and the ports on each island for foot passengers.

In both cases, therefore, it can be argued that FO's network is city to city rather than port to port and is a good example of schedule integration.

16.4.3 Integration between Modes 1

In the UK, both rail and bus are usually operated by private sector companies but tariff integration is manageable in such situations.

The Plusbus[53] add-on to rail tickets covers most companies and routes operating in an urban area and provides a significant discount to bus tickets purchased from an individual bus operator.

16.4.4 Integration between Modes 2

In Switzerland, passengers taking a flight with a member of the Lufthansa Group (including Lufthansa and SWISS) can check in baggage and receive boarding cards at over 50 railway stations throughout Switzerland.

This level of integration not only relieves passengers of having to haul luggage on and off trains but provides a more seamless journey overall.

For passengers living in Basel flying to or from Zurich airport, a free train ticket between Basel and the airport is included in the price for holders of a SWISS airline ticket.

Passengers using the train need only provide a boarding pass for the flight with a barcode included.

---

[53] http://plusbus.info/

16.4.5 An Example of Poor Integration

A contrasting example is the Alicante Tram network.

This tram system connects Alicante (population of 250,000) with Denia at the northern end of the Costa Blanca via Benidorm, Europe's largest tourist resort.

At the time of writing (December 2015), the tram and bus networks along the route were run completely independently, with little accessible information on switching between modes, let alone any sort of tariff integration.

Benidorm merits a mention for its lack of integration between modes.

A new bus station opened at the edge of the city in 2007, replacing the somewhat cramped and run-down facility within the city centre. The station is mainly used by longer distance buses but is also used by certain local services.

A picture of the station is shown in Figure 16-4.

Figure 16-4: Benidorm Bus Station

Source: https://www.openstreetmap.org/relation/341148#map 17/38.54986/-0.12340

The Alicante tram railway line, the black line, runs just to the south of this new bus station (marked by 'Mercadona' on the above map) and the walking distance to the centre of the bus station is no more than 200 metres. However, there is no tram stop anywhere near the bus station and anybody wishing to change from tram to bus or vice versa will need to take a taxi to connect between the two.

16.5 Difficulties in Defining the Market

In Chapter 6, we examined market shares for various transport operators. But in what actual market do firms operate? A transport journey has many dimensions that affect a purchase decision, including:

- Price;
- Frequency;
- Accessibility;
- Journey time; and
- Level of amenities.

Very often, there will be a trade-off in these factors, leading to a consumer selecting one mode or company over another, that companies can determine using the stated preference techniques discussed earlier in this Chapter. If we look back at the Madrid-Barcelona corridor discussed in Chapter 6, we stated that coach was not really a competitor for other modes. Let us now look at the two dimensions of price and journey-time to demonstrate this and we will examine single fares from Madrid to Barcelona, which were available for September 1st, 2015. The results of the trade-off are displayed in Figure 16-5.

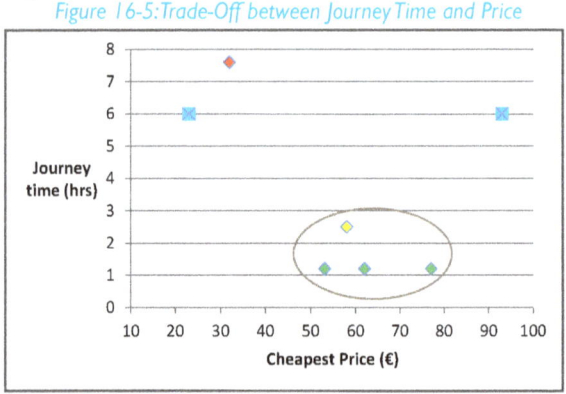

Figure 16-5: Trade-Off between Journey Time and Price

Sources: RENFE (rail), ALSA (bus), Skyscanner (air) Fares

In Figure 16-5, the red point represents the coach service. This service is clearly the cheapest public transport option, but is also the slowest. The rail service, depicted with the yellow point, is evidently much more in competition with air services (green) than coach. Perhaps rather more controversially, we also include car (blue points) in the assessment of the market. The price by car depends on three factors:

- Type of car and its fuel consumption;
- The number of people travelling; and
- The perception of "cost".

This last point is similar to the Leeds-Manchester example presented in Figure 6-2. At the lowest level, the perceived cost of the journey only includes fuel, calculated at €23 per person for two people travelling together. At the other extreme, the cost per kilometre of a car, including wear and tear and depreciation as well as fuel, is around 30 cents per kilometre[54].

On this basis, the cost per person is over €90 for the journey.

However, we are not comparing like with like. If you recall our discussion on GJT in Section 5.2, we need to adjust journey times to take account of access and egress from the terminal, be it a bus station, railway station or airport. In the example shown in Figure 16-6, we have added two hours to air journey times and 90 minutes for rail and coach times. We should ideally also add on the costs of access and egress (for public transport modes) and parking (if appropriate, for car) but we will ignore these adjustments.

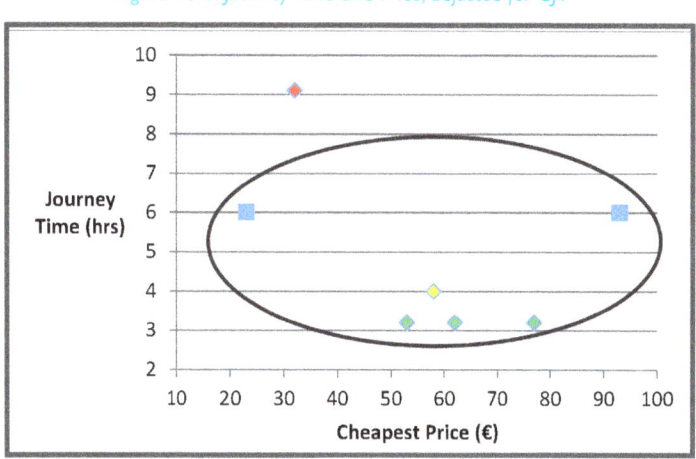

Figure 16-6: Journey Time and Price, adjusted for GJT

54 http://revista.dgt.es/es/noticias/2014/12DICIEMBRE/1201Precio-medio-del-kilometraje.shtml#.VbS-N_lWiko

The journey time gap between air, rail and car has now narrowed considerably and we can now see that, depending on the perception of car costs, the car can be a significant competitor to air and rail in this corridor whilst bus travel is still unlikely to be considered in the same market space as the other modes.

16.6 Chapter 16 Exercise

You are considering setting up a bus service between two cities 200km apart.

The service will run hourly and run between the bus stations in the two cities.

The coaches you intend to purchase or lease have toilets on-board and so no "rest stop" will be required.

No other bus service currently serves the route.

The expected journey time between the two termini is two hours and 15 minutes, although traffic congestion at certain times of day could increase this journey time to three hours.

The journey by car is a little under 2 hours but, again, traffic congestion could increase this.

There is an existing rail service, also hourly, which takes between 1 hour 45 minutes and two hours.

The trains run with two to three intermediate stops, although a few journeys at peak times are non-stop between the two cities.

- How will you assess demand for the coach service?

- What product and service will you be offering to potential customers?

17 PRINCIPLES OF MARKETING II

17.1 Overview of this Chapter

If you look at the marketing Section of any bookshop (physical or virtual), you will see books available with a wide range of marketing topics: services marketing, distribution, advertising, public relations and so on.

Only if you look very carefully, might you spot the occasional text whose prime focus is on pricing. This seems to be a strange omission, as implementation of pricing strategy is crucial to the financial health of any business. In this Chapter, we will examine some important principles of pricing and apply some of the theory of pricing that we first encountered in Section 5.1.

17.2 Overall Pricing Strategy by Mode

17.2.1 Airline Pricing

It is useful to compare pricing strategies between low cost airlines, coaches, hotels and railways. For airlines, say, a traveller will only be offered one price for standard/economy class at the time of booking between airports A and B. As the date of departure draws closer, the price usually increases, but the customer is still faced with the 'take it or leave it' approach at the time of booking of one price for each bundle of products and services. Figure 17-1 illustrates this simple choice for a one-way fare in September 2015.

Figure 17-1: Pricing Structure on Ryanair

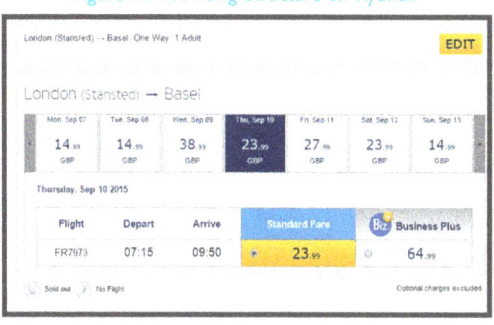

Note: enquiry undertaken on June 29th, 2015 on www.ryanair.com

Car rental companies provide a similar simple pricing structure, with the obvious difference that more expensive cars have higher rental rates.

17.2.2 Hotel Pricing

Many hotels now offer two prices for a stay. There is an advance booking option, which does not allow any changes to the reservation and a more flexible (i.e. higher) rate, which permits late cancellation and amendments to the booking at no extra cost. Figure 17-2 shows this dual pricing system for a room.

Figure 17-2: Cost of One Night in Leeds, UK

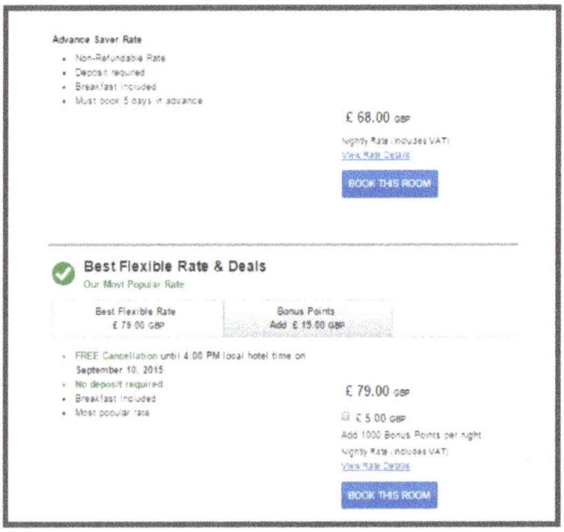

Note: enquiry undertaken on June 29th, 2015 on www.hiexpress.com

The difference between the two rates – £11 – is, in effect, an insurance premium, allowing the customer to cancel up until 1600hrs on the day of arrival. The lower tariff is also unavailable for late bookings, as it is only available up to 5 days before arrival.

17.2.3 Rail Pricing

Rail fares, by contrast, are considered confusing by many people. If we look at Figure 17-3 below, we can see that:

- Two train-specific single fares for this enquiry are much cheaper than a standard return;
- Two first class singles are slightly cheaper than a standard return; and

- The 'anytime' standard return (not shown) is twelve times the price of two 'cheap' singles.

Furthermore, rail as a mode is unique in that it is sometimes cheaper to buy two shorter tickets (A to B, then B to C) than a one longer ticket (A to C).

This anomaly has been publicised in the mainstream press and television news reports[55] .

Figure 17-3: Rail Fares between Manchester and London

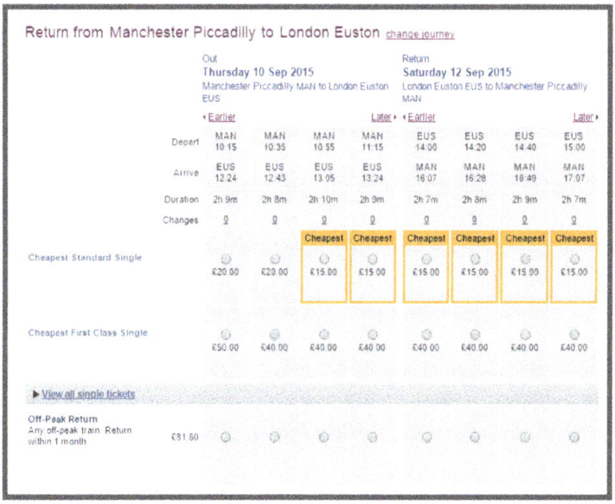

Return from Manchester Piccadilly to London Euston change journey

		Out: Thursday 10 Sep 2015, Manchester Piccadilly MAN to London Euston EUS				Return: Saturday 12 Sep 2015, London Euston EUS to Manchester Piccadilly MAN			
		‹ Earlier			Later ›	‹ Earlier			Later ›
	Depart	MAN 10:15	MAN 10:35	MAN 10:55	MAN 11:15	EUS 14:00	EUS 14:20	EUS 14:40	EUS 15:00
	Arrive	EUS 12:24	EUS 12:43	EUS 13:05	EUS 13:24	MAN 16:07	MAN 16:28	MAN 16:49	MAN 17:07
	Duration	2h 9m	2h 8m	2h 10m	2h 9m	2h 7m	2h 8m	2h 9m	2h 7m
	Changes	0	0	0	0	0	0	0	0
Cheapest Standard Single		£20.00	£20.00	Cheapest £15.00	Cheapest £15.00	Cheapest £15.00	Cheapest £15.00	Cheapest £15.00	Cheapest £15.00
Cheapest First Class Single		£50.00	£40.00	£40.00	£40.00	£40.00	£40.00	£40.00	£40.00
▶ View all single tickets									
Off-Peak Return Any off-peak train. Return within 1 month	£81.60								

Note: enquiry undertaken on June 29th, 2015 on www.qjump.co.uk

Figure 17-3 demonstrates the anomaly that if a passenger nominates an individual train for each leg of the journey, the return fare will be £30 or £35.

By contrast, introducing any flexibility into the purchasing decision would require a passenger either to book a fare more than twice as expensive – the off-peak return, at £81.60 – or else book more than one single ticket each way and let the unused ticket go to waste.

To ensure the reader that confusion on rail prices is not limited to Britain, let us consider the example below from RENFE, Spain's main railway operator.

Figure 17-4 shows four to five fares for each class (Tourist, Tourist Plus and Business) on a single screen.

Please note that this figure shows the fares for just one train in one direction.

55 See for example http://news.sky.com/story/1082173/rail-fares-call-for-action-on-anomalies

Figure 17-4: Rail Fares between Valencia and Madrid

Note: enquiry undertaken on June 29th, 2015 on www.renfe.com

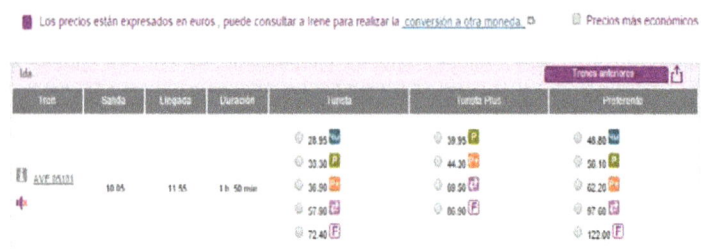

The second tourist fare from the bottom is for €57.90.

This fare claims to be a return fare (by hovering on the purple icon next to the fare) but it is still necessary to select a fare for the return train.

The number of fares shown can be reduced by ticking the 'precios más económicos' (cheapest prices) shown in the figure. The results are shown in Figure 17-5.

Figure 17-5: Valencia-Madrid Fares - Cheapest Fares

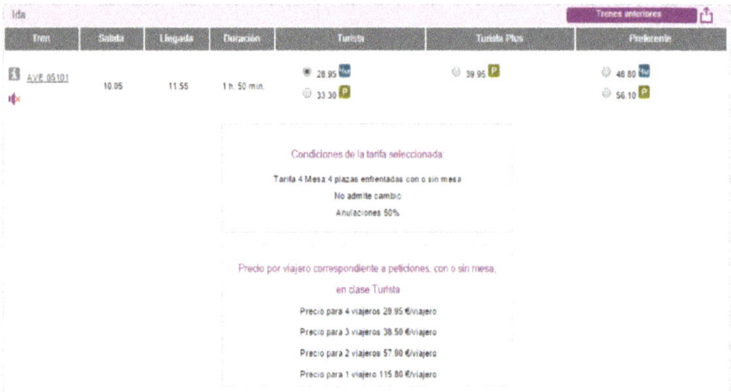

At first glance, the cheapest fare appears to be for a seat in a block of four (two seats facing forwards opposite two seats facing backwards).

The enquiry was for one person only, however and the cheapest fare is only available if four passengers are booking together.

It is not therefore apparent why the cheap fare of €28.95 each way was offered in the first place!

So, in practice, the cheapest fare is around €33 each way for an individual traveller.

17.3 Pricing and Market Segmentation

17.3.1 Introduction

We saw in Section 5.1 that being able to offer an identical product into different markets at variable prices was a key factor to developing a viable transport service.

However, as we also saw in that Section, there is a trade-off between developing a system that extracts as much consumer surplus as possible and having an over-complicated tariff system that attempts to target too many segments. In this Section, we will examine traditional segmentation methods and then those which are based on lifestyle. It is important to bear in mind that whilst product segments will usually face the same price, for services they can and do vary rather more than for products.

17.3.2 Traditional Segmentation Methods

For our purposes, we can consider highlighting the three following segments:

- Wealth/disposable income;
- Journey purpose; and
- Group size.

17.3.3 Wealth/disposable income

Wealth and disposable income are important to segmenting the transport market in two ways:

- How much a person is willing to pay for a journey; and
- How many journeys people will make per annum.

Willingness to pay per journey exhibits itself through the class system on both airlines and railways.

However, whilst railways in Britain effectively reduced travel to two classes in the late 19th century and have retained a binary choice since, airlines have moved in the opposite direction. Many full-service airlines offer (in declining price order) first, business, premium economy, economy with extra legroom and standard economy.

The number of trips a person makes per annum is also a function of disposable income[56].

---

[56] See for example http://www.masterintelligence.com/content/intelligence/en/research/reports/2014/the-future-of-outbound-travel-in-asia-pacific.html

For trip frequency, however, operators require different and more complicated measures.

Ideally, we would categorise customers according to their lifetime value (we will explore this concept in Section 18.4) but at the very least it is feasible to segment customers by their previous expenditure with the company.

For example, Lufthansa has four levels to its loyalty program: Standard, Frequent Traveller (35,000 miles per annum), Senator (100,000) and HON Circle (600,000).

As we can see, the requirements to attain the next level become more onerous but the rewards for loyalty become more valuable at each level. For franchised railways in Great Britain, however, lifetime value is a singularly difficult concept, as a franchise period usually lasts under 10 years and there is no guarantee of a franchise being renewed at the end of a franchise period.

However, 'legacy' railways, which dominate national operations have not developed loyalty programs to the same extent as airlines.

Deutsche Bahn offers rewards in exchange for points accumulated (hence similar to the many air miles' products offered by airlines) whilst there is no mention on RENFE's website in Spain of any offers in exchange for customer loyalty.

17.3.4 Lifestyle Segmentation

The Experian Mosaic system of segmentation divides the population into 15 'Level 1' and 69 'Level 2' categories.

The system is available for at least 20 countries other than the UK. The best way to explain how this system works is by example.

Category E is labelled 'Middle income families living in moderate suburban semis' and consists of the following 'Level 2' divisions:

- Comfortably off suburban families weakly tied to their local community;
- Industrial workers living comfortably in owner occupied semis;
- Self-reliant older families in suburban semis in industrial towns;
- Upwardly mobile South Asian families living in inter war suburbs; and
- Middle-aged families living in less fashionable inter war suburban semis.

Each of these 'Level 2' categories is then classified against a list of 150 criteria.

Aside from age and gender, the classification list includes household income, views on the health service, use of drugs and alcohol and, from a transport viewpoint, how each category is likely to travel to work, likely levels of car ownership and what mode of transport is likely to have been used on their last holiday.

Nottingham city council in the UK uses this system and identifies the number of household by category in each part of the city[57].

Therefore, bus and rail operators can identify the type of households living within the catchment area for specific bus routes and railway services (actual or proposed).

17.3.5 Trade-off between Segmentation & Efficiency

There is, however, a trade-off between developing sophisticated market segments and then applying this knowledge to transport demand and willingness to pay.

Let us take as an example as rail operator which has identified 20 flows (to and from its main hub and non-hub traffic) and the operator classifies people by class of travel (first or standard) and four ticket types (full, reduced, advanced purchase and commuter), which represent different lifestyles.

So, at this stage we have 160 segments.

There are two alternative solutions to assessing future demand for these segments:

- A detailed assessment of each, which would be extremely costly and time-consuming; or

- A mechanistic approach, which uses a set of 'off the peg' values (we will discuss the Passenger Demand Forecasting Handbook used by Britain's rail industry in Section 19.8)

---

[57] http://geoserver.nottinghamcity.gov.uk/live/mosaic-mapping

17.4 Segmentation Barriers

17.4.1 Overview of Barriers

One of the objectives of barriers is to develop the ability to charge different prices for different market segments.

In this section we will deal with three types of barrier:

- Time of purchase;
- Location of purchase; and
- Quantity of purchase.

17.4.2 Time of Purchase – Elapsed Time

The amount of time between when the customer purchases a good and its eventual use is a classic means of segmenting the market.

Figure 17-6 provides a snapshot of prices for various modes and, for comparison, a similar exercise for car rental and a hotel.

Figure 17-6: Sample of Prices Based on Time before Purchase

	3 months in advance (September 25th)	3 days in advance (July 3rd)
Ryanair one way, Dublin to Stansted	€37-€65	€65-€112
Binter Canarias one way, Gran Canaria to Tenerife	€32-€63	€63
Return rail fare, Manchester to London, departing early Friday afternoon, returning Saturday morning	£81.60	£75.80
National Express Cambridge-London, return as above	£14	£14
Fred Olsen Express ferry one way, Gran Canaria to Tenerife	€38	€40
Europcar, Birmingham Airport, small car, 24 hours	£40.19	£32.50
Travelodge, Farringdon, London	£80-£99	£99

Note: all inquiries were undertaken on June 10th, 2015

What is quickly apparent from Figure 17-6 is that some industry sectors are more adept at what is known as yield management than others to the point that for the hotel and car hire, it was actually cheaper to make a business-type booking (i.e. with little advance notice) than a more leisure-oriented reservation.

17.4.3 Last-Minute Bookings

One of the fallacies perpetuated by many transport operators is that it is always cheaper to book as far in advance as possible.

Operators not only gain the benefit of being able to assess demand for a specific flight or train journey longer in advance but bookings far ahead of travel also improve the company's cash flow.

However, recall from Section 12.3 that, for many transport operations, marginal costs are very low and so the operator faces a significant conundrum when faced with empty seats on the train or aircraft:

- Sell off last-minute seats cheaply. The operator will gain revenue from doing this, as once a seat leaves empty, there is no way to recoup the lost revenue. However;

- If an operator engages in this practice on a regular basis, potential customers will get wise to this strategy and will risk not booking in advance in order to pick up a cheap last-minute booking.

There is no 'one size fits all' solution to this quandary.

Lastminute.com provides an example of how hotels seek to protect the reputation of their brands through the 'Top Secret Hotel' concept. Such hotels will significantly discount late bookings but the identity of the hotel is unknown until the booking has been made and paid for.

Figure 17-7: Screenshot from Lastminute.com

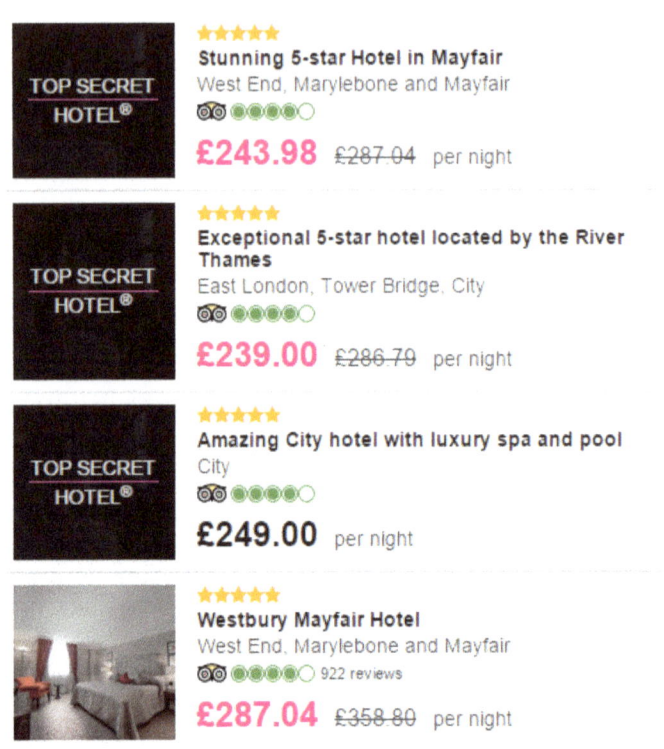

In Figure 17-7 above, we observe that all the luxury hotels listed, bar one, have elected to hide their identities. The inquiry was made for the following evening at approximately 1800hrs on June 30th 2015 for a stay a couple of days later.

17.5 Failure to Capture Markets

From an economic viewpoint, one of the more unorthodox types of segmentation is to do with time away from home. Indeed, the airline sector used to prevent cheaper fares being used by business travellers by insisting on a Saturday night being included in the period.

However, this restriction has largely disappeared now, mainly thanks to the arrival of low cost airlines whose business models are based on single fares. National Express UK (coaches) also operates on a single fares model.

To illustrate the anomaly, let us take examples of two 'off-peak' travellers but serving quite different markets. Person A wishes to travel from Guildford to Waterloo (a flow selected at random) on a Friday morning after the peak to go shopping in the West End and return at the height of the evening peak. This person can acquire a day return ticket which will cost £18. Person B, by contrast, wishes to travel from Guilford on Friday evening, stay overnight with friends and return Saturday morning.

Although person B will be travelling on two relatively lightly loaded trains, (s)he will need to buy two single tickets at £12 each. So, the fare for the person travelling with an overnight stay is both economically inefficient and could well be perceived as unfair and certainly illogical. The economic argument is that, as Person B is not using any peak resources, the fare should be cheaper than for Person A.

Certain UK rail operators have addressed this anomaly. For example, First Capital Connect had off-peak single fares and restricted the use of cheap day returns during the evening peak.

Figure 17-8: Fares for Two Types of Off-Peak passenger

	Off-peak out and return, same day	Off-peak out and peak return, same day	Off-peak out and off-peak return, next day
Guildford-Waterloo (A)	£18.00	£18.00	£24.00
St Albans - Farringdon (B)	£11.50	£18.70	£18.90 (£11 + £7.90)

So, we can see from Figure 17-8 that, although FCC had gone some way to addressing the anomalies of these different off-peak travellers,

Person B is still paying significantly more than Person A on the St Albans route simply because of the overnight stay in London.

For 'B' type passengers who have a choice of mode, a pricing structure similar to the one just demonstrated is unlikely to generate as much demand as a price that would be perceived as fairer.

18 PRINCIPLES OF MARKETING III

18.1 Chapter Overview

So far, we have examined what we mean by a product and have assessed pricing issues. In this Chapter, we will move our focus to the key differences between products and services and the implications of these differences for a transport business. We will also develop a basic framework for service businesses and provide some insight into how this framework can be used to improve the profitability of the business.

18.2 Product or Service?

Anybody perusing most marketing textbooks would come away with the conclusion that the world of commerce is dominated by products. However, a brief examination of Figure 18-1 shows that this is clearly not the case.

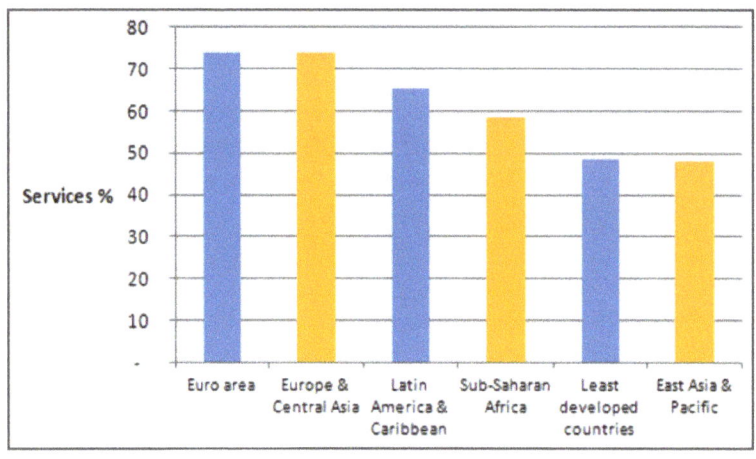

Figure 18-1: Services as % of GDP in 2014 by Region

Source: http://data.worldbank.org/indicator/NV.SRV.TETC.ZS

North America data was not available for 2014 at the time of writing but, in 2013, 78% of the USA's GDP was attributable to services.

Why is the differentiation between services and products important? From the consumer's viewpoint, there are several differences between the two that are pertinent to the transport sector:

- *Accessibility.* For many services, the consumer needs to go to the 'service factory'. For our purpose, such 'factories' include airports, bus/railway stations and ferry terminals. As we have seen in Section 5.2, the issue of accessibility is of importance;

- *Comparing quality.* Products are generally straightforward to compare. For example, we can compare the effectiveness of two floor cleaners, brands of toothpaste, the taste of ready meals, and so on. By contrast, the transport process is particularly complicated; not only does the purchase of a transport 'product' involve many stages (access to terminal, passing through the terminal, in flight, egress from the destination terminal) but also many of the stages are the responsibility of different organisations. The United States is exceptional in this regard, with airlines owning or leasing their own terminals, but this is unusual elsewhere;

- *Inseparability.* Traditionally, the entire transport 'product' needed to be produced and consumed simultaneously, from ticket purchase through check-in, security and the journey. Recent technological developments have facilitated the separation of production and consumption, Ticket purchase and check-in, the latter thanks to the development of automated check-ins, reduce overall journey times and interaction with staff. However, inseparability for the bulk of the end-to-end journey still applies;

To address these differences, we shall now examine two sets of factors beyond the traditional four 'P's' of marketing (product, price, place (distribution) and promotion.

18.3 Physical Evidence, People, Process

18.3.1 Physical Evidence

In Section 12.7, we referred to the replacement of older aircraft with newer types on cost grounds.

But there are good reasons to replace an ageing fleet with more modern equipment.

Airlines, for example, will often promote the age of their fleet as a reason to fly with them.

Similarly, new electric rolling stock on railways and new buses will be expected to have a similarly positive impact on demand.

Within the vehicle, other aspects of physical evidence are the shape and comfort of the seats, the quality of catering and the overall cleanliness of the aircraft, bus or train.

18.3.2 People

Even with the automation of ticket purchase and check-in, interaction with people forms a significant part of the transport process for many people.

Whilst a daily commuter will have little, if any, interaction with staff, leisure passengers travelling by rail, coach and air travellers will expect to come into contact regularly with service providers.

The importance of managing the contact between service providers and customers has been acknowledged for a long time.

In 1982, the then chairman of SAS (Scandinavian Airlines System) talked about the 50,000 daily 'moments of truth' each time a customer came into contact with a staff member.

Much more recently, Ryanair has benefited significantly by working to reduce the antipathy felt by the public.

Whilst their "Always Getting Better" programme, introduced in March 2014, covered a wide range of improvements, much of the programme is concerned with alleviating the highly negative perceptions felt by much of the travelling public (the author has overheard some passengers joking that the airline may have decided to replace the robots working as cabin crew with human beings!).

18.3.3 Process

Closely allied with people, the processes involved in transportation are important, especially when technology is leveraged to change and hopefully improve these processes.

As more people search and book online, a company's website – in effect its shop front – assumes a greater importance.

Not only is the look and feel of the site relevant to people's perception of the brand but a site should be easy to use and quick to load. For instance, as an example used for this, the author timed two searches for a one-way resident's fare from Lanzarote to Gran Canaria on October 1st 2015.

With Binter Canarias, the dominant operator, the elapsed time between requesting the page and filling in personal details after selecting the flight was 45 seconds, whereas using Canary Fly's website, the identical process took more than twice as long (105 seconds)[58].

In this case, the difference in booking time was attributable to the efficiency of the website, but companies for any mode will also try and reduce the steps necessary to make a booking to increase the attractiveness of their 'ticket office'.

A second process, which has changed on most low-cost carriers is that most now allocate seating either during the booking process or for free at check-in.

Ryanair was one of the last LCCs to convert to allocated seating in 2014 and the airline felt that it was at a competitive disadvantage by not offering this service.

18.4 Service Profit Chain – the 3 'Rs'

18.4.1 An Alternative Approach to the 'P's' of Marketing

The Service Profit Chain[59] suggested that a virtuous circle of satisfied, loyal employees and satisfied, loyal customers could contribute to improving the profitability of a company that was able to motivate not only its staff but also its customers to become ambassadors for the brand.

---

58 *Canary Fly resolved this issue in Spring 2016 and their website now runs at a speed similar to Binter's.*
59 *"Service Profit Chain", James L Heskett et al, ISBN 9781439108307 "Service Profit Chain", James L Heskett et al, ISBN 9781439108307*

In this Section, we will take a look at part of the service profit chain relating to how companies can get customers to not only promote their brands for them – for free – but also how to generate extra income per customer.

To this end, we will examine the following three 'R's':

- *Retention.* How can a company retain its customers rather than lose them to competing firms?

- *Referrals.* Once customers are retained and loyal how can we leverage these 'brand ambassadors' to generate more customers? and

- *Related Sales.* With unbundling of the product a major trend, especially in the airline industry, the issue of related sales, or increasing the average spend per customer, is not as challenging as increasing customer volume, once a company has gained a customer's trust and loyalty.

18.4.2 Retention

With products, customers develop a relationship with as much with the retailer as with the manufacturer, if not more.

Mobile telephony and cars are two areas in which customers will have relationships with both.

For many services, the relationship is often only with the service provider, be it a bus company, airline or ferry operator.

In highly competitive markets, companies will spend significant amounts of money to generate new customers but logically, it would be cheaper if the company could retain more of its present customer base than to try to find new ones.

Let us examine a company which has 10 million active customers and loses 30% of these per annum to competitors.

Through a range of promotional strategies, such as advertising and sales promotions, it is able to generate 3 million customers per annum to fill the gap and so the active customer base has a constant 10 million people.

We can see how this works in the first part of Figure 18-2, on the next page.

Figure 18-2: Impact of Increased Retention

	Beginning	Retention	End	New Customers
2011	10,000,000	70%	7,000,000	3,000,000
2012	10,000,000	70%	7,000,000	3,000,000
2013	10,000,000	70%	7,000,000	3,000,000
2014	10,000,000	70%	7,000,000	3,000,000
2015	10,000,000	70%	7,000,000	3,000,000
2016	10,000,000			

	Beginning	Retention	End	New Customers
2011	10,000,000	75%	7,500,000	3,000,000
2012	10,500,000	75%	7,875,000	3,000,000
2013	10,875,000	75%	8,156,250	3,000,000
2014	11,156,250	75%	8,367,188	3,000,000
2015	11,367,188	75%	8,525,391	3,000,000
2016	11,525,391			

Now, let us look at a scenario in which the company is able to improve its retention rate to 75% whilst keeping the promotional activity constant, bringing in 3 million new customers per annum. After five years, the active customer base has increased to a little over 11.5 million.

Increasing retention is much more than doling out loyalty cards to customers.

One of the elements of research, which went into the development of the 'Service Profit Chain' was the difference in consumer behaviour between customers who were merely 'satisfied' (scoring, say, 4 out of 5 in a survey) and 'very satisfied' (5/5).

The example used in the research was for Xerox, which found that very satisfied customers were six times as likely to repurchase from the company compared to merely satisfied ones[60].

18.4.3 Referrals

Referrals can be classified as direct or indirect. A direct referral is a personal recommendation from a friend or relative, whilst an indirect referral results from being influenced by somebody or a group whom the potential consumer holds in high esteem.

There are several instances of companies who value the importance of referrals.

---
60 https://hbr.org/2008/07/putting-the-service-profit-chain-to-work

For example, in January 2015, Transferwise was offering £100 to customers who recommended three friends to their foreign exchange website (obviously, these friends needed to use the service to get the reward).

An indirect referral is best exemplified with reference to social media.

If, for example, an establishment consistently has a high rank on TripAdvisor, a potential customer is more likely to try a well-reviewed bar, restaurant, hotel or other service than one which is rated poorly.

The customer does not personally know these reviewers but is influenced by them.

Let us now expand the example of Figure 18-2 (75% retention rate, 3 million new customers per annum) and see how referrals can improve the customer base.

In Figure 18-3, we will assume a referral rate of just 1%; in other words, 1 in every 100 customers recommends just one other person who then goes on to use the service.

Figure 18-3: Impact of Referrals

	Beginning	Retention	Referral Rate	Referrals	End	New Customers
2011	10,000,000	75%	1%	100,000	7,600,000	3,000,000
2012	10,600,000	75%	1%	106,000	8,056,000	3,000,000
2013	11,056,000	75%	1%	110,560	8,402,560	3,000,000
2014	11,402,560	75%	1%	114,026	8,665,946	3,000,000
2015	11,665,946	75%	1%	116,659	8,866,119	3,000,000
2016	11,866,119					

Once added to the improvement in retention rate, the customer base of this company has increased by nearly 19% in five years and around 550,000 new customers – 29% of the increase – is attributable to referrals[61].

Please note that we have implicitly assumed that the company has not expanded output or opened more sales outlets: this increase is attributable entirely to retention rate and referrals.

---

61 547,245 (11,886,119-10,000,000) = 29% (approx.)

18.4.4 Related Sales

In the airline sector, related sales are generally referred to as 'ancillary revenue' and are a significant stream of income, and this is certainly the case for low cost carriers. In the year to March 2014, almost 25% of Ryanair's total revenue was attributable to ancillary revenue, up from 20% just two years previously.

For Wizzair, an LCC operator based in central Europe, ancillary revenues comprised 35% of the total in the financial year 2014-2015.

For airlines in particular, it is important to distinguish between two types of ancillary revenue when discussing the service profit chain.

Two items of such revenue could be described as monopolistic and these refer to baggage fees and seat selection.

Not only is there no alternative supplier for these two items but, for many travellers, such purchases cannot realistically be called optional.

For example, it would be challenging, to say the least, to attempt a two-week holiday with only hand baggage and, for many people, having an aisle or extra legroom seat is a necessity.

By contrast, for travel retail and on-board retail (see below), the airline is in competition with other suppliers and can be viewed as true related sales.

Individual airlines are somewhat reluctant to provide details of the components of their ancillary revenue but IdeaWorks provided a breakdown of this revenue for airlines in 2013[62]. For non-USA full service carriers, the breakdown is shown in Figure 18-4.

Figure 18-4: Details of Ancillary Revenue, 2013

Detail of Ancillary Revenue	Share
Travel Retail (hire car, hotel, insurance, etc.)	20%
On Board Retail (food, etc.)	20%
Sales of Frequent Flier Miles to Affiliates	10%
Baggage Fees	20%
Other (e.g. credit card fees)	30%

For 2014, IdeaWorks quoted a figure of US$ 17.5 billion for non-USA full service carriers' ancillary revenue.

The top two items may be considered as discretionary

---
[62] http://www.ideaworkscompany.com/wp-content/uploads/2014/11/Press-Release-92-Global-Estimate.pdf

purchases. When booking an airline ticket, passengers always have the option of purchasing car hire, and so on, elsewhere.

Similarly, on-board retail competes with the outlets available in an airport's departure lounge or the customer's own kitchen.

18.4.5 Lifetime Value of a Customer (LVC)

We traditionally seek information on average revenue per customer per annum and this is normally a straightforward calculation to make (revenue divided by units sold).

A more pertinent question is how much a given customer is worth over his or her lifetime.

Let us examine three hypothetical scenarios to see how LVC works. See the data presented in Figure 18-5.

Figure 18-5: LVC Example

	Scenario 1	Scenario 2	Scenario 3
Spend per Trip (€)	200	250	300
Trips per annum	2	2.5	3
Profit Margin	10%	15%	20%
Years of custom	20	20	20
Discount factor	10%	10%	10%
Annuity Factor	9.51	9.51	9.51
LVC (€)	381	892	1,712

The first column shows an occasional traveller in economy class who makes an average of two trips per annum (scenario 1).

Profitability for the lowest level of service is usually relatively low, so we will assume a profit margin of 10% per trip. We will also assume that the customer has some loyalty to the service provider and will be a regular customer, contributing €40 per annum profit, over 20 years (discount, annuity factor and how the figure of €381 was attained should become clear after reading Chapter 21).

We will now change the trip frequency (2.5 per annum) and a higher spend per trip (€250). The higher expenditure may be attributable to purchasing more ancillary services or allowing him/herself an occasional upgrade on the class of travel.

Finally, we examine a very satisfied and loyal customer who again increases frequency of purchase and average spend.

The impact on LVC is significant: more than doubling between the first two scenarios and the LVC of the third customer is more than quadruple the mildly loyal, economy class customer. Indeed, we have probably underestimated the LVC of the very loyal customer (scenario 3) because we have not considered referrals that this customer will make; the likelihood of referrals increases from scenario 1 through to scenario 3.

Chapter 18 Exercise

In Chapter 16, we encountered Alicante Tram and its lack of connections with the large bus station in Benidorm. This question, by contrast, will focus on the part of the network which is within the metropolitan area of Alicante city (zone A – see http://www.tramalicante.es/descargas/pdf/PLANO%20ZONAL%20A4.pdf).

With a population of some 250,000 people, Alicante has a significant bus network in addition to the tram system (see http://www.alicante.subus.es/). This network is operated independently by a large private company, Vectalia. There is limited integration by means of multi-journey tickets which can be used by either tram or bus in the Alicante area. Roughly 30 million passengers per annum use the bus network and 5 million the tram network (stopping services) in Zone A.

If the owners of the tram (a public sector body called FGV) wished to increase usage of its network and hence increase revenue, what strategies could be used to achieve this objective?

Use the framework of this Chapter to guide your answer.

19 FORECASTING I

19.1 Introduction

One of the truisms of forecasting is that, in practice, it is impossible to forecast correctly[63]. Or, to put it another way, whilst it may not be possible to get a forecast right, it is very easy to get it wrong.

To give an extreme example of this, if a new business district were to be developed along the line of a route served by rail and close to an existing railway station, there are no plausible circumstances in which we would expect rail demand to decline as a result of this development.

Although our forecasts are going to be shrouded by uncertainty, we nonetheless need a forecast to build a case for investing significant amounts of money in a business, and it is therefore important that our forecasts are at the very least plausible and consistent.

In previous Chapters, we have examined the techniques used for forecasting. In the following two Chapters, we will put these techniques to work in developing and assessing forecasts.

19.2 Assessment of Recent Trends

A good starting point for any forecast is to examine, where possible, recent trends in demand.

Although there is no guarantee that five years of growth, for example, will induce a sixth, an understanding of what has happened in the past can provide some insights into future growth.

Let us examine the two forecasts shown, on the following page, in Figure 19-1.

---

[63] See http://www.publications.parliament.uk/pa/cm201213/cmselect/cmpubacc/464/464we02.htm for an example of Eurostar forecasts which illustrate this point.

Figure 19-1: Two Examples of Optimistic Forecasts

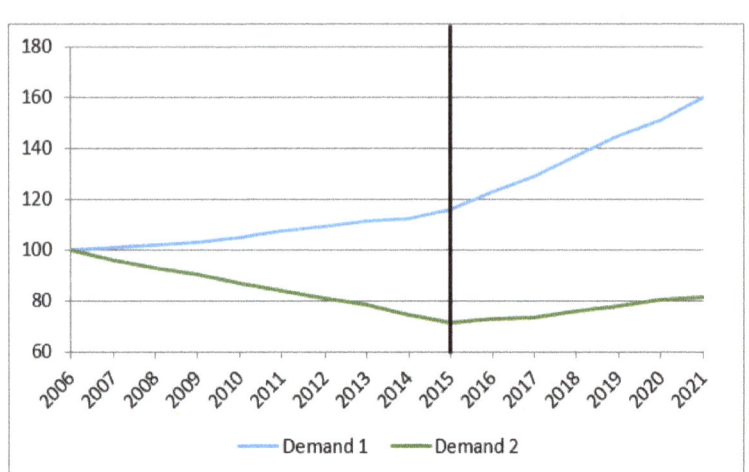

Demand 1 shows growth of between 1% and 3% per annum up to 2015. From 2016 onwards, however, the forecast shows annual growth ranging between 4% and 6%. Demand 2 has suffered declining demand between 2006 and 2015 at a rate of between 3% and 5% per annum; by contrast, the forecast for Demand 2 is growth of between 1% and 3% between 2016 and 2021.

There could be valid reasons for assuming significant improvements in demand growth for the two examples above, but it is critical that these changes be fully justified to the top decision-makers who will have ultimate responsibility for these forecasts. The technical analyst will be responsible for explaining not only why the variables underpinning demand have transformed the demand pattern but also how.

19.3 A Comparison between British and Irish Rail Demand

19.3.1 Recent Trends

Figure 19-2 shows the evolution of demand for rail travel in Great Britain between April 2005 and March 2016. A notable feature of this demand is that, overall, demand remained healthy throughout the recession which started in 2008-9 and the only sector which suffered a year-on-year decline were operators in the southeast of England.

Figure 19-2: Passenger Journeys in GB (millions)

Financial year	Franchised long distance operators	Franchised London and South East operators	Franchised regional operators	Non-franchised	Total
2005-06	89.5	719.7	267.3	0	1,076.5
2006-07	99.0	769.5	276.5	0	1,145.0
2007-08	103.9	828.4	285.8	0	1,218.1
2008-09	109.4	854.3	302.8	0	1,266.5
2009-10	111.6	842.2	304.0	1.4	1,259.3
2010-11	117.9	917.6	318.2	1.8	1,355.6
2011-12	125.3	993.8	340.9	1.5	1,461.5
2012-13	127.7	1,032.4	340.9	1.7	1,502.6
2013-14	129.0	1,106.9	350.5	1.9	1,588.3
2014-15	134.2	1,154.9	364.7	2.1	1,655.8
2015-16	136.0	1,182.9	368.0	2.3	1,689.3

Source: https://dataportal.orr.gov.uk

The contrast with rail demand in the Republic of Ireland is evident from Figure 19-3, where we can see that total passenger volume in 2014 was still well behind pre-recession levels and is no higher than that seen in 2005 (note that DART stands for Dublin Area Rapid Transit in the table below). By contrast, GB rail demand increased by 54% between 2005-6 and 2014-15.

Figure 19-3: Passenger journeys in Ireland (thousands)

	Mainline and other services	Dublin suburban services	DART	TOTAL
2005	11,068	9,556	16,256	36,880
2006	8,917	13,862	19,689	42,468
2007	10,537	13,880	20,244	44,661
2008	10,324	13,645	19,865	43,834
2009	8,877	11,768	17,520	38,165
2010	9,697	10,861	16,793	37,351
2011	10,656	9,911	15,924	36,491
2012	10,350	9,934	15,747	36,031
2013	8,144[64]	11,730	15,985	35,859
2014	8,421	12,141	16,321	36,883

Source: http://www.cso.ie/px/pxeirestat/Database/eirestat/Rail%20Statistics/Rail%20Statistics_statbank.asp?sp=Rail%20Statistics&Planguage=0, http://www.irishrail.ie/media/iarnrod_eireann_annual_report_2014_1.pdf?v=gradqpo

---

[64] Note that, in 2013, some main line services were reclassified as Dublin suburban, which makes a direct comparison of specific sectors with previous years challenging.

19.3.2 Differences in GDP

How can we explain the differences between the very different fortunes of British and Irish railways?

In section 7.3, we examined how real GDP influences demand for transportation, so, as a starting point, let us compare the changes in real GDP in the UK and Ireland between 2008 and 2014.

The results are shown in Figure 19-4.

Northern Island is included in the UK figures below but not in the rail demand in Figure 19-2, but as NI makes up just a small part of the UK, this should not materially affect our analysis.

Figure 19-4: Percent changes in real GDP, Ireland and UK

	Ireland	United Kingdom
2008	-2.61	-0.33
2009	-6.37	-4.31
2010	-0.28	1.91
2011	2.77	1.64
2012	-0.31	0.66
2013	0.17	1.66
2014	4.78	2.55

Source: International Monetary Fund, World Economic Outlook Database, April 2015

The data suggests that Ireland had a worse recession than the UK and the compounded growth from 2008 to 2014 was -2.2% in Ireland and +3.7% in the UK. However, it is unlikely that a difference of six percentage points in GDP growth over six years could explain such a large difference in demand performance.

19.3.3 Differences in Motorway Networks

An alternative explanation may lie not so much in what the different railway companies are 'doing wrong' but what might be occurring beyond the railway sector. For example, the difference may be attributable to investments in competing modes and, in a country the size of Ireland, the alternative is effectively roads.

In Figure 19-5, we can see the development in the size of motorway networks in the UK and Ireland during the period 2008-2014.

Figure 19-5: Length of Motorway Networks in km

	2008	*2014*
Ireland	423	1,224
Great Britain	3,499	3,592

Sources: https://www.cia.gov/library/publications/resources/the-world-factbook/fields/2085.html#ei, http://ec.europa.eu/eurostat/tgm/table.do?tab=table&language=en&pcode=ttr00002, Transport Statistics of Great Britain 2014, table RDL0101

We can see immediately that whilst the motorway network in Ireland nearly tripled in size over six years, in the United Kingdom it barely changed. Please note that these figures refer specifically to length and do not include widening schemes, such as England's M1. The longest distance between major cities in Ireland is the 266km between Dublin and Cork or under three hours' drive. The motorway linking the two cities was built in stages and was finally completed in 2010. The car journey time is comparable with rail, which has an average journey time of 2½ hours. However, as we have observed, if we were to calculate generalised journey time for a large proportion of rail passengers, rail's GJT would be higher than that by car.

19.3.4 Vehicle Kilometres Travelled by Car

We saw in the previous Section that Ireland's motorway network has expanded significantly in the last few years. The next question is whether the number of journeys has increased as a result.

Figure 19-6: Vehicle-km by Car, GB and Ireland

	Britain bn km	**Ireland m km**	**Ireland M7 count**
2008	395	32,592	58,126
2009	394	32,572	58,314
2010	386	32,055	58,220
2011	387	31,638	n/a
2012	387	31,076	n/a
2013	386	32,031	61,598
2014	394	31,457	62,682
2008-14	-0.3%	-3.5%	7.8%

Source: http://www.cso.ie/multiquicktables/quickTables.aspx?id=tha10_2 https://www.gov.uk/government/statistical-data-sets/tra02-traffic-by-road-class-and-region-kms (TRA0201), National Roads Authority, Ireland Note: the M7 traffic count figures are from the Naas bypass and so includes traffic to/from Limerick (M9 motorway) as well as Cork (M8).

It is notable that, compared to rail travel in Ireland, which declined by nearly 20% over 5 years, road travel has stayed reasonably constant over the same period, enforcing the view that the increase in size of the motorway network has influenced a modal shift from rail to road, as we would expect.

As Ireland endured the heavy recession that it did until 2014, a drop of less than 4% in traffic is small. An alternative means of examining competition from the road sector is the traffic count method. Figure 19-6 also shows that over the period 2008 to 2014, average daily motorway traffic between Limerick, Cork and Dublin has increased by around 8% in six years.

So, what we have are various bits of evidence which are reasonably consistent. What we may infer from what we have is that, on the key Dublin-Cork route at least, the impact of the opening of the motorway is likely to have had a negative effect on rail demand. Of course, rail travel does not exist in isolation of other modes, especially the car. "On the Move: Making sense of car and train travel trends in Britain"[65] is a document that explains trends in rail and its most competitive alternative mode.

Although data for car travel on specific routes is difficult to obtain (but not impossible, as we saw in Chapter 6), understanding how overall trends in car travel are developing – car ownership, average journey distance, car occupancy per journey, etc. – are important to support forecasts for projects where the car is likely to be an important source of competition.

19.4 Revenues

19.4.1 Introduction

Revenues are based on a projection of passengers, tonne-miles or a similar measure and often the most difficult aspect to determine in an appraisal.

Not only is it necessary to forecast passenger volume but also how this volume will be segmented and therefore what is the average revenue per passenger that the new project is likely to generate.

We covered this to some extent in previous Chapters, but we will now go into this area in more detail.

---

[65] http://www.racfoundation.org/assets/rac_foundation/content/downloadables/on_the_move-le_vine_&_jones-dec2012.pdf

19.4.2 Pricing Policy

Pricing policy will to some extent be determined by capacity. For commuter services, the PIXC criterion (passengers in excess of capacity) will influence demand; irrespective of whether PIXC forms part of an operator's agreement with the franchisor, if a service or route becomes uncomfortably overcrowded, demand and hence revenue will be constrained. In practice, demand is often forecast in two stages: the first assumes that all demand may be met and the second stage imposes limits on volume of this demand, based on, for instance, hourly capacity.

The objective of the forecast is then to maximize the revenue of this forecast if demand exceeds capacity, taking into account price caps on tickets imposed by Government or Transport Authorities.

19.4.3 Forecasting Using Elasticities

An elasticity approach is appropriate for relatively small changes to the established services with relatively large levels of existing demand and without extremes of market share. By definition, there must be some existing demand actually using the mode that is the subject of study.

So, use of an elasticity approach is not appropriate for forecasting patronage for completely new services, or where there are major changes, especially with respect to the competition.

This might be the case, for instance, for a new LRT system or new route. An operator might already be carrying almost all of the potential traffic, so that there is little more to be gained whatever the improvement, or the capacity to carry additional traffic under acceptable conditions is limited.

This might well be the case for a London commuter route, where alternatives are poor, or on a rural bus route, where even significant improvements may have little impact if the bus service is not especially competitive in terms of journey time or frequency.

19.5 Reactions of Competitors

One omission which is frequently made in forecasting is to not fully take account of competitors' reactions.

We first discussed this issue in the Bangkok-Singapore air transport market in Section 4.3.

We will now generalise the issue.

Consider a firm that wishes to enter a market or an existing firm, which decides to reduce its prices.

For short, we will call this company the 'disruptor'.

We saw in Section 5.3 that a reduced price should increase demand for the service; this is a reasonable assumption, assuming that other firms do not react.

But how likely a situation is this?

Incumbents or other competitors can react in a variety of ways. For example:

- Increase advertising spend to counter the promotional activity of the disruptor;

- Introduce price promotions. Although promotions are temporary, they would send a signal to the disruptor that the other firms will not accept the changes without a fight;

- Reduce price, in an effort to neutralise the disruptor; or

- Increase frequency and so retaliate by using some other means to improve service other than price.

We will illustrate the retaliation argument with the public transport market between Stansted airport and central London.

A summary of the shares comparing 2009 and 2013/2014 is shown in Figure 19-7.

Figure 19-7: Market Shares at Stansted Airport

	2009	2013	2014 Q1-Q3	Single Fare (£)	Return Fare (£)
Bus	22.2%	29.5%	26.1%	9.00	15.00
Rail	25.0%	22.0%	24.0%	21.20	36.60

Source: CAA Survey data, "Sustainable Development Plan", Stansted Airport (2015), rail and bus websites

Until 2004, rail transported two to three times as many passengers as bus/coach. The Stansted Express rail link has consistently been operated as a premium fare service; the price per mile is significantly higher than other services in the area and, between 2009 and 2013, fares increased by 11%, or just over 2% per annum.

In other words, Stansted Express has been a priced at a premium for several years.

However, Stansted airport rail services face intense competition from coach services into central London.

In the four-year period to 2013, Stansted Express lost passengers whilst bus and coach were clearly beneficiaries, gaining seven percentage points' share.

It appears that even the introduction of new rolling stock in 2011 was insufficient to prevent rail's reduced share.

However, rail's share showed signs of a recovery during 2014.

19.6 Scenario Planning

19.6.1 Internal Consistency

A frequently used method to test the robustness of a forecast is to apply sensitivity tests.

For example, the cost of petrol is used to forecast rail demand, as a lower fuel price would be expected to encourage more car trips and some switch away from public transport.

So, the sensitivity analysis would predict (for example) a doubling of fuel price over 10 years and its impact on rail demand assessed in the forecasting model. A more complicated option is to develop scenarios. Let us say that an airline wishes to consider the impact of a collapse in the value of the Pound (GBP) on the demand in the UK for air transport. Three of the impacts which would most likely occur are:

- Rise in inflation, as imports would become more expensive (the UK regularly incurs a trade deficit);

- Disposable income would be expected to decline, meaning that a higher proportion of household income would need to be spent on essentials such as food and energy. This would lead to less money per household available for foreign holidays (from Chapter 3, this means that the demand curve shifts to the left); and

- Higher fuel prices (crude oil is always sold in US dollars) would impact on the airline's costs, causing it to raise fares or add fuel supplements (supply curve shifts to the left).

Once all key elements of the internally consistent scenario have been developed, the forecaster is then in a position to evaluate the full impact of a reduction in the Pound's value.

19.6.2 "States of the World"

Shell was one of the innovators in using scenario planning and has been active in this field for over 40 years.

A 'state of the world' can be defined as an assessment of a likely outcome in the business environment and then assessing its impact on a specific industry or business.

If we were to take this approach specifically for forecasting transport demand, we could develop a scenario called, for example, 'New Aspirations'.

Owning a first car used to be an aspiration of many young people in previous generations, but various sources[66] suggest that this may no longer be the case.

Coupled with an increasing propensity for people to live in city centres[67], these two trends taken together have profound implications for not only private car demand but also that of public transport.

19.7 Forecasting Costs

In comparison with forecasting demand and revenue, future operating cost forecasts should be *relatively* straightforward. The operator will be required to buy or lease new vehicles, be they trains, ferries or aircraft.

If purchased outright, the operator must either pay out for the new vehicles upfront or else get a bank loan to fund the investment. The finance division of the company should advise on whether there are taxation implications in the lease or buy decision. In general, the costs of acquiring vehicles will be fixed.

Next, the operator will need to consider the impact on its variable costs attributable to the forecast demand.

There will be increased costs relating to crew, maintenance staff, fuel bills and track/airport/port access fees, amongst others. All assumptions should be made clear and the projected cost increases should be made explicit, year by year.

---

66 *See, for example, https://www.kpmg.com/US/en/IssuesAndInsights/ArticlesPublications/Documents/me-my-life-my-car.pdf*
67 http://www.economist.com/node/21559338

Although nobody can say for sure how operating costs will look in thirty, twenty or even ten years' time, there is at least a solid body of evidence available now on the costs incurred in running a transport service, on maintenance costs for infrastructure and when this infrastructure will need replacing. The risk attached to cost projections should therefore be considerably lower than to revenues.

19.8 Demand Forecasting – PDFH and Alternatives

19.8.1 GB Rail – Passenger Demand Forecasting Handbook

The industry 'bible' is the Passenger Demand Forecasting Handbook, developed over years through a wide range of market research studies, and now maintained by the Association of Train Operating Companies (ATOC). This deals very specifically with the rail context, but there is a wide body of academic knowledge dealing with transport planning across all modes, and taught to the level of Master degrees at many UK universities.

The latest version of PDFH runs to several hundred pages and was last issued in 2013 (version 5.1). It provides guideline values for planners to use in a wide range of scenarios; for example, for rail fare elasticities, different values are provided as follows:

- To or from London;
- By ticket type and/or journey purpose;
- Non-London, whether PTE (urban areas such as Birmingham or Manchester) or non-PTE;
- Whether the flow includes an airport.

In total, there are 44 different fare elasticity values to choose from, depending on these criteria.

Other Chapters of PDFH deal with frequency, crowding, punctuality and reliability, rolling stock quality, station facilities and intermodal competition.

In spite of all this detail, however, it is important to bear in mind that, in spite of the status of PDFH which is the required methodology in evaluating changes to railway services or new ones, PDFH is not a substitute for providing accuracy in demand forecasting.

19.8.2 Critique of the PDFH

Tom Worsley of Leeds University wrote a report[68], commissioned by the ORR, RAC Foundation and Transport Scotland, published in December 2012. "Rail Demand Forecasting Using the Passenger Demand Forecasting Handbook" provides a critique of the PDFH in Chapter 5 and determines how well PDFH has accounted for recent trends in rail travel in Chapter 6.

It is evident from this appraisal that, although the economic conditions prevailing in Britain since 2009 should have dampened demand for rail travel, this has not generally been the case.

As we saw at the beginning of this Chapter, rail travel in the UK has remained robust in spite of a 6% decline in GDP per head between 2007 and 2012; in Ireland, by contrast, where the recession was deeper (10% decline over the same period) demand for rail travel has conformed to the pattern of demand usually expected by analysts, with travel and wealth positively correlated (recall that we examined elasticity of demand with respect to income in Section 5.3.4).

19.8.3 Alternative Methodologies

Although the UK Government endorses forecasts undertaken using the PDFH methodology, it does also allow for alternative methods where:

- The current PDFH methodology is proven not to provide credible forecasts based on historic experience; and/or

- Alternative forecasting methodologies are considered more suitable to the specific circumstances.[69]

Alternative methods may be more appropriate when the catchment area is quite small or the impact on a specific corridor, with its own idiosyncrasies, is being examined. To give an insight into other means of how demand forecasting can be undertaken, especially in an urban context, we can have a brief look at econometric or regression methods used in New Zealand[70]. Please note that it is not the intention of this Section to suggest which methods are 'right' or 'wrong' but to identify that there are other very different methodologies available to forecast transport demand.

---

68 http://www.racfoundation.org/assets/rac_foundation/content/downloadables/pdfh-worsley-dec2012.pdf
69 http://www.dft.gov.uk/webtag/documents/expert/pdf/unit3.15.4d.pdf (page 14)
70 http://www.nzta.govt.nz/resources/research/reports/518/docs/518.pdf

Whilst the PDFH has, in fact, used these methods to derive the approved elasticities for demand forecasting, some of the material produced is derived using quite dated information. An alternative method, therefore, is to derive the required coefficients directly from raw data, as the New Zealand example below demonstrates.

In brief, the model research in New Zealand was a linear equation in the format below. This research did not examine whole urban areas but focussed on corridors.

Rail Demand = A + B * Service Improvements + C * Fares + D * Petrol Prices + E * Retail Sales + F * Employment

The objective of the equation is to explain as much of the variation in rail demand by the variation in the other factors (those shown on the right-hand side of the equation).

It is also important that the explanatory variables are reasonably independent of each other; we can do this by examining the correlation coefficients between each variable. Recall that we discussed the issue of multicollinearity in Section 9.4.2.

A similar equation was used for bus demand in the same corridor.

It is interesting to note what the researchers omitted on statistical grounds: car ownership, population (the data per corridor was deemed insufficiently robust) and, perhaps most surprisingly, data on rail service reliability.

For Auckland, the authors actually say that, "The reliability data for rail did not show any obvious association with rail patronage growth."

19.8.4 WebTAG

The Transport Appraisal Guide is issued and updated regularly by the UK's Department of Transport and provides values for a wide range of factors that need to be considered for forecasting transport demand.

For example, the November 2014 WebTAG provides projected car journey times between different regions of Great Britain.

Figure 19-8 provides a sample of WebTAG guidance for what could be termed 'inter-city' journeys to and from the Greater London area.

Figure 19-8: Long Distance Car Journey Times from Greater London

2010/11	100.00
2011/12	100.21
2012/13	100.42
2013/14	100.62
2014/15	100.83
2015/16	101.08
2016/17	101.46
2017/18	101.84
2018/19	102.22
2019/20	102.60
2020/21	102.99
2021/22	103.43

Source: WebTAG table M4.2.1

It is reasonable to assume that, as the economy grows, demand for road space will increase and thus lead to a reduction in average traffic speed and hence an increase in journey time (so, the project is for journey times to be 3.43% longer in 2021 than in 2010).

This sort of information is useful if there is no expectation of a significant change in the road network of the corridor being studied.

How would we tackle the problem of assessing demand on rail and coach services, however, if we knew that a brand new motorway was planned or a current one was to be widened?

At the very least, road congestion would decline in the short term before more traffic was generated onto the road due to lower congestion.

Let us look at a concrete example of this phenomenon. Between 2006 and 2009, the M1 motorway, one of the primary arterial roads between London and the rest of the country, was widened between Luton, some 50km from London, and the M25 circular motorway which roughly follows Greater London's boundaries. The construction work widened the road from six lanes in total to eight.

In Figure 19-9, we examine the annual average daily traffic (AADT) on two Sections of the M1: at Milton Keynes, which was unaffected by the construction work, and at Redbourne, which is south of Luton and is covered by the widened M1.

Figure 19-9: AADT per Lane on the M1

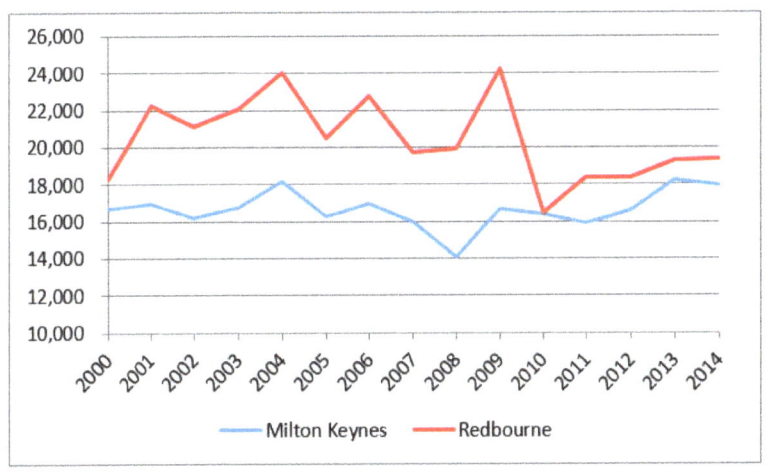

Traffic per lane was significantly higher at Redbourne, which is rather closer to London, up until 2009. After 2009, however, when the widening works were completed, there was a significant drop in traffic volume per lane, which we may take as a surrogate for speed and hence journey time.

We would expect this improvement to be reflected in some diversion from rail to car but the generic WebTAG guidance will clearly not capture these local improvements.

So, this Section is in effect a warning about taking a mechanistic approach to forecasting and emphasizing the need to examine local factors which could influence inter-modal competition.

19.9 Forecasting Rail Demand in Ireland

In contrast to the complex segmentation methodology used in British passenger rail forecasts, which aim to project demand over 100 or more market segments (differentiated by flow and ticket type), we will now examine a much simpler approach, used by AECOM, to forecast rail demand in the Republic of Ireland[71] in 2011. The regression model used was:

Passengers/Population = 4.532 + 0.143 * GNP/Population

[71] http://www.irishrail.ie/media/irishrail_28febfinal_part11.pdf

Figure 19-10 shows the fit of the model against the data for the latest eighteen years of data available. 84% of the variation in passenger demand was explained by the one variable, namely Gross National Product[72] per person, which is a very creditable result.

Figure 19-10: Actual and Modelled Data for the Republic of Ireland

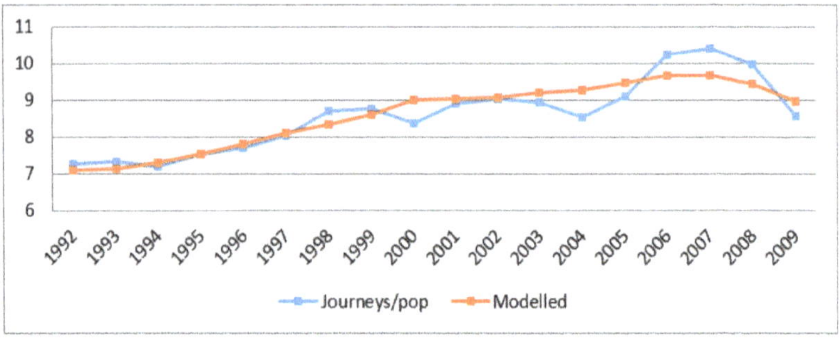

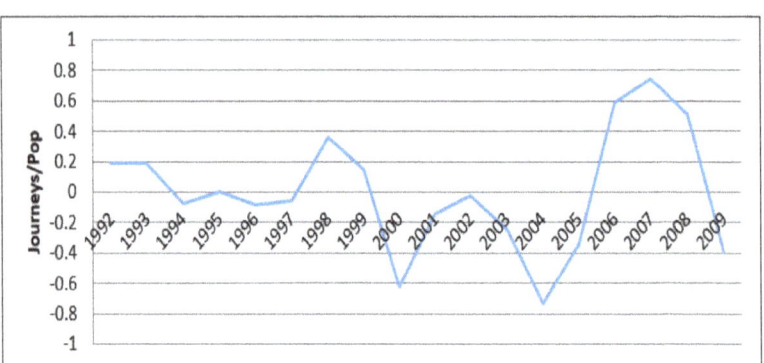

Source: Iarnród Éireann and Goodbody Economic Consultants

Inviting though this result looks, the technique involves much more than just fitting a line. A closer examination of Figure 19-10 above seems to show that, as the number of passengers per population increases, the gap between actual and predicted per capita journeys appears to widen (see Figure 19-11).

Figure 19-11: Author's calculation of the Error Term in the AECOM Model

Note: a negative value above implies that the model overestimated demand.

As well as Figure 19-11 providing grounds for concern as the error term increases in magnitude from 2004 onwards, the error appears to exhibit a downward drift from 1992 to 2004.

---
[72] GNP and GDP are slightly different measures but, for our purposes, we will treat them as the same.

This drift would not be apparent from Figure 19-10, which underlines the importance of examining the model's errors. In other words, the randomness of the error term, which is an important part of a robust model, is questionable.

If the error term had settled down in the latter years of the period observed, we could, perhaps, discount the earlier bias in the error term, but, clearly, this has not happened.

19.10 How Effective Is the AECOM Model?

The purpose of developing a model such as this is to enable forecasts in passenger demand.

As the model ended in 2009, it is instructive to see how the model performed for the five subsequent years, based on actual growth in population and GNP (as recorded by Ireland's Statistical Office, CSO), in Figure 19-12.

	Actual Per Capita journeys	Modelled per capita journeys	Error (actual – modelled)	Error (%)
2010	8.39	8.95	-0.56	-6.6
2011	8.17	8.86	-0.69	-8.5
2012	8.05	8.93	-0.88	-10.9
2013	7.99	9.06	-1.06	-13.2
2014	8.11	9.57	-1.46	-15.3

Figure 19-12: Actual and Modelled Demand on Irish Railways 2010-2014
Source: CSO Ireland, Author's calculations

So, we can see that the model significantly overestimated demand in the five years immediately following the study period and the quality of the model deteriorates over time, as the analysis of the errors in Section 19.9 suggested was likely.

Moreover, at the time that the forecast was undertaken (presumably early 2011, as the forecast was published in October of that year), the expansion of Ireland's motorway network was at the very least well planned, if not actually underway.

The lesson that we can draw from this exercise is that it is important to revisit forecasting models "after the event" to check how effective they have been.

We will return to this issue again in Chapter 22.

19.11 Forecasts for Non-existent Services / Infrastructure

19.11.1 Introduction

So far, we have assumed that forecasts are a function of current demand and/or are based on infrastructure that already exists.

What if it is necessary to forecast the demand which will be placed on yet to be built infrastructure or a new service connecting two points which to date have had no direct connection?

In this Section, we will use two examples: a direct air service between two points and rehabilitation of worn-out rail infrastructure which currently has very low demand.

19.11.2 New Direct Air Service

An airline operates flights from several hubs, one of which is A. This airline operates flights to 20 points from Hub A and knows the demand on each of these routes. The demand will be a function of various factors, including:

- Combined population and business activity between A and 1, A and 2, etc.;
- Frequency of service provided;
- Existing land-based and air competitors; and
- Average revenue per ticket, which is a function of the three factors above (i.e. whether the route is principally for business or leisure purposes, whether a high frequency is needed to attract business travellers and to what extent our airline has the ability to raise prices in the face of competition from other operators).

With this knowledge and also an understanding of the demographics and economy of city 21 (the point of new service), the airline should be able to assess demand on the new route before it is launched.

19.11.3 Replacing Worn-Out Infrastructure

Much of Africa's transport infrastructure has become dilapidated through lack of maintenance. Whether the causes of this deterioration have been management incompetence, corruption or insufficient revenue to invest in maintenance, the results are the same: a vicious circle, caused by declining revenue, insufficient funds to maintain the line and services, which in turn reduces demand and thus revenue available to invest.

An example of this vicious circle is the 1800 km-long TAZARA railway, built in the 1970s between Zambia and the port of Dar es Salaam in Tanzania, in order to provide an alternative route via Rhodesia (Zimbabwe) and South Africa; politically, the South African route was unacceptable to Zambia, as both Rhodesia and South Africa were governed at the time by minority white regimes which practised apartheid.

TAZARA also serves the Tanzanian town of Mbeya, the largest on the route with a population of some 400,000. Mbeya is some 850km from Dar es Salaam.

The line was opened in 1975 and was designed to carry 5 million tonnes of freight per annum, principally copper, from Zambia to export markets. Up until the mid-1980s, traffic of up to 2 million tonnes per annum was regularly seen but, more recently, annual freight has been much lower.

The East African Railways Master Plan was published in January 2009.

We can see from Figure 19-13 that the forecasts, seven years out from the date they were published, envisaged a tight range between the lowest and highest scenarios; in practice, the actual traffic carried in the latest financial year, to June 2015, was less than 10% of that forecast.

Figure 19-13: Master Plan Forecasts for TAZARA

000 tonnes	**2008**	**2010**	**2015**
High	594	719	1,096
Base	589	699	1,018
low	593	680	945
ACTUAL		534	90

Source: www.eac.int infrastructure index.php?option com docman&task doc download&gid 10&Itemid 70 2014-15 actual figure: http://www.miningweekly.com article tanzaniazambia railway gets 224m chinese lifeline 2015-11-10

Although no forecast could have been expected to predict such a widespread collapse in demand as 90,000 tonnes, the very narrow forecast range between high and low does suggest an absence of a scenario approach to forecasting in this case. In Africa, road haulage is usually somewhat more expensive than in Europe due to lower quality roads and bureaucratic costs at border crossings.

When forecasting railway demand in developing countries, a plausible scenario, therefore, is that the road transport sector would improve and thus weaken further demand for rail services.

This is precisely what has happened on the Zambia-Tanzania corridor in recent years, according to analysis by the Centre of Competition and Regulation at the University of Johannesburg[73]: increased competition in the supply of road haulage services has driven down prices on domestic routes (Dar to Mbeya) significantly and, to a lesser extent, cross-border trips to and from Zambia.

TAZARA is not atypical of rail projects in sub-Saharan Africa which produce consistent losses but, with one more dollop of emergency funding, the decline in traffic would allegedly go into reverse and the business would start making money. We discuss the problem of optimism bias in Chapter 21.

---

73 http://www.competition.org.za/working-papers/, Paper 2015/03

19.12 Chapter 19 Exercises

Exercise 1 An island is linked to the mainland by a subsidised ferry service and is currently used by some 500,000 vehicles per annum. The island has a significant volume of tourist demand in summer as well as being used by island residents as their lifeline to the mainland. The regional government has proposed replacing the ferries with a bridge and the proposed toll for using the bridge will be similar to the ferry tariff. You have been approached to forecast likely demand for this bridge and assess the viability of the project. What information will you request from the council in order to develop your forecast?

Exercise 2 An airline currently operates from a hub to ten different cities. In the table below, we can see the weekly frequency of flights to each destination, how long the route has been in operation and the average load factor on each route.

City	Frequency/ week	Duration (months)	Load Factor (%)
A	25	17	92
B	4	13	74
C	8	9	76
D	5	14	78
E	14	4	81
F	21	5	79
G	8	8	77
H	9	13	83
I	5	19	84
J	10	2	73

Using the regression techniques from Chapter 9:

- Determine the relationship between load factor, frequency and age of routes; and

- Comment on the quality of the regression equation you obtain.

The airline is proposing to start a service to city K, which has similar mix of population, commerce and tourism as the other ten destinations. Assuming that the new service will operate 7 times per week, what is the estimated load factor after each of the first four months of operation?

20 FORECASTING II

20.1 Chapter Overview

In this Chapter, the focus is on assessing both trends and seasonality in data. We will develop two methods to model the data and, later on, use both models to undertake short-term demand forecasts. We will then compare and contrast which model provides the better result and why.

20.2 Seasonality

When demand on a line or corridor is expected to be highly seasonal, there will be several implications that need to be considered (in addition to the pricing issues discussed earlier in this text). Examples include:

- Will the capacity of vehicles be adequate to carry loads during the peak period;

- What are the cost implications for adding capacity and staff to cope with the peaks in demand?

Time of day seasonality is clearly evident on commuter routes during weekday mornings and evenings, but we can also see seasonality on a certain day of the week (market day, for example) or holiday routes served by airlines, such as Spain, Turkey and Greece.

20.3 Time Series Decomposition (TSD)

20.3.1 Multiplication or Addition?

There are two ways to assess seasonality, which are the multiplicative and additive methods. In this Section, we will see how both work using a small example before moving onto the larger Turkish air demand figures.

Let's assume that the operator providing a bus route serving a shopping centre has collected the following data of demand by hour of the day over several days. The route operates for 12 hours per day.

Figure 20-1: Hourly Bus Service Demand

Hour	Demand	No Seasonality	Additive	Multiplicative
900	530	750	-220	0.707
1000	645	750	-105	0.860
1100	800	750	50	1.067
1200	950	750	200	1.267
1300	1,125	750	375	1.500
1400	730	750	-20	0.973
1500	470	750	-280	0.627
1600	580	750	-170	0.773
1700	860	750	110	1.147
1800	990	750	240	1.320
1900	750	750	0	1.000
2000	570	750	-180	0.760
	9,000	9,000	0	12

We can see that there is a peak in demand at lunchtime and a smaller peak early in the evening.

If there were no peaks or troughs in demand, there would be 750 passengers per hour. Note that the totals of the 'demand' and 'no seasonality' columns are identical.

First, let's look at the additive column. If an hour of the day has above average demand of 750, the figure in the column will be greater than zero and, similarly, an hour of low demand will have a negative value.

The sum of these weights must equal zero.

The multiplicative approach is a little different; for each hour, we divide the actual hourly demand by 750 in this example to calculate each hour's seasonality factor. So, for the 9am row, the factor is 530/750 or 0.707 and for the 1300hrs row, the factor is 1.5 (1,125/750).

When all the hourly factors are added together, the sum will be 12, which is the number of periods whose seasonality we are trying to assess.

Either method of calculating seasonality factors is valid and, ideally, we should use both methods to see which provides the better eventual result. However, for the Turkish air demand data, we will use the multiplicative method only.

20.3.2 Assessing Seasonality

In this Section, we will use air transport statistics to demonstrate seasonality, as data covering several years between the UK and all airports and countries world-wide is publicly available. Although aircraft have less flexibility in capacity – much to Ryanair's annoyance, standing passengers are not allowed on aircraft! – rail operators would not want to see business turned away due to overcrowding and generate bad publicity through stories of passengers being treated like sardines.

Sometimes, the seasonal effect is quite obvious. Figure 20-2 shows the monthly demand over four years between Britain and beach resort airports in Turkey (so flows between the UK and both Istanbul and Izmir have been excluded). There are two visible effects, namely an overall year-on-year increase in demand but also a high level of seasonal variation, with demand significantly higher in summer than in winter.

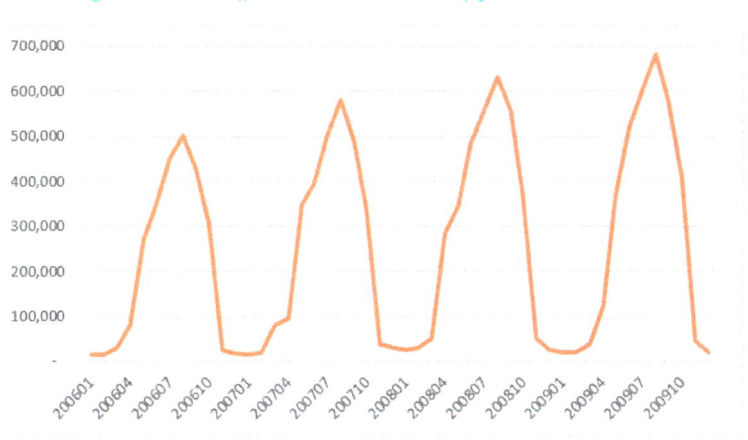

Figure 20-2: Air Traffic between UK and Turkey, Jan 2006- Dec 2009

However, sometimes the seasonal element is not quite so clear. In Figure 20-3, we can detect a downward trend, but the seasonality on routes to South Africa is somewhat less apparent than is the case with Turkey.

Figure 20-3: Air Traffic between the UK and South Africa, 2006-2010

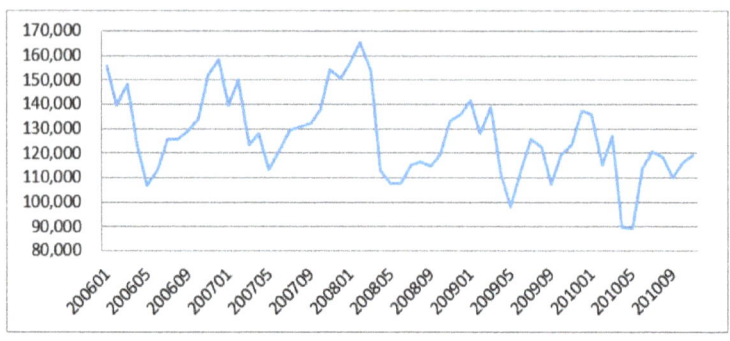

Source: http://www.caa.co.uk/airportstatistics

If a trend line is imposed on the Turkish data, the increase over the four years is around 3,250 passengers per month, as we can see from the regression line in Figure 20-4.

Figure 20-4: Turkish Data with Trend Line

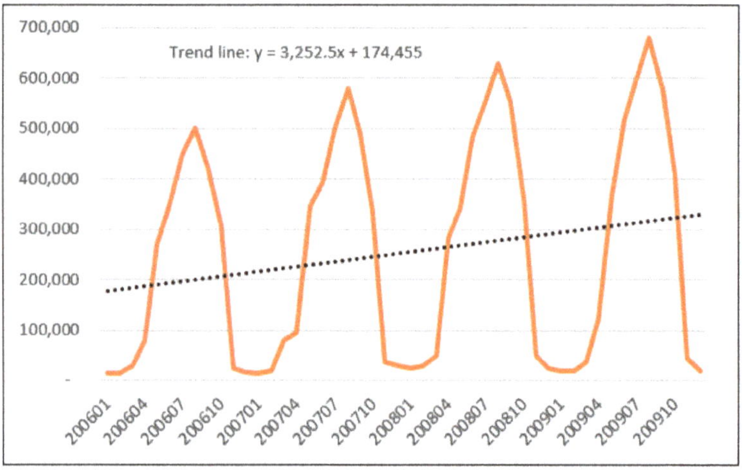

Trend line: y = 3,252.5x + 174,455

Next, we need to work out the seasonal variation. To do this, we will apply a series of weights to each month of the year. If there were no seasonality, each month would have an equal weight of 1 and so the sum of weights per annum would add up to 12, as we saw in the previous Section.

This situation clearly does not apply here – clearly, some months will have a weight close to zero and others will be much higher than 1 – so we will illustrate how we calculate the weights using all 48 months' data.

The method for calculating the monthly weights is shown in Figure 20-5.

First, add up all the January volumes (Jan-06 + Jan-07 + Jan-08 + Jan-09).

If the passenger data is in one long column, the formula can just be copied for the remaining months.

Figure 20-5: Monthly Weights for Turkish Data

Month	Passengers	Proportion of Total	Weights
Jan	68,926	0.0057	0.0678
Feb	83,492	0.0068	0.0821
Mar	192,168	0.0158	0.1890
Apr	578,393	0.0474	0.5690
May	1,327,450	0.1088	1.3058
Jun	1,741,718	0.1428	1.7133
Jul	2,106,779	0.1727	2.0724
Aug	2,391,572	0.1960	2.3526
Sep	2,048,065	0.1679	2.0147
Oct	1,414,880	0.1160	1.3918
Nov	156,714	0.0128	0.1542
Dec	88,644	0.0073	0.0872
	12,198,801	1	12

The figure of 12.198 million shows the total demand over all 48 months in our sample.

Next, we divide each monthly total by the grand total to show the proportion of demand occurring in each month; by definition, these proportions must be equal to 1.

Finally, we multiply each proportion by 12 and we then have the weights for each month.

What these weights tell us is that January accounts for a little less than 7% of total demand whilst in October, say, monthly demand is some 39% higher than average.

So, for each month, we have a trend figure and a multiplier for each month of the year. If we multiply the trend by the seasonal factor, we will attain the modelled estimate for that month's demand.

By subtracting modelled from actual demand, we can see the variation for each month.

Figure 20-6 shows the results of the model for the first twelve months of the dataset.

Figure 20-6: Calculation of Residuals – 2006 Data

Month	Passengers	Trend	Seasonal Element	Modelled (Trend * Seasonal Element)	Residual
1	14,265	177,708	0.0678	12,049	2,216
2	14,056	180,960	0.0821	14,863	-807
3	28,507	184,213	0.1890	34,823	-6,316
4	78,646	187,465	0.5690	106,662	-28,016
5	268,815	190,718	1.3058	249,042	19,773
6	346,015	193,970	1.7133	332,336	13,679
7	449,948	197,223	2.0724	408,733	41,215
8	500,307	200,475	2.3526	471,638	28,669
9	424,896	203,728	2.0147	410,448	14,448
10	308,596	206,980	1.3918	288,080	20,516
11	24,525	210,233	0.1542	32,410	- 7,885
12	17,518	213,485	0.0872	18,616	- 1,098

The comparison between the actual and modelled demand can be seen in Figure 20-7 when the exercise is carried out for all 48 months.

Figure 20-7: Actual and Modelled Turkish Demand

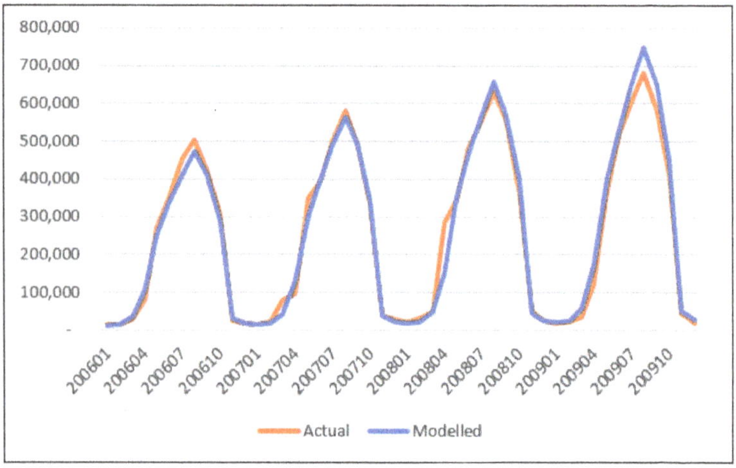

20.3.3 How Effective is the Model?

From Figure 20-7 we can see that, overall, the model works reasonably well. The model has over-estimated demand during the summer of 2009, however.

To get a better understanding of how well the model is working, we can look at a graph of the residual terms.

Figure 20-8: Residual Terms of the Mode

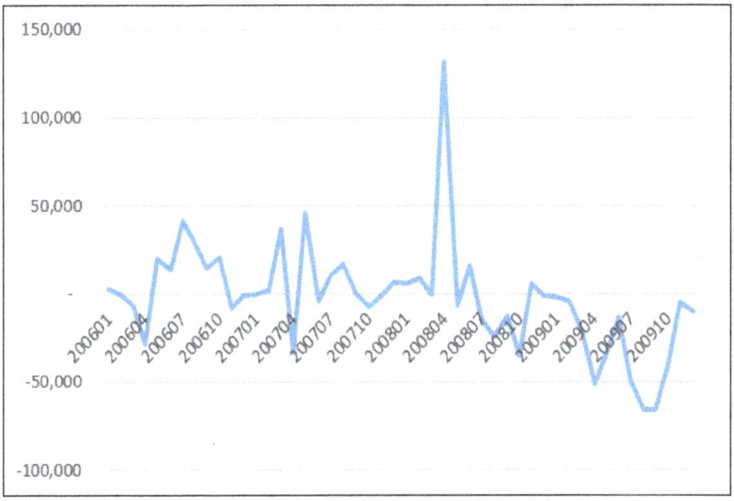

Figure 20-8 shows a spike in actual demand for April 2008, whose volumes were much higher than in either 2007 or 2009. This figure could be a data error or explained by some unknown event. The over-estimation of demand in summer 2009 could be attributable to the recession which hit western Europe late in 2008.

However, one forecasting method may not be the most effective. In the following Sections, we will introduce a very different method of forecasting and compare the efficiency of the two methods we describe. Both methods will then be used to forecast demand for Turkish resort airports for the first eight months of 2010 and compare the forecasts with what eventually occurred.

20.4 Exponential Smoothing (ES)

20.4.1 Principles of ES

With time series decomposition in the previous Section, we employed a trend line and constant seasonal factors for each month of the year, so the seasonal factor for April 2008, for example, was the same as for April 2006.

What we shall do now is demonstrate a method which explicitly takes account of previous values of demand.

Let us take a simple example in which we have eight weeks of sales data.

The output from the ES method is shown in Figure 20-9 and Figure 20-10.

Figure 20-9: Simple ES Example

	Col D	Col E	Col F	Col G
			Alpha	0.3
	Week	Demand	Forecast from Prior Week	Forecast for Next Week
Row 6	Week 1	27.0	0.0	27.0
Row 7	Week 2	31.0	27.0	28.2
Row 8	Week 3	29.0	28.2	28.4
Row 9	Week 4	35.0	28.4	30.4
Row 10	Week 5	33.0	30.4	31.2
Row 11	Week 6	41.0	31.2	34.1
Row 12	Week 7	29.0	34.1	32.6
Row 13	Week 8	32.0	32.6	32.4

Figure 20-10: Previous Table Showing Formulae

	Col D	Col E	Col F	Col G
Row 3			Alpha	0.3
	Week	Demand	Forecast from Prior Week	Forecast for Next Week
Row 6	Week 1	27	0	27
Row 7	Week 2	31	=G6	=$G$3*E7+(1-$G$3)*F7
Row 8	Week 3	29	=G7	=$G$3*E8+(1-$G$3)*F8
Row 9	Week 4	35	=G8	=$G$3*E9+(1-$G$3)*F9
Row 10	Week 5	33	=G9	=$G$3*E10+(1-$G$3)*F10
Row 11	Week 6	41	=G10	=$G$3*E11+(1-$G$3)*F11
Row 12	Week 7	29	=G11	=$G$3*E12+(1-$G$3)*F12
Row 13	Week 8	32	=G12	=$G$3*E13+(1-$G$3)*F13

The actual demand is provided in column E and the smoothing function occurs in column G.

Actually, what ES does is to state that a smoothed value in a given period is given a weight of 0.3 (in this case) of the current value and a 0.7 weight for previous values. The value of alpha must be between zero and one.

By choosing a low value of Alpha, we have given more weight to previous values than the current one.

In doing so we can see how the original dataset has become significantly smoother as a result of the ES exercise.

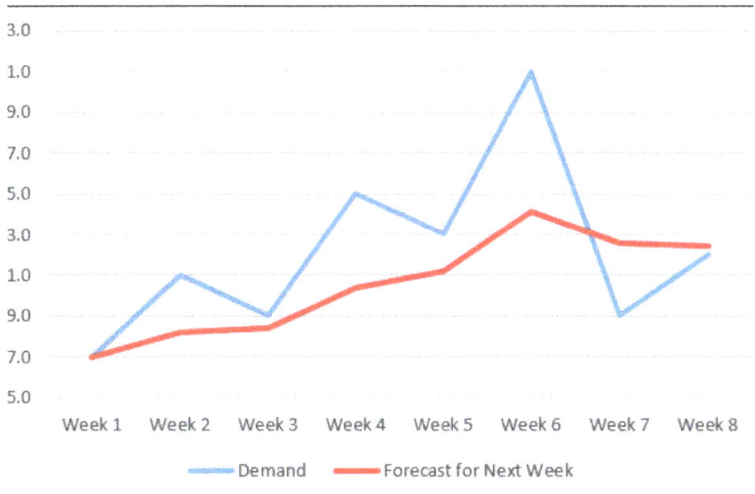
Figure 20-11: Actual and ES Data

A natural question that you may consider at this point is how do we pick the 'best' alpha?

We will address this issue in the next Section, when we apply a more complicated form of ES to the Turkish data, which takes account of both the trend and seasonality elements that we have seen are present in the data.

20.5 Holt Winters Exponential Smoothing (HWES)

20.5.1 Overview

HWES is a methodology which combines three basic elements:

- A base level of underlying demand;
- A trend element; and
- A seasonal factor for each month.

We saw in the previous Section with the simple ES method that we applied an arbitrary damping factor of 0.3 to smooth the data. For HWES, we will initially use 0.3 for all three separate factors.

The set-up of the model is a little complicated; therefore, the formulae used to develop the model are relegated to an annex of this Chapter.

20.5.2 The HWES Model

The model for HWES using the Turkish air passenger data is presented in Figure 20-12. Please note that months 19 to 46 are omitted for brevity.

Figure 20-12: HWES Model (Abridged)

Month		Passengers	Underlying Demand	Trend	Seasonals	Forecast	Absolute Deviation
Jan	1	14,265			0.07		
Feb	2	14,056			0.07		
Mar	3	28,507			0.14	Alpha	0.3
Apr	4	78,646			0.38	Beta	0.3
May	5	268,815			1.30	Gamma	0.3
Jun	6	346,015			1.68		
Jul	7	449,948			2.18		
Aug	8	500,307			2.42		
Sep	9	424,896			2.06		
Oct	10	308,596			1.50		
Nov	11	24,525			0.12		
Dec	12	17,518	206,341	-	0.08		
Jan	13	14,056	205,434	- 272	0.07	14,265	209
Feb	14	19,632	230,072	7,201	0.07	13,976	5,656
Mar	15	78,646	336,870	37,080	0.17	32,780	45,866
Apr	16	95,361	336,823	25,942	0.35	142,529	47,168
May	17	346,235	333,666	17,212	1.22	472,600	126,365
Jun	18	394,467	316,185	6,804	1.55	588,391	193,924
....							
Nov	47	45,342	326,196	5,557	0.14	44,907	435
Dec	48	18,374	294,192	- 5,712	0.08	29,512	11,138
							83,864

In the model, we can see three columns that make up the forecast, which are the underlying demand, trend and seasonality elements.

The underlying demand figure for the first December is the average of the first twelve months of data and the seasonal elements for the first twelve months only are calculated in the same way as in Figure 20-5.

The initial trend value, for December 2006, is set to zero.

Thereafter, underlying demand values are weighted with 'alpha', trend values with 'beta' and seasonality factors with 'gamma'.

20.5.3 Absolute Deviation

What we have in the model for HWES using the Turkish air passenger data is presented in Figure 20-12.

Please note that months 19 to 46 are omitted for brevity. are modelled values (labelled 'Forecast') and the actual values ('passengers').

The column 'absolute deviation' shows the difference between these two values, irrespective of sign. The average error over all 48 months is 83,864 passengers.

Please note, though, that the values for Alpha, Beta and Gamma were chosen at random. What we aim to achieve in any forecast is to minimise the difference between the actual and modelled values. In other words:

- Minimise mean absolute deviation (MAD), subject to:
  - Alpha, beta and gamma being greater than or equal to zero; and
  - Alpha beta and gamma being less than or equal to one.

If this formulation looks familiar to you, then congratulations! What we have here is a simple linear programming exercise, which we first encountered in Chapter 14.

In Figure 20-13, we can see the arguments in Solver prior to solving the problem. Please note that the solving method needs to be set to 'Evolutionary'.

Figure 20-13: LP Formulation to Solve Parameters

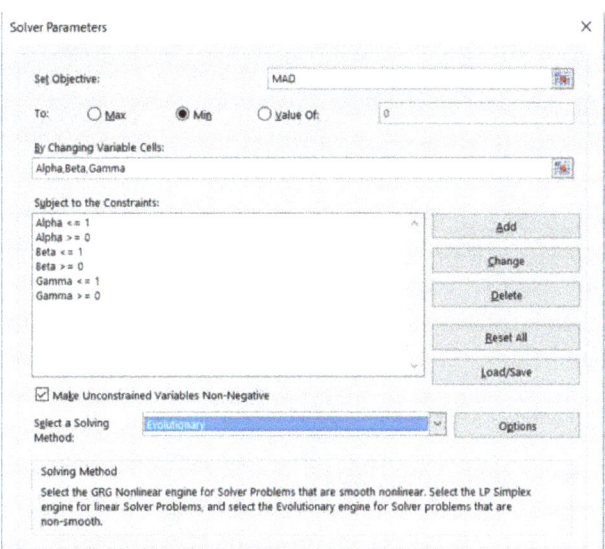

20.5.4 Optimized HWES Output

We can now see the values for Alpha, Beta and Gamma which minimise the MAD figure in Figure 20-14.

Figure 20-14: Optimised HWES Output

Month		Passengers	Underlying Demand	Trend	Seasonals	Forecast	Absolute Deviation
Jan	1	14,265			0.07		
Feb	2	14,056			0.07		
Mar	3	28,507			0.14		
Apr	4	78,646			0.38		
May	5	268,815			1.30		
Jun	6	346,015			1.68		
Jul	7	449,948			2.18		
Aug	8	500,307			2.42		
Sep	9	424,896			2.06		
Oct	10	308,596			1.50		
Nov	11	24,525			0.12		
Dec	12	17,518	206,341	-	0.08		
Jan	13	14,056	206,236	1	0.07	14,265	209
Feb	14	19,632	209,077	39	0.07	14,049	5,583
Mar	15	78,646	221,602	217	0.16	28,890	49,756
Apr	16	95,361	222,803	231	0.39	84,545	10,816
May	17	346,235	224,516	252	1.32	290,562	55,673
Jun	18	394,467	225,131	257	1.68	376,915	17,552
Nov	47	45,342	284,304	837	0.13	35,870	9,472
Dec	48	18,374	282,495	800	0.09	25,091	6,717
							19,075

Alpha 0.034671
Beta 0.014258
Gamma 0.083389

Note that the mean absolute deviation is now just over 19,000 passengers rather than the 83,000 reported in Figure 20-12.

20.5.5 MAD for TSD Method

The MAD for the HWES looks reasonable, representing less than 10% of average passenger demand per month, but as we are comparing the two methods, we need to calculate the MAD for the first method as well.

For Time Series Decomposition, the MAD is in fact slightly higher, at 20,419.

20.6 Forecasting Using TSD and HWES Methods

We now come to the crux of the Chapter, which is to test the two different models for forecasting.

We will develop the forecasts for January to August 2010 and then compare these forecasts with the actual demand for these months.

Figure 20-15: Outturn Demand Against Forecasts

	TSD	HWES	Actual	TSD MAD	HWES MAD
Jan-10	22,634	20,269	17,815	4,819	2,454
Feb-10	27,685	22,095	19,821	7,864	2,274
Mar-10	64,335	47,488	38,675	25,660	8,813
Apr-10	195,489	136,148	126,949	68,540	9,199
May-10	452,907	381,586	500,300	47,393	118,714
Jun-10	599,822	496,534	648,860	49,038	152,326
Jul-10	732,285	625,602	734,592	2,307	108,990
Aug-10	838,926	703,612	759,003	79,923	55,391
				35,693	57,270

We can see in Figure 20-15 that the HWES method significantly underestimated the summer peak for 2010 and that the MAD for the eight forecast months was somewhat higher than the TSD method.

In Figure 20-16 we can see a graph that summarises how the two methods performed.

Figure 20-16: Graph of Actual and Forecast Demand

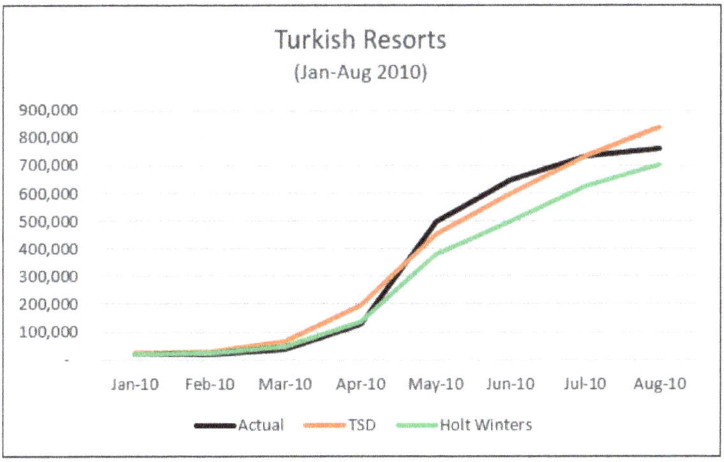

To understand why the HWES undershot actual demand the way it did, we will now examine peak summer demand for the five years for which we have data available (2006-2010 inclusive).

Figure 20-17 shows demand for the peak summer months in each year.

Figure 20-17: Summer Demand to Turkish Resorts

Summer (June to August)		
	Demand	Change
2006	1,296,270	
2007	1,474,359	14%
2008	1,668,276	13%
2009	1,801,164	8%
2010	2,142,455	19%

What has happened is that the trend element in HWES slowed down dramatically in 2009 as a result of the relatively weak increase in demand compared to previous years.

The underlying demand element, which had been increasing significantly, also started to slow down in the same year.

By contrast, the TSD method uses a constant trend figure over all periods and so the forecast was not as adversely affected as HWES.

The increase in 2010 was much higher than anything seen in the years 2006 to 2009 inclusive, which explains why the HWES method undershot more than TSD.

20.7 Lessons Learned

We have undertaken some extensive analysis in this Chapter to explain how short-term forecasts can be developed for time series.

Although the HWES model appeared to be the better choice (it had the lower MAD for historic data), it proved to be a relative weak forecaster of demand because of the slowdown in demand increase in 2009, which caused the under-estimation of 2010.

Usually, there is some visibility about bookings in the next summer season and, if demand were expected to surge in 2010, we would probably steer clear of the HWES method in this case.

A second test was run on modelling demand between the UK and Dubai for the three years 2011 to 2013 and forecasts were developed using both methods for January to September 2014.

For this second test, the MAD was a little higher using HWES for the 'historic' data but showed less errors than the TSD method when 'forecasting' demand during the first nine months of 2014.

We can conclude by saying that one of the methods is not superior to the other, as TSD turned out to be the better forecaster for Turkey whilst HWES proved more accurate for Dubai.

Therefore, forecasting requires judgement as well as using numerical tools and we need to base our judgment on the better method not just from the numbers but also the specific situation we are attempting to forecast.

20.8 Seasonality at Terminals

We will finish this chapter with what will appear to many readers as light relief after the extensive analysis of Turkish air transport demand and switch our attention briefly to terminals.

Seasonality is a major challenge for many terminal owners. Whilst airline and ferry operators can lease in extra capacity during high seasons or lease out spare capacity in periods of low demand, the capacity of terminals is fixed throughout the year.

To illustrate this, let us look at the airport of Zakynthos in Greece, an island which has a population of a little over 40,000. In 2014, the airport registered 1.2 million passengers, all but 40,000 of which were international.

In the summer months, there are a little over 100,000 arrivals per month from the UK in July and August, whereas between November and March, there are no more than 200. Therefore, the profitability of Zakynthos airport is determined by no more than seven months of the year.

By contrast, in winter months, there are usually around five flights per week and these are domestic flights to Athens using small (50 seat) aircraft.

A second example of extreme seasonality, in this case by hour of day, may be witnessed regularly at Bole airport (Addis Ababa, Ethiopia).

The dominant operator is Ethiopian Airlines and their strategy is to funnel all their flights through one morning and one evening wave per day.

In Figure 20-18, we can see that arrivals dominate between 6 and 8am, enabling those passengers in transit to catch departing flights between 8am and 11am.

After this morning peak, the airport is mainly silent until 7pm, when the next wave of arrivals and departures begins.

The morning wave channels passengers from Asian, American and European origins to African destinations (the 'southbound' wave), whilst the evening wave reverses the flow from origins south of Addis Ababa to destinations in the rest of the world ('northbound' wave).

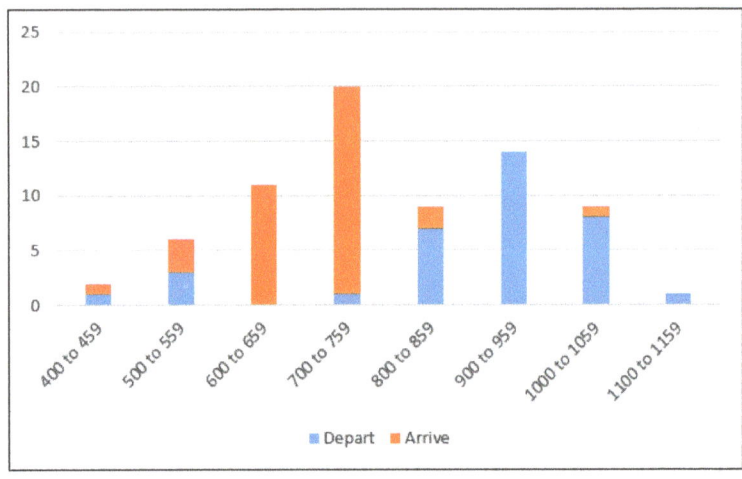

Figure 20-18: Aircraft Movements at Bole Airport - Morning

Source: www.flightstats.com. A day was selected at random for this exercise.

The graph above shows aircraft movements for Terminal 2 only; Terminal 1 was originally used for domestic flights but a small number of regional destinations were shifted to the domestic terminal in order to ease pressure on Terminal 2. This pressure is considerable: the stated capacity of Terminal 2 is 5 million passengers per annum but, in 2014, 7 million passenger movements were recorded[74]. Whilst operating at 140% of design capacity may not seem excessive, the fact that the bulk of passenger movements are squeezed into two five hour periods suggests that the hourly design capacity is exceeded by a much higher margin than 40%.

A parallel issue concerns the strategy of Ethiopian Airlines itself. Superficially, aircraft utilization on many routes is poor, with aircraft sitting on the ground for over 12 hours each day at Heathrow and Frankfurt, to name but two routes, in order to arrive back at the Addis Ababa hub for the southbound wave.

However, this strategy clearly works for the airline, given its levels of profitability[75].

74 http://www.reuters.com/article/2015/02/12/us-ethiopia-airport-idUSKBN0LG1X020150212
75 http://afkinsider.com/102462/ethiopian-airlines-make-more-profit-than-all-other-african-carriers-combined/

20.9 Chapter 20 Exercise

This question will test your understanding of regression and seasonality using real data from the Canary Islands. The data in the following table shows passenger demand between the islands of Tenerife and Gran Canaria for 58 months from January 2011 to October 2015 inclusive. The data for the exercise needs to be in three columns showing time, ferry and air demand.

- Draw simple line charts for ferry and air demand over time. What evidence can you see in terms of long term trend and seasonality for each mode?
- For each mode, undertake a simple regression for each mode separately of demand and time. What do the results for each regression tell us about the long-term trend in demand for each?
- You now need to set up four new columns on your spreadsheet. For ferry, use the regression equation to model the trend in demand and, in the next column, calculate the residual (actual minus modelled) for each month. Repeat this exercise for air demand.
- For each mode, you should now have 58 residuals. In a separate part of the spreadsheet, calculate the average residual for each month of the year. So, for example, the average January residual is the residual from months 1, 13, 25, 37 and 49.
- We now need to set up two final columns which will add together the trend effects from step 3 and the seasonality impact from step 4.
- For each mode, now graph actual demand with modelled demand (trend plus seasonality).
- You should now have two charts that show very different seasonal variations during July and August for ferry and air travel between the two islands. Why do you think that the summer variation in demand is so different for ferry compared to air travel?
- If, at this point, you have not yet lost the will to live, repeat the exercise using the HWES method and compare the results.

The data to solve this problem is on the next page.

Month	Ferry	Air	Month	Ferry	Air
2011 01	74,497	52,977	2013 06	113,300	50,353
2011 02	70,661	60,146	2013 07	121,933	46,903
2011 03	103,102	65,661	2013 08	129,196	33,615
2011 04	97,820	61,542	2013 09	102,709	44,892
2011 05	90,136	65,184	2013 10	91,923	53,585
2011 06	95,446	67,594	2013 11	84,662	52,060
2011 07	98,271	63,788	2013 12	95,838	43,930
2011 08	111,099	51,771	2014 01	73,062	47,622
2011 09	89,747	62,624	2014 02	73,508	48,997
2011 10	80,302	67,056	2014 03	92,643	53,738
2011 11	70,114	70,018	2014 04	102,884	50,678
2011 12	85,562	62,779	2014 05	100,274	54,423
2012 01	63,703	59,170	2014 06	105,247	54,586
2012 02	66,589	59,291	2014 07	116,860	51,909
2012 03	73,077	66,838	2014 08	127,730	38,710
2012 04	82,743	57,556	2014 09	98,552	50,668
2012 05	84,927	61,873	2014 10	84,664	58,064
2012 06	87,052	60,211	2014 11	70,584	53,392
2012 07	102,052	55,949	2014 12	93,173	53,489
2012 08	105,354	39,955	2015 01	76,843	46,608
2012 09	82,877	47,422	2015 02	82,197	46,475
2012 10	80,756	54,491	2015 03	89,062	55,624
2012 11	74,933	52,745	2015 04	110,398	55,139
2012 12	92,135	47,867	2015 05	99,470	55,470
2013 01	84,644	46,949	2015 06	102,071	57,059
2013 02	93,659	44,634	2015 07	128,679	54,109
2013 03	108,553	51,003	2015 08	133,928	40,839
2013 04	84,364	50,533	2015 09	98,967	50,775
2013 05	102,001	51,628	2015 10	101,045	58,841

20.10 Annex: Formulation of HWES Spreadsheet

There are three phases to setting up the spreadsheet: the initial In the second sheet view below, we can see the formula for calculating the absolute deviation and the MAD is simply the average of deviation of the 36 monthly values calculated by HWES compared to actual data. Note that alpha (J7), beta (J8) and gamma (J9) are not shown. Column B contains month labels (Jan, Feb, etc) and column C contains a month counter, with cell C4 having a value of 1, C5 contains 2 down to cell C51, which has a value of 48.

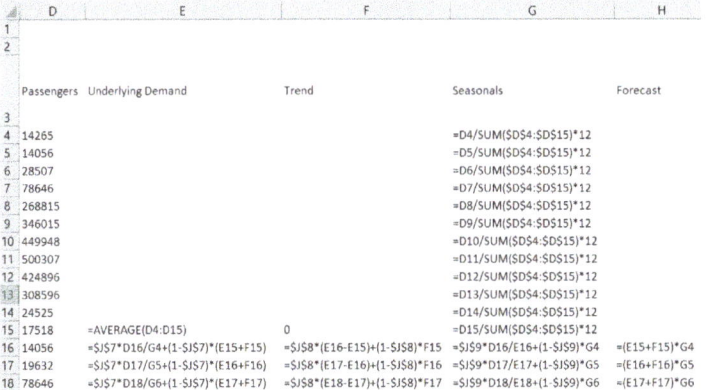

In the second sheet view below, we can see the formula for calculating the absolute deviation and the MAD is simply the average of deviation of the 36 monthly values calculated by HWES compared to actual data.

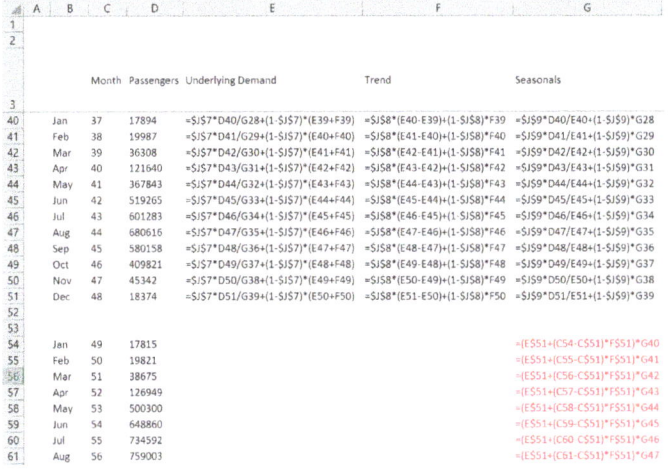

315

The forecasts for January to August 2010 (months 49-56) are shown in red text. The forecasts are a function of the final value of underlying demand (E51), a counter to represent the number of months we are away from the last actual value (C54-C51 gives us 1, for example), the final trend value calculated (F51) and the latest seasonal factor for each month, so the forecast for April 2010 (G57) uses the seasonal factor from April 2009 (G43).

The HWES method is cumbersome to set up, without doubt. However, once it has been completed, it is relatively easy to adapt to any dataset.

21 HOW TO UNDERTAKE AN INVESTMENT APPRAISAL

21.1 Overview

Very often, the most difficult aspect of carrying out an investment appraisal is to set out the information in an orderly manner to undertake the calculations. Later in this Chapter, we will undertake work on a relatively straightforward example, including a step-by-step guide on how to calculate the viability of a project.

Before we start work on this example, however, we need to discuss the time value of money.

21.2 Introducing the Discount Rate

21.2.1 General Concepts

Let us imagine that you are given a choice between €1 today and €1 in one year's time. We will assume that there is no inflation, so all figures quoted in this Chapter are in real terms. The rational response is to take the €1 on offer today, for two reasons:

- You could take the money and invest it, thus yielding somewhat more than €1 in a year's time, say, €1.10;

- Alternatively, you might consider that there is a risk that the person offering you the €1 may not be around in a year and therefore, as compensation for this risk, you would need to be offered more than €1 in a year's time to compensate you for this risk. If you require 10% compensation, you would equate €1 now with €1.10 in one year's time.

Let us now put this concept in a transport-related framework. If we invest in a new railway or rehabilitate a ferry now, this means that the expenditure incurred cannot be used for other purposes (this is known as an opportunity cost) and therefore each €1 of current expenditure is worth more to us than €1 of expenditure in the future.

For revenue, the risk argument is more apt.

As we saw in Chapter 19, there are many things that can blow demand forecasts off course and, the farther out the expected demand, the more risk we need to apply to the revenue stream to convert it to the equivalent of today's money.

21.2.2 The Discount Rate in Practice

We now need to perform a little bit of algebra! If we have determined that €1 now is worth €1.10 in a year's time, how much is €1, which we will receive a year from now, worth to us today?

$$\text{Let } €1.00 \text{ (Year 0)} = €1.10 \text{ (Year 1)}$$

If we divide both sides of this equation by 1.1, we get

$$€0.909 \text{ (Year 0)} = €1.00 \text{ (Year 1)}$$

where €0.909 is €1/(1.10) or €1/(1+10%).

Let us now generalise this formula for any discount rate and several years. In Figure 21-1, Year 0 is best viewed as when the assessment is being undertaken.

Figure 21-1: Value of €1 Over Time

Period	Value of €1
Year 0	1
Year 1	$1/(1+r)$
Year 2	$1/(1+r)^2$
Year 3	$1/(1+r)^3$
....	....
Year n	$1/(1+r)^n$

So, if we have five years' worth of revenue of €100 starting from next year (Year 1), the value of this revenue is:

$$100/(1.1) + 100/(1.1^2) + 100/(1.1^3) + 100/(1.1^4) + 100/(1.1^5)$$

using a 10% discount rate.

However, we do not need to calculate such a fearsome expression, as Excel will take care of this, as we shall see in Section 21.6.

One issue which becomes apparent early on when undertaking investment appraisals is how much revenues and costs in later years have relatively little impact on the investment decision.

To illustrate the impact of discounting on projected costs and benefits, Figure 21-2 demonstrates how the value of €1 diminishes over time and as the discount rate increases.

Figure 21-2: Current Value of a future €1

	5%	10%	15%
5 Years	0.784	0.621	0.497
10 years	0.614	0.386	0.247
15 years	0.481	0.239	0.123
20 years	0.377	0.149	0.061

Another way of looking at Figure 21-2 is that at least €2 of revenue in fifteen years' time (for example) is worth less than €1 of revenue today, using a 5% discount rate.

21.3 Net Present Value (NPV)

The NPV of an investment can be defined in fairly straightforward terms as the present value of the revenue or benefits minus the present value of the costs. To illustrate the concept, we will assume an investment of €100 now (Year 0) and benefits of €50 per annum for three years thereafter. The data is shown in Figure 21-3. We will use a discount rate of 10% to illustrate the concept.

Figure 21-3: NPV Example

Period	Cash Flow	Discount Factor	PV Cash Flow
Year 0	-100		-100
Year 1	+50	$1/(1.1)$	45.45
Year 2	+50	$1/(1.1)^2$	41.32
Year 3	+50	$1/(1.1)^3$	37.57

So, the present value of costs is €100, so unchanged from the original value, whilst the present value of benefits is €124.34, which we get by adding up the last three figures in the final column. The NPV of this project is therefore €124.34 - €100 or €24.34.

21.4 Internal Rate of Return (IRR)

If, instead of using a 10% discount rate in Figure 21-3, we had used 20% instead, the NPV would only be €5.32. Let us now ask what is the maximum discount rate that can be used in a project before the NPV becomes 0.

This figure is known as the IRR.

To illustrate this point, let us look at a slightly more complex project, which incurs €100 of costs now, followed by €15 of revenue for ten years thereafter.

Figure 21-4 shows how the NPV declines as we start the discount rate at 1% and steadily increase it to 13%.

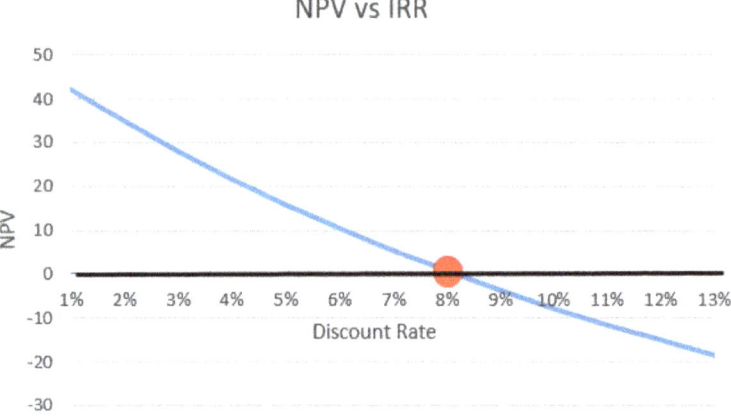

Figure 21-4: NPV and IRR Combined

The rate at which NPV is 0 uses a discount rate of 8.14%, or, in other words, the project's IRR is 8.14%. Once again, however, we will be able to calculate the IRR simply using an Excel formula.

21.5 NPV Compared to IRR: Which is Better?

21.5.1 NPV

NPV allows the evaluator to quantify what the benefits will be, as it produces a single figure in today's money.

It is then straightforward to compare one project with another and select the one with the higher NPV.

There are times, however, when the IRR and NPV methods give conflicting answers, as we shall now demonstrate.

A firm has to choose project A or Project B and the firm uses a discount rate of 5%. The results of the NPV and IRR calculations are shown in Figure 21-5.

Figure 21-5: Conflicting NPV and IRR Results

		Project A	Project B	
	Year 0	- 5,000	- 20,000	
	Year 1	2,000	7,000	
	Year 2	2,000	7,000	
	Year 3	2,000	7,000	
	Year 4	2,000	7,000	
	Year 5	2,000	7,000	
Discount rate:	5%	3,659	10,306	NPV
		29%	22%	IRR

If the firm had sufficient funds to carry out both projects and the two projects were independent, then we would carry out both. However, on those occasions where the results conflict, we would always select the project with the higher NPV.

The reason why project B is preferred is because its overall benefits are higher. Although the IRR is higher for project A, we would need to find a third project (say C) in which to invest to provide for the shortfall of 6,647 of benefits (10,306-3,659) that we have suffered from not choosing project B.

So far, we have just taken the discount rate as a given and, in many cases, this is acceptable practice (as we shall see in in Figure 21-6). But what if such guidance is not available?

A firm should ideally select its discount rate based on its weighted average cost of capital (WACC)[76] so that any project has a higher return than what it pays for its funds. The appropriate discount rate would then be the WACC plus a premium to take into account the project's specific risk.

In practice, however, the majority of firms do not undertake such a complex exercise, so the discount rate actually used may not reflect the company's cost of capital or the risks associated with the project.

21.5.2 IRR

Using IRR to evaluate projects does have the virtue of not requiring the company to assess a project – or even company-specific discount rate.

---
76 For a brief explanation of WACC, see http://www.investopedia.com/terms/w/wacc.asp

As we saw in the previous Section, however, the use of IRR alone could lead to selecting the less beneficial project. IRR has a second problem, which is often glossed over but, to explain this problem, we will have to revert to some algebra! If we look back at Figure 21-1, we will convert this table into IRR format, so that the sum of the terms is equal to an NPV of zero. In other words:

$$1 + 1/(1+r) + 1/(1+r)^2 + 1/(1+r)^3 + 1/(1+r)^4 + 1/(1+r)^5 = 0 \quad \text{(Equation 1)}$$

for an initial year plus five years of cashflows. The IRR method requires us to solve this polynomial equation for the discount rate r. However, the problem arises that if there are five years of discounting, there will be five solutions to the equation above. Some solutions will be negative, but what if there are two positive solutions that are similar? Consider the following equation, for example:

$$X^2 - 17X + 72 = 0 \quad \text{(Equation 2)}$$

Which is a similar format to equation (1). We can also write equation 2 as $(X-8) * (X-9) = 0$. We can now immediately see that this equation is solved if $X = 8$ or $X = 9$. Both are valid answers but Excel will only provide us with one solution for IRR calculations. These last two Sections have raised complex issues, the solutions for which are beyond the scope of this book, but it is important to be aware of the advantages and disadvantages of the two appraisal methods.

21.6 Applying Investment Appraisal Techniques

In this Section, we will complete an investment appraisal problem from first principles, including the Excel functions required to assess the value of the project.

A railway company has decided to run a new service between two points, A and B, starting in January. The rolling cost lease costs are estimated at £300,000 per annum and all other costs (staff, track access agreements, period advertising) have been calculated at £200,000 per annum. The service will run for ten years, after which all costs and revenue estimates will be examined once again as the lease agreement comes up for renewal. The market research experts within the company have calculated that the annual revenue from this new service will be £500,000 in the first year of operation, with £20,000 annual increases in revenue up to and including the tenth year.

Before the service starts, the operator intends to carry out a large scale promotional campaign, which will cost £250,000. The Managing Director wishes to know whether the service will be profitable or if a subsidy will be required. The discount rate to be used for this project is 12%.

The latest discount rates provided by Government at the time of writing are, in fact, significantly lower than this. Figure 21-6, an extract from the Green Book[77] (developed by the Treasury) provides for much lower discount rates than would be used in the private sector.

Figure 21-6: Guidelines for Discount Rates from the Green Book

Years from Current Year	Discount Rate
0-30	3.5%
31-75	3.0%
76-125	2.5%
126-200	2.0%
201-300	1.5%

Source: https://www.gov.uk/government/publications/webtag-tag-data-book-november-2014 Table A1.1.1

The first step (Figure 21-7) is to set out all the revenues and costs in an easy-to-follow table.

Note that 2015 is year 0 and 2016 is Year 1, and so on. It is critical to be consistent at this stage: revenues are positive figures and costs are negative.

Figure 21-7: Step 1 – Set out all costs and revenues

	Advertising Campaign	Leasing	Other Costs	Revenue
Year 0	- 250,000			
Year 1		- 300,000	- 200,000	500,000
Year 2		- 300,000	- 200,000	520,000
Year 3		- 300,000	- 200,000	540,000
Year 4		- 300,000	- 200,000	560,000
Year 5		- 300,000	- 200,000	580,000
Year 6		- 300,000	- 200,000	600,000
Year 7		- 300,000	- 200,000	620,000
Year 8		- 300,000	- 200,000	640,000
Year 9		- 300,000	- 200,000	660,000
Year 10		- 300,000	- 200,000	680,000

Next, we add a column to the right showing the net cash flow for each year.

---

[77] https://www.gov.uk/government/uploads/system/uploads/attachment_data/file/220541/green_book_complete.pdf

Figure 21-8: Step 2 – Add the annual summary of revenues and costs

	Advertising Campaign	Leasing		Other Costs	Revenue	Total
Year 0	- 250,000				-	250,000
Year 1		- 300,000	-	200,000	500,000	-
Year 2		- 300,000	-	200,000	520,000	20,000
Year 3		- 300,000	-	200,000	540,000	40,000
Year 4		- 300,000	-	200,000	560,000	60,000
Year 5		- 300,000	-	200,000	580,000	80,000
Year 6		- 300,000	-	200,000	600,000	100,000
Year 7		- 300,000	-	200,000	620,000	120,000
Year 8		- 300,000	-	200,000	640,000	140,000
Year 9		- 300,000	-	200,000	660,000	160,000
Year 10		- 300,000	-	200,000	680,000	180,000

Next, add in a discount rate. It is good practice to input the figure explicitly so it is easier to change it later if required.

In the case below, the discount rate has been input into cell Cl4.

Figure 21-9: Step 3 – Add a discount rate into your spreadsheet

	Advertising Campaign	Leasing		Other Costs	Revenue	Total
Year 0	- 250,000				-	250,000
Year 1		- 300,000	-	200,000	500,000	-
Year 2		- 300,000	-	200,000	520,000	20,000
Year 3		- 300,000	-	200,000	540,000	40,000
Year 4		- 300,000	-	200,000	560,000	60,000
Year 5		- 300,000	-	200,000	580,000	80,000
Year 6		- 300,000	-	200,000	600,000	100,000
Year 7		- 300,000	-	200,000	620,000	120,000
Year 8		- 300,000	-	200,000	640,000	140,000
Year 9		- 300,000	-	200,000	660,000	160,000
Year 10		- 300,000	-	200,000	680,000	180,000
Discount Rate:		12%				

Next, we invoke the NPV formula, which is

NPV (rate, range to evaluate).

Excel does not accept the concept of year 0 for NPV calculations, so our range to evaluate in this case is from year 1 to year 10. We then need to add on the -£250,000 for Year 0 manually to our NPV figure. The formula used to calculate the NPV figure is as follows:

=NPV(Cl4,F3:F12)+F2

where Cl4 is the discount rate, F3:F12 are the annual cash flows from year 1 and F2 is the cash flow from year 0 (in this case, the cost of the initial advertising campaign).

We do not discount this 250,000 as this expenditure will be incurred in the current year.

As a general rule, always try to avoid using numbers in formulae.

If there are several formulae on a spreadsheet with, say, the discount rate and you need to change this figure, you will have to change the discount rate in every formula in which it appears.

By contrast, using a cell reference (Cl4 in this case) rather than "12%" means only one change is necessary – Excel will automatically change all formulae where the discount rate is used.

Figure 21-10: Step 4 – Calculating the NPV

	Advertising Campaign	Leasing	Other Costs	Revenue	Total
Year 0	- 250,000				- 250,000
Year 1		- 300,000	- 200,000	500,000	-
Year 2		- 300,000	- 200,000	520,000	20,000
Year 3		- 300,000	- 200,000	540,000	40,000
Year 4		- 300,000	- 200,000	560,000	60,000
Year 5		- 300,000	- 200,000	580,000	80,000
Year 6		- 300,000	- 200,000	600,000	100,000
Year 7		- 300,000	- 200,000	620,000	120,000
Year 8		- 300,000	- 200,000	640,000	140,000
Year 9		- 300,000	- 200,000	660,000	160,000
Year 10		- 300,000	- 200,000	680,000	180,000
Discount Rate:		12%			
NPV		£155,081.78			

So, we have almost finished.

We can see that, at a discount rate of 12%, the project is worth a little over £150,000 to us today.

Unfortunately, discount rates are not always available or else they are very difficult to calculate, as we discussed earlier.

So, another question we could ask is what is the maximum discount rate, which will give us a positive NPV?

For this we invoke the IRR; this is shown in row 18.

Figure 21-11: Step 5 – Calculating the Internal Rate of Return

	Advertising Campaign	Leasing	Other Costs	Revenue	Total
Year 0	250,000			-	250,000
Year 1		- 300,000	- 200,000	500,000	-
Year 2		- 300,000	- 200,000	520,000	20,000
Year 3		- 300,000	- 200,000	540,000	40,000
Year 4		- 300,000	- 200,000	560,000	60,000
Year 5		- 300,000	- 200,000	580,000	80,000
Year 6		- 300,000	- 200,000	600,000	100,000
Year 7		- 300,000	- 200,000	620,000	120,000
Year 8		- 300,000	- 200,000	640,000	140,000
Year 9		- 300,000	- 200,000	660,000	160,000
Year 10		- 300,000	- 200,000	680,000	180,000
Discount Rate:		12%			
NPV		£155,081.78			
IRR		21%			

So, this tells us that the project will still be positive up to a discount rate of approximately 21%.

The formula for IRR is similar to NPV, but note that the range comes first and DOES include Year 0:

IRR (range, guess)

The range is now F2 to F12 (including year 0). As Excel needs a starting point to work out the IRR, you can just supply a sensible one of your choosing (such as 10% or 0.1).

=IRR (F2:F12,0.1)

As mentioned previously, the IRR gives us the discount rate for which the NPV is zero.

To three decimal places, the IRR is 20.578%.

So, to test that this IRR figure is correct, replace the original 12% in the NPV formula with 20.578%.

The results are shown in step 6.

Figure 21-12: Step 6 - Confirmation that the IRR is Correct

	Advertising Campaign	Leasing	Other Costs	Revenue	Total
Year 0	250,000			-	- 250,000
Year 1		- 300,000	- 200,000	500,000	-
Year 2		- 300,000	- 200,000	520,000	20,000
Year 3		- 300,000	- 200,000	540,000	40,000
Year 4		- 300,000	- 200,000	560,000	60,000
Year 5		- 300,000	- 200,000	580,000	80,000
Year 6		- 300,000	- 200,000	600,000	100,000
Year 7		- 300,000	- 200,000	620,000	120,000
Year 8		- 300,000	- 200,000	640,000	140,000
Year 9		- 300,000	- 200,000	660,000	160,000
Year 10		- 300,000	- 200,000	680,000	180,000
Discount Rate:		21%			
NPV		-£0.18			
IRR		21%			

We can see that the NPV is now 18p, or zero to all intents and purposes.

21.7 A More Complex NPV Example

21.7.1 The Problem

An airline has just bought a new Airbus A350 and is evaluating the most profitable way to employ it. The aircraft will be used on one of two new routes, which are to Leisuretown or Businessville..

As the names imply, these routes serve very different markets. For Leisuretown, the aircraft will be fitted with in an all-economy configuration with 470 seats, whereas an analysis of the market for Businessville suggests that a three-class configuration with 320 seats is more appropriate.

The cost of fitting out the aircraft in either layout is assumed to be the same for our purposes.

The demand forecast suggests that Leisuretown flights will have an average load factor of 90%, whilst the Businessville route will achieve 75%.

As might be expected, the average return fare per passenger is somewhat higher to Businessville (€795) than to Leisuretown (€400).

In the first year of operation, Leisuretown flights would operate once per week and Businessville twice per week.

For the next four years, each route would be flown four times per week, which would use up the aircraft's capacity entirely (both routes are long haul and a similar distance).

Costs per flight are estimated at €150,000 for Leisuretown and €170,000 for Businessville (it costs more to serve First and Business Class passengers).

Finally, promotional costs per annum on the leisure route are €1,500,000 whilst the three-class business-oriented route will incur annual costs of €1,800,000.

Assuming a discount rate of 10%, is it possible to determine which route provides the better return (measured in NPV) for the airline?

21.7.2 Summarising the Data

When a problem such as this arises, the first step should always be to summarise the information provided, as before. This step is carried out in Figure 21-13.

Figure 21-13: Summarised Data for New Route Problem

	Leisuretown	Businessville
Year 1 frequency	1 per week	2 per week
Year 2 onwards	4 per week	4 per week
Capacity	470	320
Load Factor	90%	75%
Average Fare (€)	400	795
Costs per flight (€)	150,000	170,000
Promotional Costs	1,500,000	1,800,000

Note that the cost of the new aircraft is not included in the assessment. The aircraft has already been bought and so is not relevant to the route decision itself. We will also exclude any changes in maintenance or head office costs for this problem.

21.7.3 Preparing the NPV Calculation

What we now need to work out is the revenue and profit for each flight. For the Leisuretown route, the revenue per flight is 470*90%*€400 or €169,200. A similar calculation for Businessville gives us an average revenue of €190,800.

Next, we deduct the costs per flight for each route and so we have operating profit per flight of €19,200 for Leisuretown and €20,800 for Businessville. Assuming 52 weeks per year, we can now calculate the gross profit per annum for Year 1 and Year 2 onwards for each route. However, we must also subtract the promotional costs before we reach a net profit figure for each route. The relevant figures are shown in Figure 21-14.

Figure 21-14: Net Profit Calculations by Route

	Leisureland	Businessville
Revenue per flight	169,200	190,800
Profit per flight	19,200	20,800
Gross Profit Year 1	998,400	2,163,200
Gross Profit Year 2+	3,993,600	4,326,400
Net Profit Year 1	- 501,600	363,200
Net Profit Year 2+	2,493,600	2,526,400

For Leisureland, the profit per flight is 19,200, hence 998,400 in Year 1. Once the promotional costs for year 1 are subtracted (-1,500,000), our net profit for the year is -501,600, as shown.

21.7.4 Calculating the NPV

We are now in a position to calculate the NPV of the two alternative cash flows. This is probably the easiest part of solving the problem! The results are presented in Figure 21-15.

Figure 21-15: NPV Calculation

	Leisureland	Businessville
Year 1	- 501,600	363,200
Year 2	2,493,600	2,526,400
Year 3	2,493,600	2,526,400
Year 4	2,493,600	2,526,400
Year 5	2,493,600	2,526,400
Discount Rate	10%	10%
NPV	6,729,797	7,610,498

So, it looks as if The Businessville route provides the higher NPV and the initial recommendation is to proceed with the three-class configuration to serve the Businessville route.

21.7.5 Reassessing the NPV Calculation

Before signing off on this problem, we need to address two major flaws in the analysis. First, there has been no attempt at sensitivity analysis. If the problem is set up using the three tables above, this is a straightforward exercise. The analysis is extremely sensitive to changes in the fare. If the average fare to Leisuretown increases by just €5 return, the NPV increases to €8.1 million and so is higher than the Businessville figure. If the average fare to Businessville declines by just €5 (½%), the two NPVs are virtually indistinguishable.

A more serious omission in the calculations concerns revenues and profits in Year 1. In Year 1, the aircraft will have spare capacity which can be deployed on other routes. We have not been provided with any information on what these other routes would be and how much profitability would arise. It is safe to assume that the aircraft destined for Leisuretown would be deployed on other leisure routes whilst the aircraft with high yield seats would be used on a more business-oriented route in year one in addition to the flights to Businessville.

This is a process known as normalisation. In Years 2-5, we are comparing the profitability of a fully-utilised aircraft but this is not the case in Year 1. So, it is important when undertaking investment appraisal calculations to compare like with like. Adjustments would also be required if we were comparing one route over, say, five years and another over six.

21.7.6 Lessons Learned

The more complex NPV example above sheds light on several important issues when undertaking a financial evaluation:

- Only take account of relevant costs. The price tag of the new aircraft is a red herring here, as the aircraft has already been purchased;
- Keep it simple! Extract the information in the problem and develop tables setting out the information in a clear manner. Keep the calculations simple to avoid errors;

in the original draft of this problem, there was no gross profit step in the calculations, but it was easier to insert it so that the logic of the net profit calculation was clearer;

- Ensure that the layout of the problem allows for sensitivity tests. We saw in the above problem how sensitive the NPV calculations were to very small fare changes; and
- Having excluded irrelevant information, make sure that all relevant information has been included in the appraisal. The airline is unlikely to make its new aircraft sit on the ground in Year 1 and so will be deployed on existing routes whilst demand builds up on the new ones. We need the data for the other routes flown by the aircraft in Year 1 to come to a final decision based on the NPVs of Leisuretown and Businessville.

21.8 Lease or Buy Decision

Transport operators often face a choice whether to lease or buy aircraft or rolling stock. The choice would be made through investment appraisal techniques such as those outlined in the previous Section and is dependent on the:

- Purchase cost;
- Leasing cost;
- Residual value of the asset at the end of the period being evaluated;
- Taxation policy; and
- Depreciation policy.

Detailed discussion of these last two items is beyond the scope of this book, so an example will not be presented here. However, if the reader is interested in this area, comprehensive worked examples are provided at

http://www.cimaglobal.com/Thought-leadership/Newsletters/Velocity-e-magazine/Velocity-2012/Velocity-February-2012/Model-answer--F3-buying-or-leasing-assets/

and

http://kfknowledgebank.kaplan.co.uk/KFKB/Wiki%20Pages/Asset%20investment%20decisions.aspx.

21.9 Benefit: Cost Ratios – An Alternative Approach

A business will often have two or more opportunities for investment and sometimes, a NPV calculation by itself is insufficient to determine which is the better project to select. Consider the following two projects:

Project 1: Capital costs = £6m, PV of income = £10m;
Project 2: Capital costs = £100m, PV of income = £105m.

In both cases, we can see that the NPV (present value of income minus initial capital costs) is £4 million for Project 1 and £5 million for Project 2. Our 'gut instinct' would lead us to prefer Project 2 over Project 1, as its NPV is greater. However, there are several other issues to consider:

- In Project 2, small differences between the forecasts and the actual costs or benefits might totally eliminate the NPV;

- the organisation may simply not have £100m to spend, so that Project 2 is unaffordable, regardless of its benefits; and

- even if it does have the available funding, by choosing the cheaper Project 1 it leaves itself £94m to invest in other projects with benefits of their own.

So a further issue is that of choosing between projects that all have positive NPVs when, as we have seen above, bigger may not necessarily be better, and there is not capital available to pursue them all.

The key indicator when funds are limited is the Benefit: Cost Ratio (BCR), which is defined as:

$$\text{PV net annual benefits/income} \div \text{PV capital costs}$$

For our purposes and using the simple example of the two projects quoted above, Project 1 has a BCR of 1.7, and Project 2 a BCR of 1.05.

On this basis, we would argue that Project 1 provides 'more bang for your buck' and has lower risk, due to the initial outlay of £6 million rather than £100 million.

21.10 Mitigation of Risk

There are certain techniques that are available to help keep forecasts robust and supportable.

These include the selection of the discount rate itself and scenarios.

21.10.1 Scenarios

As we saw earlier in the text, having just one forecast is very much a hostage to fortune.

If, say, demand has been calculated at 2% growth in GDP per annum but in practice it turns out to be 1%, demand is likely to be significantly lower than forecast, with unpleasant financial consequences for the company.

To give an insight into the sensitivity of growth projections, consider Figure 21-16.

Figure 21-16: Sensitivity of Total Demand to Annual Growth Rates

Growth Rate	Demand in Year 0	Demand in Year 20	Demand in Year 30
1%	100	122	135
2%	100	149	181
3%	100	181	243

*Note: formula used was 100 * [(1+growth rate (%)] ^ (number of years)*

So, over thirty years, we can see that the difference between a 1% and 3% annual growth rate is close to double the volume of demand.

One way around this is to develop a series of internally consistent scenarios we examined in Section 19.6.

What, for example, is the impact of high fuel costs?

Operating costs would increase but demand for public transport could rise as people perceive the cost of a rail or bus journey to be cheaper than the equivalent journey by car.

Similarly, a period of sustained low fuel prices would reduce the operator's cost base but could well lead to an increase in demand for motoring.

21.10.2 Optimism Bias

HM Treasury (UK) provides guidance on optimism bias, which it justifies on the grounds that project promoters have a tendency toward optimism in evaluating a project's costs and benefits. The Green Book on optimism bias[78] proposes the following methodology:

- First, assume the highest level of optimism bias, which for standard civil engineering (hence most railway) projects is 44% of the present value of the capital cost;
- Determine how these risks can be mitigated. For example, using tried and trusted contractors or having a robust business case will mitigate the risk; and
- By determining what proportion of the optimism bias is attributable to each factor, such as contractors or business plan we are able to quantify the reduction in risk for a project.

Whilst the Green Book provides specific numbers to calculate optimism bias on capital costs, it does not do so for either benefit streams or operating costs. However, the guidance recommends nonetheless that a bias factor be included for these other two streams by undertaking sensitivity analysis. It suggests asking the following questions, which are in practice just sound business practice:

- By how much can we allow benefits to fall short of expectations, if the proposal is to remain worthwhile? How likely is this?
- How much can operating costs increase, if the proposal is to remain worthwhile? How likely is this to happen?

21.10.3 What a Financial Appraisal Can Miss

Even when an investment appraisal is thorough, it is still possible to overlook wider benefits and costs. Imagine, for example, that a car company decides not to invest $11 in a safety feature to make its vehicles safer and justifies this decision on the benefits gained ($11 extra profit per vehicle) against the value of lives likely to be lost should a car catch fire.

---

[78] https://www.gov.uk/government/uploads/system/uploads/attachment_data/file/191507/Optimism_bias.pdf

This is not an imaginary case but is in fact an allegation made against the Ford Pinto, which was made in the USA in the 1970s. Irrespective of the rights and wrongs of the case, Ford's reputation (and consequent sales) suffered badly as a result of negative publicity.

Reputation is irritatingly both unquantifiable but also critical to a company's success.

For example, the line between Fenchurch Street and Southend used to be known as the 'Misery Line'. Although the current operator's performance is now one of the best in Britain, it took a long time for the line to shed this unfortunate name.

21.11 Chapter 21 Exercises

Exercise 1 A rail operator is examining an opportunity to start a new service.

To purchase the rolling stock will cost €3.5 million and annual operating costs attributable to the new service will be €125,000.

The operator expects revenue of €500,000 per annum in the first year and annual growth of 6% per annum up to the tenth year.

Assuming a discount rate of 5%:

- What is the net present value of this project to the operator; and

- What is the minimum annual growth rate for revenue necessary for the project to be financially viable (to the nearest 0.1%)?

Exercise 2 An airport has decided to build a new terminal with a capacity of 10 million passengers per annum.

The airport has a choice of two strategies.

It can build the new terminal in two stages of 5 million passengers per annum each or it can build one large 10 mppa terminal from the outset.

Each of these two options has its advantages and problems.

The 'gradual' approach will mean more significant capital expenditure is deferred for several years but the total construction costs of £200 million are significantly higher than the 'big bang' approach of constructing the entire terminal in one go (£160 million).

The gradual approach also has lower annual operating costs for the first ten years but, once the second phase of construction is complete after Year 10, operating costs are the same under either approach.

The construction of the second phase is also somewhat disruptive to operations and annual revenue is projected to fall by 3% per annum during the four years of phase 2 construction before resuming 5% annual growth once the second phase is complete. The big bang approach does not suffer this disruption and so revenue growth is stable at 5% throughout.

All figures are expressed in real terms, i.e. without inflation.

The two options are summarised in the table below.

Figures in £000		Gradual	Big Bang
Construction	Year 0	100,000	160,000
Operating Costs	Years 1-10	25,000	35,000
Construction	Year 7	100,000	-
Operating Costs	Years 11-15	35,000	35,000
Revenue	Year 1	50,000	50,000
Revenue growth	Years 2-6	5%	5%
Revenue growth	Years 7-10	-3%	5%
Revenue growth	Years 11-15	5%	5%

Which of the two options produces the higher net present value, assuming a discount rate of 10%?

Note that we would not expect the entire terminal to be built in one year, i.e. Year 0. So, if we are now in 2016, let us assume that the terminal takes five years to complete and starts operations in 2021. Year 0 is 2020 and therefore the construction costs, revenue and operating costs are all expressed in 2020 £s.

22 FROM INVESTMENT APPRAISAL TO ECONOMIC APPRAISAL

22.1 Introduction

Appraisal can be undertaken from different perspectives, depending on the objectives of the commissioning body.

The key choices are:

- A business case that requires a commercial perspective. For example, an operator may invest in new rolling stock, aircraft or ferries as a means to increase revenue and profitability; or

- Appraisal for Government or a public sector body usually considers both a social perspective as well as the commercial one. The new vehicles will attract higher volumes and therefore have a positive impact on road traffic volumes, pollution and possibly adverse effects on competing modes. Most of these extra factors would not be considered by the operator in a strictly financial evaluation.

In this Chapter, we will discuss the issues necessary when undertaking an economic appraisal as well as the difficulties involved in quantifying many of the effects.

We will also examine projects from mainland Spain, Britain and the Canarian island of Lanzarote.

22.2 Financial and Economic Appraisals Compared

A financial appraisal focuses on the gains and losses to one organisation, usually a profit-making entity such as transport or terminal operator. As we shall see below, an economic appraisal (also known as Cost Benefit Analysis) needs to take into account many more factors than a financial one.

Economic appraisal can be used to show how the (narrower) appraisals for business, government and citizens aggregate up to the social level.

They should, ideally, explicitly show the winners and losers from a scheme. For example, a new tax on rail tickets is a transfer from railway customers to Government. Although a crude solution is simply to cancel the users' loss with the Government's gain (so removing both from the cost-benefit calculus), a more complete economic analysis would explicitly show the costs and benefits to each group.

22.3 Stakeholders

23.3.1 New Airport at St Helena

Economic appraisal, by contrast, is used to show the impact (direct or otherwise) on stakeholders. A stakeholder is a group which has some 'interest' in the organisation. Let us now go through this topic in some detail, as developing a list of significant stakeholders is an important step in undertaking cost-benefit analysis.

For our example, we will use the airport of Saint Helena (SHA), one of the world's most remote islands. The airport was scheduled to open in the first half of 2016 but the commencement of service has been delayed by issues of high winds. For now, St Helena is currently only accessible by a five-day ferry trip from Cape Town in South Africa.

23.3.2 Level 1 Stakeholders

Level 1 stakeholders may be defined as those most immediately affected by a project. For SHA, these stakeholders can be considered to be:

- *Airport operating company* – Basil Read. This company is responsible for designing, building and operating the airport for 10 years, after which SHA reverts to the Government of St Helena;

- *Airport Owner*, the Government of St Helena

- *Funding organisation*, the Department for International Development (UK Government);

- *Airlines*. So far, just one, Comair, will be operating links between St Helena and South Africa; and

- *Andrew Weir Shipping Ltd*, the operator of the current ferry service.

22.3.2 Level 2 Stakeholders

We would expect that the introduction of an air service to the island will have a wider impact than just the owners and operators of transport infrastructure and operations. Here, we will explore these other stakeholders who will be affected.

- *Tourism sector.* At present, St Helena reportedly receives just 2,000 tourists per annum[79]. Once the island is connected with a weekly five-hour flight from Johannesburg, we would expect to see current operators in the tourist sector and investment in the island to raise capacity. The tourism sector also needs to include new entrants who may be attracted to St Helena as a result of the larger tourism potential that air links will provide;

- *Population.* Increased tourism will be expected to increase employment and disposable income on this island of 4,000 people, even if tourism volumes did no more than double their current level. There will be some negative effects that will have been incurred, such as noise during construction and a potential negative environmental impact, but noise from flights is unlikely to be a major issue, with just one scheduled jet service per week for now; and

- *Government.* Although the Government was included as a stakeholder under Level l, there are secondary issues to consider, such as the increased revenue, which could be expected from tourism development projects and tourist volumes.

22.3.4 Economic Factors Improve Viability

As a rule of thumb, projects that do not stack up financially can become viable once economic factors are taken into account. By contrast, it is highly unusual to find financially viable projects that become infeasible once an economic perspective is included.

Figure 22-1 illustrates the difference between the two appraisal types, using an urban rail project as an example.

---

79 http://www.sthelena-samedia.co.za/media-air-access-to-st-helena-opens-up-tourism-and-investment-opportunitiesm-media-pack.htm

Figure 22-1: Urban Rail Service: Financial & Economic Appraisal Items

Item	Financial appraisal £	Economic appraisal £
Investment Cost	-80,000,000	-80,000,000
The following figures are per annum		
Operating Cost	-1,450,000	-1,450,000
Revenue (operators)	4,300,000	4,300,000
Time savings		2,560,000
Road decongestion		620,000
Government tax revenue		-320,000
TOTAL per annum	2,850,000	5,710,000

In a financial appraisal, future costs and benefits will be subject to a discount rate, as we saw in Section 21.10. An economic appraisal, by contrast, will use the same methodology but the discount rate used would be based on factors other than strictly financial criteria.

22.4 Geographic Area

One of the challenges in economic evaluation is to determine the area affected. For the St Helena airport example which we looked at earlier, the costs and benefits are in effect limited to the island itself. For projects affecting a small region of a larger land mass, the picture can be more complicated.

Imagine, for example, that town A, a small town with limited jobs and facilities, is currently linked by rail to town B and an operator proposes a new link between towns A and C. The new rail service will include both commuter and off-peak services. Town C is the largest and A is the smallest of the three and C is roughly the same distance from A as B. The current transport network is shown in Figure 22-2.

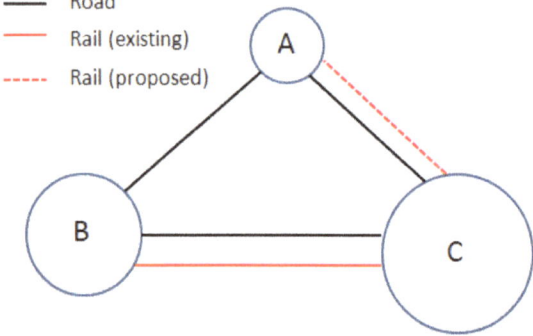

Figure 22-2: Transport Network for A, B and C

Let us now briefly examine in this hypothetical example the benefits by area. Town A is undisputedly a beneficiary of the proposed rail service as there will be rail access to the larger town for work, shopping trips and other types of journey. Town C also benefits although probably to a lesser extent, since C is more important to A than A is to C.

But what about town B? Traffic between A and C will increase, as two modes are available rather than one (we will assume 'sensible pricing', so there will be trips generated by rail as well as those diverted from road). However, assuming that the population of A remains reasonably constant, traffic between A and B could decline; in the short term, residents of A will go shopping in C rather than B so levels of commerce in B would see a reduction.

In the medium term, a higher proportion of A's workforce are likely to seek employment in town C as the larger town will have more employment opportunities. By contrast, remaining road users of the A-B road could see a benefit as traffic volume declines as a consequence of the diversion of trips between A and C. Similar benefits could accrue to the A-C road if a significant number of trips switch to the rail service.

The overall indicative results are summarised in Figure 22-3.

Figure 22-3: Benefits of New Rail Service

	A	B	C	A-B Road	A-C Road
Jobs	Improvement	Deterioration	Improvement	---------------	---------------
Shopping/Leisure	Improvement	Deterioration	Improvement	---------------	---------------
Congestion	---------------	---------------	---------------	Improvement	Improvement
Overall	Improvement	Deterioration	Improvement	Improvement	Improvement

The important issues arising here are that:

- An improvement in service can provide losers as well as winners; and
- The geographic area chosen for the economic evaluation is critical.

22.5 Stakeholders Revisited

We will use our simple example of the A-C railway project and identify stakeholders in the project. The benefits and losses identified below assume that the railway will be built.

Figure 22-4: Benefits of Interested Parties

Stakeholders	Nature of Benefits or Losses	Classification	Ease of Quantification
A-C rail users diverted from road	Time savings	Primary	High
A-C rail users diverted from road	Travel cost differences	Primary	High
Residual A-C road users	Time savings (A-C road will be less congested)	Primary	Medium
A-C rail users (brand new trips)	Operator revenue	Primary	High
Local authority A	Improved accessibility	Secondary	Low
Local authority B	Reduction in commercial activity	Secondary	Medium
Local authority C	Improved accessibility	Secondary	Low
Local authority C	Improved attraction to businesses	Secondary	Low
All road users	Less accidents	Primary	Medium
Construction workers	Jobs	Primary	High

We can see from this list of just ten benefits or losses that many of these are difficult to quantify. Figure 22-4 nevertheless gives us an idea of the wide-ranging issues, which need to be considered in an economic evaluation. There is also a column marked 'classification'. As a general rule, it is easier to quantify the impact of a new service or piece of infrastructure on those who are directly affected by it. Wider economic impacts (discussed in Section 22.9) can be a significant proportion of overall benefits, even though they are hard to quantify.

22.6 More Assumptions for the New Railway

Let us return to and add some information about the new railway line between A and C. Let us assume the following:

- The benefitting region is the area covering all three towns;

- Operating costs are £100 million per annum of which £50 million are labour costs;

- The area suffers from high unemployment, so each job created by the railway reduces unemployment by one;

- Revenues are £120 million per annum including £40 million lost by bus companies plying the routes A-B and A-C, £40 million is attributable to car users and £20 million comes from trips not previously made; and

- Time savings in generalised journey time are 10 minutes for car users and 20 minutes for bus users.

We will now discuss which elements should be included in the economic appraisal of this project.

22.6.1 Labour Costs

If, for example, all workers on this new railway were previously receiving benefits, we could reduce the gross £50 million labour cost by the amount the Government provided in benefits (which would presumably cease upon gaining employment). There are also less immediate and tangible benefits of higher purchasing power of the newly employed group.

22.6.2 Revenues

Based on the assumptions in paragraph , the £120 million is not all new money, as only one sixth of the revenue is generated by trips which would not have been made without the new railway. So, we can argue as follows:

- Revenue abstracted from bus passengers is excluded, as it is just a transfer of money from one operator to another;
- The £40 million from car users could also be excluded, as the revenue incurred is, once again, a transfer from one mode to another; and
- The revenue incurred from brand new journeys can be counted as a benefit.

22.6.3 Other Benefits

We have just seen that one of the important non-financial benefit streams is time savings.

For bus passengers who choose not to switch, there will be a time saving of ten minutes on their journey.

However, if the bus company reduces the frequency on the A-C bus service, overall journey time could increase; recall that the overall journey time (GJT) is a function of waiting time as well as journey time.

For car drivers and passengers who do not switch to rail, there are no frequency issues, so the time savings of 10 minutes can be fully included.

22.7 How are Financial and Economic Appraisals Related?

As a rule, we would expect the results of financial and economic evaluations to be positively correlated.

When more people are involved, either directly as passengers or indirectly as beneficiaries of wider economic benefits, we would expect to see both the economic and financial cases improving.

This is particularly the case where a significant proportion of costs are fixed, as with many rail projects.

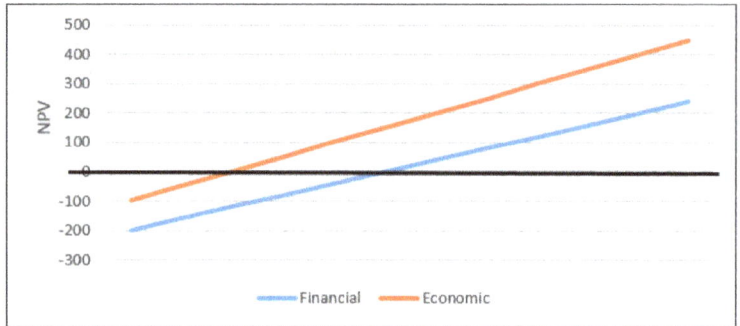

Figure 22-5: Relationship between Financial and Economic Appraisals

In Figure 22-5, we can see that, as the number of people effected by a project increases (X axis), we would expect both types of appraisal to exhibit an improvement in their net present values.

The NPV of the economic appraisal should increase at a faster rate, however, as the present value of the benefits per person is higher than in the financial evaluation.

22.8 Value of Time

Earlier in this text, we discussed how a project could be justified on the grounds of saving time.

Although one of the arguments used to promote Britain's High Speed 2 is how savings in time can be used to justify projects on economic grounds, it is important to bear in mind that a project can be similarly justified when there are very large volumes of journeys with each passenger benefitting from small time savings; for example, most London Underground lines have an annual passenger volume at least 10 times the long term forecast of the HS2 network.

In October 2013, the UK government changed its guidance on the values of time to be used in project evaluation.

The old and new figures are shown in Figure 22-6.

Figure 22-6: Changes in Value of Time per Hour (2010 prices)

Passenger Type	Type	Aug-12	Oct-13	change
Rail	Business	47.18	31.96	-32%
Underground	Business	45.90	26.28	-43%
Commuting	Non-business	6.46	6.81	5%
Other	Non-business	5.71	6.04	6%

Source: http://www.dft.gov.uk/webtag/documents/expert/unit3.5.php

The reason cited for the significant reduction in business travel time is that there is a consensus that the figures should reflect the values of time to the individual rather than the employer.

However, another issue is that journey time in many cases no longer needs to be 'wasted'.

As Wi-Fi is rolled out across rail, bus and even airline routes, business passengers can use trains as mobile offices and therefore a time saving cannot necessarily be fully counted in project evaluation.

These new, lower values could have significant impacts on projects developed in the future, all the more so with routes which have a high proportion of business travellers.

22.9 Wider Economic Impacts

Direct benefits are primarily time savings for users that are assumed to translate into a variety of forms that benefit the nation through productivity or tax.

However, benefits may be felt by those who do not actually use the infrastructure or service provided by the investment – for instance, if a rail project reduces road traffic, remaining road users will benefit from a reduction in congestion and reduction in accidents. Benefits of this sort are termed 'non-user benefits'. Wider Economic Impacts (WEIs) include:

- Agglomeration benefits (also known as clustering), which, despite popular belief that in the future everything will be done by internet and video, reflect the theory that companies in the same economic sector are more efficient if they are located in the same place, which travelling to work and for business allows to happen. Examples include hi-tech clusters in Cambridge and along the M4 corridor; and

- Labour market impacts, whereby reduced travelling time to work allows people to enter the labour market, who might otherwise be excluded from it, or to move to jobs in which they are more productive once the geographical area in which they might work expands. As mentioned above, changing job is easier if this does not involve disruption of habitual travel patterns.

Although these are difficult to quantify, they can nevertheless provide a significant contribution to the benefits of a project.

In the case of the current Thameslink project[80], WEIs were calculated at £1.3 billion compared to £9.7 billion for direct benefits.

For the High Speed 2 line, WEI benefits account for around 15% of the total (so a similar proportion to Thameslink).

Many governments now require public sector appraisals to take into account the environmental impact of projects, such as CO_2 emissions.

For road and airport projects, the impact of accounting for these emissions would most likely be negative, whilst rail projects, particularly those which are expected to divert demand from road and air, would make a positive contribution to the cost-benefit analysis.

22.10 Ex-post evaluation

The evaluation of the economic (and financial) impacts of a project should not just be undertaken before a project is executed (ex-ante) but also after a project has been completed (ex-post).

The ex-post evaluations will reveal not only relatively straightforward information such as how demand developed, in fact, in comparison to forecasts, but the impact on employment, land values, property prices and a host of other factors.

An ex-post evaluation is also a useful tool to understanding why actual results differ significantly from those expected before a project is completed. The Jubilee Line Extension (JLE), undertaken between 1993 and 2000, cost over £3 billion and, as a consequence, has been the subject of major study.

The impact study[81], published in 2004, studied the extent to which the JLE met its objectives during the first couple of years after it opened.

---
80 http://www.nao.org.uk/wp-content/uploads/2013/06/10164-001-Thameslink-Full-Report.pdf
81 http://home.wmin.ac.uk/transport/jle/wp/WP54_JLE_Summary_Report_[130904].pdf

Although a project as large as the JLE cannot be expected to see all the envisaged impacts and benefits until several years after the project's completion, the two years of data collected by the researchers was still able to provide insights into what went right and wrong and also what impacts, which have been observed since the project's completion, were excluded from the ex-ante appraisals.

22.11 Barcelona-Zaragoza-Madrid AVE Line Revisited

In Section 6.6, we examined inter-modal competition in Spain's busiest long distance corridor. We will now examine the economic impact of the new high speed railway line and how beneficial economically the project has been judged to be. The data in this Section was provided by Ginés de Rus of Las Palmas University and was published in 2012[82].

De Rus estimated total costs (in net present value terms) of the Madrid-Barcelona line at a little over €12 billion in 2010 prices. The bulk of this cost, unsurprisingly, was the construction of the line itself (€8 billion) and the remainder was for the acquisition of rolling stock and maintenance of all assets.

He reported five classes of benefit and these are shown in Figure 22-7.

Figure 22-7: Benefits of Madrid-Barcelona AVE Line

Benefit	Value (€million) in 2010
Time Savings	2,795
Generated Demand	1,076
Other Modes Cost Savings	2,936
Accidents	330
Congestion	20
TOTAL	7,158

The two largest line items of benefits were time savings for rail travellers switching from conventional to high speed rail (€2 billion) and cost savings caused by the airlines reducing frequency (€1.3 billion).

We saw earlier that wider economic impact benefits (WEI) accounted for around 15% of two rail projects in the UK.

[82] http://www.ems.expertgrupp.se/uploads/documents/hsr.pdf

De Rus did not discuss these in his paper but the geography of Spain makes it unlikely that the figure for WEI would be as high; De Rus showed that only 17% of all benefits were not accounted for by traffic between Madrid-Zaragoza, Zaragoza-Barcelona and Madrid-Barcelona.

Even if we were to add in 15% of WEI to this project, total benefits would only come to €8,421 million (7,158/0.85) and so we may calculate the benefit: cost ratio, encountered in Section 21.9, as:

$$8,421/12,422$$

This ratio is 0.68 which means that, on the basis of this appraisal, the line should not have been built. De Rus also undertook sensitivity tests and the highest ratio he calculated was 0.75. UK government guidance[83] would, unsurprisingly, rank this project as poor value for money and a ratio of below 1.5 is considered as "low", taking account of the uncertainty of the values of some of the economic benefits calculated.

22.12 Example: An Economic Appraisal in Britain

Whilst it could be argued that the Barcelona-Madrid example omitted several factors that are extremely difficult to calculate, here we present another example of CBA. The Rotherwas rail report starts with a financial appraisal before moving onto the economic evaluation (chapter 4, pp29-35).

The Rotherwas report goes somewhat farther than the factors shown in Figure 22-1. The economic evaluation for Rotherwas includes:

- health benefits (caused by walking more compared to using a car);
- reductions in mortalities and injuries;
- reductions in noise and greenhouse gasses; and
- the positive impact on absenteeism of the new rail link

In Figure 22-8, we present the annual costs and benefits identified for the project.

---

[83] *https://www.gov.uk/government/uploads/system/uploads/attachment_data/file/255126/value-for-money-external.pdf*

Figure 22-8: Annual Benefits and Costs for Rotherwas Rail Project

£000	Benefits	Costs
Subsidy		1,684
Congestion	165	
Rail Safety	13	
Tax Revenue (fuel sales)		59
Absenteeism	8	
Mortality benefits (health benefits from walking/cycling)	256	
Accidents	37	
Local Air Quality	1	
Noise	3	
Greenhouse Gases	10	
Infrastructure (less road repairs)	1	

Please note that the subsidy figure refers to 2015 and the remainder to 2010. We can see from the evaluation that many of the items covered in the economic evaluation are very small when compared to costs and revenues of the rail project itself; we can see that the six smallest benefits identified (highlighted in the above figure) total around £36,000 per annum. There is also an argument that the appraisal is extremely thorough; a more cynical view is that some of the items included smack of desperation (and you will notice that the Benefit: Cost ratio for the scheme is below 1 even after all these other factors are included).

22.13 Bus Station, Puerto del Carmen (PdC), Lanzarote

22.13.1 Objectives of a Bus Station

As a final example in this Section, we will look at a bus station that opened in 2014.

A bus station should have at least one of four direct objectives:

- Interchange between modes. This category includes bus stations attached to airports and railway stations;
- Interchange between bus lines. At a point where several buses meet, a bus station facilitates passenger interchange and moves crowds of interchanging passengers off the streets;

- Serving a large generator or attractor of passengers. The bus station at Brent Cross Shopping Centre in northwest London is a good example of this type; and

- Serving a point where several bus lines terminate. Usually, we would expect such a bus station to be present at locations with large passenger demand (such as Brent Cross), but there may be cases where it is convenient to locate such a station away from the busy city centre if such land is in short supply.

In addition to these direct objectives, we would also seek wider economic objectives such as improved accessibility for jobs, shopping and other commercial and social activities.

22.13.2 Description of the PdC Bus Station

Figure 22-9 shows the location of the bus station in relation to the town it serves and the bus routes using the station. The only public transport modes in the area are buses and taxis.

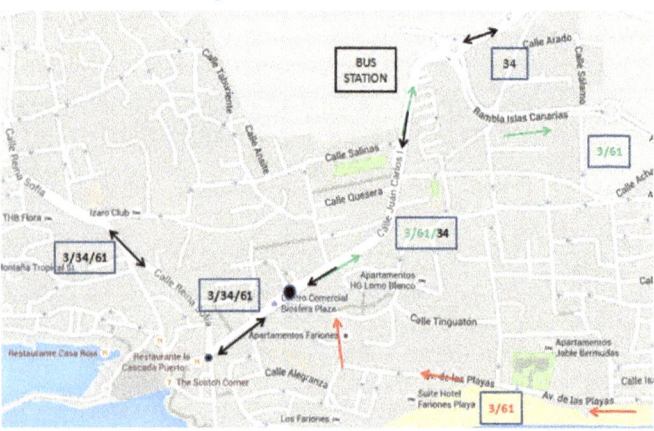

Figure 22-9: PdC Bus Station

PdC is Lanzarote's largest resort so, unsurprisingly, most of the tourist activity occurs in the areas of Avenida de las Playas (beach road) and the port area, in the bottom left of the picture. Also shown on this map is the Biosfera Plaza shopping centre. So, the bus station is on the outskirts of town and is next door to the town's secondary school. There are no other generators or attractors close by. The budget for the bus station was reportedly €500,000.

There are three routes in the town:

- 3 – this route links PdC with Arrecife, the capital and Costa Teguise, another large resort on the island. The route runs every 20 minutes for most of the day and every 60 minutes at night. However, this bus does not call at the bus station;
- 34 – the route links PdC with the town of Tías and plies the same route in both directions throughout and runs approximately every 60 minutes; and
- 61 – this airport-PdC-Playa Blanca service runs along the beach road from the airport (shown in red) but a more northerly route when travelling to the airport (in green). The route becomes bidirectional only to the west of "Centro Comercial Biosfera Plaza", marked by the large black dot. The general frequency for the 61 is every 30-60 minutes.

The bus station is therefore only served by the 34 in both directions and the 61 in one direction, namely from Playa Blanca to the airport.

22.13.3 Assessment of the Bus Station

This bus station does not appear to succeed in any of the direct objectives discussed in Section 22.13.1. Moreover, given its remoteness from any generators or attractors (other than the school, which should generate sufficient demand but only for two short periods on schooldays), any wider economic benefits suggested for this piece of EU-funded infrastructure are unlikely to be realised. Information on transport demand is relatively sparse in Spain but the bus station reportedly serves no more than 10-12 persons per day.

22.14 Further Reading – Isle of Skye Bridge

The Skye Bridge opened in 1995, linking the Scottish mainland at Kyle of Lochalsh with the island of Skye. This bridge replaced a ferry service and was initially a toll bridge. However, after a great deal of controversy, the bridge was bought by the Scottish government and, from 2004, the bridge became toll-free. A lengthy report "Evaluation of the Economic and Social Impacts of the Skye" details the economic benefits of the bridge, both with and without tolls, online at https://www.hitrans.org.uk/documents.

23 CASE STUDY ON PRICE DISTORTIONS

23.1 Introduction

This case will assess in broad terms the economic impact of the conflict between tourists and residents in the Canary Islands.

This conflict is caused by the distortions in the market generated by schemes that allows residents of the islands to receive a 50% discount on inter-island travel and travel to and from the mainland of Spain (Peninsula).

We argued in Section 15.6 that the provision of a 50% subsidy benefitting residents increased the prices of travel for non-residents both between the Peninsula and the Canary Islands as well as between islands.

In this case study, we shall assess:

- To what extent higher fares have suppressed demand, both from the Peninsula and within the Canaries;

- The impact on total tourism expenditure of this reduction;

- Assess the welfare loss of this tourism expenditure and the annual subsidy cost for Canarian residents; and

- Determine whether a better value for money solution is available that would increase the overall welfare of the Canary Islands.

Please note that 'subsidy', in the context of this case, applies only to the 50% discount enjoyed by residents of the Canary Islands for inter-island traffic or to/from the Peninsula; the assessment does not cover the Public Service Obligation subsidy paid on air routes such as Gran Canaria to Tenerife South.

23.2 Tourism Demand

23.2.1 Tourism and the Economy

Tourism accounts for 31% of the Canary Islands' GDP, according to a recent study[84].

This figure is second in Spain only to the Balearic Islands in terms of dependency on tourism for generating wealth and is also a higher proportion than the Maldives, Seychelles and much of the Caribbean[85].

For the smaller islands of Lanzarote and Fuerteventura, the proportion of touristic GDP will be somewhat higher; estimates by the author calculated the dependence on tourism as a little over 50% in the case of Lanzarote (official data for GDP or GVA by island is not available).

23.2.2 Foreign Tourists

Foreign tourist arrivals in the Canary Islands have shown consistent growth, with the exception of Fuerteventura, which witnessed an increase much higher than the other islands, and La Palma, which suffered a sharp decline.

Tourist volumes for the two years are displayed in Figure 23-1.

Figure 23-1: Foreign Tourists by Island, 2007 and 2014

	Tourists 2007	Tourists 2014	Change 2007-2014
Fuerteventura	1,012,948	1,749,743	72.7%
Gran Canaria	2,509,602	2,879,485	14.7%
Lanzarote	1,582,043	2,013,044	27.2%
La Palma	162,096	124,200	-23.4%
Tenerife	2,997,660	3,749,630	25.1%
TOTAL Foreign	**8,264,349**	**10,516,102**	**27.2%**

23.2.3 Peninsula Tourists

The picture for Peninsula tourists is the diametric opposite of that for foreign visitors, with all islands showing a significant decline in demand between 2007 and 2014 – see Figure 23-2.

---

84 http://www.exceltur.org/wp-content/uploads/2015/06/IMPACTUR-Canarias-2014.pdf
85 http://skift.com/2013/03/09/the-worlds-most-tourism-dependent-countries/

Figure 23-2: Peninsula and Total Tourists by Island, 2007 and 2014

	Tourists 2007	Tourists 2014	Change 2007-2014
Fuerteventura	121,266	102,470	-15.5%
Gran Canaria	513,748	390,862	-23.9%
Lanzarote	341,581	256,235	-25.0%
La Palma	81,691	44,274	-45.8%
Tenerife	837,187	521,247	-37.7%
TOTAL Peninsula	**1,897,238**	**1,421,364**	**-25.1%**
All Nationalities	10,161,587	11,937,466	17.5%

Source: FGATUR, Author's Calculations

The tables above show a stark contrast between the demand for Canary Island trips foreign and Peninsula tourists. If we examine the data over time, we have two very different trends apparent in the data.

Figure 23-3: Tourism Demand over Time

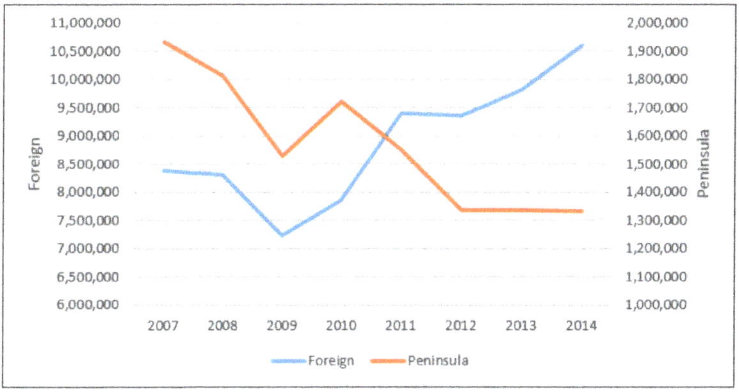

Foreign tourist volumes dropped significantly in 2009 but have been on an upward trend since. Peninsula tourists have continued to drop steadily since 2007, with the exception of 2010.

23.3 Spanish Leisure Trips Abroad

To assess whether the fall in Peninsula-Canaries traffic is attributable to economic factors specific to Spain, we will examine a control group, which is leisure trips undertaken by Spaniards to foreign countries. For the purposes of our analysis, trips to the Canary Islands can be considered as foreign, as these require a two to three-hour flight and so are different in character to domestic tourism undertaken within the Peninsula.[86] Spanish tourists travelling abroad have increased somewhat when we compare 2007 to 2014 in Figure 23-4.

[86] In 2014, 9% of domestic trips were undertaken by air compared to 61% of foreign trips (source: IET)

In contrast to the drop of 25% witnessed for tourism between the Peninsula and the Canary Islands, foreign trips abroad for leisure purposes have shown a healthy increase over the seven years. The increase in friends and family traffic seems rather high, but this could be attributable to larger numbers of foreign residents visiting their home country.

Figure 23-4: Spanish Leisure Trips Abroad

	2007	2014	Change
Friends and Family	2,388,481	3,431,828	43.7%
Holidays	6,118,027	6,262,284	2.4%
TOTAL	8,506,508	9,694,112	14.0%

Source: Instituto de Turismo España (IET)

However, even if we take the low figure of 2.4%, this still compares favourably with the 25% drop in traffic on Canarian routes.

23.4 Peninsula-Canarias Air Traffic

23.4.1 Fares

Air Europa and Iberia Express dominate flights between Tenerife, Gran Canaria and the Peninsula. Iberia Express appears to have a policy of a high minimum floor on flights to and from the Canary Islands, as exemplified by the example below, in Figure 23-5, of fares from Tenerife.

Figure 23-5: Minimum Single Air Fares from Tenerife, 2015 (€)

		RYR	AE	IBE	London 2,900 km
TF-MAD 1,797 km	20-Aug	144	208	211	277
	06-Sep	102	197	211	204
	23-Sep	30	144	211	92
	09-Oct	60	144	211	88
		RYR	AE	VU	London
TF-BCN 2,195 km	19-Aug	174	327	158	221
	05-Sep	106	134	105	218
	22-Sep	39	61	65	136
	08-Oct	46	89	85	64

Source: Skyscanner, July 16th, 2015 (RYR = Ryanair; AE = Air Europa; IB = Iberia, IBE = Iberia Express)
Note 1: Tenerife, MAD = Madrid; BCN = Barcelona

Peninsula demand shows a significant peak during July and August, yet there was no evidence of a reduction in fares during a low month such as November. By contrast, Ryanair and Vueling vary fares significantly, according to demand. Air Europa has similar minimum fares on their website but these fares can be undercut using a comparison site such as Skyscanner.

The Iberia Express policy of fixed fares does not apply to routes of similar distance, such as Madrid-Edinburgh; on the Scottish route, there is a significant difference in minimum fares between the summer peak and quieter periods. This fixed-fare policy yields perverse prices, with the lowest fares to London (roughly 60% longer than the distance of TF-MAD) often being cheaper than either Iberia Express or Air Europa.

The full service operators maintain this policy, at least on their own websites, even when they form a dominant duopoly (Gran Canaria, Tenerife) or when they would be expected to be a price follower, as in the case of Lanzarote, where Ryanair is the dominant operator to the Peninsula.

Figure 23-6 shows the number of flights to and from the Peninsula by airline for 2014.

Figure 23-6: Flights in 2014 by Island to and from the Peninsula

	Gran Canaria	Tenerife	Lanzarote	Fuerteventura
Vueling	3,418	2,999	971	453
Air Europa	3,054	6,123	1,324	354
Ryanair	2,456	2,786	2,187	814
Iberia Group	4,316	4,238	960	898
LCC share 2014	44%	36%	58%	50%
RYR share 2014	19%	17%	40%	32%
LCC Share 2007	38%	40%	36%	36%

Source: AENA Statistics (http://www.aena.es/csee/Satellite?pagename=Estadisticas/Home)

23.4.2 Load Factor

For the purposes of the above analysis, Spanair routes to the Canary Islands were designated as 'low cost' for 2007 operations, along with Futura,

Ryanair, easyJet and Clickair. Ryanair has been highlighted in the table above as its fares are generally the lowest available per kilometre and often less than half the price of the next cheapest operator.

Whilst it is not possible to determine profitability by route, it is feasible to ascertain load factors for all the key players on Peninsula flights, as they all use a single type of aircraft (the exception being Air Europa).

In Figure 23-7, we present four figures per airline:

- Total, which is all of Iberia Express' business (IE only operates to, from or within Spain), most of Vueling's and Ryanair's operations to, from and within Spain only;

- International, including all flights between any part of Spain (including the Canaries) and foreign countries;

- National, which comprises all domestic routes including the Canary Islands; and

- Canaries, which only shows flights between the Canary Islands and the Peninsula.

Figure 23-7: 2014 Load Factors by Airline

	IBE	RYR	VUE
TOTAL	73%	85%	77%
International	74%	85%	76%
National	72%	83%	78%
Canaries	78%	88%	83%

What should be apparent immediately from Canaries, which only shows flights between the Canary Islands and the Peninsula, is that flights between the Canaries and the Peninsula enjoyed a significantly higher load factor than airlines' other operations during 2014. Whilst Ryanair does not appear to be taking advantage of this state of affairs to offer higher prices (see Figure 23-5), the same cannot be said of Iberia. It is this rent-seeking behaviour that presumably encouraged Norwegian to enter the Peninsula-Canaries market in October 2015.[87]

23.5 Inter-Island Traffic

Inter-island traffic was roughly 7.4 million trips in 2007 and 6.8 million in 2014, a drop of 8.5% in seven years.

There, is, however, a very wide variation of growth between individual flows, as Figure 23-8 demonstrates.

---

[87] http://www.travelweekly.co.uk/Articles/2015/07/10/55877/norwegian-to-start-canaries-flights-from-mainland-spain.html

Figure 23-8: Inter Island Traffic: Major Flows

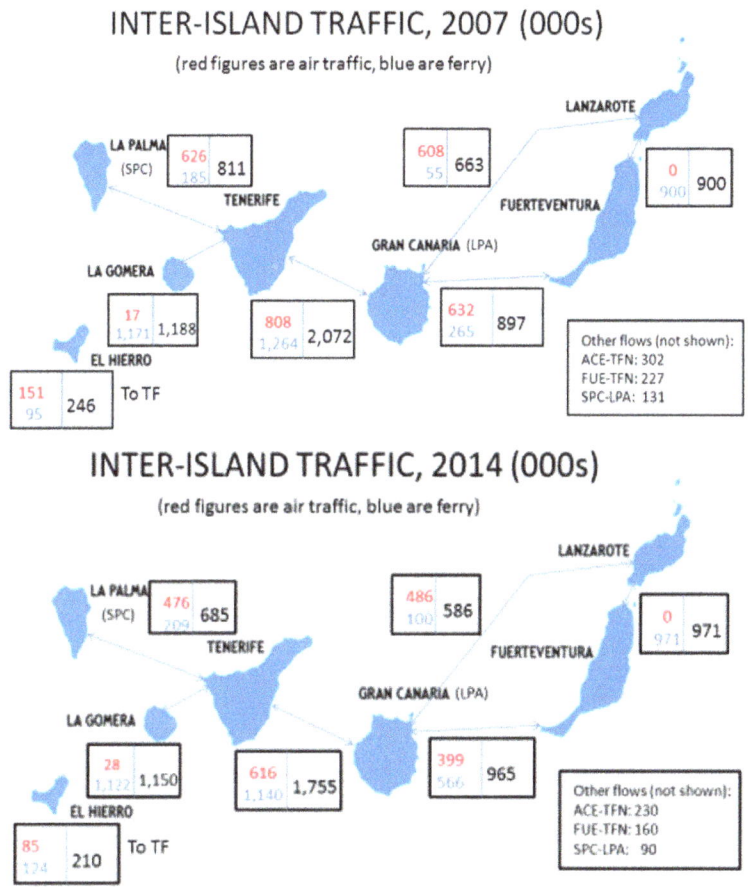

One significant flow that has been omitted from further discussion is Lanzarote (Orzola) to La Graciosa, an island with a population of around 700 people immediately to the north of Lanzarote.

In 2014, there were some 332,000 trips on this route but figures for 2007 are not available.

Inter-island traffic was roughly 7.4 million trips in 2007 and 6.8 million in 2014, a drop of 8.5% in seven years.

A reduction of 8.5% needs to be placed in the context of changes to Canadian GDP and tourism volumes over the same period.

This data is presented in Figure 23-9, using the economic data from Figure 7-12 and the tourist volume data in Figure 23-2.

Figure 23-9: Changes in Real GDP and Tourist Volumes

	Change 2007 to 2014
Real GDP	-6.4%
Tourist Volumes	+ 17.5%

On this basis, we can infer that demand performance for inter-island transport has been weak; using an elasticity of 0.7, for example, we would expect to see a reduction in demand of around 4.5% and that is before considering the significant increase in tourism volumes.

If we look at individual flows, we can see that there has been a wide variation in demand changes. The changes in the six busiest routes are presented in Figure 23-10.

Figure 23-10: Top Six Flows Demand Changes, All Modes

Route	Shortest Distance (km)	Change 2007-2014
La Gomera-Tenerife	38	-3.2%
Gran Canaria-Tenerife	68	-15.3%
Lanzarote-Fuerteventura	14	+8.5%
Fuerteventura-Gran Canaria	115	+7.6%
La Palma-Tenerife	139	-15.0%
Lanzarote-Gran Canaria	208	-11.6%

In absolute terms, Lanzarote-Fuerteventura provides the cheapest trip for tourists (€23 return) and demand has been showing a steady increase.

This route is the only one in the Canary Islands with three ferry companies competing.

La Gomera's population fell by 7% between 2007 and 2014 and so a reduction of just 3% implies an increase in tourist volumes between La Gomera and Tenerife (recall that demand with respect to population has an elasticity of 1).

There are five to six daily sailings each way between La Gomera and Tenerife, which is quite a high frequency to serve a population of just over 20,000, so tourists are likely to play a significant role in demand on this route.

The cheapest return fare for non-residents is €68[88].

---

[88] *As seen in July 2015*

Figure 23-11: Propensity of Tourists to "Island Hop"

	Population	Tourist Main Destination	Tourists' Secondary Destination
Fuerteventura	106,930	1,990,842	97,438
La Gomera	20,721	87,732	96,723
Gran Canaria	851,157	3,579.940	51,972
El Hierro	10,675	4,924	15,518
Lanzarote	141,940	2,399,667	243,776
La Palma	83,456	150,550	147,340
Tenerife	889,936	4,772,587	223,476
TOTAL	**2,104,815**	**9,409,882**	**876,243**

Source: FRONTUR

The above figure shows that less than 10% of tourists who visited the Canary Islands in 2014 visited more than one island.

This figure is consistent with EGATUR data, which showed 89% of tourists did not visit any other island. In 2007, EGATUR recorded 16% of tourists who visited at least one other island, so the situation has deteriorated over the last seven years.

23.6 Inter-Island Air Fares

23.6.1 Types of Route

Air routes within the Canaries can be classified into three types:

- Longer routes (> 170km) between Lanzarote and Tenerife/Gran Canaria, Fuerteventura to Gran Canaria and La Palma to Gran Canaria;

- Shorter routes, including Tenerife to Gran Canaria, La Palma to Tenerife and Fuerteventura to Gran Canaria; and

- Non-commercial routes, which are subject to direct subsidy (known as a Public Service Obligation), including routes from El Hierro and La Gomera. These are not discussed further.

The distinction is important because, in this Section, we will benchmark inter-island air fares against routes with a similar distance flown by Ryanair between the Peninsula and the Balearic Islands.

In Figure 23-12, we present two inter-island air fares and benchmark these against flights over similar distances operated by Ryanair to Ibiza and Mallorca.

23.6.2 Fares on Longer Routes

The fares shown in the first half of Figure 23-12 are low season fares to the Balearic Islands and bookable three months in advance, whilst the second table shows prices at the height of the peak just four weeks in advance. Lanzarote – Tenerife North (TFN) is a monopoly operated by Binter whereas the route to Las Palmas has competition from a smaller operator, Canary Fly; this explains in part the lower cost per kilometre of the shorter inter-island route.

Figure 23-12: Canarian and Balearic Air Fares

	Valencia-Ibiza	Barcelona-Majorca	Lanzarote-TFN	Lanzarote-LPA
Passengers (2014)	197,247	1,410,078	243,154	486,037
Flights (2014)	2,571	12,426	4,428	11,731
Passengers/flight	77	113	55	41
Distance (km)	174	202	272	208
Fares 10-16/10/2015	18.64	18.72	61.60	46.61
per km	10.7	9.3	22.6	22.4
including one bag	26.37	26.45	61.60	46.61
per km	15.2	13.1	22.6	22.4

	Valencia-Ibiza	Barcelona-Majorca	Lanzarote-TFN	Lanzarote-LPA
Passengers (2014)	197,247	1,410,078	243,154	486,037
Flights (2014)	2,571	12,426	4,428	11,731
Passengers/flight	77	113	55	41
Distance (km)	174	202	272	208
Fares 10-16/08/2015	45.70	50.15	82.60	46.61
per km	26.3	24.8	30.4	22.4
including one bag	53.43	57.88	82.60	46.61
per km	30.7	28.7	30.4	22.4

Note: fares for both seasons were examined on July 16th, 2015

What is not immediately explainable is the very wide discrepancy in fares at other times of the year, with the Ryanair fares at less than half the level of the cheapest Canarian ones. Even if a bag is paid for with the Ryanair flight, the cost per kilometre is significantly below that of Canarian flights (which include a luggage allowance in the price).

23.6.4 Airport Charges

To enable a fair comparison of the flights listed in Figure 23-12, we also need to consider airport charges. The two charges which are of interest here are the landing fees (based upon an aircraft's maximum take-off weight) and fees per departing passenger.

In 2015, these charges were significantly lower for inter-island flights than for domestic routes to and from the Peninsula[89]. For a Boeing 737-800, as operated by Ryanair, and assuming 170 seats occupied, the approximate difference airport charges per passenger was €4 under the 2015 tariff, or 2 cents per kilometre for a 200km trip. Therefore, the anomaly in ticket prices per kilometre is really higher than Figure 23-12 suggests.

23.6.4 Fares on Shorter Routes

In Figure 23-13, we can see the fares on the two most popular shorter routes, between Tenerife and La Palma and Gran Canaria (LPA).

Figure 23-13: Fares on Shorter Routes

	TFN- La Palma Canary Fly	TFN- La Palma Binter	TFN-LPA
Passengers (2014)	475,137	475,137	581,635
Flights (2014)	10,468	10,468	12,308
Passengers/flight	45	45	47
Distance (km)	139	139	112
Fares 10-16/08/2015	38.13	44.60	46.60
per km	27.4	32.1	41.6
Fares 10-16/10/2015	38.13	44.60	40.60
per km	27.4	32.1	36.3

Note: fares for both seasons were examined on July 16th, 2015

This figure provides some support for the monopoly pricing argument in the previous Section; please note how the fare per km, in cents, between La Palma and Tenerife is lower for Canary Fly and only slightly higher for Binter, even though the route is half as long as Lanzarote-Tenerife.

---
89 http://www.aena.es/csee/ccurl/861-788/Guia%20tarifas%20aena%20aeropuertos%202015%20ingles_ed%20marzo.pdf

Although Binter has an air monopoly on the Tenerife-Gran Canaria route, air travel between the two largest islands accounts for only one third of total demand. In Figure 23-14, we compare the ferry fares, which, in certain cases, are only slightly below the equivalent air fare.

Figure 23-14: Ferry Fares Tenerife-Gran Canaria

	Olsen	Armas
August 10-16		
Frequency	6	3
Single Fare	€ 38	€ 32
October 10-16		
Frequency	6	not
Single Fare	€ 38	available

Inter-island ferry fares are discussed in further detail in the next Section.

23.7 Inter-Island Ferry Fares

Figure 23-15 provides mid-season return (October 2015) fares for a foot passenger. Any discounts attributable to residents have been excluded from the comparison.

Figure 23-15: Ferry Prices in the Canaries and Elsewhere

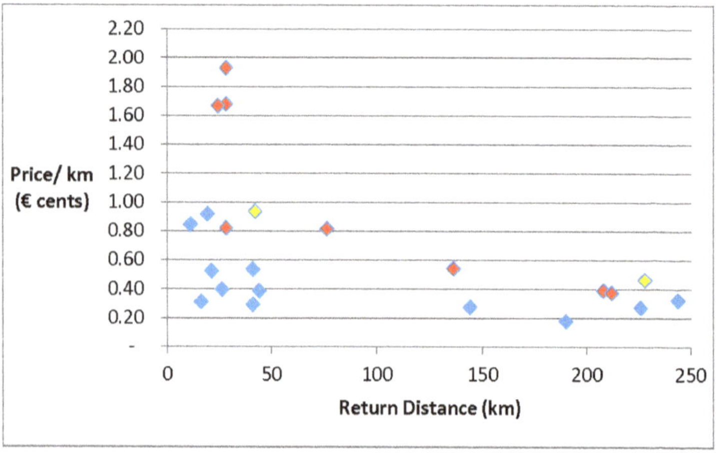

[Scatter plot: Price/km (€ cents) vs Return Distance (km), ranging 0–250 km on x-axis and 0–2.20 on y-axis]

Note: fares research was undertaken in July 2015

In the previous chart, inter-island Canarian fares are shown in red, the yellow points represent other ferry routes in Spain and the blue points are elsewhere in the world (UK, France, Italy, Malta and Australia). The chart provides evidence that, in general, the prices charged by Canarian ferry operators are somewhat higher for similar distances than in other countries.

23.8 Operators in the Canaries

23.8.1 Airlines

There are three major and two minor transport operators plying routes in the Canary Islands. Binter Canarias is the dominant air operator and provides links between all the minor islands and Tenerife, Gran Canaria or both. Its flagship route has traditionally been between Gran Canaria and Tenerife with 14 flights per weekday each way in summer 2015. In terms, of frequency, this route is matched by La Palma-Tenerife (14 per weekday) followed by Lanzarote-Gran Canaria (13) and Fuerteventura-Gran Canaria (11).

A second operator, Canary Fly (CF) commenced operations in late 2013, effectively replacing Islas Airways, which went bankrupt in October 2012. As of summer 2015, CF effectively competed with Binter on just two routes: La Palma-Tenerife (4 per weekday) and Lanzarote – Gran Canaria (3). CF stopped serving Fuerteventura early in 2015. CF also flies between Gran Canaria and Tenerife but only three times per week, so its market share is negligible.

Therefore, the three top air routes all have a combined frequency of roughly 16-18 flights per day each way.

23.8.2 Ferries

The two dominant ferry companies are more evenly matched in terms of frequency but with the exception of Tenerife-Gran Canaria (the two ferry companies use different ports in Gran Canaria so their shares can be quantified), it is difficult to say which one dominates in terms of demand.

Unlike Binter, the ferries generally operate a network within the individual provinces of Tenerife (Tenerife, La Palma, El Hierro, La Gomera) and Las Palmas (Gran Canaria, Fuerteventura, Lanzarote) and between the two large islands, but not otherwise between the provinces.

A summary of the major routes is shown in Figure 23-16 below, along with air shares where appropriate.

Figure 23-16: Market Shares by Route

Route	Operators	Mode/Operator Shares in 2014
La Gomera-Tenerife	FO, AR	Ferry (98%)
Gran Canaria-Tenerife	BI, FO, AR	Air (33%), FO (43%), AR (24%)
Lanzarote-Fuerteventura	FO, AR, LR	Ferry (100%)
Fuerteventura-Gran Canaria	BI, FO, AR	Ferry (58%), BI (39%), CF (3%)
La Palma-Tenerife	BI, CF, FO, AR	Ferry (31%), BI (61%), CF (8%)
Lanzarote-Gran Canaria	BI, CF, AR	AR (17%), BI (76%), CF (7%)

BI: Binter Canarias, CF: Canary Fly, FO: Fred Olsen Express Ferries, AR: Acuas Ferries, LR: Lineas Romero Ferries

23.8.3 Spotlight on Fuerteventura to Gran Canaria

Looking back at Figure 23-8, it is noteworthy that the route between Fuerteventura and Gran Canaria has bucked the trend and shown a significant increase in demand. This Section highlights total demand and modal split in detail between 2011 and April 2015.

In 2007, demand on the route was almost 900,000 passengers per annum and by the end of 2012, demand had fallen to around 770,000 annually.

Since the end of 2012, however, demand has increased markedly, by around 25% in just two years.

The impact of the 2012 changes (particularly the improvement on the ferry service) is evidenced by the steady increase in overall demand during 2013 and the switch in ferry's role from being the minor to the dominant mode.

In Figure 23-17, we have highlighted events over the last three years that have influenced demand on the Fuerteventura-Gran Canaria route.

Figure 23-17: Events of the FUE-GC Route

Action	Date	Results
Fred Olsen introduces promotional fares	June-12	Shift to ferry, demand increase
FO introduces fast ferry	August-12	Reduced ferry journey time, shift to ferry
Islas Airways goes bankrupt	October-12	Demand constant, shift to ferry
FO doubles frequency	December-12	Generalised journey time by ferry declines, greater capacity on route, overall demand increases
Canary Fly (CF) inaugurates Fuerteventura-Gran Canaria flights	Late 2013	Air traffic increases but ferry traffic has doubled in a year
CF pulls out of FUE-GC route	February 2015	No discernible change to date in total market size or air's market share

The impact of the 2012 changes (particularly the improvements on the ferry service) are evidenced by the steady increase in overall demand during 2013 and the switch in ferry from the minor to the dominant mode.

Figure 23-18 shows that ferry has maintained the lead role into 2015, with a market share consistently around the 58% level. It also shows the evolution of demand on a MAA (Moving Annual Average) basis.

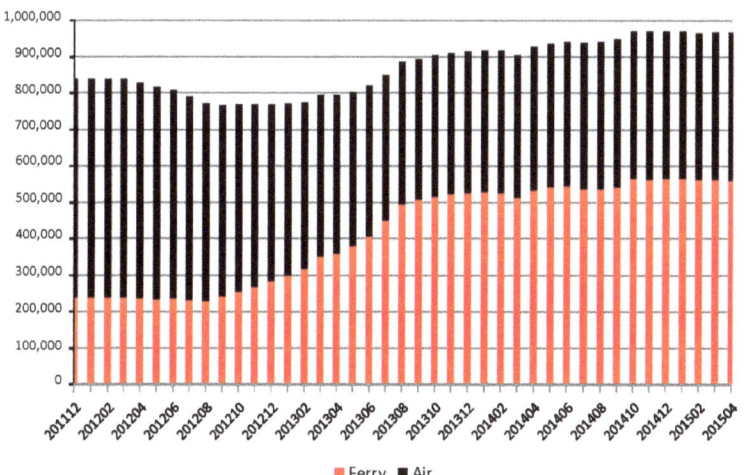

Figure 23-18: Demand by Mode on Fuerteventura-Gran Canaria

23.9 Subsidies to Residents

23.9.1 Inter-Island Air Trips

We saw in Section 7.3.3 that inter-island traffic had not grown strongly when compared to GDP.

Also, when compared to growth in tourism of nearly 16% in seven years, we may draw a similar conclusion.

Recall from Section 15.4 that non-residents of the islands pay double compared to residents of the Canaries.

To highlight the low incidence of tourist trips on inter-island travel, we can examine the number of inter-island air-trips subsidised for the latest three years for which data is available.

The results of this exercise are shown in Figure 23-19 on the next page.

Figure 23-19: Total and Subsidized Air Trips

Route	2010	2011	2012	2010-2012
TF-LPA	712,943	757,076	714,644	2,184,663
ACE-LPA	536,879	590,899	504,081	1,631,859
FUE-LPA	525,128	599,049	482,773	1,606,950
ACE-TFN	258,749	285,890	259,134	803,773
SPC-TF	575,578	620,705	530,360	1,726,643
FUE-TFN	176,264	193,253	158,471	527,988
SPC-LPA	105,266	115,074	91,077	311,417
El Hierro	169,663	169,155	151,021	489,839
La Gomera	32,057	31,723	10,428	74,208
TOTAL Trips	3,092,527	3,362,824	2,901,989	9,357,340
Subsidised	2,817,645	2,141,733	2,833,211	7,792,589
Subsidy (€m)	85	61	83	229
	91%	64%	98%	83%

Please note that the subsidies were those paid in a given year rather than the number of trips actually subsidised in the year of travel. There were delays in payment for 2011 travellers and the arrears were presumably paid in 2012, explaining the very high figure of 98% for that year. Therefore, the average figure of 83% for the three years (or five trips out of every six) being made by residents is probably a best estimate. The average subsidy paid over the three years was €76 million.

A second distortion impeding inter-island travel is a legal barrier to entry. The two incumbent airlines are legally protected from competition and, as a result, fares are somewhat higher in the Canaries than on routes of similar length elsewhere in Spain.

We saw in Figure 23-12 that passengers able to fly from Barcelona or Valencia to the Balearic Islands pay well under half per km compared to Canarian passengers over similar distances.

The Canarian system is especially inefficient as the average load is barely over 40 passengers per flight compared to 71-77 on the smaller Valencia-Ibiza market. It is also interesting to note that, although the Barcelona-Majorca market is more than double the size of Lanzarote-Las Palmas, the number of flights per annum is no more than 20% higher. So, overall, the cost per available seat-km on the Canarian route is somewhat higher because smaller aircraft (68 seats) are used throughout.

By contrast, we can compare the cheapest fares between Lanzarote (for example) and Madrid, which is more than seven times as far as Gran Canaria. In October 2015, the cheapest one-way non-resident fare on Binter was €49.60, whilst a single fare (also non-resident) with Ryanair was available for €43 on several days, including one day at €29.

Demand on the Balearic routes is much higher in summer than winter (by contrast, Canary inter-island transport has relatively little seasonality) and so fares during the summer peak to and from the Balearic Islands are almost on a par with Canarian fares.

Figure 23-20 shows the difference in seasonality between traffic between the Peninsula and the Balearic Islands and inter-island Canarian traffic for both modes. The seasonal variation (of the highest and lowest values) for Balearic island traffic is nearly double that of Canarian demand.

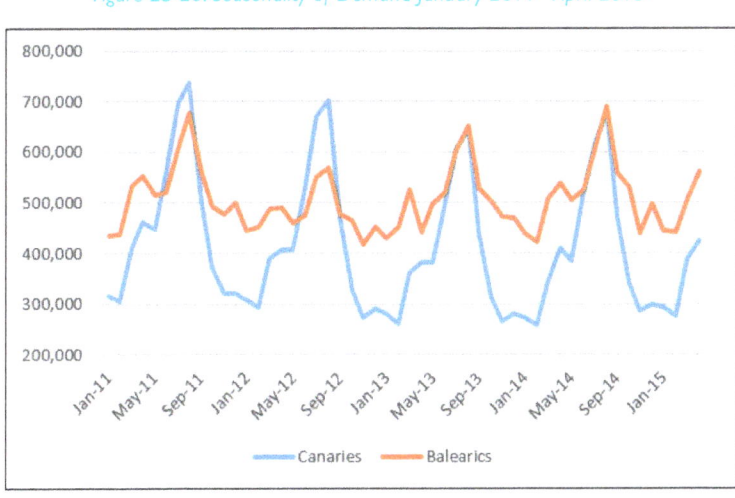

Figure 23-20: Seasonality of Demand January 2011 – April 2015

As we have mentioned previously, service provision with a higher level of seasonality is more expensive, and this certainly applies for immovable infrastructure, which needs to recover its costs over a shorter part of the year.

23.9.2 Air Trips to/from the Peninsula

As might be expected, given the distance involved, subsidies on Peninsula air fares consume the highest amount of money.

Since 2012, total traffic fell farther in 2013 and 2014, but was showing signs of growth in 2015. So, traffic in the current year is running at roughly 2012 levels.

23.9.3 Ferry Trips

Data on ferry subsidies is somewhat harder to come by, so we need to make some estimates. The best estimate is that ferry subsidies for residents are reportedly running at approximately €60 million per annum[90].

The figure under the "441M" programme (see the footnote) combines subsidies for the Balearic and Canary Islands as well as Ceuta and Melilla.

Given the populations and distances involved, we expect that most of this subsidy is spent on the Canarian network.

23.9.4 Summary of Subsidies

Piecing together the available evidence, the subsidies totalled around €266 million on average for the period 2010-2012.

Total annual expenditure by the Canarian government was around €6.7 billion in 2014 and a similar amount is projected for 2015.

By contrast, the bill for subsidising Canarian residents' transport costs is currently budgeted at €300 million, or a little under 5% of the regional government's expenditure.

Please note, however, that the subsidies come from central government rather than the regional one.

23.10 Tourism Expenditure Losses

23.10.1 Quantified Costs – Peninsula Tourists

---

90 http://www.sepg.pap.minhap.gob.es/Presup/PGE2015Ley/MaestroDocumentos/PGE-ROM/doc/1/3/14/2/3/N_15_E_R_31_117_1_1_3_1.PDF

We will now assess the extent of tourism expenditure in the Canary Islands attributable to the drop in Peninsula-Canaries traffic.

There are two benchmarks we can use for this exercise:

- The volume of foreign tourists visiting the Canary Islands; or
- The volume of Spanish tourists travelling abroad on leisure trips.

We will use the second of these benchmarks as the growth in Spaniards travelling abroad (14%) is somewhat lower than the increase in foreign tourists holidaying in the Canaries (25%).

So, our estimate can be perceived as conservative.

Tourism income is generated by three factors that can be described as the tripod of tourism income, as expenditure by tourists in a holiday destination depends on all three factors:

- The volume of tourism arrivals;
- The average length of stay per tourist; and
- The daily expenditure of each tourist for each day that they are on holiday.

The 'Emisor' column shows the annual number of Spaniards travelling abroad for the purposes of a holiday or visiting family and friends.

The data has been smoothed from the original dataset as it was subject to unexplained jumps between various years.

'Peninsula' is the number of tourists aged 16 or older as recorded by EGATUR to the Canary Islands and 'Penisula2' is the number to be expected if the trajectory of tourists to the Canary Islands has been similar to the number of Spaniards travelling abroad.

The difference between the actual and expected tourist volumes is shown in the 'Lost Tourists' column.

Figure 23-21: Lost Expenditure from Peninsula Tourists

The revenue lost is the product of these lost tourists, their average stay and average daily expenditure as recorded by EGATUR. To put these figures into context, EGATUR estimated total tourism expenditure in the Canary Islands at €4.22 billion in 2014.

	Emisor	Peninsula	Peninsula2	"Lost Tourists"	Average Stay	Expenditure per Day	€m lost
2007	8,506,508	1,933,978					
2008	8,575,422	1,813,654	1,949,646	135,992	7.4	47.84	48
2009	9,437,456	1,528,555	2,145,632	617,077	7.1	48.77	215
2010	9,873,126	1,723,520	2,244,682	521,162	7.3	49.68	189
2011	9,326,081	1,550,404	2,120,310	569,906	7.7	47.62	208
2012	9,920,037	1,338,454	2,255,348	916,894	7.3	46.8	312
2013	9,699,069	1,335,963	2,205,110	869,147	8.1	45.27	317
2014	9,694,112	1,333,105	2,203,983	870,878	7.7	45.21	304

23.10.2 Wider Economic Benefits

We have seen from previous Chapters that tourism expenditure is based on the three factors of arrivals, average length of stay and average daily expenditure.

We have also seen that less than 10% of all tourist arrivals visit two or more islands. Data is not available on whether tourists who visit more islands spend longer in the Canary Islands, but it is not unreasonable to assume that they do.

So, let us now pose the following question. Of the 10.5 million tourists who visited the Canary Islands in 2014, what if 1 million of them spent an extra day on holiday as a result of visiting another island (assuming that fares were lowered from their current level)? If we work on an assumption of €40 per tourist per day for incidentals (food, drink, local transport, tourist sites) etc., these extra guest nights would generate an extra €40 million per annum or 1% of actual tourism income.

We noted in Section 23.5 that there were around 6.8 million one-way trips on inter-island routes in 2014.

Therefore, the impact of 1 million extra tourists undertaking a return inter-island trip would increase demand by around 30%. It is unlikely that the increase would be evenly spread, however, and would be focused on shorter routes with more tourism appeal, such as Tenerife-La Gomera and Fuerteventura – Lanzarote/Gran Canaria.

Wider economic benefits also include what is known as a multiplier effect.

If, for example, you spend €100 in a store and the owner makes

40% profit, the owner will then have extra disposable income.

Let us assume, for example, that this owner saves half of his or her profit and spends €20 elsewhere.

This cycle continues until the sums become negligible.

At each stage, the sum available is 20% of the value of the previous stage).

Using the figures in the above example, the initial expenditure of €100 becomes 100*/ (1-0.2) which is €125.

Although we will not attempt to calculate the multiplier effect here, it is important to be aware of its existence.

23.11 Alternative Uses for Funds

23.11.1 What Funds Are Available?

We have seen from previous Chapters that there is a loss of around €600 million per annum, half of which is government expenditure on subsidies and the remainder is money not injected into the Canarian economy.

In this Section, we will be very cautious and assume that only €300 million is available to be spent elsewhere.

23.11.2 Change from Unlimited Subsidy per Person

We saw in Section 15.6 that there was no limit on the amount of subsidy that an individual receives for inter-island travel or trips to and from the Peninsula.

There is also sufficient evidence that wealthier people travel more and so we end up in the perverse situation that the subsidies flow more to people with a higher propensity to travel.

The perversity is amplified by the fact that the full subsidy is available to business class fares as well as economy.

There is no publicly available data on the frequency of subsidised travel and there are certainly cases for which a subsidy might be appropriate for frequent travel, (many businesses treat Lanzarote and Fuerteventura as one market, given the two islands' proximity) but there remains a case for assessing the necessity of subsidies for frequent travellers.

That said, the advantage of the current, unlimited system is that it is not overly bureaucratic and the subsidy is nowadays applied automatically via a database which checks residents' eligibility for the discount.

23.11.3 Abolition of Subsidy

If the hypothesis proposed earlier is correct, namely that the resident's discount increases the normal fare, one option is to remove the subsidy entirely and allow the market to set all fares. This proposal would also apply to routes that are unable to support a commercial air service but, even on these routes, the differential between residents and non-residents would be abolished.

The argument for subsidies is reduced somewhat if average fares decline. In November 2015, Norwegian, a new carrier scheduled to start Peninsula-Canaries operations, is offering fares at around one quarter of the Iberia Express price. IE's costs per available seat kilometre were broadly in line with Vueling and easyJet in 2012 but above Ryanair's.[91]

So, this is a further argument that fares could be reduced by allowing the market to work and for flights to and from the Peninsula market to operate on a fully commercial, market-driven basis. Even during periods of low demand – November was the weakest month in 2014 – the airlines' load factors held up and, in fact, both Ryanair and Vueling had above average load factors for Peninsula routes during the month.

So, a further argument against subsidies is why routes with several hundred thousand passengers per annum and operated by modern, efficient jet aircraft need subsidies in the first place.

This is particularly true for flights between the Canary Islands and Madrid or Barcelona. Inter-island flights, by contrast are run with small aircraft and high frequencies. This system, unsurprisingly, increases operating costs and the average number of passengers per flight on inter-island routes rarely exceeds 50.

The short distance is not a reason for running smaller capacity aircraft; for example, between Bahrain and Dammam (Saudi Arabia) Gulf Air runs several Airbus A320 aircraft per day and the distance between the two airports, at 86km, is shorter than any inter-island route flown today, with the exception of Lanzarote-Fuerteventura.

---

91   http://centreforaviation.com/analysis/liberia-a-new-hammer-can-crack-an-old-nut-but-sometimes-the-new-ones-taste-better-109589

24 ANSWERS TO EXERCISES

Chapter 2 Exercise 1

The initial satisfactory outcome for explaining the data is the table provided in the question. As a starting point, we can simply graph the volume of demand by mode over each year as follows.

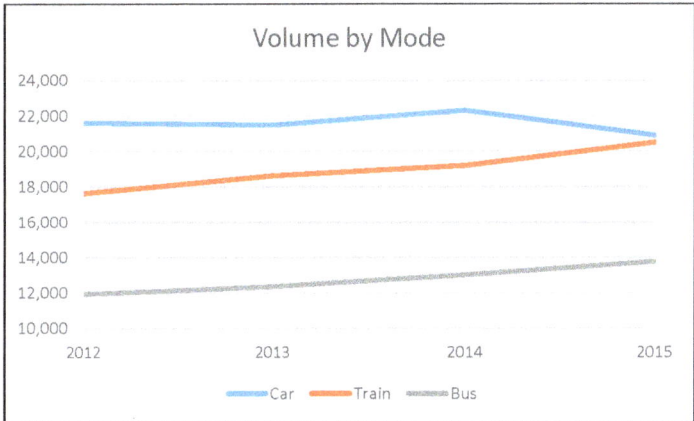

This first version shows us how train and bus have increased demand throughout but car volume dropped in 2015. However, it tells us nothing about the size of the total market. Alternatively, we could have used a stack bar chart.

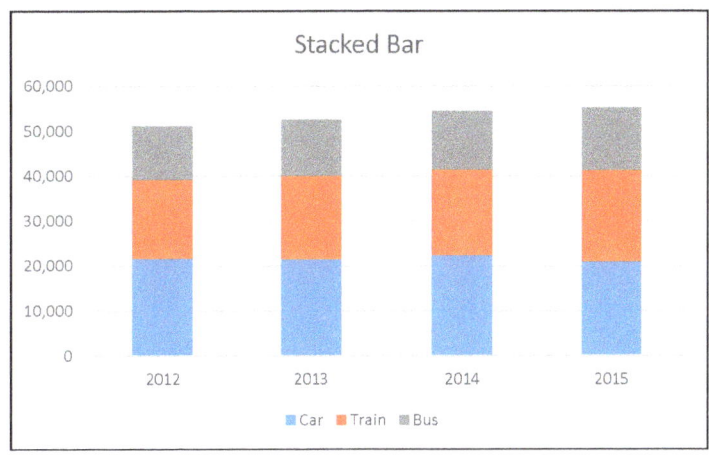

We can now see how the market has steadily grown over the three years but the stacked bar chart does not give us any indication about market shares. Instead, we can draw a pie chart that provides us with market size and share for a specific year as shown below.

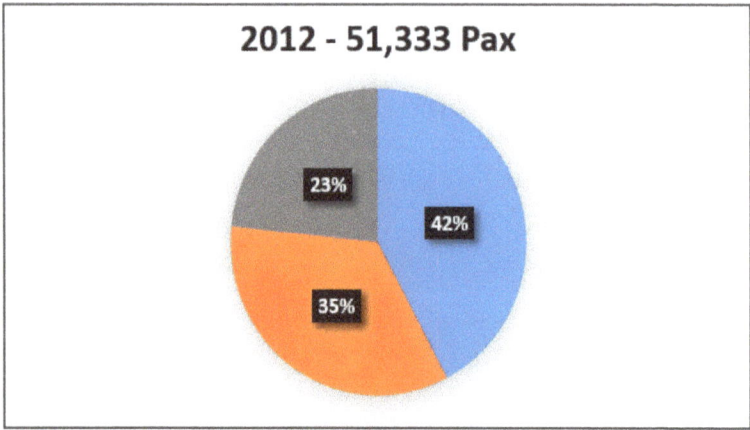

In the above chart, the total market size was added manually to the title and we can now see the share of each mode.

We could undertake a similar exercise for 2015 and see how market size and shares have changed.

The pie chart method will not use any data from intervening years, however.

There is, in summary, no 'best' chart; it really depends on the message that the author is trying to convey to the audience.

Chapter 2 Exercise 2

We are asked in this question to compare two types of tourist to Tenerife. Here we present the first two versions.

The first is just the raw data as provided in the question and the second version sets the number of tourists visiting in January 2011 from both the UK and Spain to 100.

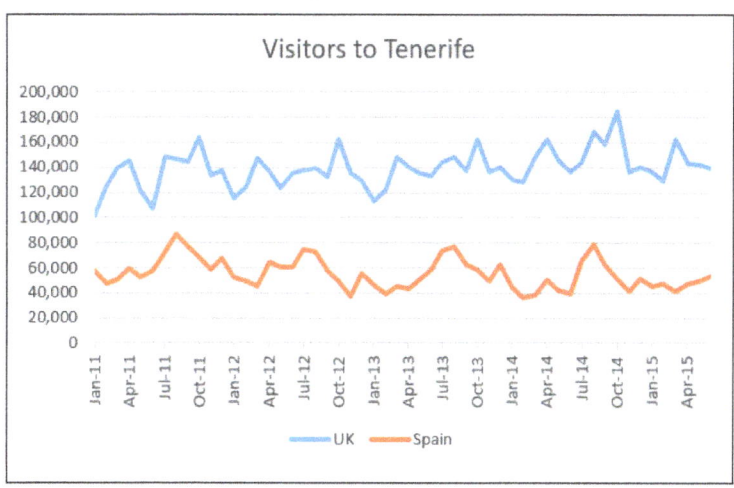

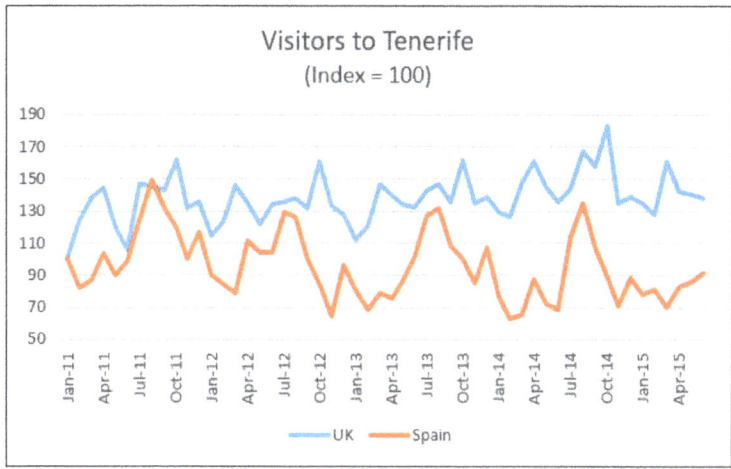

The value of the index system is that we can see that there has been some sort of divergence in trend between UK and Spanish tourists. Note also that the Y axis starts at 50 so there is less 'white space' on the chart.

For Spanish tourists, it looks as though there is a seasonal peak in summer, which is unsurprising.

To assess whether numbers overall are increasing or decreasing, we can convert the data to a moving annual average (MAA) format, so the first data point is the average value of Jan-11 to Dec-11, the second is Feb-11 to Jan-12, and so on.

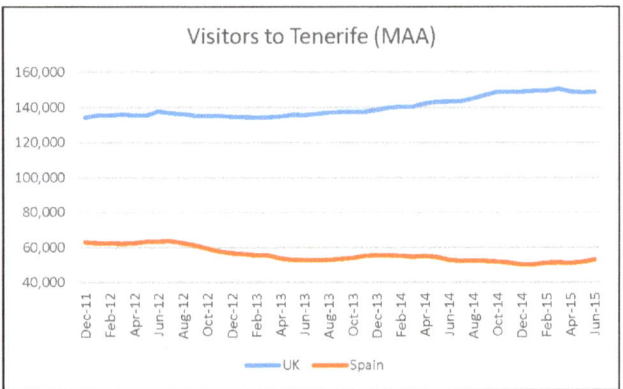

This third chart confirms that UK tourists have increased over the 4½ years and Spanish ones have declined, but there is a wide space between the two lines. So, we can employ either a second Y axis for the Spanish data or – the author's personal preference – index the data again.

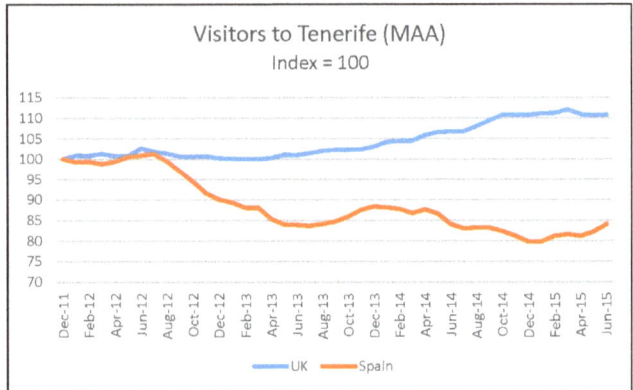

We can now say that demand from both UK and Spain was stable until mid-2012, at which point UK tourists increased by some 10% up to late 2014, whilst Spanish visitors declined by around 20% over the same period. Since then, the Spanish market has shown signs of recovery whilst growth from the UK has been negligible.

Chapter 3, Exercise 1

Demand curve shift:

- income change. If incomes rise faster than inflation, there will be higher disposable income. This, in turn, would be expected to lead to a higher propensity to travel and shift the demand curve to the right;

- The Chapter discussed how the curve would shift if a substitute good to rail (say, an express bus service) changed its price. The same applies to complementary goods. So, if railway station car parks increase prices, the overall impact of rail travel would be negative and shift the demand curve to the right.

Supply curve shift:

- Technology. In air travel, for example, the unit cost per seat-km has declined as larger aircraft have been introduced. This has shifted the supply curve to the right, resulting in an equilibrium point of higher quantity of air travel and lower prices. A similar argument can be made about the introduction of low cost carriers, with much of the process now being self- service, resulting in lower unit costs;

- Consumer preference. For many people, public transport is perceived as being an attractive option compared to the expense and pollution caused by owning a car. Suppliers would respond to this change of perception and increase supply accordingly, so the supply curve would shift to the right.

Exercise 2

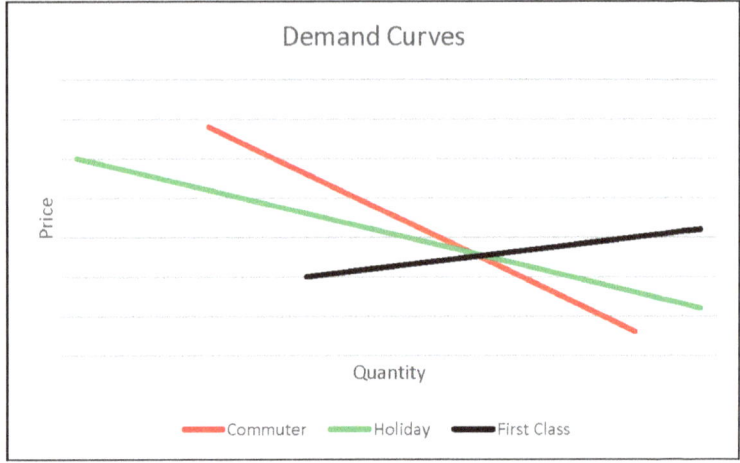

The commuter line should have a steeper demand curve than the holiday route.

Commuters often have little choice but to travel by rail, which is one reason why the government controls season ticket fares.

By contrast, if a certain holiday route becomes expensive, holidaymakers can switch to another route or decide not to travel.

The first-class line is more controversial and is a classic case of a luxury good. As the price increases, demand may increase as people perceive a certain cachet in travelling first class. By contrast, if first class service is provided cheaply by an airline with a weak reputation, many potential customers will perceive the good as being inferior.

Chapter 4, Question 1

I would personally argue that grocery shopping does not offer perfect competition for the following reasons:

- Each chain will have a different range of goods and the prices are unlikely to be identical;
- A consumer is likely to be more inclined to visit a supermarket 5 minutes away rather than a half-hour drive; and
- Stores can and do differentiate themselves through their opening hours.

Plumbers and dry cleaners both provide a service and, once quality of service factors come into play, there is a case for arguing that the rules of perfect competition do not apply.

A plumber can be chosen at random from Yellow Pages or by personal recommendation. Most users of plumbers are not experts in plumbing, so we will select one based on the recommendations of friends and family.

Were the plumber's charges considered reasonable?

Did he or she turn up on time?

Is the plumber friendly and personable?

Were any supplementary visits required to remedy work?

If, say, a dry cleaner X starts to provide a home delivery service, then X is offering a service which competitors Y and Z do not.

There is nothing to prevent the other two from copying the home delivery service, granted, but X could then up his game and offer delivery according to an hourly slot rather just morning or afternoon.

So, in this way, X is still able to differentiate his overall offering from competitors.

Chapter 4, Question 2

When considering transport markets, frequency and distance (or journey time) are key determinants when assessing competition, in addition to price.

For London-Yorkshire services, Virgin East Coast dominates the market in terms of frequency.

Grand Central, for example, offers four services a day between Kings Cross and Doncaster whereas VEC operates over 20 services just in the mornings.

So, both GCR and HT must work harder and offer lower fares to compensate for the inconvenience of much lower frequencies.

Between Manchester and Liverpool, there is not a great deal to choose between the rail companies in terms of journey times, fares or frequencies (although in Summer 2016,

Trans Pennine Express offered both cheaper and faster services.

National Express offers a frequent service from £3 one way but takes at least 65 minutes for the journey (double the time of the fastest trains).

Chapter 5, Exercise 1

The two GJT calculations are shown below.

Monday - Saturday

		Town Unweighted	Residential area Unweighted	Town Weighted	Residential area Weighted
Wait for bus	2	7.5	0	15	0
Time on bus	1.5	15	0	22.5	0
Walking	2	0	10	0	20
Wait for train	2	5	5	10	10
Time on train	1	30	30	30	30
		57.5	45	77.5	60

Sunday

		Town Unweighted	Residential area Unweighted	Town Weighted	Residential area Weighted
Wait for bus	2	7.5	0	15	0
Time on bus	1.5	15	0	22.5	0
Walking	2	0	10	0	20
Wait for train	2	15	15	30	30
Time on train	1	30	30	30	30
		67.5	55	97.5	80

For Monday-Saturday, we assumed that passengers arrived at random, but is this likely to occur on Sunday? Walking may be the least pleasant mode of transportation – this is reflected in its weight of 2.0 compared to 1.5 for bus and 1.0 for rail – but it is also the most reliable! If a train departs every 30 minutes, and assuming the service does not leave early, most passengers who walk to the station will arrive, say, between 1 and 10 minutes before the train departs (assuming that they are familiar with the rail timetable!) and so 80 minutes is probably an overestimate for the residential GJT on Sunday.

For those passengers who need to use a bus to reach the railway station, much depends on how reliable the bus is and how well the schedule of the bus dovetails with the railway timetable.

Chapter 5 Exercise 2

The individual effects of each change are shown in the coloured cells. Please note that, if we added up the individual effects, we would have a net increase of 80 passengers.

However, more normal practice is to multiply the effects and, when we do this, the projected increase in demand is around 6.6% rather than 8 %, so we would expect demand to increase by 66 passengers on the rail service.

1000	passengers per day
20%	rise in incomes
0.8	Elasticity
16%	rise in rail passengers
160	extra passengers
10%	fare increase
-0.9	elasticity
-9%	rise in demand
90	reduction in rail demand
5%	rise in bus fares
-0.2	elasticity
-1%	decline in bus passengers who will switch to rail
10	bus passengers switching to rail

Combined demand:

116%	incomes
91%	rail fares
101%	bus fares
106.6%	multiplication of all factors
66.156	so approximately 66 passengers extra

Chapter 6 Exercise 1

HKX offers a very low frequency compared to the other modes. In Great Britain, open access rail operators usually offer several services (3-5) per day, seven days per week. The lack of frequency is likely to inhibit HKX from developing its demand and, unless a passenger is using just part of the route (say Köln-Düsseldorf), day return trips are not possible on HKX.

On the core Köln-Hamburg route, a table of fares and frequencies looks similar to the table below (the fares below were examined for a trip eight weeks ahead).

	Fares	Frequency (per day)
HKX	€18-€34	0-1
Deutsche Bahn	€29-€59	every hour
Flixbus	€16-€23	7-9
Germanwings	€33-€100	3-7

Given the availability of air travel and the four-hour journey time by rail, it is likely that Germanwings would dominate the day trip market between Köln and Hamburg.

The extension to Frankfurt could be considered a surprising move. Not only was the frequency extremely low (two trains per week) but the journey time was slower even than the bus service. The extension also took place nearly three years after long distance bus deregulation and so, in terms of frequency and journey time, HKX failed to make an alternative viable offer to the travelling public. The single fare on HKX between Köln and Frankfurt was significantly lower than bus, however (€9 compared to €14).

Chapter 6, Exercise 2

For the day in question, the one-way non-resident adult fares from Gran Canaria to Tenerife port/Tenerife North airport were as follows:

One month in advance

	Minimum	Maximum	Journey time (hh:mm)
Fred Olsen	€40	€40	1:20
Armas	€32	€32	2:30
Binter	€35	€44	0:30
Canary Fly	€31	€31	0:30

3 days in advance

	Minimum	Maximum
Fred Olsen	€42	€42
Armas	€32	€32
Binter	€63	€63
Canary Fly	€45	€45

The first three operators have several frequencies per day, but only Binter has different prices depending on departure.

As the passenger demand figures in the question suggest, Canary Fly has the smallest operation (two trips per day) and this is reflected in its price.

To all intents and purposes, there is no difference between Binter and Canary Fly except frequencies and price.

Fred Olsen's fare may be perceived as surprisingly high.

The company operates from a remote port called Agaete, which is 40km from the centre of the capital, Las Palmas.

The airport, by contrast, is 25km away.

So, although FO offers a free bus service for passengers from Las Palmas, their fares are higher and the journey times longer than travel by air.

Armas has the slowest journey time but does operate from the port close to the centre of Las Palmas.

For this individual day (September 6th, 2016), there is surprisingly little variation in fares, given that four companies plying different routes are involved.

Looking at the short-term fares, the ferry companies follow a very different strategy to the airlines. Fred Olsen's fares are €2 higher and Armas shows no change.

By contrast, both airlines have significantly higher fares just three days ahead but Canary Fly's offering, on its one available flight that day, is now significantly cheaper than Binter.

Given the different fare strategies by mode and the differential between the two airlines, there is no real evidence from the information presented of any fare co-ordination between the companies.

Chapter 7 Exercise 1

There are a few challenges for this exercise. First, it is necessary to convert the revenue and cost inflation figures to 2015 levels. This is done by dividing the first two rows of the red block by the third row.

Next, we need to work out demand and ticket prices separately. We can see that the ticket price declines by roughly 1% in real terms in 2016 (the 0.99 figure), so demand will increase by 110% of 1%, or 1.1% (0.011). So, demand increases by 0.011 * 500,000 or roughly 5,500 (note that the figures here are rounded).

We can see this increase in the top row of the yellow block.

	2015	2016	2017	2018	2019
	500,000	505,340	510,628	515,864	521,050	52
	10.00	9.90	9.81	9.71	9.62	9.5
	5,000,000	5,004,336	5,007,608	5,009,846	5,011,080	5,0
	4,000,000	4,077,670	4,156,848	4,237,563	4,319,846	4,
	1,000,000	926,666	850,760	772,283	691,234	60
Revenue Inflation	100.0	102.0	104.0	106.1	108.2	110.4
Cost Inflation	100.0	105.0	110.3	115.8	121.6	127.6
General Inflation	100.0	103.0	106.1	109.3	112.6	115.9
Real Rev Infl		0.99	0.98	0.97	0.96	0.95
Real Cost Infl		1.02	1.04	1.06	1.08	1.10
Price reduction		-0.010	-0.019	-0.029	-0.038	-0.048
1+ Price Reduction * Elasticity		0.011	0.021	0.032	0.042	0.052
		505,340	510,628	515,864	521,050	526,186

We can see that although revenues have increased by £11,000 over the five years, costs have increased at a rather higher rate (£404,000).

Therefore, if the operator has been hiring extra staff to cope with the extra demand, the board should reconsider its strategy.

Chapter 7, Exercise 2

One year's accounts

The principal complication for an international business such as this is the host of currencies involved: the Norwegian Kroner, the British Pound, the US Dollar (fuel and aircraft purchases) and the Euro. We saw the challenges in accounting for aircraft fuel alone, in the Chapter.

Several years' accounts

An extract from the annual report is shown below.

(Amounts in NOK million)	2015	2014	2013	2012
Operating revenue (MNOK)	22 491	19 540	15 580	12 859
EBITDAR (MNOK)	3 694	1 184	2 784	1 822
EBITDA (MNOK)	1 481	(662)	1 500	789
EBIT/operating result (MNOK)	348	(1 411)	970	404
EBT (MNOK)	75	(1 627)	438	623
Net profit/loss (-)	246	(1 070)	319	457
Basic earnings per share (NOK)	6.99	(30.42)	9.15	13.08
Diluted earnings per share (NOK)	6.92	(29.89)	9.02	12.99
Equity ratio	9%	9%	19%	20%
Cash and cash equivalents (MNOK)	2 454	2 011	2 166	1 731
Unit cost (CASK)	0.42	0.42	0.42	0.45
Unit cost (CASK) excluding fuel	0.31	0.29	0.29	0.31
ASK (million)	49 028	46 479	34 318	25 920
RPK (million)	42 284	37 615	26 881	20 353
Load factor	86.2%	80.9%	78.3%	78.5%
Passengers (million)	25.8	24.0	20.7	17.7

We can see at the bottom of the table how Norwegian has grown so, if we are going to examine revenue and profit per passenger km (RPK), for example, we would need to take account of the airline's size over time.

A second problem we have concerns inflation, but what inflation rate is appropriate?

Norwegian has become less dependent on Norwegian traffic over time, with sizeable bases outside Norway (Gatwick, Stockholm, Madrid, etc.). so, the inflation rate faced over the network is a very challenging figure to calculate!

Next, the nature of Norwegian's business has changed dramatically.

The table below shows the average length of haul for three years.

	RPK (million)	Pax (m)	Average haul (km)
2005	2,703	3.3	819
2010	13,774	13.0	1,060
2015	42,284	25.8	1,639

We can see that the average length of haul has doubled in ten years, as Norwegian has been growing its long-haul business.

So, ideally, we would split the data between short-haul and long-haul aircraft, but there is insufficient information in the annual report to do this. Finally, we need to visit the issue of exchange rates once more. If the home currency falls (as has happened to the NKR during 2016), then revenues earned in other currencies will be flattened when they are converted to NKR. We can see from the figure below, for example, that, whilst €1 of revenue would have been recorded as NKR 7-8 in 2012-13, the Norwegian currency has fallen considerably since, so that €1 of revenue in 2016 will be recorded as around NKR 9.5.

Figure: Euro: NKR Exchange rate

Chapter 8, Exercise 1

a) You have recently purchased 10 vehicles and wish to find out the mean and variation in fuel efficiency of your new fleet;

The answer here is SD. Our entire world, so to speak, consists of these 10 vehicles.

b) You wish to compare the results from a) with the manufacturer's stated fuel efficiency;

SEM. We are testing the mean of our fleet of 10 vehicles against what the manufacturer says the fuel efficiency should be.
So, we have a sample of 10 vehicles.

c) The Board of Directors of a ferry company wishes to know how many vehicles are loaded per crossing during May.
There are 30 sailings in all;

At this stage, the directors are just interested in May data.
So, we would produce the mean and SD over the 30 sailings that occurred during the month.

d) The Board then asks whether demand during May was significantly different from the long-term average demand.

Here, we are testing whether the mean number of vehicles per sailing in May is significantly different from the company's long term average.
So, May data is now a sample of the total population and therefore we employ the SEM to test whether the results are different.

Chapter 8, Exercise 2

This is a small-sized sample, so we need to balance obvious segments with the need to have a reasonable number in each (at least five, perhaps up to 10 people per segment).

As the journey is two hours long, we are unlikely to see any business or commuting travellers on the line.

So, the criteria that could be used to select respondents are age, income and journey purpose.

If each of these categories is limited to two possible responses (young or old, 'rich' or 'poor', etc.) the maximum number of options is eight, which is the maximum number for a small sample such as this one.

If we limit ourselves to people on board, we are not considering either former customers who now use another mode or people who have never travelled with this company. Ex-customers in particular can be a mine of useful information about what people do NOT like about the service.

Chapter 8, Exercise 3

Part 1

If 75% of our sample is satisfied, this means that our standard error of the proportion (SEP) is $\sqrt{[(0.75 * 0.25) / 40]}$ or 0.0685.

Our T value for creating the confidence interval is 2.023 [TINV(0.05,39)].

If we look at the upper limit of the confidence interval, we get

$$0.75 + 2.023*0.0685 \text{ or } 0.75 + 0.1384.$$

This falls short of the 90% we require so we would conclude that the company is not meeting the 90% satisfaction criterion.

Part 2

By far the easier way to carry out this task is through trial and error, but it is not difficult if you set up a small model on Excel to carry out the task. First, we need a cell which provides us with the number of satisfied customers in the SECOND batch only.

Using the 36 in the example below, we now have 30 from the first batch and 36 from the second batch, so the proportion satisfied is 66/80 in total, or 0.825. The proportion dissatisfied is 1−0.825 or 17½% (cell D6).

	Col B	Col C	Col D	Col E
Row 3	Change this number		36	second batch of satisfied respondents
Row 4				
Row 5	Proportion satisfied		0.825	total proportion
Row 6	Proportion dissatisfied		0.175	
Row 7				
Row 8	New critical T Value		1.99045	79 TINV value for a sample of 80
Row 9				
Row 10	SEP		0.042482	
Row 11				
Row 12	SEP * Critical Value		0.084558	
Row 13				
Row 14			0.909558	sample proportion satisfied + SEP * TINV
Row 15				
Row 16	Greater than 90%?		YES	

Our sample size is now 80, so our critical T value using 95% confidence interval is 1.99045.

The SEP is calculated as before: $\sqrt{[(0.825 * 0.175) / 80]}$ or 0.0425. Note how this figure is rather smaller than before, as our sample size is somewhat higher.

So, what we require is that 0.825 + (SEP * Critical Value) > 0.9. The lowest number of respondents in the second batch that makes this possible is 36, which is the answer to the question.

The version of the model with formulae is shown below.

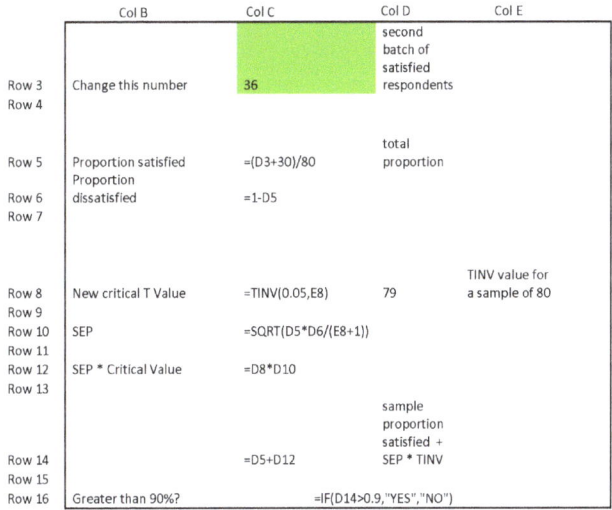

	Col B	Col C	Col D	Col E
Row 3	Change this number	36	second batch of satisfied respondents	
Row 4				
Row 5	Proportion satisfied	=(D3+30)/80	total proportion	
Row 6	Proportion dissatisfied	=1-D5		
Row 7				
Row 8	New critical T Value	=TINV(0.05,E8)	79	TINV value for a sample of 80
Row 9				
Row 10	SEP	=SQRT(D5*D6/(E8+1))		
Row 11				
Row 12	SEP * Critical Value	=D8*D10		
Row 13				
Row 14		=D5+D12	sample proportion satisfied + SEP * TINV	
Row 15				
Row 16	Greater than 90%?	=IF(D14>0.9,"YES","NO")		

Chapter 9 Exercise 1

Part 1

The regression output should look like this.

SUMMARY OUTPUT

Regression Statistics	
Multiple R	0.817498
R Square	0.668303
Adjusted R Square	0.633388
Standard Error	56041.27
Observations	22

ANOVA

	df	SS	MS	F	Significance F
Regression	2	1.2E+11	6.01E+10	19.14063	2.7992E-05
Residual	19	5.97E+10	3.14E+09		
Total	21	1.8E+11			

	Coefficients	Standard Error	t Stat	P-value	Lower 95%	Upper 95%
Intercept	693727.5	80742.49	8.591852	5.71E-08	524731.535	862723.496
Bus Passengers	-0.3436	0.101889	-3.3723	0.003199	-0.5568539	-0.1303437
Main Line	0.60913	0.103766	5.87022	1.18E-05	0.39194519	0.82631542

Part 2

Branch = 693,727 + -0.344 * Bus Passengers + 0.609 * Main line passengers

Intuitively, the equation makes sense; as main line passengers increase, so do branch line volumes. Also, as bus passenger volumes change, rail passenger numbers move in the opposite direction.

1,000 extra main line passengers should yield 609 trips on the branch line. If bus passengers increase by 1,000, we would expect to see a decline of 344 rail branch passengers.

Part 3

Around two thirds of the variation in branch passengers is attributable to the independent variables, which is a decent result. Also, in all cases, the P-value of the coefficient is less than 0.05 so we have confidence that these coefficients are robust estimates and are significantly different from zero.

You may also pick up on the fact that demand is highly seasonal; this fact, although useful to observe, does not bear directly on the task in hand.

Part 4

Comments on the chart below: the model seems to follow the actual data reasonably well and reflects the rise and fall in actual passengers (although the variation in the model is more muted than the actual data).

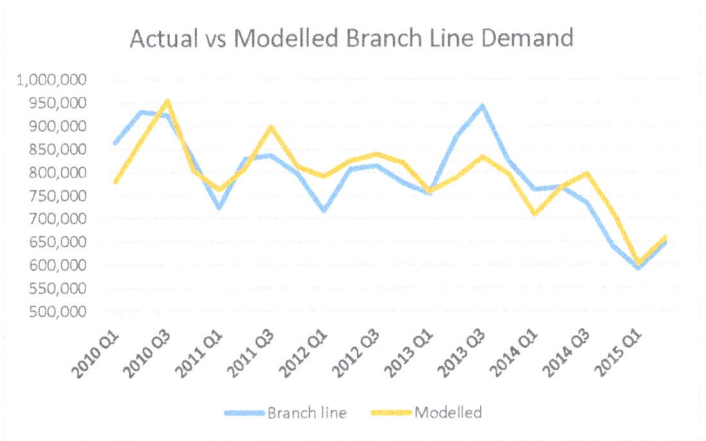

If we carry out tests on the errors, we see that we have a reasonable sprinkling of positive and negative error terms (although there are some fair-sized blocks).

Also, there is no evidence that the errors increase as volumes get larger, which is a positive point (see the following table).

Main Line	Model	Error 2
612,418	601,501	-2%
630,824	761,867	-5%
653,368	707,802	7%
691,075	656,451	-2%
696,709	713,897	-12%
732,647	758,286	-1%
752,451	790,214	-10%
775,452	767,226	0%
797,510	803,983	3%
807,745	779,278	10%
819,028	807,525	3%
842,831	811,822	-2%
848,159	788,087	10%
848,389	795,567	4%
852,695	824,923	-2%
860,263	819,786	-5%
947,402	868,844	7%
1,007,681	795,957	-9%
1,133,207	833,164	12%
1,135,171	838,485	-3%
1,198,652	896,898	-7%
1,308,203	953,915	-3%

Part 5

Car ownership data, employment levels (may be available), traffic counts on competing roads should all be feasible to acquire.

Chapter 11, Exercise 1

To use the equations, we need to define λ (lambda), the arrival rate per time period and μ (mu) the rate of service.

Our time period is five minutes and we have been told that $\lambda = 3$ and $\mu = 4$. Using the equations in the Chapter, you should get the following results.

Number of customers in the system (waiting and being served)	3.0	
Mean time spent from arrival to departure	5.0	minutes
Mean waiting time	3.8	minutes
Number waiting to be served	2.3	customers

Chapter 11, Exercise 2

Here is one run of the simulation showing the first hour of service at the ticket office.

Time	Queue	Arrivals	Potential service	Actual service	Unserved
600	0	1	4	1	0
605	0	2	4	2	0
610	0	2	4	2	0
615	0	5	4	4	1
620	1	1	2	2	0
625	0	1	4	1	0
630	0	4	4	4	0
635	0	2	3	2	0
640	0	0	4	0	0
645	0	5	5	5	0
650	0	3	4	3	0
655	0	1	4	1	0

We can see that, in this snapshot, it is likely that new customers will arrive and be able to be served immediately or soon after they arrive.

The two probability distributions which generate the number of arrivals and people served per five-minute period should look like this.

	Col G	Col H	Col I	Col J	Col K	Col L		
			per 5 minutes					
	Arrivals	3	period		Probability	Cumulative		
Row 3		Dists!$J$3	------->	0	0.0498	0.0498	<------	Dists!$L$3
Row 4		Dists!$J$4	------->	1	0.1494	0.1991	<------	Dists!$L$4
Row 5		Dists!$J$5	------->	2	0.2240	0.4232	<------	Dists!$L$5
Row 6		Dists!$J$6	------->	3	0.2240	0.6472	<------	Dists!$L$6
Row 7		Dists!$J$7	------->	4	0.1680	0.8153	<------	Dists!$L$7
Row 8		Dists!$J$8	------->	5	0.1008	0.9161	<------	Dists!$L$8
Row 9		Dists!$J$9	------->	6	0.0839	1.0000	<------	Dists!$L$9
Row 10								
Row 11								
Row 12				Served	Probability	Cumulative		
Row 13	Service	4	per 5 minute period	2	0.1	0.1		
Row 14				3	0.1	0.2		
Row 15				4	0.5	0.7		
Row 16				5	0.3	1		

You will also see the cell references for column J (the number who arrive) and column L (the cumulative probability of 1 or less arriving, 2 or less, etc.)

Below is the formula for the first arrival value (1, at 0600hrs). The formula is tedious but not overly complex. Just make sure that the number of left and right hand brackets is the same.

=IF(Rands!A1<Dists!$L$3,Dists!$J$3,IF(Rands!A1<Dists!$L$4,Dists!$J$4, IF(Rands!A1<Dists!$L$5,Dists!$J$5,IF(Rands!A1<Dists!$L$6,Dists!$J$6, IF(Rands!A1<Dists!$L$7,Dists!$J$7,IF(Rands!A1<Dists!$L$8,Dists!$J$8, IF(Rands!A1<Dists!$L$9,Dists!$J$9,Dists!$J$10)))))))

In this solution, the random numbers are located in a separate sheet of the Excel file called Rands.

The formula states that, if the random number is less than 0.0498, one person will arrive; otherwise, if the number is less than 0.1991, 2 will arrive, and so on. The formulation for the number of people served per five-minute period is very similar.

Chapter 12, Exercise 1

The important calculation for this exercise is the number of bus-kms run per annum, which is 1.8 million (10*500*360). The cost of each category per bus-km is shown below.

Driver and maintenance	420,000 €
Op Personnel per bus-km	23.3 cents
Fuel	20.0 cents
Spare parts per bus-km	0.7 cents
Depreciation per bus-km	11.1 cents
Head office fees	4.4 cents
License fees	0.6 cents

Marginal costs per bus km	20.7 cents
Operating costs per bus km	55.1 cents
Total costs per bus km	60.1 cents

For marginal costs, we can argue that personnel, head office, license fees and depreciation can be perceived as fixed in the very short term, so the short-term marginal cost comprises just fuel and maintenance parts.

Once we take a longer term, annual view, we need to include drivers, maintenance personnel and depreciation. This brings our costs up to 55.1 cents.

Finally, we have fixed costs of €90,000 (head office, license fees) which need to be absorbed. With 1.8 million bus-km per annum, this is equivalent to adding 5 cents per bus-km to attain total costs.

Chapter 12, Exercise 2

In order to compare like with like, we would need the following information as a minimum:

- Length of routes, so we can compare costs per km;
- Age and depreciation costs of the two ferries;
- Maintenance costs per ferry, which can then be converted into costs per ferry-km;
- Port fees at each end of both routes;
- Staffing costs per route;
- Demand per route, so we can calculate labour costs per passenger;
- Fuel costs. Is there a difference in fuel efficiency between the two ferries?

Chapter 15 Exercise

Although elasticities are often expressed as a single number for a given mode, there is no reason for this to always be the case. For example, leisure passengers will have a more elastic demand than business travellers. In the case of the distance bands, we can argue that the price cut for short distance passengers will be heavily promoted and so have a significant impact. Walking is also an available option over a short distance. By contrast, demand for longer distance travellers will be less elastic, based on a combination of willingness to pay and the expense of alternative modes (say, driving and parking).

Miles	Passengers	Old Fare	New Fare	Elasticity	New Pax	Old Revenue	New Revenue
0-1	400,000	2.00	1.20	-0.7	512,000	800,000	614,400
1-2	900,000	2.00	1.50	-0.5	1,012,500	1,800,000	1,518,750
2-3	1,600,000	2.00	2.00	-0.3	1,600,000	3,200,000	3,200,000
3-4	600,000	2.00	2.00	-0.3	600,000	1,200,000	1,200,000
4-5	300,000	2.00	2.50	-0.2	285,000	600,000	712,500
5+	200,000	2.00	2.50	-0.2	190,000	400,000	475,000
	4,000,000				4,199,500	8,000,000	7,720,650

This first set of proposed new fares actually reduces customer demand (albeit very slightly), increases revenue and so reduces subsidy to €655,000. The principal beneficiary is therefore the local authority, which is able to reduce expenditure on bus subsidies, but may be able to divert the €345,000 saved to other schemes which improve the welfare of the local authority's residents.

Miles	Passengers	Old Fare	New Fare	Elasticity	New Pax	Old Revenue	New Revenue
0-1	400,000	2.00	1.50	-0.7	470,000	800,000	705,000
1-2	900,000	2.00	2.00	-0.5	900,000	1,800,000	1,800,000
2-3	1,600,000	2.00	2.00	-0.3	1,600,000	3,200,000	3,200,000
3-4	600,000	2.00	2.50	-0.3	555,000	1,200,000	1,387,500
4-5	300,000	2.00	2.50	-0.2	285,000	600,000	712,500
5+	200,000	2.00	3.00	-0.2	180,000	400,000	540,000
	4,000,000				3,990,000	8,000,000	8,345,000

The second, lower set of fares has achieved an increase in ridership, by roughly 5%, but at a price. Revenue has declined somewhat and the required subsidy would be roughly €1.3 million. As we saw in Chapter 7, there could well be economic benefits involved that may make the increased subsidy acceptable. For example, assuming that a significant proportion of the extra journeys have been diverted from road, there could be less road congestion and also a reduction in fatalities and accidents. The residents are also beneficiaries as a result of lower fares overall.

Chapter 16 Exercise

Demand will come from three sources:

- Existing rail passengers;
- Car drivers/passengers; and
- Generated demand

The volume of rail passengers between the two cities will not be publicly available so assessing rail demand on the corridor is a challenge. The bus company might be able to employ people to count passengers boarding or alighting trains at the termini or the rail line may have a history of overcrowding or poor reliability, either of which would be reported in the local press or on social media.

Demand will also be determined by price and the extent to which the bus service will undercut rail fares.

The second point is inextricably linked to the first. There are two generic strategies available here, namely cost leadership (CL) and product differentiation (PD). Under CL, the company would offer a simple city-to-city link like the train but at a significantly lower price. This lower price is necessary for no other reason than the journey time by bus is slower than by train, but a low price will also attract journeys not previously made by rail. Bus would also have a guaranteed seat, which could be important if railway passengers have to stand sometimes.

This strategy is high risk, however, as the railway could easily retaliate with a low fare of its own. As long as the railway's marginal costs remain very low (so no new staff or rolling stock would be necessary to cope with extra demand), the rail fare could match bus.

Alternatively, the bus company can pursue PD. The most obvious way to pursue this is to extend the route into a dense suburb at each end of the route and allow these residents a through journey, which is unavailable by rail. The fare yield could be higher, as an acknowledgement of the lower generalised journey time higher consumer surplus that such passengers would enjoy.

Finally, the bus company could combine the strategies and allow internet ticketing only, have no physical sales office, and so on.

Chapter 18, Exercise

Using the framework in this Chapter, there is a great deal to do to improve demand for the tram service.

Note that not all categories are included below. For example, referrals are unlikely to play a major role in a frequent use, low price purchase such as urban public transport.

Physical Evidence

On the Tram Alicante (TA) website, there is no evidence at all that a complementary bus network even exists! Measures to improve physical evidence include listing which bus routes are available at each of the forty tram stops in Zone A on the website and also providing this information at each physical station and stop.

Process

The multi-ride tickets mentioned in the question are widely available around the city (http://www.alicante.subus.es/puntos-de-venta/), but there is no mention on the tram's website of where to buy these cards. TA would need to address this issue as a matter of some urgency if demand increased through increased brand awareness of the combined tram and bus network.

Consideration should also be given to extending the range of through tickets available to single journeys, as not all public transport users are frequent customers.

Retention

Perhaps THE major requirement for retention is to be able to develop a customer database. One means for a transport company to develop such a database is through time-based season tickets. The operator can then send out renewal reminders, newsletters and so on. TA does not seem to have a Facebook presence, which could also be useful to develop followers for the company.

Related Sales

Both the FB page and the customer database could be used to offer customers discounts for events taking place in the vicinity of the line or flash sales from third party companies. Both the operator and the third parties stand to benefit if such promotions are undertaken.

Chapter 19, Exercise 1

The first step is data on demand. Ideally, we should have information by month (to assess the seasonality of demand to ensure that there are sufficient toll booths) and also what proportion of demand is based on the island. Monthly data is important because, if demand were turned away in peak months, we would need to assess how much traffic, previously suppressed, would now be able to travel. The origin of ticket sales could also be important if the current ferry tariff or future bridge toll needs to offer concessions for residents of the island.

A somewhat more challenging aspect of forecasting demand for the bridge is generated traffic. Consider, if a bridge were in place now rather than a ferry, how much higher would traffic volume be? If the mainland government has undertaken similar studies or projects with other islands, the data and methodology used may be applicable for the current ferry replacement project. Otherwise, we could resort to international benchmarks.

So far, we have considered historic demand and the present. If we accept the link between GDP and the propensity to travel, economic forecasts for both the island and the mainland region should provide an insight into how much traffic might change in future as a result of these forecasts.

A further request to the regional government concerns land use. If, for example, the island has a small hospital, which the government is considering closing and expecting island residents to visit the mainland; now that accessibility to the mainland is improved, demand for the bridge would certainly increase.

Once we have all this data, we will require the specifics of the ferry tariff and bridge tolls (including any concessions) and whether the government will continue with the subsidies that it provided for the ferries. Coupled with construction and operating costs for the toll bridge, we would then be in a position to assess the value of the toll-bridge's operations.

Chapter 19, Exercise 2

Below is the regression output for load factor as a function of frequency and the amount of time that the route has been operating.

SUMMARY OUTPUT

Regression Statistics	
Multiple R	0.9119049
R Square	0.8315706
Adjusted R Square	0.7834479
Standard Error	2.6145418
Observations	10

ANOVA

	df	SS	MS	F	Significance F
Regression	2	236.2492	118.124599	17.28022	0.001960934
Residual	7	47.8508	6.83582895		
Total	9	284.1			

	Coefficients	Standard Error	t Stat	P-value	Lower 95%	Upper 95%
Intercept	66.40105	2.414881	27.4966152	2.16E-08	60.69076429	72.11134
Frequency/week	0.5622875	0.124991	4.49860998	0.002803	0.266729835	0.857845
Duration (months)	0.6894246	0.15487	4.45164564	0.002966	0.323216188	1.055633

So, the equation is:

LF (in %) = 66.40 + 0.56 * Frequency + 0.69 * Duration

This equation looks logical, as load factor generally increases as a route gets more established. The role of frequency is a little more complex: whilst higher frequencies are more attractive to customers, the airline is adding extra seats which need to be filled! If we plug frequency 0 7 and Duration values of 1 to 4 in the above equation, we would get the following results.

Frequency	Months	Load Factor
7	1	71.0
7	2	71.7
7	3	72.4
7	4	73.1

In other words, we are predicting that, with seven flights per week, load factor in the first month would be 71.0%, rising to 73.1% in the fourth month. Please note, however, that each destination will have its own local factors. So, whilst the regression model provides a useful starting point, we should not take the results as a rigid certainty.

Chapter 20, Exercise 1

It is always worthwhile looking at the data first to understand what is happening.

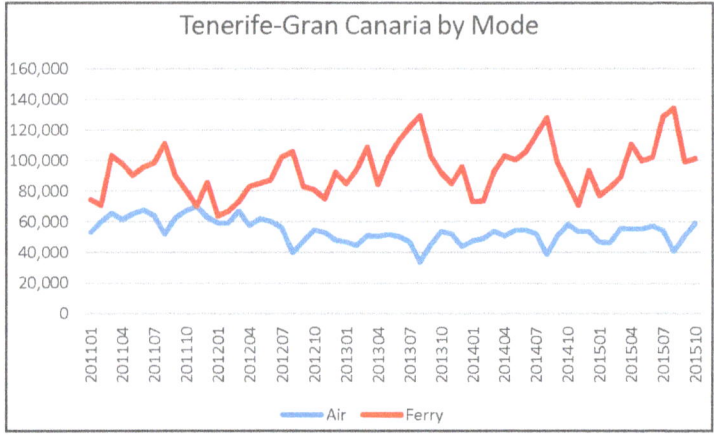

The trend for ferry demand is reasonably clear: aside from the seasonal elements, which we will deal with later, there is a gradual upward trend in demand from 2012. By contrast, air travel declined until the end of 2012, but has not dropped farther since.

Next, we need to develop the trend regressions. To do this, we just need to renumber the months 1,2,3, and so on. You should get the ferry and air demand regressions as shown below. Note that, although the trend for ferry demand is clearer, the regression for air demand is actually more robust. This anomaly is most likely due to the higher levels of month to month variation in ferry traffic.

SUMMARY OUTPUT — Ferry

Regression Statistics	
Multiple R	0.3642
R Square	0.1327
Adjusted R Square	0.1172
Standard Error	15520
Observations	58

ANOVA

	df	SS	MS	F	Significance F
Regression	1	2063132239	2063132239	8.565148	0.0049432
Residual	56	13489013932	240875249		
Total	57	15552146171			

	Coefficients	Standard Error	t Stat	P-value	Lower 95%	Upper 95%
Intercept	83241	4129	20.1598	0.0000	74970	91513
Count	356	122	2.9266	0.0049	112	600

SUMMARY OUTPUT   Air

Regression Statistics
Multiple R	0.4805
R Square	0.2309
Adjusted R Square	0.2171
Standard Error	6777.7060
Observations	58

ANOVA

	df	SS	MS	F	Significance F
Regression	1	772137507.7	772137508	16.80851	0.000134964
Residual	56	2572488690	45937298		
Total	57	3344626198			

	Coefficients	Standard Error	t Stat	P-value	Lower 95%	Upper 95%
Intercept	60254	1803	33.4153	1.12E-38	56641.65	63866.06
Count	-218	53	-4.0998	0.000135	-324.45	-111.46

Next, we need to model the trend, month by month, for each mode (the "Reg Ferry" and "Reg Air" columns below) and calculate the residual for each month.

The two tables below show the seasonality factors (multiplicative) for each mode, calculated by dividing the average actual January value by the average trend value for each of the twelve months.

Ferry	Actual	Trend	Seasonality
January	74,550	92,148	0.8090
February	77,323	92,504	0.8359
March	93,287	92,861	1.0046
April	95,642	93,217	1.0260
May	95,362	93,573	1.0191
June	100,623	93,929	1.0713
July	113,559	94,286	1.2044
August	121,461	94,642	1.2834
September	94,570	94,998	0.9955
October	87,738	95,355	0.9201
November	75,073	93,573	0.8023
December	91,677	93,929	0.9760

Air	Actual	Trend	Seasonality
January	50,665	54,805	0.9245
February	51,909	54,587	0.9509
March	58,573	54,369	1.0773
April	55,090	54,151	1.0173
May	57,716	53,933	1.0701
June	57,961	53,715	1.0790
July	54,532	53,497	1.0193
August	40,978	53,279	0.7691
September	51,276	53,061	0.9664
October	58,407	52,843	1.1053
November	57,054	53,933	1.0579
December	52,016	53,715	0.9684

So, to calculate the modelled value for each month, we multiply the trend value by the seasonality factor and the result is shown in the modelled column (see the example below) and the absolute deviation is the absolute value of ("Ferry" – "Modelled").

Ferry	Month	Count	Ferry	Trend	Seasonal Factor	Modelled	Absolute Deviation
January	201101	1	74,497	83,598	0.81	67,632	6,865
February	201102	2	70,661	83,954	0.84	70,176	485
March	201103	3	103,102	84,310	1.00	84,698	18,404
April	201104	4	97,820	84,667	1.03	86,869	10,951
May	201105	5	90,136	85,023	1.02	86,648	3,488
June	201106	6	95,446	85,379	1.07	91,463	3,983
July	201107	7	98,271	85,735	1.20	103,261	4,990
August	201108	8	111,099	86,092	1.28	110,488	611
September	201109	9	89,747	86,448	1.00	86,058	3,689
October	201110	10	80,302	86,804	0.92	79,871	431
November	201111	11	70,114	87,160	0.80	69,928	186
December	201112	12	85,562	87,517	0.98	85,418	144
January	201201	13	63,703	87,873	0.81	71,091	7,388
February	201202	14	66,589	88,229	0.84	73,749	7,160
March	201203	15	73,077	88,585	1.00	88,993	15,916

What this shows us is that, whilst ferries enjoy higher demand in summer and much weaker levels of demand in the winter months (October to February), air traffic between the two islands goes down markedly in August. Note also that the seasonal ferry figure for December is somewhat larger than the other winter months; this may be attributable to a small increase in demand over the Christmas period.

Here is the result of the modelling exercise for ferry demand.

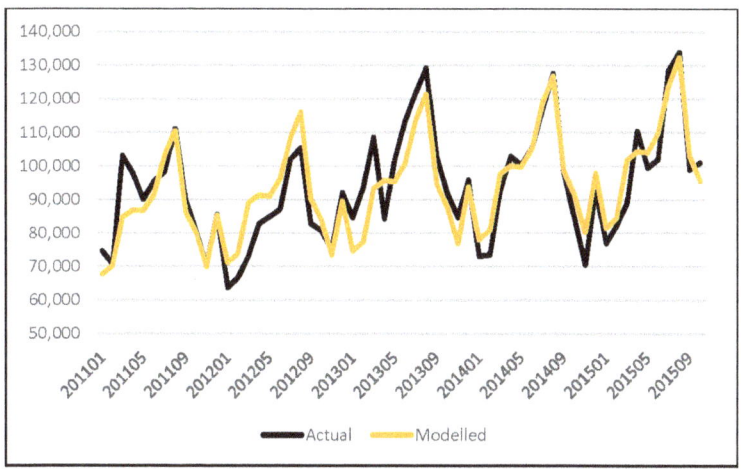

Using the same methodology for air travel, we can see that the overall fit is rather weaker than for ferry travel.

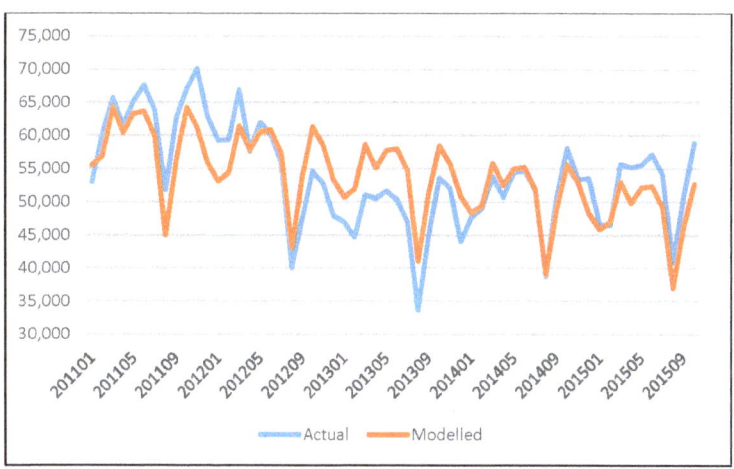

We can see that, overall, the fit is reasonably good, although the ferry model provides a closer fit to actual demand than the air model does. It would be worth carrying out an investigation to see why the model consistently underestimated demand for both modes in 2012 and overestimated it in 2013.

For completion, the next page show extracts from the results of the Holt Winters Exponential Smoothing analysis for both air and ferry traffic.

Ferry

Month	Count	Ferry	Underlying Demand	Trend	Seasonals	Forecast	Absolute Deviation
201101	1	74,497			0.84		
201102	2	70,661			0.79		
201103	3	103,102			1.16		
201104	4	97,820			1.10		
201105	5	90,136			1.01		
201106	6	95,446			1.07		
201107	7	98,271			1.11		
201108	8	111,099			1.25		
201109	9	89,747			1.01		
201110	10	80,302			0.90		
201111	11	70,114			0.79		
201112	12	85,562	88,896	-	0.96		
201201	13	63,703	84,823	-	0.80	74,497	10,794
201202	14	66,589	84,491	-	0.79	67,423	834
201203	15	73,077	77,696	-	1.06	97,992	24,915
201204	16	82,743	76,905	-	1.09	85,496	2,753
201205	17	84,927	79,073	-	1.04	77,977	6,950
201206	18	87,052	79,707	-	1.08	84,899	2,153
201207	19	102,052	83,695	-	1.16	88,113	13,939
201208	20	105,354	83,886	-	1.25	104,599	755

Alpha 0.316283
Beta 0
Gamma 0.472217

Air

Month	Count	Air	Underlying Demand	Trend	Seasonals	Forecast	Absolute Deviation
201101	1	52,977			0.85		
201102	2	60,146			0.96		
201103	3	65,661			1.05		
201104	4	61,542			0.98		
201105	5	65,184			1.04		
201106	6	67,594			1.08		
201107	7	63,788			1.02		
201108	8	51,771			0.83		
201109	9	62,624			1.00		
201110	10	67,056			1.07		
201111	11	70,018			1.12		
201112	12	62,779	62,595	-	1.00		
201201	13	59,170	66,787	139	0.87	52,977	6,193
201202	14	59,291	63,935	40	0.94	64,307	5,016
201203	15	66,838	63,827	35	1.05	67,108	270
201204	16	57,556	60,814	- 66	0.96	62,788	5,232
201205	17	61,873	59,985	- 91	1.03	63,260	1,387
201206	18	60,211	57,524	- 170	1.06	64,677	4,466
201207	19	55,949	55,950	- 216	1.01	58,448	2,499
201208	20	39,955	51,480	- 357	0.79	46,096	6,141

Alpha 0.572847
Beta 0.03309
Gamma 0.696208

Chapter 21, Exercise 1

This exercise is a straightforward NPV and IRR calculation. The results are shown below.

	Rolling Stock	Op Costs	Revenue	Cash Flow
Year 0	- 3,500			- 3,500
Year 1		125	500	375
Year 2		125	530	405
Year 3		125	562	437
Year 4		125	596	471
Year 5		125	631	506
Year 6		125	669	544
Year 7		125	709	584
Year 8		125	752	627
Year 9		125	797	672
Year 10		125	845	720

Discount Rate 5%

NPV 506

IRR 7.6%

So the NPV is €506,000 and the maximum discount rate which provides a positive NPV is 7.6%.

Chapter 21, Exercise 2

The key figures from the question are reproduced below. This exercise is as much about layout as it is about NPV calculations.

Figures in £000		Gradual	Big Bang
Construction	Year 0	100,000	160,000
Operating Costs	Years 1-10	25,000	35,000
Construction	Year 7	100,000	-
Operating Costs	Years 11-15	35,000	35,000
Revenue	Year 1	50,000	50,000
Revenue growth	Years 2-6	5%	5%
Revenue growth	Years 7-10	-3%	5%
Revenue growth	Years 11-15	5%	5%

First, let's examine the gradual approach. We calculate revenue by inserting an annual growth factor in the fourth column and we take two hits, in Year 0 and Year 7 on construction costs. We are told that operating costs increase once phase 2 of construction is complete, starting in Year 11.

	Cost (£K)	Growth	Operating Costs	Revenue (£K)	Cash Flow
Year 0	-100,000				-100,000
Year 1			25,000	50,000	25,000
Year 2		5%	25,000	52,500	27,500
Year 3		5%	25,000	55,125	30,125
Year 4		5%	25,000	57,881	32,881
Year 5		5%	25,000	60,775	35,775
Year 6		5%	25,000	63,814	38,814
Year 7	-100,000	-3%	25,000	61,900	- 63,100
Year 8		-3%	25,000	60,043	35,043
Year 9		-3%	25,000	58,241	33,241
Year 10		-3%	25,000	56,494	31,494
Year 11		5%	35,000	59,319	24,319
Year 12		5%	35,000	62,285	27,285
Year 13		5%	35,000	65,399	30,399
Year 14		5%	35,000	68,669	33,669
Year 15		5%	35,000	72,102	37,102
					88,648

So, the NPV of the gradual approach is £88.6 million. Next, the big bang approach.

	Cost (£K)	Growth	Operating Costs	Revenue (£K)	Cash Flow
Year 0	-160,000				- 160,000
Year 1			35,000	50,000	15,000
Year 2		5%	35,000	52,500	17,500
Year 3		5%	35,000	55,125	20,125
Year 4		5%	35,000	57,881	22,881
Year 5		5%	35,000	60,775	25,775
Year 6		5%	35,000	63,814	28,814
Year 7		5%	35,000	67,005	32,005
Year 8		5%	35,000	70,355	35,355
Year 9		5%	35,000	73,873	38,873
Year 10		5%	35,000	77,566	42,566
Year 11		5%	35,000	81,445	46,445
Year 12		5%	35,000	85,517	50,517
Year 13		5%	35,000	89,793	54,793
Year 14		5%	35,000	94,282	59,282
Year 15		5%	35,000	98,997	63,997
					76,108

We can see that the NPV is somewhat lower in this case, at £76.1 million. In essence, Big Bang never really recovers from the larger upfront financial requirement and we also have significantly higher operating costs in the first ten years. The additional revenue in "Big Bang" is insufficient to make this option viable compared to the approach of construction by phases.

Readers are invited to check whether a somewhat lower discount rate (say 5%) would alter the decision.

INDEX

A

Addis Ababa 312
AECOM 289, 290, 291
AENA 81, 84, 122, 123, 357, 369
Aéroports de Paris 51
Air Asia 47, 48, 49
Air Berlin 46
Air Corsica 52
Air Europa 356, 357
Air France 52
Alicante 274
Alicante Tram 274
Armas 366, 385
Arrecife 235, 351

B

Bangkok 47, 48, 49, 54, 281
Bangkok Airways 54 Barcelona 77, 79, 80, 81, 82, 83, 84, 85, 347, 348, 356, 374
Benidorm 249, 274
Binter 268, 362, 363, 365, 366, 385
Blabla 77
Blue Islands 50, 51
Blue Islands Air 50
British Airports Authority 52
British Airways 50, 201, 246
Brussels 77, 78
Buzz 214

C

Canary Fly 268, 362, 363, 365, 366, 385
Canary Islands 64, 95, 122, 123, 248, 313, 353, 354, 355, 356, 357, 358, 360, 361, 364, 365, 370, 371, 372, 374

Carrefour 177
Channel Tunnel Rail Link 187
Charles de Gaulle 51
Chiang Mai 54
Civil Aviation Authority 55
Condor 46
Copenhagen 37, 38
Crossrail 187

D

Department for Transport 176
Deutsche Bahn 69, 86, 258, 384
Dubai 219, 220, 222, 232, 233, 310, 311

E

easyBus 66
easyJet 50, 51, 52, 75, 126, 229, 357, 374
EGATUR 355, 361, 371
Emirates 206
Essential Air Services Program 52
Ethiopian 312
Eurostar 78, 79, 275
Experian 258

F

First Great Western 230
First Group 215, 242
Flixbus 86
Ford 335
Frankfurt Airport 46, 86, 177, 312, 384
Fred Olsen Express 64, 67, 248, 366
Fuerteventura 354, 360, 361, 365, 366, 367, 373, 374

G

Gandía 177
Gatwick 50, 51, 52, 55, 124, 126
Gatwick Airport 50, 51, 52, 55, 122, 124, 126, 177, 387
Germania 46
Germanwings 86, 384
Gozo 227
Gran Canaria 33, 64, 86, 248, 268, 313, 353, 361, 363, 365, 366, 367, 384
Green Book 323, 334
Gulf Air 201, 374

H

Hamburg-Köln Express 86, 384
Heathrow 48, 52, 55, 186, 201, 202, 207, 312
Hull Trains 56, 215

I

Iberia Express 356, 357, 358, 374
Ibiza 361
IdeaWorks 272
Indonesia 235
Ireland 277, 278, 279, 286, 289, 290, 291
Islas Airways 365
Isle of Skye 351

J

Jersey 50, 51
Jetstar 49
JFK 51
Jubilee Line 346
Jubilee Line Extension 346

K

Koh Samui 53, 54

L

La Gomera 360, 361, 365
Lanzarote 122, 123, 219, 235, 246, 268, 337, 349, 350, 354, 359, 360, 361, 362, 363, 365, 373, 374
La Palma 219, 220, 222, 223, 361, 363, 365
Lleida 82
London 43, 48, 50, 51, 56, 63, 65, 66, 75, 77, 78, 79, 152, 165, 174, 215, 216, 230, 232, 233, 236, 243, 255, 263, 281, 283, 285, 288, 289, 350, 357, 381
London City 50, 51, 165
Los Cristianos 248
Lufthansa 46, 248, 258
Lyon 74, 77

M

Madrid 75, 77, 80, 81, 82, 83, 84, 85, 186, 236, 256, 347, 348, 356, 357, 374, 387
Mallorca 46, 197, 198, 361
Malta 227, 365
Monarch 126, 130

N

Network Rail 189, 190, 225
Newark 51
New Zealand 286, 287
Norwegian 37, 97, 126, 374, 387, 388

O

Orly 51, 52
Ouigo 76

P

Paris 51, 52, 74, 76, 77, 78
Passenger Demand Forecasting Handbook 259, 285, 286, 287
Plusbus 248
Port Authority of New York and New Jersey 51
Puerto del Carmen 349, 350, 351

Q

Qantas 49

R

RENFE 250, 258
Rotherwas 349
Ryanair 37, 205, 206, 214, 241, 245, 247, 253, 267, 268, 272, 356, 357, 358, 361, 362, 374

S

Santa Cruz 248
SAS 37, 267
Scoot 48, 49
Scotland 75, 216, 286
Seville 75, 84, 85
Singapore 47, 48, 281
Singapore Airlines 47, 48
SNCF 76
Song 215
South Africa 293, 300, 302, 338
Stansted Express 282, 283
St Helena 338, 339, 340
Stockholm 37
Surat Thani 53, 54
SWISS 248
Sydney 233

T

TAZARA 293, 294
Ted 215
Tenerife 33, 36, 64, 86, 248, 313, 353, 356, 360, 361, 362, 363, 364, 365, 369, 377, 384
Thameslink 56, 66, 203, 346
Tiger Air 48, 49
Tuifly 46
Turkey 70, 217, 228, 297, 299, 300, 301, 302, 305, 310, 311
Turkish Airlines 217

V

Vueling 219, 357, 358, 374

W

WebTAG 287, 288, 289

Z

Zaragoza 79, 80, 82, 83, 84, 347, 348

www.ingramcontent.com/pod-product-compliance
Lightning Source LLC
Chambersburg PA
CBHW040326300426
44113CB00020B/2672